Is 53:4-5	**JESUS CHRIST** ↑	Rev 1:3 BLESSED IS HE WHO READS AND THOSE WHO HEAR THE WORDS OF THIS PROPHESY, AND KEEP THOSE THINGS WHICH ARE WRITTEN IN IT; FOR THE TIME IS NEAR.
Matt 2:1-12		
They saw HIS STAR		

REV 13:18
$\sum ???????$ =
'COSMIC' 666
Identifying the
SECOND BEAST WHO
IS A MAN!!!

Remember Ananias & Sapphira, Acts 5:1-10

Read Proverbs 9 & 10 too

TIME IS DYING / GEN 1:14-18

This Book offers YOU the very EVIDENCE that GOD of the Holy Bible is ONE and the SAME, CREATOR GOD of the entire Universe and all 'life' that is in it.

GEN 1:1

DO YOU WANT TO BE AMONGST THE PRIVILEGED TO FIND THIS OUT YOURSELF HOW??? THEN YOU WILL MOST CERTAINLY DISCOVER THIS AWESOME BRIDGING TRUTH RIGHT HERE IN THIS BOOK.

" 'You shall love the LORD your GOD with all your heart, with all your soul, with all your strength, *and with all your mind*' and 'your neighbour as yourself.' "   Luke 10:27

HINT: THE EARTH' AXIS ROTATION IS SLOWING DOWN AT A RATE OF 1/1000TH SECOND EVERY 100 YEARS. THIS SCIENTIFIC ESTABLISHED FACT IS USED AMONGST OTHERS IN THIS BOOK TO ESTABLISH THE 360 DAY YEARS TO BE OCCURRING IN OUR 'BIBLICAL HUMAN FUTURE' TO COME AND CONSEQUENTLY THIS IN TURN HAS BEEN USED TO CALCULATE OUT THE UNIQUE SUM THAT TOTALS THE COSMIC GENERATED 666, AS TITLED. THIS UNDENIABLY FROM THIS PERSPECTIVE REFERS TO THE SAME IN REV13:18.

GEN 1:1 IN THE BEGINNING, GOD CREATED THE HEAVENS AND THE EARTH. THIS IS THE UNDERPINNING BIBLICAL CONNECTION THAT LINKS THE GOD OF THE HOLY BIBLE TO BE THE ONE AND THE SAME CREATOR GOD OF THE ENTIRE UNIVERSE AND ALL 'LIFE' IN IT.

YET, "WHERE IS THE COSMIC CONNECTION ITSELF THAT ACTUALLY EXHIBITS AND UNDENIABLY BRIDGES EVIDENTLY THESE TWO TOGETHER???" IT IS ONE THING TO UPHOLD GEN 1:1, WHICH IS ABSOLUTELY AND IRREVOCABLY CORRECT, BUT WHAT DO WE HAVE FROM WITHIN THE UNIVERSE ITSELF TO BE ESTABLISHING THE SAME???

THAT' THE QUEST WHICH IS ANSWERED IN THIS BOOK!!!

'THE BIBLICAL 360 DAY YEARS & THE SCRIPTURAL COSMIC 666'

The main purpose for embarking on such an arduous journey, which it was as you can easily appreciate as evident from the very title of the book and to complete it through sheer GOD fearing determination was to bring to you a deeper understanding to this Satanic schemed initiative for the final annihilation of all Mankind, if at all this was possible from Satan' world view. This book however may on the way chip at a few generally accepted traditional Christian teachings. This as an example will contend against the current understanding of the Biblical generated concept - the **'End of Days'.** This would be the case by default due to some of my own inevitably derived and developed eschatological elements that are included, as I journeyed in this discovery as titled. This also does include the scientific concept of the same and the underpinning singular and most important cosmic acquisition of biblical proportions, that is in my opinion, being this unique 'cosmic number set' as evidently revealed here; to be sum

totalling to the Biblical Revelation **13:18 666.**

GCFM ©

GLOBAL CHRISTIAN FAMILY™ MINISTRIES

WWW.GLOBALCHRISTIANFAMILY.COM

E : gcf@globalchristianfamily.com

FIRST EDITION copyright © 2012 CHARLES ALPHONSO

'THE BIBLICAL 360 DAY YEARS & THE SCRIPTURAL COSMIC 666' was first conceptualized before this 21st Century had even begun i.e. before the year 2000. The title was first registered under ISBN on 25 July 2001 a few years after I had started on this adventure. The Book was finally completed with GOD' GRACE on this Day of the LORD, 1 September 2012 and published accordingly in the same month. All rights reserved. No part of this publication may be reproduced, stored in a retrieval system, or transmitted by any means, electronic, mechanical, photocopying, recording, or otherwise, without having the prior written permission received from the publisher.

THANK YOU
FOR OBSERVING THIS

'THE BIBLICAL 360 DAY YEARS
&
THE SCRIPTURAL COSMIC 666'

SELF-PUBLISHED

International Standard Book Number

ISBN 978 – 983 – 40720 – 2 - 5

All Scriptures used are quoted or referenced from the Spirit Filled Life Bible (New King James Version) – Thomas Nelson Publishers, Nashville, USA, copyrighted 1991. I also quoted a few verses from 2ESDRAS, which were taken from the Good News Bible - Catholic Study Edition which has the Deuterocanonical/Apocrypha also included. This Bible was formerly published by the Catholic Bible Press, a division also of Thomas Nelson Publishers.

The Deuterocanonical/Apocrypha Section that is used here was copyrighted by the American Bible Society in 1979. This Bible is now currently called as the Good News Translation - Catholic Study Edition and is currently being published by the American Bible Society, with the full range Deuterocanonical/Apocrypha Section included.

I wish to extend my personal thanks and courtesies to the American Bible Society, for receiving their kind approval in permitting the quoting and making reference of the relevant verses as taken from the Biblical Book, 2ESDRAS, verbatim according to their PUBLICATION.

DEDICATION

THIS BOOK IS RESPECTFULLY DEDICATED TO ALL THE VERY DEAR SOULS, WHOM WERE SO UNFORTUNATE TO HAVE BEEN AND MANY ARE STILL BEING **MURDERED** IN THE MOST DESPICABLE NAME OF WICKED RELIGIOUS IGNORANCE. THIS HAPPENING, TIME AND TIME AGAIN THROUGH ONE GENERATION JUST PAST, FOLLOWED BY ANOTHER THROUGHOUT THE AGES BY THOSE THINKING THAT THEY WERE ACTUALLY INDEED CHAMPIONING THEIR CAUSE & THEIR RELIGION.

EVEN AS CURRENTLY, THOSE WHO HAD NARROWLY ESCAPED DEATH ARE STILL BEING PERSECUTED DAILY UNDER DIRECT TORTURE AND OTHERS UNDER VARIOUS OPERATIVE DISGUISES. SOME OF THESE METHODS ARE THE SHACKLING OF HUMAN FREEDOM SUCH AS IN SPEECH, IN POLITICAL CHOICE, AND ABOVE ALL IN THE EXERCISING OF OUR GOD GIVEN FREE WILL. THIS IS PRIMARILY TO CHOOSE WHOM WE WANT TO WORSHIP, MARRY AND CONGREGATE WITH, IS JUST SIMPLY AGONISINGLY ATROCIOUS. THIS IS TO SAY THE VERY LEAST THAT IN THIS MODERN DAY AND AGE OF UPHOLDING HUMAN RIGHTS SOME TWO THOUSAND YEARS AFTER OUR LORD AND SAVIOUR JESUS CHRIST WHO HAD THROUGH DIVINE GRACE, MERCY AND AGAPE LOVE – LITERALLY, PHYSICALLY AND SPIRITUALLY, HAS ENSHRINED IT BY DIVINELY SETTING **ALL** MANKIND FREE. YET WE ARE STILL BEING SUBJECTED TO EVERY PHYSICAL SHACKLE OR MIND TRAP CONCEIVABLE BY OUR HUMAN OPPRESSORS, WHO BEING UNDER THE CONTROL OF EVIL SPIRITUAL BEINGS AT WORK; TO KILL, STEAL AND DESTROY NOT ONLY OUR BODY BUT ALSO OUR VERY SOUL.

CONTENTS

COPYRIGHT DETAILS vi

RECOGNITION & THANKS TO AMERICAN BIBLE SOCIETY vii

DEDICATION viii

PREFACE - LETTER FOR MY NEIGHBOUR 11

OPENING INTRODUCTION 21

PREVIEW PROPER 27

BOOK ONE: 'THE BIBLICAL 360 DAY YEARS'

REVELATION 13:18
PART ONE

REVELATION 13:18 47

'THE 360 EARTH DAYS ORBITAL YEARS'
PART TWO

'THE 360 EARTH DAYS ORBITAL YEARS' 89

ADDENDUM OF PART TWO & BRIDGE TO BOOK TWO 149

MORE ANCIENT & MODERN CIVILIZATION TIME SEQUENCE
RELATIONSHIPS 215

BOOK TWO: 'THE SCRIPTURAL COSMIC 666'

THE COSMIC BASED CONSTRUCTION, LEADING TO THE 'NUMBER' OF THE BEAST
PART THREE

THE COSMIC BASED CONSTRUCTION, LEADING TO THE 'NUMBER' OF THE BEAST 269

THE UNVEILING OF THE 'NUMBER' OF THE (SECOND) BEAST
PART FOUR

THE UNVEILING OF THE 'NUMBER' OF THE (SECOND) BEAST .... 345 - 394

APPENDICES:
18 MILESTONE ACHIEVEMENTS AND CHARTS .... 395 & 396

The unintentional but misleading and erroneous Christian teaching by our teachers, through which most of us were made into believing that the number that would be received by those willingly i.e. through willfull consent would be the number 666; is yet another common taught fallacy amongst us indeed. For in fact, it is the **number that would sum total 666** would be the correct Biblical accentuated version, as clearly expressed within the Rev 13:18 Scripture instead!!! Check it out yourself and do confirm this for yourself. Better still, do inform all your loved ones and friends about it too and get this book for more **'discernment learning'** that you will certainly experience and which will fortify you, for your further sharing with your family and friends alike, as we journey through this world together. PRAISE BE TO GOD ALMIGHTY.

Here is wisdom. *Let him who has understanding* **calculate the number of the beast, for it is the number of a man: his number is 666.**

Rev 13:18 Spirit Filled Life Bible - NKJV

LETTER FOR MY NEIGHBOUR

The biblical work that I had embarked on as titled more than a decade and a half ago, is in fact loaded with a good combination of science related established documented facts (astronomical & cosmological), ancient and modern. Together with several new intriguing cosmic possibilities, which I had very meticulously derived from within several relevant biblical scriptural texts, spanning across a few referenced canonised Biblical Books from within the Holy Bible that had enabled me to complete this challenging endeavour. The title in itself so aptly describes and answers what this book is entirely about. There is no ambiguity whatsoever about it.

Also, blended into this mix, includes, several specific and relevant necessary references made to scientist authored books and written articles such as 'Just Six Numbers' by Sir Martin Rees; some established and accepted theories of the Cosmologist Dr Stephen Hawking - The 'BIG BANG'; also the super genius Albert Einstein; Dr Samuel A. Goudsmit–Physicist; Astronomer Gerald P. Kuiper; Alan Gunt – propagator/originator for the 'Theory of Inflation' relating to the very beginning ('BIG BANG') of the Cosmos; Hipparchus – early Greek Astronomer; well known acclaimed Gordon Lindsay (Christian Writer and Evangelist) for his 'God's Plan for the Ages'; the great Indian Mathematician and Astronomer - Aryabhata and a few others too.

Based on what the title describes, I must state at this very outset that as far as my knowledge is regarding to this matter, there is no current or past evidence for it having been presented and/or authored by anyone in this original uniquely linked perspective. This is especially for the obtaining of the unique singular number set, which I have proposed in this book, that indeed sum totals the 666 as expressed and revealed per the scriptures in the Biblical Book, REVELATION - Rev Chapter 13 verse 18 refers and confirms. This amazingly had been derived jointly through my own applied understanding of several relevant scriptures that I had engaged for the intents and purposes as described in this book, coupled together with some very interesting scriptural mysteries that have been revealed here of the COSMOS in its very expansion through the GOD measured 'Universe Space' for itself. This specific cosmic connection was fundamentally derived through a fresh understanding of these relevant referenced scriptures. I am of the sincere opinion that this was only possible through divine guidance carrying me through all the way. Praise be to GOD.

There were, however, some in the past who had skirted with the issue of the '360 Days Years'. This was from their perspective of the supposedly globally disruptive impact that the Biblical Noah' Flood had which was compounded with their other proposed possible calamity contributors at the similar time that had actually caused as per their understanding, the lengthening of the planetary orbit of our Earth from its supposedly assumed original 360 days to what it is now - 365¼ days years since then. Yet none of these were from my perspective involved in the biblical sound happening for the 360 Days Years, which also readily links up with the generating of the unique singular number set that remarkably produces for us the intriguing cosmic based yet biblical sum total **666**. Thereby, my perspective has nothing in common or having any consensus with their perspective of the '360 Days Years'.

You would be continuously challenged to think through carefully what you had just read and what you would be reading in every next page in the book. Nothing has been written in this book to unnecessary waste precious time but to consistently stir up the curiosity, the intellect and the emotion to keep you motivated and captivated to read on and to be justly rewarded step by step, stage to stage, as you progress through the unveiling and the deciphering of several biblically encrypted scriptural mysteries for the very first time ever. Yes, that' right. FIRST TIME EVER!!!

The main purpose for embarking on such an arduous journey, which it was, as you can easily appreciate as evident from the very title of the book and to complete it through sheer GOD fearing determination was to bring to you a deeper understanding to this Satanic schemed initiative for the final annihilation of all Mankind, if at all this was possible, from Satan' world view. This however may on the way chip at a few generally accepted traditional Christian teachings, which directly pertains to the current understanding of the Biblical generated concept - the **'End of Days'** with some of my own inevitably derived and developed eschatological elements that are included, as I journeyed in this discovery as titled. This also does include the scientific concept of the same and the underpinning singular and most important cosmic acquisition of biblical proportions, that is in my opinion, being this unique 'cosmic number set' as evidently revealed here; to be sum totalling to the Biblical Revelation 13:18, **666**.

This last emphasis having been particularly so elusive, steeped and veiled in biblical mystery, shrouded in such marvellous divine scriptural encryption and as such almost having been totally ignored or missed by the biblical; the secular and the theological scholarship fraternity, is therefore not so surprising after all. With this in view, I wish to declare with the sincerest humbleness though, that, "I HAVE DISCOVERED IT AND WANT TO SHARE IT WITH YOU, MY NEIGHBOUR."

This will be primarily what you would be benefitted with besides a string of others, which would make you to become much more sophisticated in your awareness to being renewed in the spirit. Also, to have a refreshed revival once again, attesting that the Holy Scriptures held within a 'Library of Books', being the Holy Bible itself, is indeed the untainted and true word of our LORD GOD ALMIGHTY and that you can live your life by this very STANDARD with the salvation hope of heaven being the ultimate reward that awaits each of us on the 'Day of Judgment'. **PRAISE BE TO GOD**

It is through this very perspective, that it is important for us to have a book of this genre to be timely published for unfettered public consumption. This being across all borders, especially in these recent times, when there are many difficult episodes of Bible bashing and Christ bashing in books and movies, which also includes this daily over the internet chatter and other media too. This also, as lifestyles have become somewhat removed from being GOD-Centred living to worldly-centred living. This is where sex, money, self-gratification, self- interest gains and power position seeking only profits, are all that matters for fulfilling our existence here with no care of the afterlife, of which has been taken by many, a far backseat, in this all-testing single journey GOD given human life.

> In addition to this discovery of the Cosmic 666, I was fortunate enough to also obtain in bonus, so to speak, when I also had found out that the strikingly important biblical numbers such as: One hundred and forty four thousand (12 X 12,000 = 144,000); forty-two months (42); one thousand two hundred and sixty (1,260); time, times and half a time; and the number, one hundred and forty four (144), all of which are as mentioned in the Biblical Book of Revelation; The Book of Daniel and other relevant biblical scriptures have specific connections to the 'number set' sum totalling 666. These were all also so intricately intertwined with the 'Scriptural Solution' as obtained for the 'Cosmic Construction' of the 'number' of the second beast, sum totalling 666.

I sincerely do hope, as you begin to read through this book, that you do not think that it is just a process of establishing when actually would 'The Biblical 360 Days Years' begin for us as a natural solar planetary cosmic event for our Planet Earth. For it does have besides this, direct ramifications to the traditional Christian teachings for the 'End of Days'. This effort substantiates and reveals this based on the relevant referenced scriptures that do support it. Also, dispelling the currently accepted long standing notion that the Noah' Flood had indeed been the very cause for the Earth, to have been thrown into a 365¼ days orbit around the Sun, based on their very own traditional perspective of the original 360 days years Earth orbit. For according to my biblical researched findings with regards to the 'Biblical 360 Days Years', these have yet to happen in our Biblical Human History!!!

Their previous understanding would be proven to be inaccurate here and that it needs to be corrected urgently for the very benefit not only of the 'Christian World', but also for the world at large. This may sound to being very gutsy on my part, but the fact of the matter is that it is indeed the case as you will discover in this book.

It is important to do so, because, this has inevitably unearthed such great and severe ramifications as just mentioned, which involves more than what meets the 'eye'. This directly affects the very sanguine 'Institution of Christianity' amongst others, which was and still is built upon the Holy Scriptures for our doctrine and religious teachings as found in our Holy Bible according to our interpretations of it.

Obviously, no such similar traditional biblical interpretation in our Christian teachings should be acceptable anymore, once we do realise the error. However, it is definitely excusable for having done so as previously, but hopefully and prayerfully should be rectified and remedied accordingly as soon as possible, if it is actually found to be in gross error by YOU. That' right, **YOU!!!**

The writing of this book would be an excellent way to be bringing this 'argument' to light. It is also immensely important for the public at large too and not only so within the 'Global Christian Family', because, this subject 'End of Days' should also be of great importance to others too. I know my task at hand is indeed an uphill struggle but some 200 years or more ago there was the Italian Astronomer/Physicist Galileo Galilei who was indeed in a much more peril situation with the Church. His accomplishment was indeed in the aspect, when he had with evidence presented the heliocentric theory to the papacy, when he was summoned to their court. This in his time back then had caused such uproar so loud that it could have had rocked the very 'Seat of the Roman Catholic Empire'. To quash this from happening, the Church quickly decided to quash him!!! However, with due respect to the Church, they did not kill him for he was old, feeble and probably close to being blind too at the time and thereby, was subjected instead to house arrest, if I stand correct.

Galileo had supported the Copernican Sun-Centred view that the Earth was indeed the Planet together with the others in the Solar System that were orbiting the Sun and not the other way round. Unfortunately, the Roman Catholic Church at the time had infamously adopted to some extent the earlier Aristotelian (Aristotle, 384 - 322 BC) Greek Philosophy together with the Egyptian Greek Astronomer, Claudius Ptolemy's Earth-Centred System. This had inevitably placed the Earth in the very accolade esteemed centre from our human perspective, due to the Church' coupling of this Earth-Centred System by consolidating it with their gross misreading of the relevant Biblical Scripture as found in Joshua 10:12a – 14. This had then steadfastly confirmed the very position of the Church with regards to the Sun revolving around the Earth instead.

Joshua 10:12a - 14
"Sun, stand still over Gibeon;
And Moon, in the Valley of ᵇ Aijalon."

13 So the sun stood still,
And the moon stopped,
Till the people had revenge
Upon their enemies......................................14

The subsequent evidence supported Galileo' heliocentric proposition was therefore in exact reverse to this and thereby, inevitably becoming in direct loggerheads obviously with regards to the Church' acceptance at the time, which is now a universal scientific established fact. This also has now been fully accepted and recognised as such by the Church, but not too long ago though.

However, this declaration on Galileo' part back then was just HUGE!!! It was religious blasphemy, heresy in those terrible days of old, which I am so deeply grateful would not be branded as such in these more tolerant and modern times that we now do have. For now very much anything can be debated and argued in intellectual discourse without one being imprisoned, whipped, hanged, or to be burnt at the stake; well in most places at least.

In conclusion to this heliocentric proposition at the time, in fact it was Aristarchus of Samos (310 BC – ca 230 BC), ancient Greek Philosopher and astronomer, who was actually the very first individual to have presented the first model which had indicated that the Sun was indeed in the very centre, with the Earth revolving around it. However, this was strongly overshadowed by the widely accepted Aristotle Philosophy then and thereby was rejected totally until Copernicus long time later, followed closely by Galileo who had re-established the heliocentric system.

With the 'Biblical 360 Days Years' having been established in the first part of my work, I was then able to remarkably continue into my second and perhaps even more important part. This was in my ongoing effort to be able to construct this unique singular set of numbers as derived from the Cosmos, which uniquely sum totals 666; the same sum total as indicated in Rev Chapter 13:18.

> The unintentional but misleading and erroneous Christian teaching, through which most were made into believing that the number that would be received by those willingly i.e. through willfull consent, would be the number 666; is yet another common taught fallacy amongst us indeed. For in fact, it is the **number that would sum total 666** would be the correct Biblical accentuated version, as clearly expressed within the Rev 13:18 Scripture instead!!!

You can easily check it out for yourself, whether this statement just made above, which also actually underpins the very crux for writing this book, is absolutely correct or not, by reading intently and very carefully this quoted Scripture.

It is this unique singular number set that I have been so fortunate to have been able to propose here, amazingly being derived from the very Cosmos and yet Scriptural based, culminates my entire effort in this work. It is as already mentioned before, to my present available knowledge, that it is the very first of it' kind ever to be successfully computed and it is indeed verifiable through many channels, and is as written for your very benefit and spiritual well being at heart.

In the very process, this also fortunately dispels with the popularized and current notion for some that the world would be ending sometime in December, 2012. This fortunate outcome is yet another subsequent result or spin off from this work amongst several others.

I do sincerely hope that you will take up this very challenge to get this book to ensure that together we would succeed in this divine ordained commission as expressed in Rev 13:18. This is not a scientific based written book but definitely a scriptural based written book with scientific connotations. It is indeed another Christian book that hopefully many would read for their added spiritual benefit to enhance and to further fortify their belief that the Holy Bible is indeed the **TRUE WORD of ALMIGHTY GOD**.

It is especially for the neighbour who does not want just to believe blindly when taught that the 'WORD OF GOD' is indeed true in any which way you want to cut it. It is intended for that extra bit of push or rather gentle nudging pull that it can be proven to be so in our individual walk to inherit eternal life. This is not just with the heart, and of our own spiritual experiences and/or of others, although this is equally important, but also with the convincing of the **discerning mind**. For it is as such, revealed in the Scripture, Luke 10:27 which reads:

> " 'You shall love the LORD your GOD with all your heart, with all your soul, with all your strength, **and with all your mind**' and 'your neighbour as yourself.'"

This would catapult us onto standing on more solid ground, which I would prefer to refer to it as being, **'Faith Prosperity Ground'**. This could probably be better for some of us rather than just sheer emotion which could be shaken and swayed by convincing well crafted theories against our very belief system whether intended or unintended as clearly orchestrated by many in the past and even more so prolific in our present times.

My book, is also written for somewhat similar purposes, if I could take the liberty to say so, that being in parallel to some extent to what the sub-title of Josh McDowell's 'A Quest FOR ANSWERS' does against the absurdly manipulated but well crafted claims having been made in Dan Brown's 'The DA VINCI CODE'. And of course Dan Brown is in his right to do what he desires within the law, even in presenting his investigation as such in his book, though not being of the same view as ours. The problem is that 'The Da Vinci Code' is so well crafted that it could mislead and betray the trust that many have in our LORD and SAVIOUR JESUS CHRIST, into believing what he is establishing, especially amongst those who are not well grounded with the 'WORD' that we take exception and deep concern.

My effort and very attempt in my book is also somewhat echoed in the underpinning biblical scriptures of PROVERBS 9 and 10, which are aptly titled respectively as - 'The Way of Wisdom' and 'The Way of Folly'. For your convenience a few verses of both are shown here as taken from the Spirit Filled Life Bible - New King James Version (NKJV), Holy Bible; Thomas Nelson Publishers.

These scriptures being quoted right here, also quite inadvertently exposes my intended target audience, but certainly all are welcome to be equal passengers on this journey of biblical discovery and discernment.

The Way of Wisdom

Proverbs 9:
8   Do not correct a scoffer, lest he hate you; Rebuke a wise man, and he will love you.
9   Give instruction to a wise man, and he will be still wiser; Teach a just man, and he will increase in learning.
10 "The **fear** of the LORD is the beginning of **wisdom**, And the knowledge of the Holy One is **understanding**.

The Way of Folly

Proverbs 10:

16 "Whoever is simple, let him turn in here"; And as for him who lacks understanding, she says to him,

17 "Stolen water is sweet, And bread eaten in secret is pleasant."

18 But he does not know that the dead are there, That her guests are in the depths of hell.

This 'wisdom' and 'understanding' as described above in Proverbs 9, is also anchored in the very scriptures that began my journey in the first place for writing this book, as clearly expressed in Rev 13:18 as follows:

Here is wisdom. *Let him who has understanding* **calculate the number of the beast, for it is the number of a man: his number is 666.**

This particular Revelation Scripture also does similarly and inadvertently so, describes the only necessary credentials that I or anyone else embarking on this journey, would need, to reach out to the intended target audiences – which are all those who are seriously in search for 'Answers to Difficult Asked Spiritual Minded Questions'.

This book will cause some controversy too I am sure, science and religion wise, which I am afraid would take place so unfortunately, but hopefully and prayerfully these same people would arrive at some point in their 'argument' to see the truth behind this effort. For it was written fundamentally to reveal some very important and relevant hidden cosmic facts all wrapped up in particular scriptural mysteries that have been embedded in biblical encryption and till to-date has remained as such. It does not in any way **contort** or **manipulate** these biblical facts to be tailored for this effort. It is in fact bringing out and revealing these hidden mysteries for our added wellbeing and for our continued Christian walk towards our obtaining of the ultimate GOD provided Salvation.

It was engineered for the public interest and their welfare at heart with some Christian Spiritual undertones that do not offend but hopefully would invigorate the very soul to action in getting to know our LORD and SAVIOUR, Jesus Christ, in a more defining and rewarding intimacy. I sincerely hope that it will have a serious impact on the discerning mind and would be another important 'Christian Agent for Change' for those who may come across it. Also, importantly yet, another added testimony, that our Holy Bible is indeed the true and attested WORD of our LORD GOD ALMIGHTY being the Creator of the heavens and the earth and everything in it as confirmed by GENESIS 1:1.

Basic details of the Author: Graciously married with two sons. I am in no doubt, above everything else, still an ardent and with greater passion than before a very committed student of the Holy Bible. My humble credentials, if I may say so again, are as fortified and as exhibited by this very Scripture and others like it, i.e. in Rev 13:18; Proverbs 9:10.

First time author using gratefully and carefully this very platform to reach out to YOU, so together, to pave the way forward for each of us and for those following closely behind to be liberated from any shackles that may inhibit us from attaining our potential in CHRIST JESUS. Thereby, to be further richly enabled through the refreshing and renewal of our discerning mind to understanding the greater things of our **LORD GOD ALMIGHTY** has intended for each one of us. Hallelujah.

PRAISE BE TO GOD who first loved us even whilst we were yet sinners **Romans 5:8** refers and confirms.

The reason that it had taken me this long to complete this work as dated ending 1 September 2012, i.e. in the unravelling of the biblical intrigues as embedded in a maze of scriptural mysteries, was for the many times, that I just did not know how to continue the work. This is the honest truth and my testimony too. This was simply because I was stumped and stupefied for the solution to progress to the next higher level or link.

However, thank GOD ALMIGHTY, I had prevailed and that I had stayed on the course, to eventually be able to receive the necessary revelation and help from GOD THE HOLY SPIRIT. This I do sincerely and humbly believe such was the case to continually keep me correctly linked up and well aligned accordingly to the very completion of this book. THANK YOU JESUS CHRIST.

I hope you do find the rest an encouragement to challenge you to further strengthen your belief in our ALMIGHTY GOD, through HIS HOLY BIBLE - HIS WRITTEN WORD. Amen.

You may contact me at my email address:
E: gcf@globalchristianfamily.com

OPENING INTRODUCTION

> THIS IS YET ANOTHER ADDED TESTIMONY THAT OUR HOLY BIBLE IS INDEED THE TRUE AND ATTESTED WORD OF OUR LORD GOD ALMIGHTY BEING THE **CREATOR** OF THE HEAVENS AND THE EARTH AND EVERYTHING IN IT AS CONFIRMED BY GENESIS 1:1.

In the beginning GOD created the heavens and the earth.

DISCOVER yet another new and amazing glimpse of the awesome & complex mind of GOD, behind these earth bearing future cosmic events to happen, which GOD had set into motion, when GOD had first created for us, even before having us; the Universe.

DISCOVER for yourself, this amazing complexity, as I unravel for you, these future cosmic earth bearing events that have never been understood nor having been known about in this unique way, ever before.

THESE also, ranking amongst the very top echelon of the numerous scriptural mysteries and of important future scriptural events, will be revealed to you, "How it uniquely involves the Divine Workings in the very cosmos".

DISCOVER particularly, how several key prophesies, as found in the Biblical Book of Revelation and others, were divinely designed into the ongoing and progressive cosmic development of the Universe and it' most unique Solar-Earth System.

THESE new discoveries and new realization in itself, provides us with significant cosmic evidence loaded testimonies, for the ultimate 'Supreme and Divine Authorship' of the Universe by GOD ALMIGHTY, which in turn welds itself inseparably with the 'Divine Inspiration' of GOD ALMIGHTY being evidently attested behind the numerous writers of the Holy Bible.

YOU will see many of these 'evidential linkages' being revealed to you, as you progress through this book. These very same would hopefully, also negate and/or make it extra difficult for all those who adamantly still continue confronting us with the absurd accusation and debate, that the Holy Bible is merely just a concoction of our 'Christian Belief' or the one that we currently have is adulterated and a corrupted text of the 'lost original'.

THESE future earth bearing cosmic events, involving scriptural mysteries are found embedded cryptically in the Holy Bible Biblical Books, although being in plain sight. This having somehow enabled these 'mysteries' despite the centuries of Biblical Scholarship scrutiny to escape all previous detailed studies of the Holy Scriptures, gives me then this wonderful opportunity, to decipher as many that I am able and privileged to do so in this very book that is now being offered to YOU.

SO, ARE YOU READY TO ACCEPT THIS PRIVILEGE TOO AND TO RECEIVE NOW THESE AWESOME HOLY REVELATIONS OF MIGHTY COSMIC DIMENSION???

THESE will not only give you, another important and valuable affirmation to the 'Divine Truth' in the Biblical Scriptures, but also, must follow to surely further enhance your awareness, your belief, your faith and your ever readiness. This is especially, when the impending challenges due to the inevitable dangers that would come our way, which the 'Revelation End Times' and/or even the 'personalized end times' in our own individual lives will definitely and certainly bring.

THIS 'Revelation End Times' happening, according to the Holy Scriptures, will be certainly orchestrated by Satan himself, the fallen though once the most esteemed Archangel in the heavens. In the final phase of Satan' strategy, this will then eventually be executed through his own human appointee:

'THE BEAST FROM THE EARTH'
Revelation Chapter 13 refers.

> **MY BOOK IN THE COURSE OF IT' PROGRESS WILL ALSO PROVIDE YOU WITH DETAIL EXPLANATION OF WHEN, HOW AND WHY, THE EARTH WILL EVENTUALLY OBTAIN THE BIBLICAL 360 DAY YEARS AND HOW THIS IS DIRECTLY LINKED TO THE ESTABLISHING OF THE SCRIPTURAL COSMIC 666. THIS IS EXACTLY WHAT THE VERY TITLE DOES EPITOME.**

> ALSO, EMPHASISED HERE IS THAT THE '360 DAY YEARS' HAVE YET TO OCCUR, WITHIN OUR WELL KNOWN AND WELL DOCUMENTED 'HUMAN BIBLICAL HISTORY'. THIS IS THE VERY CRUX OF THE MATTER THAT SEPARATES MY BIBLICALLY RESEARCHED FINDINGS IN THIS BOOK; REGARDING THE 360 DAY YEARS, WITH THAT POSSIBLY OF THE OTHERS, WHO MAY HAVE BEEN TO SOME, NARROW EXTENT, ON SOMEWHAT A SIMILAR PATH.

IT is also very easy for one to confuse this very effort of mine to being that of the past civilizations and ancient peoples/nations designing and using a 360 Day Calendar. This is no way similar to what I am proposing here through this book. They were actually trying to design a calendar system which would be as accurate as possible to be in-sync with the climatic seasons and also the flooding cycles of their respective rivers prevailing in their region or land. This was to mainly accommodate their agricultural efforts in when to sow; what to sow; and when to harvest periodically throughout the year. It was also pertaining to their hunting and their nomadic cyclic lifestyles, and for maintaining religious & civil events. However, this was not possible for the many short comings in their system which had not taken into account the various motions of the Earth at different times and its relationship to the Moon and the Sun that had made their Lunar Months not to mesh with the Solar Year and their daily observation of the day and night rotation cycles.

AS you very well know, the Solar Year has indeed approximately 365.2422 days per year. This actually means that the Earth takes 365.2422 days to complete its annual orbit or journey around the Sun. So, in order to compensate for the various calendar short comings, they made adjustments. This they did by adding what is called intercalary days at the end of their calendar year or as the case may be intercalary months during specific years in the cyclic periods of their calendar. This they did to bring back the Solar Year to be as close to their calendar system so the seasons and their other needs as mentioned above could be predicted more accurately. All of this is already common knowledge and has been researched very thoroughly in the very greatest of detail as clearly evident from the numerous books over the decades and centuries that have been written on this, together with the numerous internet websites today being dedicated to this subject. Anymore research in this similar direction could be easily likened to that of 'flogging a dead horse'.

ON the other hand, what I am writing about here is on an entirely different subject. That the Earth will at some distant future time in our human biblical history-future would also be taking exactly and precisely 360 days to complete its very orbit around the sun. This would be the case annually, at that future time, for quite a number of years, before predictable i.e. you can calculate out these planetary changes would once again occur to prevent this from continuing indefinitely as such.

THIS means no more necessity of intercalary days from 5, 5¼ to 30 days or more over short and longer periods of time for seasonal adjustments to be made to the annual calendar. For in this case our Planet Earth would then be needing exactly and precisely only 360 Days to complete it' annual orbit around the Sun. For these at that future time would be indeed the natural occurring 'Perfect Years'.

BIBLICAL Scholars and theologians have been calling these long before this actually coming to pass, as being 'The Prophetic Years'. Through their reading of the relevant scriptures, they have also informed us that these very same 'Prophetic Years' have indeed already taken place. In fact, they have informed us through their Scholarship that the 'Prophetic Years' have already been completed in full. So my understanding of the same would then not be 'too friendly' to what they have been teaching us, all this while past.

YES, the 'Prophetic Years' with annual lengths of 360 Day Years will surely happen as having been foretold in our Holy Scriptures. However, these have yet to occur as per my very understanding of it, which I am most eager to share with you in this book. This will take place, by the very rules as revealed through the revelations that I have introduced or conveyed here. Well anyway, this is my personal conviction as underpinned by my scriptural derived understanding on this matter.

THIS however, giving us yet another great platform for good intellectual discourse, for a better perspective; being accompanied and supported with strong verifiable substantiated written argument, as written in this book, which is in-line with the relevant referenced scriptures.

> THIS IS FOR THE CHRISTIAN AT LARGE AND THE SAME TOO FOR OTHERS OF DIFFERENT FAITHS, WHO DO SHARE MANY ASPECTS OF OUR HOLY SCRIPTURES.

THEREFORE, the crux for the reality to this matter is that these specific Holy Scriptures are indeed substantiating that there will indeed be coming a time in our 'Human Biblical Future', that our Planet Earth will be experiencing these 360 days year orbit around the Sun for a specific number of years at the time. Now this is indeed a very different kettle of fish to be contending with, which I am having the wonderful and blessed privilege to be swimming in for a time and a season.

IN my book, I will also lead you through an amazing step by step process; how the obtaining of the 360 days year will be directly linked to the generating of a very unique and interesting **'cosmic number'**, that will and must be singly attributed to 'the beast from the earth'. You will undoubtedly learn this with greater amazement and be even awestruck; for it will uniquely sum total **666**. And hopefully, this will be the very same number, which Rev 13:18 was coaxing us to eventually calculate.

THIS linked understanding is indeed greatly paramount in being the very key for you to know exactly what this book is all about. Also, the generating of this unique 'cosmic number' in it-self provides us with the amazing biblical know-how to this purposefully GOD designed planetary process. This also, being readily linked to the overall expanding Universe, as it continuously unfolds before us, whilst we obtain the required 'cosmic number' which biblically sum totals 666.

ALSO, in retrospect, this cosmic in-built difficulty for obtaining this unique number set is absolutely fitting to the taking up and the fulfilling of this 'Divine

Commission Undertaking', as openly offered in the Book of Revelation. Rev 13:18 confirms as follows:

Here is wisdom. Let him who has understanding calculate the number of the beast, for it is the number of a man: His number is 666.
(Spirit Filled Life Bible - New King James Version)

HOWEVER, having said all of the above, I must confess right here and now, there were many times over that I had felt really most silly and completely hopeless to the extent of even thinking probably that I was going out of my mind, bonkers in wanting to continue on with this awesome and challenging effort. This was primarily based on the very realization that the hypotheses being presented here could be so easily shattered and done away with by any mediocre scientific mind, or even one amongst the rest of us, as being completely baseless and unfounded by any standard. This is despite these being directly derived through the relevant referenced Holy Scriptures; for yet these are still coming through my very own applied understanding of the same. This is in particular, with our own Solar Planetary System, when I personally do not have any such academic credentials at any level per se to be making any such 'Scientific Weighted Proposals' even only in theory. However, if I am humbly privileged to claim what the Rev 13:18 Scripture has indeed established the very ground rules for the taking up of this 'Open Divine Commission' i.e. the only necessary prerequisites to back me up to be convincing enough to be allowed to come up with such hypotheses, being the very understanding as underpinned by the associated wisdom, then the hypotheses will stand the scrutiny from any quarter.

This is what is most scary of the entire journey through this arduous effort. Many times, I felt utterly defeated by this very thinking and was indeed ashamed even to carry on, not of being ridiculed as such, but due to my own realization of whether this could be indeed really possible. However, despite this doubting, as I continued to steadfastly persevere on, even through this inner struggle and inner nagging turmoil that was constantly and consistently ravaging on unrelentingly in my mind, throughout the entire effort, (perhaps this was Satan' attacks upon my mind), I became to also realize graciously, the many **'coincidences'** that the Holy Scriptures had with this proposed cosmic happening.

These very **'coincidences'** in particular, involving our Sun, Earth and Moon with the several relevant referenced Scriptures that have been engaged here, had indeed been paramount in having kept me to be most diligent and most adamant to continue pressing on to it' very completion.

PRAISE BE TO GOD ALMIGHTY
AMEN

GENESIS 1:14

> Then God said, "Let there be lights in the firmament of the heavens to divide the day from the night; and let them be for signs and seasons, and for days and years;

PREVIEW PROPER (FOR BOOK 1 & 2)

The Hebrew word for **signs** as per Strong's Concordance #226, gives us the following meanings besides others such as evidence, mark, a signal etc. Therefore, based on these meanings it provides us with the obvious linkage, that we could also take the **'number'** of the beast as being a sign; as it is to be placed on the forehead or on the right hand, as the case maybe per the victims choice – Rev 13:16-17 refers. This is done to provide the evidence for all to see, both spiritual beings and human alike, that when the victims are marked as such, they have indeed come under the full authority of Satan and his beasts. In spiritual terms, they have cashed in their souls for a few personal 'TIME-LIMITED' liberties.

Therefore, although it may come as a mighty big surprise to many, that the 'number' of the beast has indeed a '**Cosmic Based Construction**' and evidently through this effort also **derived through relevant referenced Scriptures,** you will quite certainly realize for yourself, as you study through this book, that it' discovery is well within our human ability – as Rev 13:18 is our testimony to this very possibility.

All this had initially begun for us when GOD had described to us as indicated in the Scriptures of Gen 1:14 - 18; that the lights in the firmament, especially the Sun and the Moon and even the Stars, let them be for **signs.**

Now, you may want to question, "What is so important, interesting and different about my book on the subject of the beast through its number?"

If my explanation in the Preface was not good enough convincing for you, then in order for me to properly answer this anticipated question, I need to bring your attention first and foremost to my first book, 'THE BIBLICAL 360 DAY YEARS', which I will simply refer to here as being Book One and is in fact included here for your personal benefit. It is made up of two major parts, to which an important 'Addendum' to Part Two was later added. This 'Addendum' is also an important 'Bridge' to link you up and to help you to successfully crossover to Book Two, which is 'THE SCRIPTURAL COSMIC 666'. Also included in Book One, is an interesting section describing some relevant ancient and modern civilization time sequence relationships; some in more depth than others for our specific intent and purposes.

Through Book One, you will discover, how it would be possible for Planet Earth to experience for the very first time in our Biblical Human History/Future the 360 Day Years. This will be primarily accomplished through the use of a good blending of Biblical Scripture, some quite basic Science and prayerfully a lot of divine guidance.

These first 'Two Parts' in this Book One are predominantly pertaining to the development of the Biblical 360-Day Years. This according to the proper understanding of the relevant Biblical Scriptures will be experienced by the Earth for the very first time, i.e. ever since Adam had walked on this Earth in this human era. I am staking my claim: This would definitely take place and through this book, will be providing you with concepts structured, based on the very understanding of the relevant referenced Scriptures from the Holy Bible. This means, as far as I know, no one has actually written on these very subjects as titled, using any of my original structured concepts and also to providing you the reader, with the convincing solution, in support to this Cosmic Solar Planetary event actually to be taking place. Now this partly answers the above question.

Now, I am fully aware that there have been several references made to the 360-Day Years by others too, in the past. This is besides those whom I was first referring to in the Preface and also in the Opening Introduction. In this secondary case, it seems that it was made in reference to their main writings, which were based on a completely different subject. To further elucidate on this, for example: They were probably writing on the Noah' Flood or events relating to it or even probably making some references to Daniel' 'Seventy Weeks of Years' or Revelation' 42 months and 1,260 days.

The Noah' Flood in particular is a well-known and well-read Biblical event. This was their subject or main evidential reference, as they agreed with the others that the Noah' Flood was indeed responsible in upsetting the Earth' system of motions, whereby it caused us since then to have 365¼ day long years instead besides causing the Earth' axial axis to tilt too.

They made reference to Noah' Flood with regards to this replacing of the previous and original 360 Day Years. This is what they thought had taken place and still most of the 'Christian World' do preach and teach this very thinking.

Others went on to add that a large astral body, probably a sizable asteroid, which they believe came quite close to the Earth at the precise time the Noah' Flood was to have begun; thereby upsetting the Earth' motions. They did not confirm that the asteroid had actually entered the atmosphere of the Earth and had crash landed into us but that it had come real close and this proximity at that opportune time as proposed by them, also resulted in the probable and possible cause for the lengthening of the Earth' orbit around the Sun. These were their theories or hypotheses and based on these together in turn became the key contributing factors to cause the Noah's Flood as they had thought to become of such magnitude to cause global devastation and annihilation of the global population. This was indeed the case according to their understanding of the subject matter except for the precious Noah's eight (including himself) to have remained through the Flood and after the Flood to re-procreate the human race to once again through their generations to eventually repopulate the entire world globally. So they say. This directly means, in a way, we are all descendants of Noah's Family.

This global flood devastation according to them, progressed in turn to be also the direct cause for the tilting of the Earth' very axial axis as already mentioned, as to what it is currently now, 23° 26' 15" (i.e. 23 degrees 26 minutes 15 seconds or not more than 23½ degrees) off it' centre. This dramatic axial axis planetary earth movement change was then subsequently used by them to link the very beginning for us to have the annual seasons of varying climates since then. According to them, all of this coupled together, had resulted in us having the 365¼ days since then, instead of the previous and probably Earth' original 360-Day Years. No intercalary calendar adjustments necessary here though, unlike in the previous first group, as already been discussed in the Preface and in the Opening Introduction

All of this, is centering on the Noah' Flood. This was their subject. Here they were trying to justify the magnitude of the Noah' Flood, as they believed it was global in destruction. They were actually trying to offer the reader and believer, some reasoning to understand the then prevailing belief, which is also widely the current belief amongst most of us Christians; that the Noah' Flood was indeed globally reaching. This was how they and their predecessors understood it from their study of the relevant Holy Scriptures in the Bible. They were probably offering those of us who were having several doubts on this global devastation, some basis to accept this and to reconfirm to us, that the Noah' Flood was indeed globally reaching in devastation. In fact there are scientists even currently still doing research on this very understanding of a globally devastating Noah' flood. They are trying to unearth the evidences through land and marine archaeology. I do wish them good fortune in their committed and continued search for the answers, but I do however, beg to seriously differ with these two hypotheses not that it were not possible, but that these were not the very reasons for the Earth to have acquired the 365¼ day years annual orbit around the Sun and also similarly to have acquired this pronounced Earth' axial axis tilt. This is what my book will also actually stand to prove had not been the case indeed, against those of whom had made the claims as per their reading of the relevant biblical scriptures in Genesis Chapters 6 – 8 that it had been globally destructive.

> *Of course my findings and the evidences for supporting my proposition against that of the others is all locked up in biblical scripture too and will be revealed to you accordingly.*

Pastor and Evangelist James Gordon Lindsay, in his spectacular prophetic book 'God's Plan of the Ages' had indeed proposed continuous and ongoing periods of varying number of years of 360 and 365¼ day years. This being spread over varying cycle lengths of 360 years and 365¼ years, respectively. These two types of differing year length cycles, according to Gordon Lindsay, and as to my understanding of his book; each cycle signals the beginning that means it began with important and significant Biblical events and even with regards to some significant secular events. These have indeed become milestones in our human and biblical history.

These both types of significant events seem to coincide with the very changes in the cycles, i.e. one to the other from being 360 switching to the 365¼ day years. It is this very linked speculative reasoning from my perspective, as propositioned by Gordon Lindsay, that in my evaluation of his work, gives rise to us with such similar consensus (if there are any out there too) to question its very validity and soundness.

The reason I stated this linking as being speculative, besides the linking itself, is because, it directly ignores the very important 'Solar Planetary Cosmic Forces' in play, that would actually and eventually bring this event to happen in due course. Of course to be fair with Gordon Lindsay, this cosmic possibility would not have been known at the time by him and that is the reason why he possibly was channeled into this thinking as proposed in his book to obtain the desired outcome. Also, the fact is that no one else would have also known about this Solar Cosmic possibility to be happening, that would bring about for us some time in the future our very own 360 Day Years. The reason for this too, is that it has not yet been discovered, and thereby, only through this book that I am discovering this very possibility myself and most willing to similarly share this with YOU.

Yet, then again his proposed linking is essentially the basis of his book to reveal to us these repeating cycles of time in years through certain specific cycle lengths that he suggests and proposes to have some significant impact regarding some secular events and also similarly in some of our biblical events. Furthermore, it becomes a little more complicated, as these cycles also interweave with each other and also comprising of other cycle lengths such as the 40 year cycle lengths; Israel Jubilees cycle lengths; the 450 year Judgment Cycle lengths; Seven Times Cycles lengths; Daniels 70 Weeks cycle; the four 490 year cycle lengths of temple worship.

This was what Gordon Lindsay had established and evidently had concluded in his book with reference to the switching from the 360 to the 365¼ day years and vice versa in his periodically switching theory from one time cycle length to another time cycle length as just mentioned above.

In his book, he describes 13 cycles of 360 years and 26 cycles of 365¼ years in varying time length cycles. As I understood it, in total 39 such interweaving cycles, covering a period of exactly 7,049 Solar Years. This of course incorporates the 'Biblical Creation Week'; the continued Biblical History since then; across the Noah' Flood and even into our Biblical Future to come, until the very 'End of Days'. All this is remarkably packaged by him in a very short period of just 7,049 Solar Years.

Somehow, his 39 interweaving cycles worked out to be representing 13 cycles of 'Calendar Years' (i.e. 360 day years) and exactly double that i.e. 26 cycles **in 'Solar Years' (365¼ day years). However, even in disagreement, I must respect** his perspective, just as much as I would like mine to be given a chance for each of you to decide, in agreement hopefully, or to be otherwise, as the case could possibly be too.

> In conclusion, in my personal capacity, he had in fact indeed written a very interesting and fascinating book. His Christian walk and Christian work had accomplished so much during his tenure on this Earth, having benefitted hundreds and perhaps even thousands of people worldwide, including myself too. I am indeed totally humbled having come to know about him and his ministry through his book.

My disagreement with his book besides the reasons already given is primarily due to the simple biblical derived fact as described in my book, that we are **yet to have** our very first 360 Days Year in our entire past Human Biblical History. And yes, I am expecting it to occur for the very first time in our distant future.

This then quintessentially falls upon me to offer the substantiated scriptural backed evidence for my justified disagreement. This I am trying to exactly accomplish here in writing this book to be providing you with a platform for evidential verifiable argument to hopefully overcome such unintentional misinformation from the several sources that many of us had been exposed to from our very early childhood that is through our Catechism or Sunday School. Many of us have also grown up with this thinking and will not let go of it, as we do sincerely believe it to be correct as such. Well I do hope this book of mine, will make this CHANGE to happen for YOU, when you see the very merits for my argument.

With this in focus, I am confident to express and to even singularly claim that my work is indeed an original perspective through and through. This is because the subject itself that I am writing about in my Book One and subsequently in my Book Two as well, is essentially based on the 'Biblically Derived Cosmic Progress' in the development of our advancing Solar Planetary System. This is however limited to be specifically focusing only into the area of it' cosmic development that would produce for us in a relatively short period, in comparison to that of the overall age of the Universe, our very first 360 Days Year here on Planet Earth, ever since we human beings had first begun walking upon it.

Thereby, I do humbly believe and sincerely hope that my two books under one ISBN title as being presented here, amongst the thousands of Christian Books that have already been written on various subjects and topics by Biblical Authors, would hopefully bring to the Christian World and the world at large, an all new and refreshing understanding both academically and also hopefully spiritually. This also further enhancing and fortifying from this fresh perspective; that GOD' WORD as expressed in the Holy Bible, is absolutely true and perfect in every which way you want to cut it. This is despite the several biblical interpretation hiccups that we have encountered along the way due to the unintentional but nevertheless erroneous interpretations (a few as from my perspective) that have indeed misled and caused division within and without our Christian Global Family.

From all of my above presentation, it may appear to you being all so very high flying, especially, it coming from an unknown, untried or unrecognized source (that' me in a nutshell). Yet, be rest assured that you will be able to comprehend it quite easily with an open mind and to draw your own conclusions at the very end of it. Hopefully, this meets in unison with my own effort here.

There are no mathematical or scientific propositions used as such in my book that are indeed overwhelmingly complicated. Only the use of very simple math and basic understanding would be required. This is the other wonderful thing about reading this book.

Now, I need to complete my answer to the question that had been anticipated.

During the process of writing my first book, 'The Biblical 360 Day Years', I began to realize that I could also obtain for the very first time the unique 'number' of the beast, through a cosmic approach, but yet again scriptural derived. Now although, it is quite clear that many in the past have written about this 'number' as it is of the beast, but they had one thing in common and that was they had calculated the 'number' of the beast, based on the mystic and occult system of Gematria. According to Wikipedia – the free internet encyclopedia, this Gematria was essentially first practiced by the Tannaim who were the rabbinic sages during the Mishnaic period, which lasted for about 130 years from approximately 70 – 200 CE. According to their tradition, the Tannaim was the last generation in a long sequence of oral teachers that began with Moses.

Gematria is a system of numerology which exchanges an alphabet, a word, a phrase even that of Scripture with numbers that when sum total may represent a coded message to them of some past, present or future significance. There are many such methods which fix the numerical value for these exchanges and you have to be very familiar with the subject to understand which method is applicable for what purpose.

However, in more recent times, spread through the past several centuries or so until even now, those opposing the Church (The Roman Catholic Church) came up with numerous combinations of numbers, each set manipulated in such a way to sum total 666. These were and still are specifically describing the various positions of office as held by the Pope and thereby labeling them as being the Anti-Christ who is mentioned and identified as such in the Book of Revelation. This was their way (those opposing) of attacking and protesting against the Holy See (The Pope) and it' very Institution, by wickedly attempting to bring it into disrepute, through any which means as much as possible. I will go into this subject with somewhat greater detail as we progress through Book One.

> So, through all of these decades and centuries past, the calculation for the 'number' of the beast was centered on this one occult driven system of Gematria.

I will stand corrected; if it could be proven that there were others using dissimilar methods or systems for this very purpose. Novels and short fictional stories wrapped up in secular fantasy, which have been written on this overall subject of the 'End Times', are quite definitely not to be taken into serious account for obvious reasons, even though of it' convincing and entertaining reading indeed.

> So, again with this in focus, my second book, 'The Scriptural Cosmic 666' comprising of another Two Parts, which can be simply referred to as Part Three and Part Four, are also original in concept, perspective and content.

However, I came to quickly realize that the Two Parts of my first book, 'The Biblical 360 Day Years' takes on a completely enhanced higher meaning and impact, when I discovered that the Solar Planetary Earth' development towards its 360-Day Years together with the expanding Universe is in fact progressing also towards the establishing or rather to the generating of this unique 'number' of the second beast, which sum totals 666. As a consequence, I felt it best for you to have both of these books at the same time, under a combined title. This evidently from my perspective does conclude my answer for the first anticipated question.

Yet many may want to still question: "Why bother finding out the 'number' of the beast in the very first place???" Well, it is like this.

"**Why** did and still people do aspire to climb up Mount Everest or to swim the English Channel or to repeatedly break the World Records in any field of sports or of human achievement???"

"**Why** did people aspired to have manned missions to the Moon and indeed against all odds eventually had achieved it six times to date for the greater glory of all mankind???"

"**Why** is there so much of continued human effort just to save the Great Panda from becoming extinct or for that matter the Great Whale or even the spotted Leopard, etc???"

"**Why** did we need to decipher the Human Genome revealing our very own Human Genetic Code???"

Now, all of these and the like are of Earthly things and have their great importance in their own right. However, in my opinion, with the finding out of the 'number' of the beast, this too becomes ten-fold or perhaps even a hundred-fold more important for us to know regardless of whether you are Christian or not. For in my personal point of view and hopefully eventually yours too, it is more important, relatively speaking, because this finding out of the 'number' of the beast has indeed direct implications on our life as it potentially affects our eternal spiritual future. It is from this very perspective that I have stated that it is even more important than secular discoveries. Another way of looking at it is besides this; the very realization of the truth and the impact of the 'End of Days' too, at that time and also in the immediate, than merely being just of our Earthly achievements, makes it, relatively speaking more important for many of us to know.

Furthermore, as our LORD GOD ALMIGHTY had expressed it through REV 13:18; that we should seriously attempt finding it out, then it must surely be very important for having us to do so. Even if you are not interested or do not believe in the 'Christian Afterlife', please do read these books, for it may challenge you to change your perspective to this very possibility. Also, that the Holy Bible is to be taken as it had been in the past i.e. the 'OLD TESTAMENT' was the orally handed down inspired 'WORD OF GOD', having later to have been written down by men but yet not of their own invention but that solely of GOD. Amen.

Hopefully, after you have gone through these two books that I have written, you too will perhaps with an added twist or more onto the 'Rope Of Truth', further enhancing that the Holy Bible is indeed the 'TRUE WORD of GOD ALMIGHTY' in it' entirety which also includes the 'NEW TESTAMENT'. This in humbleness is my sincerest and most expectant HOPE that these books would also in some way help someone to see the 'Light'. This in itself would make it all to be worthwhile.

FOR GOD IS THE LIGHT AND THE VERY SALVATION IN OUR LIVES

Psalm 27, brings this out so beautifully. This is further emphasized amongst numerous others, as in John 1:4-5; 1:9 & 1John 1:5 – NKJV.

Now, if you are still somewhat skeptical of how would it be possible that the 'number' of the beast could be or rather is indeed to be generated through the 'Cosmic Mechanisms' which GOD ALMIGHTY had created and initiated in the very first place in the Universe; then allow me to gently nudge you with a bit more heavier stuff into the right direction.

According to Sir Martin Rees, British Astronomer and author, reiterates what other scientist have already discovered, that the Universe is indeed possible, only because of just six fundamental constants. I am sure you do immediately recognize that the number of fundamental constants being six is indeed the only digit that was used in the sum total of the 'number' of the second beast being 666.

We are informed that even small changes in any of these six constants, could even be responsible to the very extent for our Universe becoming non-existent.

> **Could you just imagine that our LORD GOD ALMIGHTY with such fine delicateness, this massive fragileness could be ingrained in such a large almost unfathomable dynamic body, as the Universe? This just blows your mind to smithereens.**

To give you one of his examples: Sir Martin Rees explains to us in his book, 'Just Six Numbers', that the first fundamental constant, is the number we get when we divide the strength of the electrical force, which holds atoms together, by the universal force of gravity. This had determined the formation of galaxies and stars, planets and even their very orbits. The value of this constant is 1, followed by exactly 36 zeros. Sir Martin Rees tells us that if this fundamental constant had fewer zeros, meaning that the Universal gravity was stronger than the above situation, this would have resulted in a short-lived and a very much smaller Universe; a Universe in miniature.

On the other hand, if I do understand it correctly, if the same fundamental constant had more zeros, this meaning that the Universal gravity was weaker than the original situation as indicated above, then matter itself would obviously not be assembled together, after the possible 'trigger' for the Universe expansion i.e. after the 'Big Bang' had occurred.

This means the subsequent formation of the 'Universal Bodies', such as the galaxies and the stars, definitely would not have been able to take place, if there were more zeros after 1 of this constant which already has 36 zeros. For the complete examining of these six fundamental constants, please do read his book.

> **However, before we leave Sir Martin Rees; a question does crop up: How did these six fundamental constants come to being precisely as they were and still are, which had made possible this Universe of ours and all the 'life' that we know of, which currently exists as far as we know, only on Planet Earth and that all of these six fundamental constants are still being maintained as such???**

The answer, if you have not come to it is just simply – our LORD GOD ALMIGHTY. Well anyway while you are still pondering on this, I made reference to Sir Martin Rees' book, 'Just Six Numbers', to further enlighten you that the entire Universe was indeed put together and is still maintained as such by a precise mathematics which clearly exhibits to us that behind it all is a purposeful GOD-MINDED design for its possible existence. This GOD' design, which evidently was inculcated into the creation of the Universe had in actual fact, also produced all the so called 'mathematics' which includes the physics and all the other contributing sciences that we now have and do know about as is being discovered as such by our very learned scientists; yes you are right, just basically through numbers.

Therefore, in anticipation, do not be too skeptical of my very suggestion and proposal that our LORD GOD ALMIGHTY had also designed into these complex 'Cosmic Mechanisms', the very construction of the 'number' of the beast. This if you really do think about it, is indeed a very clever and yet higher way of also testifying to GOD' divine authorship of the Universe itself.

> **For through this very precise mathematical designed construction of the Universe, it possibly could offer us yet another verifiable perspective, for the unmistakable proof as underpinned by the cosmic evidences for GOD' workmanship. This being GOD' Divine Signature, that the Universe had not just come about by sheer chance association through a chaotic system, but that it was of HIS very own 'GOD Doing' that had made all of this indeed possible.**

Also, through my own perspective of it being definitely verifiable through biblical scripture, if you know how to resource from it appropriately; this Universe construction design and all the life created in it, evidently exposes simultaneously, both the 'Hand of GOD' in it and to an extent a glimpse of the 'MIND of GOD' in it too. I will certainly show you precisely, and in the process, hopefully remove your expected skepticism or at the least as much as possible, how this was indeed established in this very book. This is from the perspective of the 'Cosmic Number Construction' as derived and developed through the relevant Scriptures, for the obtaining of the unique number set of the second beast, which remarkably sum totals 666!!!

It is as mentioned also an 'Open Public Divine Commission', as declared in Rev 13:18, which reads:

> **Here is wisdom. Let him who has understanding calculate the number of the beast, for it is the number of a man: his number is 666.** (NKJV)

So for me, it became just simply to obey and to accept this 'Open Public Divine Commission' outright not by personal choice or by personal intent though, but probably it was my destined 'calling' to do so, even without realizing it at first, as already mentioned before. Please take note that there is no conceitedness in this statement, although you may perceive it to be so.

This 'Divine Commission' does not demand a PhD in Theology or in Divinity or even in the Sciences, but only the vital and relevant **'understanding'** being applicable to calculate out the 'number' of the beast. I am spiritually glad that I had some twenty years ago, through personal choice, after careful deliberation had willfully become a born again Evangelical 'Pentecostal' Christian. I am also spiritually grateful for having been brought up well through very strong traditional grounded Roman Catholic roots and their Christian teaching; for I was born into it, as my entire family were Roman Catholic from several generations past. At least three generation past, I am sure, making my children to be the fifth generation. I thank my beloved father and my beloved mother for being such devoted Roman Catholics and for bringing me up as such. Their love and care for me and for my siblings in every aspect of our living is just immeasurable. I also personally do believe in my heart, in my mind and above all deep in my very soul, that the switching to being an Evangelical 'Pentecostal' Christian had actually made it possible for me to better understand GOD's WORD through the more intent with purpose and direction the study of the Holy Bible. This inevitably, as I believe now, had also set me onto the path to be able to receive this 'calling', if I may humbly say so again. And in the process make it my definite 'mission' to do so, i.e. in the revealing of the number of the beast that sum totals 666. Well that is what I do think not for humility sake I say this, but that it must have been the case and I am truly humbled by this mission. You are of course entitled to your own opinion. GOD BLESS.

Through the pursuit of discovering, when we would finally experience the '360 Day Years' and the calculating of the 'number' of the beast, through this very 'Cosmic Construction', as described in this book; I also discovered the following:

(a) The possible Scriptural 'Age of the Universe' and of the Earth, as derived through the proper understanding of some relevant scriptures in the Holy Bible.

(b) When the Earth' Axis Rotation Speed Switchover or EARSS for short actually does take place. This is a new and fundamental concept, which I originally had developed in the process of writing these books.

(c) There is a 'Universal Time' (UT) out there in the Cosmos and there is also a 'Local Time'; this depending on where you are located in the Cosmos, in relation to this UT.

This is another new fundamental understanding with regards to our existing concepts of 'Time' which I had developed during the process. So, for the time being, our focus regarding this 'Local Time' would be with our Planet Earth i.e. 'Earth Time' (ET) in relation to this UT.

(d) I had also discovered how these are related to one another and how we can convert one time system (ET) to the other time system (UT).

(e) Also, had found out that there are specific time linkages with how the Babylonian; the Maya; the Indians of India and possibly also the Chinese and even our current observation of time and time periods are actually all similarly linked together to a singular common source of reference. This despite having been developed independently through the various civilizations of the past to the very present.

And many more interesting possibilities that will be revealed to you accordingly, as you do proceed on, through these two books having been combined under a single title.

This for me personally, could be the very culmination, when an English woman, my parent' friend, had presented me with the Holy Bible, whilst we were then residing in Sheffield, England for a good period of years. Nothing wrong with the giving of this gift, except this was way back, when I was just about four years of age. And yet at that time, having the fullest of knowledge that I was only able to speak 'baby' words, whilst other children of my age were already quite fluent in communicating indeed!!! For awhile, my parents were noticeably afraid and quite concerned that I may remain as such with a speech impediment at best or worse still end up being a mute and therefore, had already taken me to see several doctors for this 'handicap'. I was informed by my parents though, some years later, that the doctors had however assured them that nothing was wrong with me except perhaps that I was just a slow starter/learner. Yet at the time, this 'silly' action by the English woman had naturally and not surprisingly so, must have had startled my parents out of their very wits, when she being their friend, had found it fitting at the time, to give me such a difficult and awesome book to read by any standard, when I could barely call out properly to my own mother!!!

I was neither dumb nor deaf, or for that matter, not able to understand what was happening around me or what was being said to me; for all of this was just real fine. Yet, I had this real problem of not being able to speak and/ or to verbalize to any understandable level what I wanted to communicate. Therefore, my parents must have thought this English woman, at the time, really was quite crazy. For I do still remember my mother telling her off, "You do know that my son is not even able to speak properly as yet; how is he going to be able to read a book such as this at this very young age when he can't even read out aloud the alphabet!!!" Well it was something like that having the intended impact. Mamma Mia, my mother was on a roll there for a moment. She goes on to say, stretching my imagination and memory of the incident, "Could you have not given him a child' toy to play with instead?" I am quite certain at the time that I would have agreed with my mother too without question.

Yet somehow, although this had happened way back then, I do still remember the English woman reassuring them, though prophetically in hindsight, that I will be able to speak and that I will be able to read this Holy Bible at the right time. And she must have said this with such conviction and gumption, which in a way I do believe now, would have had settled and brought some very needed comfort to my troubled parents, instead of the utter embarrassment that they would have surely had felt at the time. For, if you do seriously think about it, in hindsight, it could have been taken to be a very sarcastic and nasty thing to do at the time. Yet most surprisingly, not long after, I did begin to speak, a bit slow at first but eventually overtook my friends quite quickly and have not stopped ever since!!! Alleluia. **ALL PRAISE BE TO GOD ALMIGHTY. THANK YOU JESUS CHRIST. THANK YOU HOLY SPIRIT.**

So, there you are, someone had planted the very 'seed of faith' into my life but first and foremost into my parents' life, so many years ago. This was when my beloved father (from Malaya, which it was called at the time), was given a British Colonial Government scholarship to go over to Colonial England for a period of four years or so, to complete his studies as a Radiographer being involved in the treatment of Cancer. In those days being given such a scholarship or for that matter any scholarship was really a very BIG thing indeed. It was a period in our Country' history when there were really not that many people who had the opportunity to have a proper education, let alone to be awarded with a scholarship to study overseas, especially to Colonial England, our ruling masters at the time. Those were the very early days of Cancer Research, study, discovery, diagnosis and treatment. My father must have been someone very special and above all must have been very hard working to be given this very opportunity. And indeed he was recognized as being **the pioneer** (very first individual) for receiving this special training and education (in our country' medical services), for having been sent over there for this very purpose.

Well there you have it, an inner secret from my early childhood in England, which probably to-date no one else still really knows about except for my loving and beloved mother, who has already turned 84 this year (2012), and yet she still remembers this event very well. And yes, I do still have that Holy Bible, which was presented to me, by that dear English woman in Sheffield, England. Of course, it took me many years before I did realize it' very importance and the part that it would eventually play in my own life. Amazingly, it has somehow escaped having been misplaced; destroyed through mishandling by myself or by my siblings; or by wear and tear; or having been simply lost or even having been thrown away through the years and the many times that we had to shift home over these last five decades or so.

Equally remarkable was, "How did she come up with that 'strangest of ideas' to give this 'handicap boy' at the time, this very precious gift, instead of the expected regular child' toy or for that matter even a simple basic nursery rhyme picture book?" This looking from all circumstances would have been the very sane and correct thing to have done at the time. Notwithstanding, to being ridiculed herself, she took it upon herself to do this very thing. Yet in hindsight now, through my Christian thinking, she may have been carrying out her own Christian duty in obedience to the inner promptings of the Holy Spirit. This could have been the very driving spiritual coaxing or influence, when she felt it quite appropriate, despite probably having thought of it through with regards to my young age and in double jeopardy, my having been at the time 'handicap', to have actually gone ahead to present me with this special gift. This is truly remarkable. Well anyway, If I do stand correct, neither of my parents had their very own Bible at their age and time and yet here I was holding in my hands barely four years of age, probably the **family's first Holy Bible** in fine Shakespearean English, or if you rather prefer, in Old English!!!

Besides the very 'obedience', if this was indeed the case, of the English woman, this had to simply have been from my Christian perspective too, the work of the Holy Spirit in my own life, setting in motion my very 'mission' way back then. I do sincerely hope in this engaging mission, though humbled to the core, that I would be able to live up to this spiritual expectation, if this is indeed the case. And of course, the expectation of **YOU** too, my neighbor, being as important to me, whilst I am attempting to meet my own spiritual undertaking through this 'spiritual assignment' so to speak.

> In a way what **YOU** do draw from these books, if it helps **YOU** in your life, will ultimately decide whether I too hopefully in **Christ Jesus**, would also be meeting my destined Christian mission and individually assigned spiritual expectation, if I have perceived it correctly, being as required by **GOD ALMIGHTY**.

Alternatively, if I have not done so for some rhyme or reason, or even perhaps falling short in fulfilling this spiritual assignment, then I do sincerely hope that at the very least, it would set off some other, to take up this mission and hopefully provide us with the correct avenue to resolving this scriptural mystery, as having been laid down before us by GOD ALMIGHTY for our own well being as in REV 13:18.

Anyway, that bible gift was published by, 'The Syndics of the Cambridge University Press', Bentley House, 200 Euston Road, London, N.W.1. American Branch: 32 East 57th Street, New York 22, N.Y. (Printed in Great Britain, in the English Tongue). This is what is actually printed in the inside cover.

> Also, this entire effort in writing these two books have practically consumed almost two decades of my life from the very time that I had begun the very first concept outline in the early 1990' to it' very completion this year, 2012.

It may seem to the uninitiated, as if GOD ALMIGHTY had introduced a spiritual related puzzle into the Holy Scriptures, for us to unravel or to decipher just for fun; but this is not the case as scripturally confirmed by REV 13:16-18. There is definitely a divine structured spiritual purpose for this having been included as such and it obviously has great considerable and very devastating consequences, if we do not attempt to unravel it soon accordingly. This is because our very GOD given salvation could be unnecessarily interfered with and even blocked totally by Satan' very hand, robbing us of our eternal life being our other 'Gift' from GOD just as Satan had done very much earlier through a deceiving lie on Adam & Eve way back then.

On another front: These are books through which the Author also wants to make a serious attempt, to initiate a paradigm shift in the prevailing thinking of some Christians, which had been carried forward from the past with regards to the wicked stigmatizing of the 'number' of the beast onto the Popes of the Roman Catholic Church and in turn they in retaliation onto other Christian leaders which included in particular, the once Catholic monk, Martin Luther, the 'reformist' himself.

> This paradigm shift is also for an eye opening cosmic but scriptural derived solution, which should be for all intents and purposes, for those who do not believe in a 'GOD Created Universe'.

These '360 Day Years' together with the number construction which is cosmic related and indeed sum totals 666 does indeed have greater implications on Christendom than that generally expected, understood or even have come to be known. For it has several related Biblical and Scriptural importance, directly pertaining to our very own future, in the secular and more so in the spiritual sense. Although, we cannot change history, but we still can change to some greater extent, the course that we would take for our immediate and near future. Yet the biblical future in itself, as having been foretold i.e. prophesied by our LORD GOD ALMIGHTY, cannot be changed though, unless GOD does wish to do so for GOD reasons.

This is what the Author also prayerfully hopes to accomplish in some way, through these books. For it is every Christian' duty to bring back a greater sense of 'Christian Unity' amongst us all, through every aspect of our relationship, even to including, the readily encouraging and accepting openly inter Christian faith marriages as a norm rather than being more of an exception. Yet this is so evidently lacking, as we continue being wicked; greedy; selfish; power crazy and just plain evil-driven against each other, even to the extent of using the very 'PULPIT' at times, to cause division by planting seeds that grow into 'Spirits of Enmity', ridicule and loathsome contempt, even deep-seated hatred against other GOD fearing Christians in the Body of Christ. All of this will not hold any of us in good stead, to enjoy the heavenly privileges of our GOD given salvation.

> This sadly exists, despite the fact that each Christian Denominational Group, is strangely, worshipping the One and the same GOD: GOD THE FATHER, GOD THE SON (JESUS CHRIST) and GOD THE HOLY SPIRIT. The Three in the GODHEAD, collectively and commonly called through the scriptural mystery, as the 'HOLY TRINITY'.

Yet, despite this supposing to being an important bonding apex, we have gone against each other, especially in the past, with such violent ferocity, even to the extent of brutally killing and maiming each other. This had been done though in the past, and at times even in the recent; without showing any degree of mercy, or any bit of remorsefulness, for then the 'Christian', still being able to go back to prayer, worshipping the same GOD ALMIGHTY!!!

Contrary to some believers thinking, this is definitely not the plan of GOD to split HIS Globally INTENDED CHRISTIAN FAMILY, in any way whatsoever. Shocking as it may seem this is what some Christians today, currently do believe. This is their ill-gotten skewed justification for allowing the continuing strife between the major traditional Christian denominations.

Thank God that the Apartheid in South Africa is also over, though long in the making, with countless number of innocent lives having been lost in pain and needless human suffering. For this too was atrociously implemented & brutally enforced; YES, by CHRIST BELIEVERS!!! Not forgetting all the other 'HOTSPOTS' that were at one time the focus point of global attention to the domestic violence steeped in anger, hatred and political divide, etc., as it was as such in these examples – The breaking up of **INDIA** into two separate nations – **INDIA & PAKISTAN** – and the rivalry still continues though somewhat subdued by political civility**; THE CONGO, NORTHERN IRELAND – BOSNIA – RWANDA's** tribal cleansing MASSACRE; **NORTH & SOUTH VIETNAM** just to name a few. Today, there are still other 'HOTSPOTS' that are fiercely raging on all around the world; too numerous to even mention

Do you seriously think that in such circumstances, our GOD ALMIGHTY, will accept our hymns; songs & praise; prayers; devotion and worship, as a pleasing and sweet aroma to HIMSELF??? Are any of us fulfilling the LORD' PRAYER, as we continue to strive against each other, with such despicable condemnation, hatred and brutal violence and many doing this in the NAME OF GOD???

Do you seriously think that as Christians, we are all following the same divinely prepared path and format, as revealed to all of us through GOD' WORD by our LORD and SAVIOUR JESUS CHRIST, when HE said to Thomas in John 14:6 the following:

"I am the way, the truth, and the life. No one comes to the Father except through Me.

Who are we kidding???

Finally, this is a book that wants to shout out loudly, but in a more personalized way, with regards to our very own and immediate eternal future, just as Rev 1:3 proclaims so wisely:

> **BLESSED IS HE WHO READS AND THOSE WHO HEAR THE WORDS OF THIS PROPHESY, AND KEEP THOSE THINGS WHICH ARE WRITTEN IN IT; FOR THE TIME IS NEAR.**

"YES, MY DEAR NEIGHBOUR, IT IS TIME TO WAKE UP, FOR OUR TIME IS HERE AND NOW AND IT IS AT HAND. TOMORROW MAY BE JUST TOO LATE FOR MANY OF US". (charles alphonso)

REMEMBER, ANANIAS & HIS WIFE SAPPHIRA!!! (**Acts 5:1-10**)

PRAISE BE TO GOD ALMIGHTY
Rejoice and GOD Bless.

If the need arises relating to this book, you may contact me at:
E : gcf@globalchristianfamily.com

THE *BIBLICAL* 360 DAY YEARS

BOOK ONE

"I DO NOT FEEL OBLIGED TO BELIEVE THAT THE SAME GOD WHO HAS ENDOWED US WITH SENSE, REASON AND INTELLECT HAS INTENDED US TO FORGO THEIR USE"

GALILEO GALILEI, 1564 – 1642

Some Important Introductory Notes:

Since, I will be using a few selected and relevant Scriptural verses from the Deuterocanonical, also being referred to as the Apocrypha Books, of which I will be referencing one such book - **2ESDRAS**; I felt it would be of help to you, to be given some background to this particular Biblical Book, for your better understanding.

We are informed through the Preface, as written in the Good News Bible, that there are two series of Books making up the Deuterocanonical/Apocrypha section in the Bible. The first series consists of: Tobit; Judith; Esther (Greek Text); Wisdom of Solomon; Sirach; Baruch; Letter of Jeremiah; Song of the Three Young Men; Susanna; Bel and the Dragon; and finally, 1 Maccabees and 2 Maccabees. The other series consists of: 1ESDRAS, 2ESDRAS and the Prayer of Manasseh.

With the exception of 2ESDRAS, these two series of Books, formed part of the **Septuagint (LXX)** being the Greek Text of the Old Testament. We are informed that the Septuagint was in circulation during the time of our LORD AND SAVIOUR, JESUS CHRIST. In the Good News Bible, edited by Robert Weber (ISBN 0-8407-1231-6; 1st edition, 1969), the text for the Biblical Book, **2ESDRAS,** was taken from the Latin Text printed in the Biblia Sacra.

Also, according to the 'Introduction' in relation to this Biblical Book, as found in the Good News Bible, which is now being published by the American Bible Society under it' new title at the time, Good News Translation - Catholic Study Edition; we are informed that it is primarily an apocalypse that was written by an unknown Jewish author in Hebrew or Aramaic. This was translated into Greek and an Introduction and Appendix of Christian origin were added. We are informed that the original and the Greek translation have disappeared and the text is now preserved primarily in Latin. It mainly covers the seven revelations that were given directly to Shealtiel, who is identified as being Prophet Ezra and it answers questions pertaining to the problem of evil; suffering; persecution; the end of the world; judgment and the new world. I hope this would be of some help to you.

PART ONE

REVELATION 13:18
Here is wisdom, *Let him who has understanding* calculate the number of the beast, for it is the number of a man: His number is 666.

I discovered by accident or rather as I believe, led by the hand of divine providence, that there is indeed a cosmic based solution to the generating of a specific single set of numbers, that when added together results in the sum total **666**. Equally important is that the **'number'** is not derived arbitrarily but through a purposefully designed 'Cosmic Construction'. This includes in-building into this construction, very relevant scriptural number values, as expressed in the Book of Revelation, the Book of Daniel and also other scriptural facts pertaining to the 'End Time' revelations as found in one of the Deuterocanonical Books - 2Esdras. All these Books are found arranged, as being part of the Holy Bible. So, in this particular Biblical Deuterocanonical Book, I will be making special reference to only **Chapter 14** and the last two verses of Chapter 13.

Please take note and also do not be perturbed that some bible translations have separated the Deuterocanonical Books within it as a separate section and placed it in between the Old Testament and the New Testament and while others have taken them out completely.

In addition to these Biblical Books, I will need some help from very basic astronomical science, regarding a few important astronomical facts concerning our Solar System. In astronomy as far as I am concerned, nothing seems to be very basic indeed and thereby, can get to be very technical i.e. very deep into Physics and into very higher mathematical computations which is way beyond my ability to cope and perhaps for some of you too. Anyway, we still need to have some 'basic' understanding particularly when relating to our Sun, Earth and Moon. This should come with little surprise, for if you have read **Revelation** in the Holy Bible, you cannot help but to surely realize, that most scriptural events described in it have a cosmic bearing and in fact even in the heavenly places. The scriptural events relate to the 'happenings' in the very, 'Throne Room of GOD', and the Heavens during the 'End Time', which also involves the Stars, Sun, Earth and Moon. This also includes the actual detailed description of the 'happenings' that will also be going on here on Earth itself, during the similar 'End Time' period. Isn't this Biblical Book of Revelation, an awesome 'Gift of GOD' to mankind?

I sincerely hope that what is being established in this book, which I am currently researching and writing would further enhance the magnificence and extreme importance of this last arranged Biblical Book – 'The Revelation of

Jesus Christ'. With great humbleness and with sincere well placed hope, this effort, would hopefully meet and be the required scriptural outcome needed. Amen.

Anyway, my quest into this endeavour, however, did not first begin with the search for this cosmically intertwined **beast-number** combination. It never even crossed my mind, at the time.

> I truly did not even know in the very first place, that there was suppose to be a specific single set of numbers as clearly confirmed by scripture, earthly bound or otherwise, which would indeed sum total three score and sixty six. For I always had thought that the number **666**, was indeed this identifying number of the beast in question.

In other words through this new revelation, well any way for many of us, the **'number'** that they who will decide to worship the image of the beast and who amongst them would decide to receive the **'number'**, instead of the other two choices also available to them, will not be receiving the number **666** – Rev 13:15-17 refers. I state that again:

They will not be receiving the number 666.

For the **'number'** that they would be receiving either on their right hand or on their forehead, would actually be the specific single set of numbers, as attributed uniquely to the beast **(second beast)** and to him only. I now understand that when each of these numbers, making up the entire 'number' set, whether they are of single digit values or even more, are added all together correctly, it must sum total **666** - as confirmed by Rev 13:18.

It is also common scriptural knowledge, that at the appointed time, this specific number combination would somehow be used to identify and expose the identity of the second beast, who is a man. 2Thess 2:3-4; Dan 7:25; 8:23-25 confirms this very truth. This man would be the ultimate false prophet – the antichrist in this evil triune of Satan.

With one beastly endorsement received and also the choice to choose either one of the two locations to receive this beastly endorsement, – Rev 13:16-18 refers; they would obtain for themselves:

(1) Their continued liberty of movement, as they would not be exposed to the constant danger of being killed by the beast at his first opportunity.

(2) Their continued liberty to conduct businesses, i.e. to freely engage in trade & commerce, but strictly between one and another only. This by way of multiplicity would involve organizations with organizations, countries with

countries, provided such jurisdiction and recognition of such sovereignty, i.e. still being an independent country would exist at that future time.

If it does not exist at that future period; I would not be at all surprised. For we are already being made aware daily, that we are indeed moving towards a border-less society, besides the already well advanced progress achieved as a **cash-less** society, through the various types of credit & charge cards, debit cards and other cash-less transactions possible now, in and between many countries.

The **border-less** society is also fast becoming a reality. This is due to primarily the invasion of computer technology into our very homes and the integrating of it into our daily living. This is brought upon us with the expanding services available as such through the Internet; through telecommunication & multimedia services, which already have reached almost every nook & corner, far and wide in our world. This is absolutely necessary for building the required essential backbone network usefulness, for various beneficial purposes and for the expected border-less business environment which would give us an entirely new way of 'buying and selling'. In fact this new business environment has already begun some time ago and today it is generally called as e-commerce and/or e-business. Anyway, the terminology seems to becoming more and more complex these days or perhaps more simple for some who are cyberspace savvy.

I do not foresee anything being able to stop this exponentially accelerating progress towards a borderless society. Compounded with these technological benefits and that **Globalization** being the buzzword today, having the 'politico-legalistic authority empowerment' backing i.e. through the World Trade Organization (WTO), this will be definitely implemented and eventually enforced worldwide.

There are already 138 countries in it' membership at the time of my first editing of this book. We in Malaysia, like many other countries in the region, expect to be drafted into the WTO by the year 2010. Whether it would be the case, would left to be seen. (This has not happened as yet, although we are now in the year, 2012). This would in turn speed up even more rapidly, the further disintegration of government centered trade & commerce jurisdictions within, across regional and even to distant but important international borders. Each country somewhat forced to accept this worldwide economic & business integration accessibility.

Also, many becoming exposed to be re-colonized somewhat, by the very same colonial masters of history. Not joining in could precipitate suffering the fate of being castrated from the International Community and doomed eventually to economic failure and possible social chaos.

Therefore, although it may be a bit too early to state this, but the WTO, could one day soon become even more powerful under a single jurisdiction administration, having effective control over the world populace; not so much through fire power but through economic means, which is in turn enhanced and protected by the major implementers themselves.

However, the WTO also has its merits in this implementation. For it breaks down the economic controlled trade barriers which had been set up by local governments through which they have successfully prevented outside competition from unbalancing the local manufacturers and local services to be able to continue to be viable within their own country borders. However, this outside competition, if allowed in would bring variety, quality and even goods and products at lower prices due to lower tariffs being imposed than the former very much higher tariffs due to protectionism.

Of course on the other hand, there are several valid reasons for this local domestic 'trade control'. One obviously is to provide protection, so that the local industries have opportunities to grow and succeed, within their controlled borders at least.

This is particularly important for most developing countries, so that their government in the overall sense, can govern the economic resources for implementing infrastructure; developing their own expertise in the various technologies emerging; essential services; etc., and to distribute the economic opportunities generated to it' people for the general wellbeing of the Nation. In this way, if excesses and abuses are avoided and prudent governance adhered to; a Nation should prosper both economically as well as socially and eventually in due time be able to compete successfully in the international market place as well. Above all, it provides self-determination for the people by the people.

Yet evidently, in most developing and other third world Nations, governments have constantly failed to manage prudently and fairly for the benefit of the general populace, instead this is just for the privilege few that have found favour with them. This reduces a high proportion of these Nations' populace over the decades, to be marginalized in all areas of human development, social, religious and economic progress. They are in most cases, ruled with fear constantly hanging over their heads, and thereby, removing any possible challenge to be coming from them against this very self-interest seeking government administration. Many countries even find themselves in abject poverty, resulting in many cases of untold suffering, dismay and hopelessness due to this poor governance. This deplorable situation lumbers on and in many cases mostly having gone unnoticed intentionally by the more affluent international governments who are busy expanding their own interests elsewhere, where it may be more profitable and easier to do so in the circumstance. This then eventually in most cases leads to civil unrest, breakdown in such governments, and unfortunately only to be replaced by a similar one with a different face only. This usually continues until the country has been utterly destroyed economically and torn apart in it' social fabric, identity, freedom and wellbeing at which time the affluent nations then seem to suddenly be awaken from their slumber and come to their aid making international news for weeks and months and even for years. As an observation, all this too has several hidden agendas. For these very same affluent international nations then glory in their political victory in these such matters, although still in credibility, as driven by the international humanitarian will and though 'hindered' in quite late coming to rescue these ravaged countries.

And, these very same stricken nations then usually snowball into constantly having to be at the mercy of benevolent Nations, under the auspices of the United Nations for their every day to day basic needs, which includes healthcare and even to police their security and to also manage their natural resources, if any.

An editorial in our local newspaper NST, dated 14 August 2000, stated that countries no longer covet territories but markets in other lands for their products and produce. Gaining market share is the overriding theme. They want to win economically and this is the foreign policies of the rich and the powerful nations, as well as the developing which have good governance, if I may add.

However, in my opinion, how successful will the developing and underdeveloped countries be in their efforts, when most of the time, many are in the midst of toppling their corrupt governments and at most times, they are in some state of civil chaos?

There are those who are of the opinion that the WTO, through it' legislation and backers is indeed directly and indirectly, forcing markets open for the 'big boys' (Multinational Corporations) of the former 'Colonial Masters'. Some of these former 'Colonial Masters' are also 'Super Powers' currently. This means they have more than enough fire power, capital, political will and other resources to **'influence'** these very WTO trade legislations onto the rest of the world, and they with their very close allies, becoming the eventual beneficiaries of the 'huge successes' of the WTO.

The only reason, I am using the WTO as the possible target in these examples of mass effective control, is because the Scripture in Rev 13:17 is also directly pertaining to the control of Trade & Commerce on an enlarged International Scale!!! Therefore, it is quite obvious to target the **WTO**, as this international Organization, is currently in the running, being at the top of the list so to speak to bring this Scripture possibly at some point in the future to pass in truth.

In fact, the irony at the moment from a Scriptural perspective is that many countries are trying to get into WTO and even deem it as a privilege, so that they would not be left out of the mainstream global economic prosperity. Whilst some countries do welcome their inevitable entry into the WTO with open arms, some are doing it with great apprehension. However, one country, which wants in badly, is the Super Power – China. Their inclusion is expected but it is quite difficult to tell exactly when this will happen. We are now already in the second half of 2001 at the time of writing this. However, this should take place, after they duly accept the WTO General Agreement on Tariffs and Trade and other political & trade issues to be settled. This of course if I understand it correctly must have been mainly engineered by the Mega Super Power – the USA, in consensus with it' other key partners and together being the drivers behind this agreement. This for China would be the prerequisites to be accepted into the WTO.

> Latest in at this time: China has been accepted as the 143rd member of the WTO, immediately followed the next day by Taiwan, being the 144th. The formal accession will be December 12, 2001 for China and January 1, 2002 for Taiwan. For China, it was a long and arduous 15 years or so wait.

Inevitably, even in the pre-development stages and in the subsequent on-going progress of the WTO, there would be the 'merging creation' of globally reaching Super Mega-Corporations at the very top of the 'Pyramid of Global Business', and so creating inevitably oligopolies in each specific Industry and Service. These would ultimately own and control Trade & Commerce in practically everything and everywhere, irrespective where you may be residing or even be citizen of. We are witnessing this happening right now, as evident in the Super Mega Mergers being made in the Corporate and Industrial world today. Such as taking place within the Banking & Finance Institutions; Telecommunication; Insurance; Airlines; Oil & Gas Exploration (Upstream) and the Oil & Gas Industry (Downstream); Chemical; Pharmaceutical; Advertising; Management Consulting & Audit; I.T. & Multimedia; even Stock Exchanges and Stock Brokers; and etc.

They are probably doing all of this in order to consolidate their strengths and to weed out every possible weakness, in order to enhance further streamlining and pooling of all resources in their combined operations. This they do quite obviously to face the even greater challenges of the new business competitive environment. This is certainly expected to materialize under the auspices of the WTO. There will be very little or no place for the small independent business operator. I only hope that many of these Super Multinationals would be in the hands of Godly centered people; but is this possible, considering the **'evil'** behind most large businesses.

To name just one big evil: **Corruption** - This has it' hand in every level of governance being the result of the economic expansionary needs and requirements which are ironically a necessity for Nation building and economic prosperity. This corruption is indeed fuelled and driven by big businesses, as they compete against each other for these lucrative contracts, which many a time were and are even first initiated and nurtured by their 'undercover front men' influencing those in 'high up places'.

This is done so that they can later come in directly being above all suspicion of having meddled in the affairs of the ruling government or any authority as the case may be, and bid for these same contracts that they had created or initiated in the very first place. Sometimes this 'strategy' is given the guise of the respectable lobbyist.

In turn ironically, it is this very **'Corruption'** in many cases, becoming the unlikely but important 'Engine for Growth' in many countries that have indeed even good stable governments!!!

Am I providing a positive side to **'Corruption'**???

Am I condoning **'Corruption'**???

Of course, I am not, but if you seriously do think with an open mind about this situation, you may come to realize too, that it is the very case in many countries all over the world. In other words, nothing takes off or moves if the appropriate people involved in the decision making process at any level do not get a piece of the action one way or the other. Of course in these cases, the very cost of development then skyrockets artificially which in turn directly affects the Nation' wealth building as the artificial increase in costs then unscrupulously is transferred to these crooked individuals. This in my personal opinion is tantamount to committing treason of the highest order against the entire citizenry.

By a yardstick, the more the government is corrupted, this would be more the very reason, "Why many governments around the world, do not want to accede power and will do everything under the sun to avoid being outvoted at the polls". This they will do even it be to the very destruction of many of their own general populace through bloodshed; poverty; lack of basic amenities; constant intimidation; gross human rights violations; the application of manipulated laws for their own benefit; undermining the independence of the Judiciary resulting of course in criminal & civil injustices to the highest degree, across all sectors of their administration and their people"

All of this boils down to simply enhancing and promoting **'Corruption'**, which feeds those to increase in their power and greed without any restraints or fear as the checks and balances have all been silenced at every level by their 'smart' governing.

> Sometimes, these 'manipulations' are not so easily evident or even noticeable, because it is very carefully **camouflaged** by crafty governments.

So, since big businesses in general cannot be in the hands of GODLY centered people, then the people who resist worshipping the image of the beast and resist the receiving of one of the second beast' endorsements, would be inevitably facing the full onslaught through the stranglehold this will have over World Trade & Commerce. **This is Biblical**.

The stage and platform for the beast to achieve this, as explained above is possibly being set up right now under our very noses and openly at that, under the possible guise and character such as that of the WTO.

An organization such as the WTO, which is backed by the United States and other Super Economic Powers, could be an eventual ideal target for control takeover by the beast for the very purposes of dominating Trade & Commerce on a global scale.

If the beast does get the very vital control of such an organization, this would provide it with an entirely effective global controlling system. This then would become the ideal and excellent platform avenue, for the beast to enforce his destructive and final objectives of evil dominion, over the global populace quite extensively, as foretold by the reading of the relevant Revelation Scriptures.

There could also be other avenues open to the beast besides the present offering in sight. The International Monetary Fund and the World Bank could also be part and parcel of this effective global controlling system and perhaps there are other avenues not even formed as yet. Some may possibly even be coming from the East or Asian origin, instead of a Western source of influence.

So, it must not be construed as being my personal agenda in anyway whatsoever, that it is my very intention to single out the **United States** and the **WTO** or any other Western sponsored Organization for that matter.

Of course, the beast must in the first place, be able to take full control over this 'System' and to my understanding this is highly possible. For less we forget, the beast is indeed a man (2Thess 2:3-4 confirms, besides it being revealed to us in Rev 13:18) and behind every leader in power, you have the 'king-makers'. It will be no different with the beast, as **Satan** is his 'king-maker' and will have many willing and enrolled supporters, in the likes of powerful and crooked politicians, many well heeled individuals and other 'evil' linked people, all around the World who stand to gain in all of this, following not too far behind though. The 'Satan worshippers' will be of course in ecstasy. However, all that they will gain is only for a time and a season. In other words, this clearly means limited at maximum, by their physical life spans.

Despite of what I am was saying above, I have great respect for the American People and the other major free western super powers. Their overall leadership and overall contribution to the world' wellbeing, on many fronts, especially over the last two centuries or so more, not only in peaceful times but also even in war time is really commendable. This also includes naming a few areas: Of course technological and medical advancements shared with the world; humanitarian aid across all barriers/borders even to hostile governments during their national catastrophes; Christian Evangelism; and etc.

Mind you, millions of Americans and those in the other super powers of our world will also suffer the same fate, as those described in the relevant Scriptures. For as already mentioned, those who decidedly refuse to worship the image of the first beast and also similarly refuse to receive the **'sign'** of the second beast, will suffer the same fate.

So accordingly, on the other hand, I could very well propose an entirely different scenario from the previous, altogether. The United States of America and the other friendly Nations could become the one major effective people group offering a really viable strongly based resistance, against the 'free running accesses' of Satan himself, which he had in fact been operating, through his own evil power base.

This evil power base having been fuelled by **Satan' evil influences,** over the global populace, through his ever persistent building-up of his 'network of evil offerings, to the easy way of sin; has it' very beginnings from the time of Adam and Eve, when they were so craftily duped into disobedience against GOD Almighty.

This 'evil network' as clearly evident today, has been also exponentially accelerating in reaching epidemic proportions. Ironically, this is being aided by the very 'technology driven economic systems', engineered by the very same 'affluent nations' for the so-called betterment of the world.

However, this entire 'evil network' is mainly 'entertainment' oriented and does not control world trade in it' true sense, as yet. However, included in this 'entertainment' is the ample availability of harmful narcotics on a worldwide basis. This would then also include 'Organized Crime' together with it' many other underworld activities which in turn increases crime overall.

However, Satan would still need a more dynamic and sweeping control over all the populace and not just over those who have been brought into his 'evil entertainment network' although this too I envisage is already very large and quite alarming indeed. Take note, in his progressive successes, even in this, the ruling governments are indeed ultimately responsible.

So, due to the 'entertainment' limitation of this 'evil power base' in his overall implementation of control and takeover of as much of the global commercial and trade activities; Satan needs another avenue to operate from within. This is where the previously mentioned **'effective global controlling systems'**, as a suggestion would lock in, to help meet Satan' overall objectives, as described to us in Revelation 13: 15 - 17. With these Scriptures and the possible scenario in focus those who refuse to worship the image of the first beast and who refuse to receive one of the second beast' endorsements, as mentioned in the Scriptures, would then have in particular trade sanctions strictly enforced against them.

In addition to this trade embargo, the imposing danger of being killed by the second beast at any time possible would be also very real indeed. Obviously, the second beast will have plenty of help from his fellow evil cohort human network.

It is also my opinion that it would be highly unlikely that the people who do decide to **resist**, would be acting alone, singly, but rather as an organization of people, such as possible under the network of Churches, Christian Organizations, etc. Since this book is based primarily on the Scriptures of the Holy Bible, I am restricting myself only to Christians being mobilized to defend themselves against the beast. Therefore, other people groups, in their own way and who also believe that there will come a time when the beast would take such a Biblical or similar action will also possibly mobilize themselves to resist the beast. Who knows, we may even do this jointly, when the beast finally dawns on us all. It would be great to particularly see the Ishmaelites, joining forces with the Isaacs. After all, if you do remember, Ishmael and Isaac did come together in unity, to bury their common father-parent, Abraham. This is Biblical, for Ishmael did come back despite his earlier banishment, which was not due to his own wrong doings though, to carry out their father Abraham' burial, jointly. This being quite commendable indeed, what Ishmael had done, when he willingly and rightly so, participated in the burial of their father Abram. Abram after Isaac' birth had been renamed by GOD to become Abraham as we have come to know of him in the Holy Scriptures, being the Great Patriarch of the 'People of Promise' and not before.

Trade sanctions and embargoes have already been enforced in the past and even as presently. It is a very vital political, psychological and international 'War Weapon'. For it is engineered to weaken, punish and to succumb the enemy group or the rogue nation. This will eventually destroy their resilience to continue **'misbehaving'**, particularly, with their immediate neighbours and against the wellbeing of the other international communities in these modern times.

We also cannot escape but to become critically aware through the media, of the very damaging affects these sanctions have on the people of these countries. This is especially with the very **young children**, the very old and the very sick. Also, not forgetting, this directly weakens their overall economy, which is the main target of these trade and other sanctions.

These sanctions have a crippling affect on the economy of the particular nation under sanction, which ultimately and unfortunately drills down to the common people of that nation. For those in power seem to be unscathed for a time and a season and for some even until death do them part, as they continue doing whatever evil they do.

Therefore, it is not surprising that according to the current interpretation of **Revelation 13:17**, the beast would himself employ this very effective strategy. Of course the sanctions in place now have nothing to do with worshipping the image of the beast or refusing to be beastly endorsed. For most if not all the time, these sanctions have been brought upon them due to their own political ambitions, economic issues and even because of religious ambitions, etc. Well anyway, it is not my place to offer comments or views on these complex political, historical and even possibly religious driven motives by their Executive or rebel leaders.

Yet the very trade sanctions on some nations today, do give us a window to see and understand the possible scenarios of human suffering, bearing in mind that it would be magnified many-folds then, when the beast reigns in control over globally reaching economic based powers.

At that time, when the beast takes over, those who worship and receive one of the beast endorsements, which openly declares them to be **under Satan' authority**, will form one group and be marked accordingly. All those who would still continue to be steadfast in their worship of the only **ONE TRUE GOD ALMIGHTY**, the CREATOR of the Heavens and the Earth and of all life will possibly be standing together against Satan' group. Neither of the opposing sides will recognize any neutrality nor will they tolerate the fence sitters.

I sincerely tried to offer you, through the above pages, some understanding to the foundational truth and the subsequent implementation that must and will be carried out, according to the Holy Scriptures of Revelation 13:16-17. However, if I have come short to convincing you, or if you think you could do a better job in this part of the First Chapter; then please do not hold it against me, but feel free to satisfy yourself in adding or taking away, as you may feel fit in your mind. However, do not change the main theme or the concept of this First Chapter. For what I have attempted to do here was to re-emphasize, that it would take a really large and powerful organization, with such extensive economic clout and military supremacy itself, or have similarly the necessary backing to finally and effectively implement what the 'Revelation Scriptures' have indeed prophesied to us long time ago.

In reference to the statement at the very top of the second page of Part One: I do not know how many of you perhaps, do share with me the same **'ignorance'**. I do somehow hope that I am not amongst just a few. If you happen to be a Pastor or a leader of a group of Christians, or simply have access to them, it would be good for you to find out, how many in your congregation actually know that the **'number'** which would be received by those consenting to have it is definitely not the sum total **666**. Even if you are not in leadership, you still could ask your Christian friends and even your immediate family. As a suggestion, you could ask them:

"What is the number that would be received on the right hand or on the forehead, by those who accept to follow the beast???"

A simple survey through a show of hands, such as this, could provide a valuable statistic to gauge the Christian general awareness of the beast. Firstly, that he being a man; secondly, his modus operandi; thirdly, also of the **End Times** and fourthly, that **666** is indeed not the **'number'** that would be received by all of those consenting and to accept this mode of identification. Many Christians in general, though unfortunately, but understandably have not paid much attention to the Book of Revelation. For like the Book of Genesis which for many could be somewhat tiresome to read in following the sequences of thought and biblical historical events; and perhaps for others to even be boring, the Book of Revelation is also not so an easy or simple book to be read and to be easily understood.

As for me, I began to realize that the sum total number **666** was indeed not the **'number'**, as I just happened to stumble upon it, or as I stated much earlier, through the hand of divine providence; whilst pursuing an entirely different quest whilst writing my first book.

The quest that I was pursuing or wanted to pursue in the first place was to discover, if there could be any scientific based support or even any possible theoretical evidence for a Scriptural derived 360 Days Solar Year.

This was described as a scriptural reality in our traditional sense of understanding the Holy Scriptures and also is the current interpretation of the Revelation Scriptures as in 11:2-3; 12:6 and 13:5. Bible Scholars and other Christians already knowing this will support that these relevant Scriptures in Revelation do indeed describe 360 Day Years. However, the problem is that many of these people are also of the view that prior to the **Noah' Flood** or deluge, we were already having 360 Day Years in our Human Biblical History.

This is a view **that I just cannot share** with them and I will substantiate this in detail in Part Two of this book; the reasons why we will only have this sometime far in the biblical future. In other words, it has not happened as yet in our 'Human Biblical History'.

I did not know at the beginning of this very quest to discover the evidences for the future happening of these 360 Day Years, would indeed be intertwined with my almost simultaneous 'cosmic' discovery of the specific single set of numbers, which would sum total to 666 and yet also be scriptural derived.

This is the definite distinction, as you will learn soon as below, that sets this **very scriptural cosmic derived 'number'** apart from any of the other arbitrary derived set of numbers especially those that can be put together to sum total **666** through gematria or even by any junior school going person.

> In addition to this unsolicited discovery, I was fortunate to also obtain in bonus, so to speak, when I also found out that the numbers: one hundred and forty four thousand (12 X 12,000 = 144,000); forty-two months (42); one thousand two hundred and sixty (1,260); time, times and half a time; and the number, one hundred and forty four (144); as mentioned in Rev 7:4; 11:2,3; 12:14, Rev 21:17 respectively and subsequently in Rev 14:1,3; 12:6 and other relevant scriptures, were all also so intricately intertwined with the 'scriptural solution' for the cosmic construction of the **'number'** of the beast sum totalling to **666**.

GOD ALMIGHTY being omniscient and therefore even pre-knowing that we could and would be able to calculate out this **'number'** of the beast, if GOD only points us or nudges us in the right direction. This is why I believe that GOD ALMIGHTY gave us these hints although all wrapped up in Biblical Scripture, specifically in Revelation, the Book of Daniel and also in 2Esdras. However, unraveling and understanding these divine hints have indeed a very high degree of difficulty built into it and there must be a divine reason for this too.

As I had said earlier, it never even had crossed my mind that the number **666** was indeed supposed to be the sum total of a single specific combination of a set of numbers. Yet, I knew that the sum total **666** was indeed extremely significant at some period in the future. For this unique number has a direct relationship to the **'End Times'**, as evidently described in the Biblical Book of Revelation.

Even so, this is indeed quite embarrassing, for the fact that I am Christian and I believe also, an ardent bible student/reader. Therefore, I cannot offer any excuses for not knowing this at the time, for the **'number'** has indeed serious and more than a significant impact in our 'Scriptural Belief' of the 'End Times', which is also directly associated with our Salvation and our eternal spiritualized life after our physical death has taken place.

However, I do know now, that for most of us, our misreading of the Revelation Chapter 13 verse 18 does provide us or rather channels us to the precise prevalent thinking and interpretation, as held amongst our very own 'teachers' for decades, and in fact, even for centuries past. However, having said this, their thinking or at least for many of them in the know at the time, this was and currently is that the number 666 is indeed a sum total of a set of numbers attributed to the alphabets making up the **name** of the second beast.

Remarkably, many through their exposé of this in the past seem to exhibit as if they did know without the slightest shadow of doubt, who the second beast was during their time and day. This they had 'accomplished' through their using of this kabalistic method, Gematria; which actually attributes numbers to letters of the alphabet. Since it being a man developed system, though of much intrigue, it is therefore highly possible to have been manipulated to arrive at a certain foregone conclusion or pre-determined result. Worse still, people are so readily duped into believing such crap as an observation and only are able to be doing so because of the culture & thinking prevailing at the time just as fortune telling, palm reading and other forms of astrology, which still prevails in our time and day having the same affects as such practices in the days gone by. Or is it still being practiced even today too???

You would soon learn that I do understand this above inadvertently quite differently with regards to the number that would eventually sum total 666. So be prepared to paradigm shift from the prevalent thinking as just described above.

I have come to be aware that many people in the past, who have worked in this search for the beast' **'number'**, have come to the very conclusion that the Pope, his Titles of Office, and his Papacy have direct connections with this **'number'**. They provide many possibilities of number combinations that are as mentioned above, alphabetically derived naturally, to arrive at this sum total of **666**. This directly results in branding the Pope, of all people, as the second beast. Simply ridiculous and totally absurd as far as I am concerned and hope so you too concur alike. YOU JUST CANNOT BE SERVING TWO MASTERS AT THE SAME TIME – this is scriptural.

The **'number'** according to them was to be derived based on the name of the beast itself. Some have taken this to mean 'Titles of Office', instead of the name of the actual individual holding that office.

Perhaps, they knew very well that there would be many people in the world at any given time, to have possibly the same name; for some of them to have even suggested that his name was not important, but his 'Office' would be instead. This would obviously, narrow the field.

This I suppose, according to them would eliminate the others or set him apart from those who perhaps had a similar name to him at the same material time. I am not even bringing their evil agendas into contention here as yet. This may overcome their obvious 'failure', but identifying his 'Office & his Titles' and similarly connecting these to the sum total **666**, shows up other failures and weaknesses in their proposition; mainly for the reason that it was **not GOD' Open Commission,** as so evidently scripturally defined FOR US by Rev 13:18.

Also, it is quite obvious or perhaps they had overlooked in their over eagerness to attack the Roman Catholic Church during those troubled times; that different people will hold the 'Office & Titles' in question, at different times in continuity, as long as that office exists. This would cause great difficulties in identifying who the beast really was or is or will be, as the case may be.

Obviously, they cannot be suggesting that all the individuals, let alone any of them (the Popes), are the beast. For it has already been scripturally established that the beast is indeed one particular individual man and therefore, obviously, does not involve a multitude of people. Rev 13:18; 2Thess 2:3-4 reveals this, and besides also confirms, **he is yet to come**. This will become clearer to you, only if you allow yourself to be open to the very understanding of all of these relevant Scriptures correctly.

Therefore, the above prevailing thinking on this issue cannot be accepted in any way, shape or form, as being the way to identify the second beast for these obvious shortcomings. This would be further expounded in this book, as you will surely find out, as you continue through it.

So, according to my understanding of the same referenced Scriptures, the points to note here are: Firstly, it needs to take only one specific combination, to be the precise set of numbers, when added appropriately and accordingly, must then total the given Scriptural sum result of **666**.

You will further find out in this book that not only that it takes one specific combination, but that the respective number values making up this specific combination, have indeed a definable scriptural linkage to each other, though derived cosmically separate, but yet having a strong common relationship to one another. Is this confusing??? Don't worry, just proceed on.

This then takes this precise and specific cosmic number combination to even another much higher level or dimension, which surpasses any and every human capability through all time, of being able to ever setting up. For **GOD** had done this so creatively and completely unmatchable in every aspect conceivable by any human being.

> In other words, it is not humanly possible to come up with such a precise cosmic design, that when unfolded would mathematically exactly sum total **666**. You will be given the full opportunity to discover for your own-self, this **human inability** in this very book, and hopefully to come to the very same conclusion that I had just emphasized as above. Maybe, I am being overly presumptuous here, but I genuinely believe that you too will conclude the same. Well I do certainly hope so.

This human inability then gives the appropriate divine dignity to the setting of the Divine Challenge or the Divine Commission, as scripturally having been written down in Rev 13:18.

Secondly, I also would like to state that these numbers are unique to that particular individual, whoever that may be for the specific cosmic way it was established.

With the combining of these two basic principles, it would make it extremely difficult for someone, to attempt discounting this specific interrelated cosmic established scriptural derived unique number combination, as not being the actual identity of the second beast.

In comparison, this is unlike an individual' given name, which from the beginning could have been anything, what the earthly name provider had decided at the material time. For it is obvious, the giver is in final and full control of that circumstance, each and every time; unless it was at first, Divinely established. We have read several times in the Holy Scriptures, where GOD had indeed provided the name for the new born child. This was always made known to the Biblical personalities involved, **even before the child** had been born or had even been conceived and thereby, even identifying the child' gender, if you had not taken notice of it before!!!

So, it is not as currently being thought, that the number is to be derived from the name itself. No, it is definitely not the case, as far as this proposal is concerned.

However, it is absolutely correct to associate the 'number' to the individual or directly put; it is his number, identifying him and setting him apart from any other individual for that matter.

If it was as they had thought that it was, i.e. to be derived directly from his name, or rather the letters of his name; then what would the purpose be for GOD ALMIGHTY to incorporate this 'challenge' or to openly commission those who have the wisdom (the knowledge) and the very understanding – Rev 13:18 refers; to be able to calculate out his **'number'**???

> For in their case, you would have to in the first place, know his very name. This in itself would actually identify who he is??? Think about it for awhile or have I missed something that you may know regarding this matter. Please do let me know then.

In other words, he would have already been identified through his name and therefore, be also identified as being the beast, when someone comes along with that given name. So, unless this was pre-provided to you, through the Scriptures, i.e. divinely inspired and written down as such, already into the Holy Text; "How are you on Earth going to know his name in the very first place???

You just cannot go on and design it yourself for the obvious, as this would be completely erroneous for it' sheer human interference and obvious manipulation.

Furthermore, anybody can come forward and simply suggest any name for that matter that they want or fancy and through number manipulation, allow this to also sum total to **666**.

Even more profoundly is that, "On what Scriptural basis, would you then associate specific numbers to specific Hebrew/Aramaic and Greek alphabets being the languages of the Holy Bible???"

The key and most important qualifying criteria here, is that: Is it **Scriptural**??? In other words, was this system of associating numbers to the alphabets of the written languages of the Bible, approved and supported by Scripture, itself???

If you can show me, how this could be scripturally justified and verified, then it would cause me to take another more serious look into this gematria methodology.

So, they quite glaringly had overlooked this very obvious logic or sensible argument, as exposed in the above pages, when they thought that they had indeed fulfilled the 'Open Commission' of Rev 13:18. Ironically, their version was quite readily accepted by those who had left the 'Mother Church', being the Roman Catholic Church, for the obviously appealing and vengeful reasons; well it seemed at least to them at that time. This perhaps may have been the very reasons, why no one of the 'New Movement' at that time, had challenged or cared to challenge this absurd methodology.

Even those who at that time still believed in the Roman Catholic Religious System did not do so, but came out with their own 'finger pointing' of whom they thought was the beast in this 'New Movement'.

> On the other hand: If you do **not** know his name, which directly means that you have not the foggiest idea who the individual is to start off with, and thereby, attempting to calculate out his 'number', **on a predetermined scriptural encrypted process,** should be the **only manner** this individual should be finally exposed. Well anyway this is the case as proposed in this book.

> In other words, once the calculation process has been duly completed, finished and proclaimed; then to wait for that period in time in the future when this cosmic derived number would be able to be directly linked to the particular individual would be biblically correct. This individual must also at the time exhibit all the necessary attributes that would confirm this number linkage directly to him and unmistakably **identifies** specifically that he is the unknown second beast. This makes more sense not only of the process itself, but also of the relevant Scriptures in Revelation that began all this searching for the **'number'** of the second beast in the very first place.

One important scriptural fact that you may not have seen in the referenced Revelation Scriptures ever before, is that the second beast, has no choice whatsoever in not having himself to be identified by this calculated out number in one way or the other. You will understand this thinking and revelation better, as you proceed on. There is much more to this, then has generally has been known, even as currently to this ultimate **'Saga of the Heavens'**!!!

I think that by the time he is finally recognized as being the second beast, i.e. this 'number' that was calculated out and found to be definitely his number; he would have already established himself as being the head of a powerful organization, poised to accelerate his evil strategy. This would be in accordance to just as it was revealed to us, through Revelation.

So, in essence through his further actions, he will also eventually be revealed as having the necessary attributes of being the second beast in question. It is of course a foregone conclusion that the second beast would not be a small town kindergarten school teacher in some remote place or just an ordinary municipal janitor now would he???

Since he would have been already quite established as being a very powerful individual, would this defeat the very purpose of identifying the beast??? The answer to this question is quite definitely, on the contrary, no. For it would open the very eyes of those believers at that material time, to first realize, the 'Revelation Scriptures' have finally become true in real time terms. Secondly, that the individual in question is indeed the second beast; for there were quite a few in the past and there will also be such in the future that have and will behave like beasts. Thirdly, their consideration to taking the appropriate steps to overcome this evil would be well placed, just as the beast prepares his final moves in the 'End Times' too.

If the Scriptures have been accurately interpreted and understood, then the believers should take all the necessary evasive courses of action, which will eventually overcome this evil beast driven by Satan himself. What evasive actions these could possibly be, would be left to be seen.

Yet the question that may be raised, would be, "What actually is this 'number', which we are so certain that it can be linked to an individual. In other words what is this number that can be associated to a human being?

It is already a common practice for individual identification or verification as the case may be, to be accomplished by numbers rather than just by our given name. Our National Identity Cards, ATM cards and our Credit & Charge Card identification process, would be an ideal example amongst many, which uses electronic recognition of the specific set of numbers assigned to us, and through PIN numbers we get access to our various finances and other processes. For some time now, even various types of vital information pertaining to the manufactured and/or processed products have been identified through a numbering system, which also establishes the resale value of the item concerned and for other tracking reasons too. This has been very well technologically refined and is called Bar-Coding

---

With this in view, if you were to carefully consider my concept of thinking or suggestion of identifying the second beast through his **'number'** as **Revelation** had expressed; then the number can be no other than the numbers which constitutes the **actual date and the actual time that any individual is actually born into this world.**

An individual' date and time of their birth should be able to be constituted as being that individual' most personalized attributed number. This can then be subsequently used for identifying the person too. Even in a larger and greater sense into this very Universe and it is constructed by just numbers. This is when the event of the birth being actually time-stamped by this specific set of numbers that were attributed to the 'Time' that the birth had actually occurred.

This is the **significance** that it is actually **'Time Stamped'** by the very Stars in the heavens. To be specific in the more local sense, one particular Star, which is our own Sun being of course, in conjunction with the Earth and the Moon.

This was indeed the specific cosmic relationship that I was trying to emphasize a few pages back, with regards to this specific and very precise combination of numbers have with each other. Also, being born into this Universe is indeed a truly and awesome event for anyone of us. For there is nowhere in the entire Universe, where this awesome event has taken place other than on our Planet Earth. This is as confirmed by our current and available information on this matter, being mostly biblical of course.

Sorry, I cannot rely on the gradually increasing momentum in the speculative theories, that there is 'physical life' somewhere out there, even if it is scientifically proposed. Solid evidence is definitely required, as far as I am concerned on this very high profile issue. This means showing us a 'being' or living thing, plant or animal or some other living creature as the case may be, that is currently living or even fossilized on some other planet. Until that can be established, 'physical life' only occurs in one tiny island in the vast ocean of Space and that is in our very own Planet Earth.

Perhaps one day in the future, man would be able to set up house in other planets in our own Solar System or even in other Planetary Systems. Though, that would be only transferring the location of the particular human life and other Earthly 'life', yet, this too should definitely be considered a major feat indeed for mankind, considering the numerous 'special conditions' that surely needs to be first overcome.

Therefore, what I am trying to say here is that there is no such life or for that matter any other type of life out there in the Universe.

On what authority or thesis do I state this so firmly and boldly??? Not because God is unable to start 'life' in any other location or locations under any 'prevailing conditions' in our Universe. For the fact remains, that the **Holy Bible** incorporated into it the very **'Creation Accounts'** painstakingly, if you have noticed, though in acute briefness for the entire Universe. This is somewhat like describing the 'Creation Accounts' in **'Divine Summary'**, if I could comment on it as such.

This is the authority by which, I state the above; the Holy Bible. God was indeed describing within it, this very creation to us, even from the very **beginning** of creation. Nothing was left out. Even the very creation or the by-product of creation i.e. of the **'light'**, which had set the very pulse of the entire Universe i.e. it' 'Time' into motion and which is kept synchronized for our very own purposes, as per our own local perspective from Earth by a complex triune based time operating system was also very timely included.

This involves the Earth & Moon employing this very 'light' from the Sun; coupled with their many other motions whilst orbiting the Sun, to give us our own sense of 'Earth Time' and the various seasons too.

This entire 'mechanism' has an important bearing on our calculations as when will the Earth indeed begin to have the 360 Days Solar Years. The Bible also reveals to us that besides the 'physical life' that was created on the Earth, each type having it' own limited period of time to live on Earth, there is also the 'eternal life' after death existence, for each one of us human beings. This spiritualized 'life' of each one of us, will continue for eternity and if we are judged worthy on the 'Last Day', which is the 'Day of Judgment'; then we will be fortunate to enter into heaven having escaped the second death. Otherwise, we will be condemned into the eternal fires of hell, which is the second death.

JESUS CHRIST will return at the appropriate time to decide this very matter, when HE comes again for the second time. This time HE will be coming in the capacity of HIS 'Divine Judgment' of us all. This would be unlike the first occasion when HE came here being our GOD given Saviour. He will come to judge both those who have already died and those who would be living at that time.

> The Bible also reveals to us that before all of this physical matter and physical life was even ever created, the **Spirit Life** in the Kingdom of Heaven had already existed.

From what we understand directly from the Holy Scriptures, which is to be read in its entirety; this **Spirit Life** never had a beginning with regards to Almighty GOD.

This is the 'heavenly world' which is not of this Universe; where GOD and HIS Angels and the other privileged heavenly Spirit Beings, primarily are most of the time.

This does not mean in the least thinkable way, that the heavenly world confines GOD; for GOD is omnipresent and only GOD is omnipresent.

This directly means that the Angels and the other Spirit Beings are definitely not omnipresent. Amongst these, there are also other Spirit Beings there, worshipping God continually. In fact the Biblical Book of Revelation, describes in greater detail the "Throne Room of GOD ALMIGHTY", in the Kingdom of Heaven. This description begins from Revelation Chapter 4 onwards however my earnest suggestion is for you to read the entire Book of Revelation, if you had not done so previously. Also, read carefully the first two Chapters in the Book of Genesis, which is another Biblical Book that is important here for our intents and purposes. These are directly regarding to the 'Creation Accounts', and these clearly describes the 'physical world', that we have even as of now.

With all of this detail description of these both 'worlds', the physical and the Spiritual; there was never once mentioned or hinted that there is, will be or was life in any physical form whatsoever in the rest of the Universe. This then provides for the singular exception for the Planetary Earth in this Solar System, which being one of many such systems in the Milky Way Galaxy, but yet being the solitary one with life residing in it.

> **Therefore, we now can conclude with the 'Scriptural Confidence' well in place, that other than what was, i.e. those creatures and animals that have become already extinct & the creatures and our human race that are currently found on Planet Earth; are all the 'physical life' that there is currently, in the entire Universe.**

The physical conceiving of a baby is in itself an awesome event. Also, when the child is born at that precise moment and introduced into this world, beginning for the very first time in it' life to breathe, that precise moment is indeed very significant and worthy to be recorded as such. As already indicated, it is even registered by the very heavens.

We have been informed sometime way back in 1994, that the birthrate was 2.8 babies every second in the world; 171 per minute; 10,241 per hour and 245,786 per day. Can you imagine, almost a 1/4 of a million brand new Human Beings, every day!!! This according to these statistics would increase the global population by 89,712,000. This was the actual statistic as was provided by Marie Stopes International in 1994, based on a UN estimate with regards to the increase for that year.

Another UN report for the same year indicated a slightly higher figure of increase, 94 million. At that time the estimated world population was 5.66 billion. The report also indicated that we could expect a world population of 8.5 Billion in the year 2025, which is a whopping 49.47% increase from 1994. **In comparison to this envisaged 8.5 billion population, in 1950, the world population was only 2.5 billion.** This was just two years short before I too like so many others, was graciously given the divine opportunity to enter also into our GOD' marvelous creation; for this was the year that I was born. Hurrah for me. Go ahead and do give yourself a clap offering to GOD ALMIGHTY for you too to be here.

Thank You, MY DEAR LORD GOD ALMIGHTY, for granting me my very life and for giving me through your most gracious and precious love for me, this most awesome opportunity to be in Heaven too someday together with all the Hevenlies. Yes, I do accept my Salvation, which had been paid in full by the most precious BLOOD of our LORD and SAVIOUR JESUS CHRIST. And I do most earnestly desire with all of my heart, with all of my soul, with all of my strength and with all of my mind to be walking accordingly to be found judged fitting to be receiving this in TRUTH; the priceless eternal GIFT from our GOD ALMIGHTY. I humbly do acknowledge, for YOURS is the KINGDOM, the POWER and ALL the GLORY, FOREVER AND EVER, AMEN. YOU are SOVEREIGN over everything in the physical and in the heavens too all the time.

With the birth having been so miraculously and successfully accomplished, the human being born may one day become an important contributor to this world, impacting millions of lives with his or her contributions. This is how important every birth is to Mankind on the whole. Of course the risk in reverse to this is also highly possible, as **Satan** is always at work in destroying lives. However, the point I am trying to drive home here besides the miraculous happening and the possible contribution is that the infant' entry into this world is heralded, being **Time Stamped by the very heavens.** This registering is possible only because of the Sun and it' Sunlight, coupled together with the relevant motions of the Planet Earth, including it' very own rotation on it' axis. This motion records **days** and it' orbit around the Sun records our **years**. Of course, we cannot leave the Moon out of this 'time stamping' equation, for it records the months in a Year. You will also find out later, that the Moon plays an even bigger role in conjunction with the Sun' affect on it. This together, directly affects the speed of the Earth' rotation on it' very own axis.

These effects causes not only short term but also long term changes to the very length of our day, which directly affects the 'number of days' it takes for the Earth to orbit the Sun.

This seems to establish a somewhat 'inseparable triune relationship', not only vital to the establishment of 'Local Time', as we record it here on Earth from our perspective but also life itself. It was set into motion by our LORD GOD ALMIGHTY. Thereby, GOD also set into motion, an important **significance** in it' playing (i.e. Sun-Earth-Moon) a vital part in the process of a human birth, i.e. **'Time Stamping'** it' very entry into the Universe.

This registering or recording is accomplished by no other means but with **numbers;** the values of which have been established and universally accepted. These are the very vital foundational building blocks for every science and mathematics discipline. These very 'numbers', we have all come to learn, represents specific 'values' such as zero, one, two, three, ………ten,……one hundred……ten thousand…etc., are value fixed the same throughout the world. In other words it does not change due to it' various applications or the usage by other peoples; differing cultures; differing language or even in different locations. The name or word that is used to call the number is of no consequence either, for it' the basic value which is attributed to it that is significant and universal. So, the important fact to appreciate is that the **'value'** is globally the same everywhere, for each number or combination of numbers.

This establishes, I hope the **'understanding'** to my linking of the date & time of birth numbers, which is made possible only through this **'Time Stamping'** significant process for each individual. This becomes for all intents and purposes, our unique cosmic identification. It is our number, just as it would be for the second beast too, who is a man – REV 13:18 confirms.

In other words, it becomes the specific cosmic number of our given name, no matter whatever that it may be. For it irrevocably and specifically identifies us throughout our life.

This 'understanding' is to provide the avenue for the reasons to paradigm shift the current thinking from associating numbers to the letters of our name, as was done in Gematria, to this Cosmic approach. As explained this dates our very birth into this Universe. For it is indeed independent of any human or evil interference and/or of wicked manipulation, as conveniently being possible, through the application of Gematria.

However, the 'number' to be calculated that sum totals to 666, which is the 'cosmic number' of the beast, is much more complex in constructing though. This I found out, whilst in the process and progress of writing this book than the 'simple' birth date-time number, which is being currently used to identify us today.

GOD as you must remember designed time directly as a by-product of the Universe-Solar Planetary System creation. 'Time' has become the very pulse of the Universe, as our LORD GOD had set it into motion, as clearly described in Genesis 1:14 - 18.

This now begins to set the stage, to prove the accuracy of the 'cosmic number' of the beast, which is unique to him alone, being generated

through this 'Cosmic' approach.

In fact, you may already know that many people around the world hold the date and time that an individual is born, as being very sacred. For to them, it clearly plays a defining, definite and even pivotal part in the individual's entire possible progress in his lifetime, as they employ Astrology, Fortune Telling and other methods that they do follow to chart the 'life'. In fact this is still prevailing in several cultures and was the case across every Civilization in establishing the individual' significance and their possible future destiny. This is done not only at the time of birth, but also throughout the many phases of growing up, which also amongst other events in their lives, includes his or her passage into marriage. It had a hold even on Kingdoms when they wanted to wage war on another. In fact every aspect of their lives was dictated by this.

On these particular issues, personally, I am not concerned with nor do I subscribe to it in any way whatsoever, but I referenced it just to show you that our **'cosmic number'** is held as important or even more so, than your given name. This is recognized as such in several cultures and civilizations, which as an example includes the Hindu; for they use it together with palm reading and astrology to chart out their very destinies throughout their lifetime.; well for most I think.

This **'identification'** especially now in modern times is to further establish that you are indeed the 'One', that is called by that name. For many would share your name, but it is more unlikely that any would share your exact date of birth when it is coupled together with your exact time of birth. This can even be stretched to a greater degree of accuracy, to further distance us, one from another, if needed. This is to further reduce the remotest of possibilities, for any to share your unique 'date & time' of birth precisely similarly. We can accomplish this quite easily, if we further qualify the exact time of birth to a **thousandth of a second** or even more as an example. This preciseness today can be quite easily accomplished, through the abundant availability and at the very minimal cost for the appropriate digital time-pieces.

Of course, we need to acknowledge that there is every possibility for human error in recording the actual time of birth and also due to incorrect timepieces. Also, there is that very possibility that the time is not even recorded for many, for various reasons prevailing in their particular situation, as often is the case in remote villages of third world countries presently. However, this too will improve with time, education and economic progress in these locations. Despite these setbacks and operational problems, we still can acknowledge that the process of identifying an individual, through their 'date of birth', coupled with the precise 'time of birth', is indeed a legitimate, valid and relatively easy implementation globally. In fact, this has been and is currently the case besides the given name. If I had not mentioned earlier, this does not include our thumbprints and other identifications, for my proposal here, is totally dependent on 'numbers'.

You will also begin to see that in this particular 'Cosmic' solution for the obtaining of the number that sum totals 666, it can only be discovered through additional means. These are as provided by the relevant though basic levels in the Sciences of Astronomy and Cosmology of the Universe, besides the direct engagement of the relevant referenced Scriptural verses. This is the only way for us to be able to accomplish this 'Cosmic' approach, which ultimately leads us to the solution and the process in finding out the **'cosmic number'** totaling **666**.

In fact our LORD GOD in Revelation 13:18, does inform us that the **'number'** is calculable even by us; provided we have the understanding. This 'understanding', which our LORD GOD was telling us about that we would need, I personally would think also encompasses the very use of the 'Sciences', as it develops through the ages in human thought and discovery. This then would be the acquired knowledge necessary, coupled together also that which is divinely inspired. This together, would give us the necessary associated **wisdom,** i.e. which would be required to **understand,** how to actually calculate out the 'number' of the beast. Apparently, as Revelation exhibits, our LORD GOD wants us by all means to do so.

We are also informed that the second beast is a man. Our LORD God wants us to expose this beast, this man, to the world to be readily recognized for all to see. To be made prepared and aware of him and his ploys.

This goes on to imply by inference, although, he would be quite easily recognizable due to his high profile global position as an important, powerful, well respected and *'well backed individual';* his modus operandi would be very subtle, very enticing, even seemingly to be so rewarding at first that so many would fall victim to willingly consent to receiving his mark. *This is permanent mind you, in all it' intents and purposes.*

GOD reveals to us that Satan through the second beast is strongly suggesting, as in the relevant Revelation Scripture, that everything he does is entirely for our benefit; for all people, small and great, rich and poor, free and slave. Also, obviously these benefits can only be obtained after one becomes a member and membership is obtained very easily. Absolutely no qualification whatsoever is required. No authorization is required; no pre approval is required. No form to be even filled up. Just simply, identify oneself with him, through the receiving of a mark; or of his name or the number of his name. This should specifically be carried out on the right hand or on the forehead, as one may prefer - Rev 13:16 - 17 refers.

This is also **free**; only for the process mind you. For you will pay for it in the end, with your very own life i.e. your **eternal life** after death.

This is why, it is important for us to 'identify' this individual, so that we will be made aware that he who occupies that 'high profile position', to be established in due time and season, is indeed the second beast and not just any aspiring, capable, global citizen, appointed to look after the people' needs in a global context.

Now, I do not personally claim that I am amongst those, if there are anyone else that is, who have been given the privileged **'understanding'** to calculate out the **'number'** of the beast. Besides, I was not even on this quest in the very first place, but by 'accident', stumbled upon the path to obtain the probable solution. I also say probable, not because I have doubts that it isn't, but it is for each of you to decide, whether this could be indeed the *'cosmic number'* of the second beast. This you need to do by thinking through on all of the supporting evidences and arguments, as provided for you in this book.

Yet the fact however remains that I am able through this 'Cosmic' approach, to calculate out such a 'cosmic number', which does indeed sum up to 666!!!

This was in part accomplished by engaging the relevant and significant Scriptures in Revelation, a Biblical Book, which itself is described as being a **'Cosmic Pageant'** – an elaborate, colorful series of tableaux, accompanied and interpreted by celestial speakers and singers. This description is according to the Spirit Filled Life Bible, page 1956.

We need to combine these Scriptures, with the derived understanding of Scriptural facts, as drawn out from the Deuterocanonical Book - 2Esdras Chapter 14:9-12. Read the whole Chapter, but better still read the entire Book; it will really enlighten you and may even further inspire you to becoming a better JESUS IS GOD believing Christian.

> Coupling all of this 'understanding' together, jointly with key though quite basic astronomical data relating to our Solar System and the Universe at large; then using all of this complexity to finally be able to construct the *'cosmic number'* that sum totals to **666,** is surely something worth investigating into and debating about. "Do you not think so???"

This should be especially the case, for those who are interested and concerned regarding matters of the Apocalypse and the Armageddon. Also, for those **Roman Catholics**, who for so long have been trying to defend the misguided onslaught that still goes on branding the Pope and his Offices as being the beast and the Offices of the beast. They who oppose the Papacy do this, in some ways through the application of Gematria (more on this to come).

The Roman Catholic Church in retaliation, in the past, had branded **Martin Luther** who had been recognized as being responsible for the Reformation, which subsequently triggered the split in the Church, creating a 'Christianity' at that time that is collectively called as 'Protestantism'; members of which are commonly called as 'Protestant', as being the beast of Revelation – the **antichrist**.

Perhaps this *'Cosmic'* approach could offer both major groups, including all the other Christian groups, who think somewhat similarly on this issue; the *'solution'* out of this undignified and unchristian impasse.

This had plagued them for generations in the past and will continue as presently and probably also into the distant future, unless they change their stand. Even more importantly in truth, their thinking on this matter as per my humble opinion, has been totally misguided, unfounded and **without any scriptural basis** whatsoever at all.

Their employing of **Rev 13:18** rather **wickedly**, in venting out their anger and hatred which had also resulted in the unnecessary bloody violence and killings brought upon each other, because of this very issue, directly and indirectly; in my opinion was and is purely a waste of precious life and a huge loss to Mankind. Worse still, the total blatant undermining of GOD' great commandment: John 15:12..... **that you love one another as I have loved you**.... is seriously appalling.

Now, without being bias against any legitimate GOD fearing Christian Group that declares openly, that JESUS CHRIST is GOD; that the HOLY SPIRIT is GOD and the FATHER is GOD and these THREE PERSONS are One in the GODHEAD, upholding the fundamental Christian generated belief as in the 'Holy Trinity', then I would like to state the following: As my early roots and late adult life until the age of 40 were indeed Roman Catholic (RC), which I thank our LORD GOD for several reasons, must declare unequivocally, "That it really does not and should not take much effort for us to understand, there has got to be an hidden agenda, for 'them' to somehow with their deft number manipulations, calculate that the Pope in his official and Spiritual capacity, being the Head of the Roman Catholic Church, which is and has always been at the very forefront of establishing, promoting and evangelizing Christianity around the whole wide world since it' inception, establishing LORD GOD' Salvation Message; to be then wickedly stigmatized to be indeed the second beast is really appalling to say the least. This also makes him to be according to the relevant Revelation Scriptures by simple default, the antichrist. This is really too much to condone and yet we must forgive!!!

At the time of the Reformation, Protestants quite generally held that the Pope was indeed the antichrist and reciprocating to this attack, as previously mentioned; Roman Catholics regarded Martin Luther, who they held responsible for triggering the Reformation, similarly. Also, in the other controversy between the Roman Catholics and the Greek Orthodox Church, the name was brutally applied to those Popes and to those Byzantine emperors in opposition to each other at that time, accordingly. Please refer to the Encarta Encyclopedia or other similar references on the subject for more details.

Before I do miss this opportunity, I need to let you know that I am now currently enjoying the 'Born Again' Christian experience. There is also no greater joy than to be able to bring even just one lost soul to CHRIST our LORD and SAVIOUR, who had through the Cross, made readily and freely available this **Salvation** for all peoples of the Earth. Those who choose to receive this Salvation and subsequently having received it, continue to be in this 'State of Salvation', or to get back into this 'State', before death do us part, would be set free from all condemnation and be saved from the eternal fires of **hell.** AMEN.

PRAISE BE TO GOD

We are informed that there are also other individuals in history besides the Pope, whom they have associated with their 'Gematria established Numbers', sum totalling to **666.** Just for your information to name a few: **Caesar Nero, Diocletian, Julian and Caligula** - all Roman emperors, are some who are also on their list. In fact it may not be surprising that these emperors are also actually included in this list, for many actually behaved also like beast, in their governing of the people. The List also includes the Samaritan, called Simon Magus; who is mentioned in Acts 8:9-24. I really do not know why he too had been targeted as such.

In more recent times, Saddam Hussein, Bill Gates and even **Batman!!!**, have not been spared in their charade. Can you just imagine how these people are indeed able to come up with such crazy and manipulative even outlandish accusations??? Even the cartoon legend, Batman, had not been spared!!! Other names that have been included in their 'List' are just too blasphemous in the context of those belonging to other religions to be mentioned here. For it is in the context of involving their very founders. So, I am going to just skip this and move on.

By the way, the Latin titles of the Pope, to my knowledge which have been associated through Gematria, with the sum total **666,** are as follows:

Vicarius Filii Dei; Dux Cleri; Ludovicus; Ordinarius Ovilis Christi Pastor and Dic Lux.

Some of them in the English translation, carry the meaning; In place of the Son of God (on Earth, obviously) or Vicar of the Son of God or Vicar of Christ; Captain of the Clergy and Vicar of the Court, respectively.

They have also equated their 'Gematria established Numbers' sum totalling to **666** to Hebrew words such as Romiith, which means the Roman Kingdom; Romiti, which means the Roman Man.

In Greek, they have chosen a few ancient Greek words such as Lateinos, which means the Latin speaking man; He Latine Basileia, which means 'The Latin Kingdom'; Italika Ekklesia, which means Italian Church (referring specifically to the Roman Catholic Church) and the Greek word, Apostates.

These people and those still under the influence of these 'Gematria established number associating system', must realize, more so now than ever, that their calculations being based on Gematria i.e. Numbers associated with the letters of the alphabets, either of the Hebrews, Greeks or Romans (Latin); were indeed man-made devised systems. These have an occult or mystic foundation used by the Cabalist (Cabalism) for their own expressions in interpreting the 'suppose to be' mystical hidden meanings in words and whole sentences. It is just like someone reading tea leaves to tell you your destiny or reading the liver of animals freshly cut out to announce whether the harvest is going to be a good one or the spirits are going to be happy this time with what is at hand.

You just cannot equate GOD' way of doing anything with that which has to do with the occult or divination or satanic things as this would be solely the modus operandi of those in cahoots with the evil one.

In fact the Arabs and the Chinese have also somewhat similar systems for cabalism calculations.

Therefore, with all of this above in view, in this specific case for the calculation of the **'number'** that sum totals to **666**, it must definitely be based on more divine methods. After all, it was also sanctioned by our LORD GOD Almighty, for us to calculate out this number which sum totals 666.

Therefore, by using a **man-made** system, which is indeed manipulative by this mere fact, and also it is very well known that within these alphabet associated numbering system, there are more than one numbering value system. This quite obviously, would inevitably give rise to openly manipulating the system, so to design it to fit and suit the objective at hand.

Therefore, with this in view, this cannot be taken seriously to any degree whatsoever. For example, in following the Hebrew or Greek alphabet, you can follow Gematria in 'N' or in 'n'. This indeed doubles, trebles or even more times the manipulative possibilities present in this Gematria System.

According to one definition: Gematria which comes from the Hebrew word 'guematria', is the process used mainly by the Cabalists, which consists in substituting the letters of a word or a whole sentence by their numerical assigned value and then totaling these assigned values to arrive at the final total; which they interpret as depicting a specific meaning.

I understand, there are more than two assigned value systems, as there are several schools of thought on the attributing of numbers to the alphabets of these languages including the Roman (Latin), which has the Genetic System; the Beatus System; the Common Tenth Century System, as choices.

Therefore, in this Gematria example pertaining to the total **666** of the **'number'**; it means there are at least two distinct differing numbering values applicable to the alphabet, depending on which one you adopt for your purposes. For example, the name of the Hebrew alphabet, kaph in Gematria 'N' has a number value of 20 and in Gematria 'n' the same alphabet name has the number value of 11. Also, if the letter kaph appears at the end of a word, it has a value of 500 in the 'N' Gematria system and only 23 in the 'n' Gematria system.

This could give you some understanding, for the many opportunities and possibilities open, to those who use this system to manipulate the Gematria, to meet the objectives of these people who are against you. On what basis were the assigned values chosen for a particular system, are subject again to speculation and perhaps even to the extent of ridicule? I am quite certain that the adding and taking away of values can be done quite easily. Yet seriously, this should not really be of any relevance here, because it being purely a human creation and not of God, has no authority or basis in our subsequent quest to discover the **'number'**, sum totaling **666**; which is primarily based on Holy Biblical Scripture.

> It was the Biblical Scriptures that would somehow eventually lead me to seek as my second quest, the unraveling of the **'number'** of the second beast, by remarkably employing the very Cosmos to derive it' construction.

Therefore, I conclude in the first place that even those Bible Scholars, who had earlier perhaps suggested that the 'number' of the name of the beast, could be calculated by relying on Gematria, as it was practiced in ancient Biblical times by some of the Hebrews, is in my opinion *not to be taken seriously here*.

Now someone may raise this question, "Why did GOD then not give us the name of the second beast in the first place and spare all of us this terrible dilemma"???

Surely, our LORD God knows who the second beast would really be. For the fact that our LORD GOD is the CREATOR of all things and being all knowing i.e. omniscient, but for reasons that our LORD GOD only knows, this was not to be revealed to us. So it is left entirely up to us to find out for a specific purpose.

As previously mentioned, there are three ways to be identified with the second beast or rather with the man; by the receiving of:

(1) His mark; whatever that is, for this too has not been revealed to us.

(2) His name; this too has not been revealed to us except for knowing that he is the second beast, although being a man.

(3) The **'number'** of his name. This we know to some extent and that is it sum totals to 666.

We are informed through Scripture that an individual can be identified together with the second beast, that is to be subject to him, by receiving any one of the above **'identifications'** on the right hand or on their forehead. However, I am only focusing on the third option. You need to know that if you let any one of the three options to be applied to you directly, you would have also quite obviously permanently associated yourself with him and in turn directly with Satan.

As I had mentioned above, I also understand based on my own study from the overall interpretation of Revelation 13:16-18, that when any one of these 'identifications' is finally received by those living at the time; it would be **permanent.** This confirms that you have in finality, chosen your final destiny of accepting and following Satan, instead of following our LORD God ALMIGHTY.

The modes of delivery for the receiving of any one of these identifications have not been indicated though in the Scriptures. However, many have already suggested several possibilities for the **'number'** to be received, such as a simple tattoo, to implants of microchips which are encoded with his **'number'**. In fact such microchip identification techniques are already being used in animals to establish ownership and other details. It would be the same for them intending to accept this ending.

Receiving the 'mark' of the beast would not be the same as committing a forgivable sin, i.e. if you sincerely repent it with a contrite heart.

Then what about a 'change of heart' at the very end i.e. when it is decided by the individual to renounce Satan and all that he stands for; we may ask???

Would this be acceptable to GOD after one has received the 'mark'???

I really do not think so, for I propose this receiving of the 'mark' of the beast is similar to an abomination to our LORD God. This is unforgivable to the very end of time, even into everlasting eternity. Furthermore, it is unlikely that one could have a change of heart, because you also have lost your GOD given freewill. This would be taken over by Satan himself and you at that point in time onwards belong to him. So, the very hypothesis of possibly having a 'change of heart' at some point after this beastly acceptance; in my opinion, does not apply anymore.

While you are chewing on this, it is indeed very 'generous' for the beast to provide the individual one of three choices of how to be identified with him and his works – Rev 13:16-18 refers. The devil always makes the path to him, his tormented house, which is **hell** – the lake of fire and brimstone; easy, enjoyable & pleasurable, straight and smooth, until you arrive in **THERE**.

> This would then become what we Christians have come to know, as being your *second death*, which will be for all eternity. No escape from this one.
> *BEWARE* **BEWARE BEWARE**

I only do hope and pray that if the beast' time is anytime now in our own lifetimes, then you and I, would be found spared besides those 144,000 of the 12 tribes of Israel whom would be receiving the 'Seal of GOD' - Rev 7:3 and 9:4 refers.

So the bottom-line for this book then becomes that the **'number'** which sum totals to **666**, would be obtained through a **'Cosmic'** approach, as I had personally found out. For it does uniquely sum total to *666* and simultaneously being also the auspicious **date of birth** so to speak, as it would be the beginning of the 360 Day Years for the very first time in our Biblical Human History.

This 'Cosmic approach obtained series of numbers' sum totalling to 666 in part would represent the exact time that the Earth would first begin to have a 360 Days Year, which is a perfect year or called as a Calendar Year. The **other part** in this series or set of numbers would also be revealed to you accordingly, as you do progress on.

The 360 days year is called a Calendar Year, because each of the 12 months are exactly of the same length of time and thereby, accordingly, is 30 Earth Time days each.

Therefore, it makes the perfect calendar on a day to day basis and subsequently on a month to month basis, which does not make the year to be ahead or to fall behind in the seasons. Bible scholars have aptly termed this type of year as the **Prophetic Year**.

> I just cannot help but to re-emphasize again and again, this would be the very first time in our Earth's Biblical Human History, that we would eventually have the 360 Day Years. It will be further substantiated in the second part of this book.

This will also, therefore, be offered to inevitably refute and reject all the previous claims by all quarters that have claimed outright the following:

Before the Noah' Flood had occurred, the Earth' orbit around the Sun was always 360 days in length. This then however became immediately changed in the very same year that the Flood had occurred to be the 365¼ days orbit. They citing, that it was because of the direct effects of their globally devastating Noah' Flood, that had lengthened or had caused the Earth' orbit around the Sun to be increased to 365¼ days; as evidently it is now..

> I also naturally do reject this totally and hope that by the time you finish reading PART 2, you too will also hopefully agree with my view.

As previously mentioned in the Preview of this book, some quarters have even suggested this change could have been caused by the very gravitational disturbances of some **astral body,** passing by us at that very time in the past. This caused the Earth' orbit around the Sun, to have increased in it' distance of about a million miles more. This additional orbiting distance required this additional **5¼** days period of time, so that the Earth could complete it' annual orbit around the Sun, which previous to the Flood, had only taken the original 360 days. So according to their proposal this was the original length of the year in the pre-Noah Flood days.

Now, If Noah had commented this was also what had taken place; that is before the Flood it was **360 day years,** but after the Flood it had become **365¼ day years,** then quite definitely we will not be having this discussion. For you may very well know that he was the key witness to this supposed happening together with the rest of his family. This evidently meaning, if this was stated as such somewhere in the Biblical Book of Genesis; then I too would have also accepted this without any question. And mind you Noah had lived after the flood for another 350 years, as attested by Gen 9: 28-29. He died when he was 950 years old. Surely, during this long period of time, Noah and the rest of his family would have come to realize this very fact. That the very lengthening of the supposedly 360 day years at the time before the Flood, to the 365 ¼ day years immediately after the Flood or even some years after the fact. Evidently, this was not the case during the next 350 years, and this is why nothing was also mentioned as such by them in the Holy Scriptures. For as I conclude from this basis, it was 365¼ days Pre-Noah and Post-Noah at that time and still is as clearly evident today. Not affected by the Flood at all!!! This should be considered as 'new evidence' being presented for this case. For it has never been presented as such before, and besides, the several other perspectives that I have also presented here in this book, against their proposal, is just simply overwhelming; to say the least. Let us look at another situation to this as follows:

The gravitational disturbances caused by the near passing of the astral body, they say; was also naturally and simultaneously responsible for the greatly increased magnitude of the Noah' Flood. This was then directly contributive to the widely accepted global devastation of the Noah' Flood.

> This caused some even to go on to claim, that it was because of this, i.e. the widely supported globally devastating Noah' Flood; that the Earth was then extensively tilted on it' very own axial axis. The Noah' Flood in other words was the cause of even this!!!

I personally do not have the necessary academic credentials to substantiate clearly and to out-rightly refute this above additional claim. However, in my humble opinion, this was not the way these cosmic matters in question had evolved i.e. by way of the astral body and in turn the subsequent effects of the Noah' Flood in the tilting of the axial axis.

Please take note, I am not challenging the possibility of an 'Astral Body' being able to causing a change in the Earth' Orbit. Neither am I challenging the Scriptural authenticity of the Noah' Flood from having taken place as revealed to us in Genesis of the Holy Bible. What I am challenging though in two fronts, is (1) with regards, to their 'astral body' theoretical proposition, being in turn used to provide a plausible answer for the 'religious claim' that the Noah' Flood was indeed global in magnitude and (2) that in turn this too caused the tilting of the Earth' axial axis to what it is as evident today.

The 'special insight' that I had employed or gained to fortify this conclusion or rather to make this very counter-proposition in refuting their claims, as well as the associated 'religious claim', which is in contention above, is extensively argued and well documented as such in this very book. Therefore, it is obvious that **I am of the opinion that the 'tilt' was there even before the Flood had even occurred.** Please allow me to further elucidate, as you do progress through this book, till the very end. Thank you.

However, for the time being in brief, we need to understand that they possibly did not know at the time of their proposition, that the orbit of the Earth around the Sun and the speed with which the Earth orbits the Sun have been from time immemorial, remaining almost constants; as this is exactly what Scientific Scholarship have informed us for some time now.

Furthermore, as you study the other Solar Planets and find out that these have axis tilts too, should further explain, why we just cannot and in fact should not accept this earlier view regarding our Planet Earth on this tilting phenomena to have been exaggerated as such by the Noah' Flood. For the fact is that Planets having axis tilt is quite a common characteristic in our Solar System and as such, there has to be another validated cosmic reason for this planetary tilting phenomenon.

Therefore, the 'Planetary Tilt' as astronomically observed and studied in depth in each of our respective Solar Planets through our learned scientific community, to my conclusion, did not come about by that chance association in close passing of 'astral bodies'. Even more coincidentally having the required particular size to generate such a specific cosmic affect on our Planets accordingly to bring upon it (especially the Planet Earth) the most required seasonal changes in the climate that has provided us with such a vast diversity in plant and animal life and which is also crucial for our own continued existence here.

My humble verdict on this for what it is worth is that the tilts were all naturally occurring and came about during the formation process of the Planets. Also contributed by the interacting affects of the Sun on its Planets, perhaps through it' magnetic fields, gravitational affects, etc. Besides all of this possibility, we need to finally address the most important of them all. It is that all of this had come about by intended design. That is directly by our LORD GOD ALMIGHTY' cosmictecture (coining a new word here).

For GOD declared very clearly in Gen 1:14, that we will have the **seasons**. And we know for a fact that without the tilt, coupled together with the Earth' rotation on this angled axial axis; these **seasons** that we currently have all around the world would not have occurred, if we did not have the tilt and the rotation during it' orbit around the Sun.

This directly means that each Planet had it' unique tilt from the very beginning it began operating as an integrated Planet of our Solar System; to fit itself appropriately into the overall cosmic solar planetary design that we evidently currently do have at this material time. Thereby, with no doubts in my mind; fulfilling obviously the Creator' cosmictecture plans; if I could put it in this manner.

Through this book, you will also find out just as I had, of another cosmic generated possibility, which has also contributed to the required 'Solar Planetary Cosmic Parameters', in order to provide us, with all of the necessary changes in our Solar Planetary System. This in particular is pertaining to our own Planet Earth, which would eventually accommodate and bring about our future 360 Day Years.

Whether, this may go on to suggest that the second beast' time, will only materialize on the Earth when we have a 360 Days Year at some far distant future; may not necessarily be the case, as I read it at the moment. What is clear, however, that is through this book, we will be obtaining the very 'number' of the second beast in question, which will sum total to the Biblical sum total of 666. This was calculated solely through a **'Cosmic Construction',** which was also directly derived through the appropriate understanding of relevant referenced **Biblical Scripture**. This cosmic related 'difficulty' in obtaining it, but yet entirely being developed and generated through Biblical Scripture, gives this particular effort, the required authenticity and perhaps even the divine accreditation in my pursuit, for it to be recognized as being the very **'number'** of the beast.

Before I close this Part One, I would like to take this very opportunity to include here a poem, if you can call it that, subscribing to an abstract viewpoint of, 'Time' is Dying. This I wrote sometime way back, whilst I was still in my very late teens around 18 years old at which time, I had originally named it - "What is TIME???". I have however over the years until now, as I went back to it several times, made several changes to it each time; even adding and rearranging some of the verses or stanza around. Yet, all the while, maintaining the main original framework and concept of this poem, intact.

I personally, felt it appropriate to include it here now, as it certainly describes 'TIME' in a somewhat different light than what we know of it as commonly, and currently. As this book is also in a way dealing with the subject of 'TIME', as you will see, I thought that it would be quite alright to include it in here for your added benefit. Please do bear with me through the next few pages. Thank you.

'TIME' is DYING

IN THE VERY BEGINNING, *'TIME'* WAS AT A TOTAL
STANDSTILL - AGE-LESS,
SILENT, POWERLESS,
EVEN SIDELINED; YET EVER PATIENTLY WAITING FOR
THE EVIL MASTER' CRAFTY HAND TO ENGAGE
WHEN GOD , BREATHED LIFE INTO ADAM,
AND ADAM' EVE,
THROUGH A SATANIC CONSEQUENCE
SLAMMED US ALL - GIVING BIRTH TO OUR *'TIME'*
SO *'TIME'* SET FREE BY EVIL AND OUR
WRONGDOING
TO TIDE
NOW BEING
AN EVER WINDING ONE WAY SPIRAL STAIRCASE
THOUGH WE PROCLAIM, WAITS FOR NO MAN
YET RETARDS IN SLEEP
STOPS IN DEATH..........WELL ALMOST
FOR YET AGAIN, WE LIVE ON AND
ON AND ON............FOR ETERNITY
YET DESPITE THE EVIL HAVING BEEN ACCOMPLISHED;
'TIME',
MIRACULOUSLY IS ONCE AGAIN AFRESH
IN ANOTHER BEGINNING; SINCE THE **CROSS**
YET ALL THROUGH CONSUMING ITSELF
MORE AND MORE BECOMING FRAGMENTED,
AND MORE AND MORE BECOMING FRAIL,
WHERE ONCE IN THE VERY BEGINNING, BEFORE THE
EVIL HAND
TOOK HOLD
IT WAS JUST SIMPLY AGE-LESS
FOR NOW *'TIME'*, IN IT' VERY ESSENCE, IS EVER SO
SLOWLY
DUE TO THE SINGULAR SATANIC CONSEQUENCE

DYING

WE ALSO, IN TURN ARE TO BE BLAME, IN GIVING
'TIME'
IT' VERY OWN UNDERSTANDING;
FOR NOW, IT KEEPS ON TICK-TOCKING AWAY FROM
US
ALL – RICH AND POOR;
KING AND SERVANT; FREE AND
SNARED
NO MATTER
FOR *'TIME'* HAS NEVER
BEEN A RESPECTOR OF THE ELEMENTS
BUT REGIMENTALLY OBEDIENT
TRANSPORTING LIFE UNDER GUARD TO OUR VERY
DEATH-BED
BUT IT WAS NOT SO .... AT THE VERY
BEGINNING
EVEN BEFORE THE BEGINNING
FOR **THEY** WERE INDEED *'TIME'* IN ITSELF;
LOCKING IT AWAY EVEN
FROM THE REST OF THE UNIVERSE;
WITHOUT ANY MEASURE,
WITHOUT ANY CARE OR OF ANY CONCERN
WHATSOEVER!!!
YET SHOCKINGLY, NOW *'TIME'* HAS EVEN
OUTREACHED US,
OUTPACED US; AND HAS BECOME UNASHAMEDLY
INDEPENDENT OF US ALL
JUST AS IF A NEBULOUS LIFE HAS SOMEHOW
EMERGED IN
'TIME' ITSELF
AND MOST TRAGICALLY; WE OURSELVES ARE
BEING
FOUND NOW,

MORE AND MORE CAUGHT UP IN BETWEEN THIS
VERY
SAME WINDING SPIRAL
BEING RELENTLESSLY, WITHOUT ANY COMPASSION
WHATSOEVER
BEING SWEPT
ALONG IT' RAPIDS OF
SECONDS, MINUTES AND HOURS
FROM THE TIME OF LOVE,
TO THE TIME OF TEMPORARY REPOSE,
TILL WE ALL STAND,
THOUGH SOME VERY EXPECTANTLY
AND MANY
EVEN EVER SO DEFIANTLY AT THE VERY JUDGMENT
TIME CROSSING
AS THEY ENTER INTO THE SECOND DEATH
UNLIKE THOSE BLESSED,
ENTERING INTO THEIR
SALVATION MERCY
FOR ALL ETERNITY
AAAH YES, LESS WE FORGET,
ALL OF THIS BEING DUE TO THAT SINGULAR
SATANIC CONSEQUENCE,
HAVING SHAKEN THE VERY FOUNDATIONS OF THE
ENTIRE UNIVERSE
AND YES TOO, THE VERY HEAVENS OF ABOVE
REACHING EVEN INTO THE VERY SACROSANCT
THRONE ROOM OF OUR LORD GOD ALMIGHTY
THIS CHANGING GOD' COURSE FOR ALL MANKIND SO
DISASTROUSLY - (GEN 3:1-24; JOHN 3:16-17 REFERS)
ALL OF THIS, HAPPENNING THROUGH,
THE UNFORTUNATE ADAM' EVE
HAVING GIVEN BIRTH TO THE ONCE STANDSTILL
'TIME'
AND SO, WHEN WE BECOME NO MORE,

DUST TO DUST TO RETURN, AS COMMANDED BY OUR
LORD GOD ALMIGHTY – (GEN 3:19 REFERS)
'TIME' WILL ONCE AGAIN BE BROUGHT TO A
STANDSTILL
KEPT AT BAY
SILENCED IN OUR ETERNITY;
FOR SOME, IN THE BLINDING DARKNESS;
DISMAL PITS OF
GORING PAIN;
BURNING AND BURNING WITH UNTOLD
SUFFERING;
MUCH
MORE BEYOND THAN
WHAT THE HOLOCAUST PERPETRATORS COULD EVER
HAVE CONCEIVED THROUGH THEIR DEPRAVED MINDS
OR TO BE
EVER IMAGINABLE BY ANY MORTAL
AND YET ALL OF THIS SUFFERING PALES TO THIS;
NO GOD TO COMFORT
EVER.................
BUT ONLY TO SHARE IN THE TERRIBLE HORRIFYING
WRETCHEDNESS
WHAT WAS PREPARED IN THE VERY FIRST PLACE
FOR THE FALLEN ANGELS AND NOT FOR MANKIND
EVER!!!
AND SO FOR THE BLESSED, THOUGH GRASPING ONTO
BY THEIR
VERY DEAR SOULS, THE JESUS CHRIST SALVATION,
TO THE VERY END,
WILL BE EVER SO BASKING
IN HIS MOST WONDERFUL
AND GLORIOUS LIGHT;
REJOICING, SINGING PRAISES;
IN WORSHIP
CONTINUALLY IN THE PRESENCE OF OUR LORD GOD

                            ALMIGHTY
             AN ETERNAL REFRESHING EXPERIENCE LIKE
                      NO OTHER COULD EVER BE
             AND FINALLY ON THIS EARTH AT *'TIMES'* END,
                             WHO IS
                         GOING TO CARE
                            ANYMORE
                              FOR
             THAT GRAND OLD FATHER............. *'TIME'*
             ONLY US AT ONE TIME THEN, WHO HAD ONCE
                           FLUTTERED
                         SO FLEETINGLY,
             UNDER THE ONCE WATCHFUL MAJESTIC HEAVENLY
                              STAR

                                            (charles alphonso)

I do sincerely hope that through HIS GRACE and HIS MERCY for all of us, I have in some way been able to ignite & perhaps even to have kindled your very interest this far into a blaze, and that it will spur you on, to continue steadfastly, until the very end. Please let me know without any hesitation whatsoever, if and when, you have any difficulties in understanding this part of the book.

PRAISE BE TO GOD, WHO had first loved us, even whilst we were yet sinners!!

Thank you, my LORD and SAVIOUR JESUS CHRIST

Contact me if any need arises:

E : gcf@globalchristianfamily.com

PART TWO

The 360 Earth Days Orbital Years

I believe that the number of the name of the beast or directly put, the **'number'** of the beast and for that matter, for anyone, should be no other than the specific set of numbers that are directly associated with the date and time of an individual' birth. This is indeed indicated by none other than our own Star, the Sun, in conjunction with our Earth and it' Moon. This should be the right 'number' then to be associated to self and therefore can similarly be referred to simply as being your number. For this number is not established arbitrarily, but indeed specifically fixed for each individual at the time of his birth. However, you will find out, as I begin to reveal to you, the calculation for the very construction of this particular cosmic number, is taken to an even greater degree of accuracy and preciseness, in the case of the **'number'** of the beast.

Even in the Divine Birth of our LORD AND SAVIOUR JESUS CHRIST; HIS Divine Birth was according to a predestined or fixed time. This was divinely calculated and divinely appointed to the very instant together with the designated place that JESUS CHRIST, the MESSIAH was to be born into this earthly world. This as you may very well know was recorded in exacting detail, as such, in the Holy Scriptures, as found written in our Holy Bible.

> It was so, because it had to fit precisely into the fabric of GOD' WORD, that were indeed first spoken thousands of years ago, foretelling all the events that were to take place, accordingly, including that of HIS BIRTH as in Micah 5:2.

We are informed through the Book of Isaiah, in fact through the write up on this Book, as written in the Spirit Filled Life Bible – NKJV, Thomas Nelson Publishers; that 17 of the 66 Chapters in it contain prophetic references to CHRIST.

> According to this write up CHRIST is spoken of as the "LORD – BRANCH OF THE LORD – IMMANUEL – WONDERFUL, COUNSELOR – MIGHTY GOD – EVERLASTING FATHER – PRINCE OF PEACE – ROD OF JESSE – CORNERSTONE – KING – SHEPHERD – SERVANT OF YAHWEH – ELECT ONE – LAMB OF GOD – LEADER AND COMMANDER – REDEEMER AND ANOINTED ONE".

> All of this was indeed written down about **700 years before** the event of HIS DIVINE BIRTH.

Isaiah Chapter 53 also describes the 'Way of the Cross' - THE CRUCIFIXION, which JESUS CHRIST would have to ultimately journey through this world for each one of us and in scriptural fact for all of MANKIND across all borders, divides and times.

The most famous referenced is of course Isaiah 53: 4-5 which reads as follows:

> 4   Surely, HE has borne our griefs
> And carried our sorrows;
> Yet we esteemed HIM stricken,
> Smitten by GOD, and afflicted.
>
> 5   But HE was wounded for our transgressions,
> HE was bruised for our iniquities;
> The CHASTISEMENT for our peace
> Was upon HIM,
> And by HIS stripes we are healed.

Apostle Peter who had been credited for writing the First Epistle of Peter i.e. 1Peter, describes in 1Peter 2:21-25 in the NEW TESTAMENT, the exact same biblical events as above which further testifies and confirms the above as he was indeed a witness to these events.

Other older Scriptures were first handed down through generation to generation through the 'Oral Tradition', until it was possible to be in written form in parchments and then in scrolls, as such were the case mostly with the 'Old Testament' Books. Amongst these that were recorded, were the impending scriptural events that were to take place in relatively recent times, as it had come to be accomplished in the 'New Testament', as already mentioned with regards to JESUS CHRIST.

If it had not taken place accordingly as having been predestined and which was prophesied precisely as in the Old Testament, then it would not have fit into the jigsaw of biblical and secular events of history and the many that are yet to come in the future. This Divine Birth was even revealed in the New Testament, in real time terms, in such a glorious and magnificent manner, to the particular group of wise men; none other than by a Star. For they said in Mathew 2:1-12, that they saw **His Star**. This was indeed precisely timed to the spectacular moment of His Divine though humble Birth. Luke 2:8-20 refers.

Coming back to the problem at hand, as indicated from the very beginning of Part One; I would first need to find out, when the Earth would begin to have for the very first time, a '360 Days Year' in it' cosmic biblical human history/future. Somehow, these very two events are inseparably linked so closely together, i.e., with regards to the 'time construction' of when the '360 Days Year' would actually take place in the future and the precise 'cosmic construction' of the **number** of the beast sum totaling 666.

So, as I had mentioned in Part One, I was looking at first for the answers to support a 360 Days Solar Year.

Although later, when I found out the answers to support the **360 Biblical Earth Days per Orbital Year** instead, I decided not to change the quest, as stated in Part One. I did this, so that you would not be confused too much with several conceptual changes, at the very beginning of this book. I also wanted to first establish some definite lines of thought, which were clearly defined to you in Part One. This I wanted to do before I even attempted to further introduce to you, my entirely new developed concept of 'Biblical Earth Days' producing Biblical Earth Years.

There is a subtle but yet quite a substantial difference between these two types of Years being the Solar Years as currently being observed & my Biblical Earth Years which was originally used in the biblical times. However, both do obtain their time in years, as the Earth describes it' annual orbit around the Sun. It is very important for us to quickly understand and recognise this being as such, right now.

Somewhere along the way, I somehow realised that the original pursuit was not going to get me any nearer to my first quest, based on the present understanding and calculations for the establishing of the 365.242199 Solar Days in a current Solar Year. This is because according to Scientific Scholarship this is indeed getting longer and it is made up of *mean Solar Days*. It is longer than a Sidereal Day (Earth DAY) of 23 hours 56 minutes 4.10 seconds of mean solar time, because of the travel motion of the Earth in it' orbit during the two periods between two transits of the Sun.

This means that the Earth must complete more than a whole revolution on it' axis, in order to have the Sun once again at the meridian. This is due to the other simultaneous motion of travel, as it orbits around the Sun.

Also take note that the 23 hours 56 minutes 4.10 seconds, which is the length of a current Sidereal Day, is in fact the Earth' Axis Rotation Period (EAR for short) as at the Vernal Equinox. So in other words, this is the shortest time length of the EAR period as at the Vernal Equinox in this period of time, as the Earth orbits the Sun.

Therefore, I quickly realized, the only way I could continue my quest successfully, was to first switch to begin looking for the evidences in support of the *360 Biblical Earth Days,* instead. For the former, which was for the 360 Day (based on Solar Days) Years, as you will learn soon enough, is indeed **increasing in length** from it' present 365.242199 Solar Days. This is as being presented currently by the astronomical community. This evidently makes the realisation of the former 360 Solar Days/Year quest, quite obviously impossible at the stage of my understanding of it.

It was for this very reason besides others, that I wanted the quest to remain as such in Part One, so that I could explain this subtle but substantial difference in this Part Two more effectively. As it was based on this fundamental difference that the previous i.e. the first quest had to be changed accordingly, yet still keeping and even more so, in complete alignment with all of the relevant referenced Scriptures.

This was indeed the big Scriptural understanding breakthrough, which came at the very most appropriate time. For this is indeed crucially necessary, to allow me to begin my very first baby steps, to be achieving any positive and any encouraging progress, towards this very Biblical realization.

> This is to be recognised quite naturally, as being my very **'First Milestone Achievement'**, amongst many more to come, in this quest of finding out, when would we finally have the 360 Earth Day Years.

As you go along through this book, you will find out many more 'Milestone Achievements'. Each and all are equally crucial in their own right, to bring this 'Biblical Work', if I am graciously permitted to call it that, to a successful completion.

I would actually like to call these special Biblical Years, as being the:

> 360 Earth Days Orbital Years

from which the title of this PART TWO was obtained.

This means in essence going back to the very roots i.e., for the initial biblical method for Day and Year time measurements.

Although, for the uninitiated, at first, there may seem not to be any difference between these two time measuring systems, as both also use the very same Earth' Axis Rotation to establish each 'day' and also, both as having already been mentioned, use the Earth' orbit around the Sun to establish the year.

However, the uninitiated will soon find out that a 'day' in these two systems, represents entirely different concepts in telling the time and the amount of time involved in each differs quite considerably indeed. It is within this very context of this understanding, which irreconcilably sets them apart from each other.

As already explained on the previous page; a Solar Day, is the time taken during the two periods between two transits of the Sun, as the Earth rotates on it' own axis and simultaneously travels in it' orbit around the Sun to also subsequently establish the Solar Year. **Scientists have been telling us that the EAR (Earth' Axis Rotation) has been slowing down for some time now** This inevitably makes the Solar Day longer and this is also reflected subsequently in a longer Solar Year.

While my proposed 'Earth Days', which makes up the Biblical Year is only directly concerned with the **changing number** of Earth Axis Rotations that the Earth needs during it' similar orbit around the Sun; as it also goes through all the four seasons in a year, which naturally and of course biblically constitutes a 'Biblical Year'.

So, keeping your mind' eye open (analytically thinking), you will see there is a subtle and definite difference between these two time systems. Well anyway, you will find out soon enough.

By making this very timely switch, I just narrowly accomplished my initial objective. I really mean this, as it was tough going all the way. This is because I had to over several times, understand, although pertaining to very basic astronomical data, but somewhat differently from the norm, and to even **formulate new concepts along the way**!!! This was of course particularly very scary indeed for me. Therefore, it is up to you my neighbour to either refute these new theories and new concepts, as having no basis at all, or to offer any support which I eagerly do welcome, sincerely.

As just mentioned above, 'Scientific Scholarship' had informed us that the Solar Day has indeed been progressively increasing or lengthening by their calculations;

$1/1000^{th}$ **second per every 100 years**
This is due to the slowing down of the EAR

This rate is referenced from the Microsoft Encarta Encyclopedia '96, on the subject of Ephemeris time (i.e. Orbital Time). Just for your information, Ephemeris Time is based on the annual revolution of the Earth around the Sun, as from the Vernal Equinox and back again to it.

The above rate change, obviously depends directly on the similar rate of reduction, as presently is the case, in the speed of rotation of the Earth on it' axial axis.

This has to be so, for it is well known, this motion is directly responsible for the length of each Solar Day, coupled together with it' other motion of annual travel around the Sun. It is also well known, this particular Earth Axis Rotation motion is governed by several 'change causing factors', operating within the Solar System.

With regards to our quest, this is in particular, the very cosmic relationships such as the gravity affects of the Sun exerting on the Earth-Moon and vice versa; the affects that the Moon has on the Earth' ocean tides on a daily basis; and etc. These very affects then causes the very duration of the Earth' Axis Rotation to become quite varied in the length of time that it takes to complete each rotation, as it continues around the Sun. Therefore, the EAR then directly becomes somewhat unreliable for us to derive an unchanging 'value' for a second of time measure, for us to be able to depend upon it consistently and precisely.

In the book, 'The Earth', by Dr Arthur Beiser (a Geophysicist - a former Associate Professor of Physics at New York University; a former Vice-President of the Nuclear Research Associates, Inc. amongst other illustrious appointments and other achievements), which was published by Time-Life International (Nederland) N.V. - he states on page 164:

At present the Earth' rotation period i.e. on it' axis is lengthening at the rate of about **25 thousand-millionths of a second each day**. This seems little, but after about 5,000 million years, it will give the Earth roughly a **36 hour day**.

As far as Dr Arthur Beiser Earth' rotation period is concerned, this is also similarly echoed by the other article, that I had just referred to in the previous page. That is as in the Microsoft Encarta Encyclopedia '96 on the subject of Ephemeris time (i.e. Orbital Time). This is, with regards to the overall lengthening of the day by **1/1000th second per every 100 years**; though it may seem very small initially but over a really long period of time, it would then become really significant.

> According to my understanding, this very small Earth Axis Rotation rate change, which has long been well supported by Astronomical Science, will gradually and surely have an effect on the number of days or rather with regards to our specific interest; the **'number of Earth Axis Rotations'**, which would be necessary for the Earth to orbit the Sun completely, each time.

What I did not know at the time of discovering this important understanding, is this too, would have a very important influence and direct impact on my subsequent cosmic based construction for the **'number'** of the beast. This is besides my current quest, of attempting to resolve the elusive scriptural mystery pertaining to the 'Biblical 360 Day Years'.

Also, my above understanding, with regards to the 'Number of Earth Axis Rotations', was first derived through a somewhat different interpretation or if you like, understanding, based on the already available scientific data as mentioned above:

That the Earth' rotation on it' axis is gradually slowing down at the rate of **1/1000th of a second, every 100 years.**

It is different because Scientists have been stating: "This translates to a **longer Solar Year"**. This is simply because the Solar Day is indeed becoming longer, due to this slowing down of the Earth' Axis Rotation over time, as scientifically also reflected in Dr Arthur Beiser' proposal. I don't think you need to be a Rocket Scientist, to figure this one out; however, this too can get a little tricky mind you.

> **Isn't it right also, to state that the speed with which the Earth is orbiting the Sun has remained the same; despite the slowing down of the Earth' rotation on it' own axis?**

This was in fact established as a scientific fact long ago. In 1939, the English astronomer, **H. Spencer Jones**, stated that Orbital Time (Ephemeris time), which was based on the Earth' revolution around the Sun, did not vary, although the spinning of the Earth (Axis Rotation) was not keeping time and varied noticeably during the day and during the year.

I referenced his scientific statement in the book, 'Time', page 104, by Dr Samuel A. Goudsmit (who was a Physicist at Brookhaven National Laboratory; Visiting Professor at the Rockefeller University; discoverer in 1925 that electrons spin on their axes, and helped to establish modern atomic theory), which was published by Time-Life International (Nederland) N.V.

This was what he had stated, as I understand it, with regards to the short term or more immediate variations to the Earth' Axis Rotation. We can also take this to mean as the Earth journeys annually in an **unchanging** orbit around the Sun; it' speed in this annual journey remains the same though the spinning of the EARs on a daily basis was not keeping time as it should have been. This varied noticeably as established by the Astronomer, H. Spencer Jones. This daily variation is however not referring to the overall slowing down or the possible increasing (I am proposing this possibility too, based on my own assumptions in this book which I am writing) of the EAR as mentioned a few pages earlier.

'Orbital Time' as we understand it does not vary even though the Earth' rotation on it' axis is varying in both of these situations; one being immediate and temporary and the other changing gradually through a much longer period of time with a consistency in it' rate of change. Then based on my very own understanding pertaining to the 360 day years; shouldn't then the **number** of Earth Axis Rotations to complete each orbit (referring to the second long term duration situation) of the Sun **reduces** or **increases** accordingly, as the case may be, at the material time???

Scientific Scholarship has already established that currently, the Earth' Axis Rotation is indeed slowing down, as already mentioned several times before. This means ongoing even through the present 365.242199 Earth-Solar-Time days or rather **the 365+ Earth-Axis Rotations.** It would be **reducing even into the future for quite awhile,** as per my above understanding and the usage of the same applicable scientific data as already mentioned.

> Scientific Scholarship having become so singly concerned **only with the length of the day**, with it' subsequent affect on the duration of the year, missed focussing or rather missed the significance of the consistent EAR slowing down over a really long period of time that would eventually change **the number of Earth-Axis Rotations needed** to complete the similar orbit.

> This understanding above is paramount in realising my own efforts in my book that is currently being written on the subjects as aptly titled.

Would I be making a very serious assumption with regards to the above understanding??? May be so to some of you, but I do hope that the following statement somewhat justifies this though:

They were specifically focussing on the variations and the increasing length i.e. duration or the increasing time taken for an Earth' Axis Rotation to be completed during the course of any year. Of course, this in turn will progress as currently the Solar Day even further. This as per their current astronomical data would quite obviously be indicating an **increasing** trend in the duration of the year.

Therefore, following this very relevant Scientific Scholarship, we will have the consistent and continuous lengthening of the year, as the Solar Day is indeed becoming longer due to the current phase of reduction in the speed of the Earth' Axis Rotation. This is as scientifically also had been reflected in Dr Arthur Beiser' 36 hour days. Also, if we are going to have these 36 hour long days, as suggested by Dr Arthur Beiser, in the very distant future at the end of 5,000 million years or so, then I would like to propose that we could have had such long hour days also, in our Earth' cosmic ancient past. In this stage of the book, I compute that ever since the ancient past began in regards to our Earth;

the EAR has been speeding up. This has progressively continued until it had reached a particular EAR Period probably a 24 hour period, when it began to slow down as it is currently. This hypothesis is based or derived from the very understanding of Dr Arthur Beiser' proposition as above and the currently accepted scientific data that the EAR is indeed reducing per day, at the rate of **25 thousand-millionths of a second each day** or 1/1000th second every 100 years. This progressive reduction has been going on for thousands of years now.

Therefore, you can clearly understand why, I stated very much earlier, that my interpretation differs from that of Scientific Scholarship.

> **Yet, please do take note, not going against their interpretation nor refuting their interpretation in any way whatsoever, but representing the facts in regards to the same scientific data used on the currently slowing down phase of the Earth' rotation on it' axis, quite differently based on a different perspective.**

So based on the above, the Earth' Axis Rotation may have begun slowing down probably from the 24 hours Earth Axis Rotation Period. I would like to name this referenced Period as the 'Earth Axis Rotation Speed Switchover' base or **EARSS** for short. We will learn later as we progress on, that there are in fact two such periods in the Earth' Axis Rotation Speed Switchover cycle, which are fixed 12 hours apart. This is also provided that Dr Arthur Beiser is indeed correct, that the Earth will have an axis rotation period of **36 hours** or rather 36 hour long days at the end of 5000 million years.

As you can read from all of the above, I am also quite interested with the present increase in the duration of the Solar Day and the resultant lengthening of the Solar Year. However, by actually understanding it in reference to the presently supported unchanging speed and the unchanging distance in the Earth' journey around the Sun; the number of days or rather the **number of Earth Axis Rotations** for each orbit around the Sun, as already emphasised previously, would be gradually and consistently reducing in this phase. In fact it had been reducing for a very long time now, based on this hypothesis from the 'Referenced Base Position' (RBP) of 24:00; which I have also named as being one of the Earth Axis Rotation Speed Switchover (EARSS) Bases.

Only with these understandings firmly in place, would enable me to unravel the computation for you of this long-standing mystery; the **360 Biblical Earth Day Years** or simply put in it' correct perspective - the 360 Day Years.

> This would then establish for us, my **'Second Milestone Achievement'**, in our computation progress towards obtaining the 360 Day Years.

In fact, the information derived from establishing this **360 Biblical Earth Days Orbital Years,** provides us with some spin-offs. These spin-offs could be in turn used to further fine-tune the present-day secular Calendar System and possibly, provide us with an even more precise dating of the Solar System and the Universe; if proven to be correct.

I know you may be slowly coming around to think that I must be crazy to be suggesting this possibility, with such a limited knowledge of these matters, and even practically no academic standing whatsoever myself. However, I can assure you that I am not out of my mind yet, so bear with me and keep plodding on.

You will come to understand that these spin-offs and the basis why these spin-offs could be possibly correct, when you have gone through this book. You can be rest assured that we will surely have indeed the 360 Day Years and it is not just some idea or event to remain buried and hidden in the various relevant Books of the Holy Bible.

> Sometime in the distant future, this will surely happen. It is also not just based on a calculated assumption or some theory that I had developed, for this will happen as a Solar System event i.e. it is another definite cosmic reality.

Also, this is not the same as when the **Sumerians** used a schematized Calendar System of 360 Days Solar Year; although it does provide us with another supporter for our proposition.

However, it was somewhat erroneous for that time. This was obvious, as it affected the timing of their festivals and their agricultural cycles. This made subsequent and other civilizations to employ another Calendar System which was a Lunar Year, i.e. they had developed and employed a 'LuniSolar Calendar System'.

However, this also had to be adjusted accordingly, to accommodate the additional days of the Solar Year which they did not know at the time was 365¼ days with the shorter 12 Lunar Cycles/Year, which they also probably did not know was 354 Lunar days only. This as can be seen obviously, did not mesh identically into each other.

So yet again, this too was not absolutely accurate and subsequently, in the progress of our calendar making history, this too had to be readjusted several more times over the centuries.

> It is to be noted though, that the **Egyptians, Greeks and the Maya**, did not employ a LuniSolar Calendar System.

To recap:

The corresponding lengthening, or similarly, the corresponding reduction in the Solar Days per Solar Year at a rate of $1/1000^{th}$ sec per every 100 years is directly due to the reduction or increase in the speed of the EAR as the case may be at the time.

Therefore, following this similar rate of change as above, would eventually with the appropriate time provided cause effective changes to **the number of EAR** (Earth Days/Sidereal days) in reduction or in increase, as the case maybe, which the Earth would need to complete one orbit (i.e. One Biblical Year) around the Sun.

To put it more simply:

1) As the EAR **reduces** in speed at the rate of $1/1000^{th}$ second every 100 years, this would then cause the Solar Day to also naturally to be **increasing** in it' time duration accordingly. Correspondingly, this would in turn naturally **lengthen** the Solar Year.

2) As the EAR **increases** in speed if this could be the case too at the similar rate as above, this would then cause the Solar Day to also **reduce** in it' time duration. Correspondingly, this would in turn **shorten** the Solar Year.

Following this above understanding strictly, we would be able to calculate when the Earth will first begin to exactly axis-rotate **360 times within one Earth' orbit** around the Sun.

> This would establish for us our *'Third Milestone Achievement'*, on our ongoing computation progress to obtaining; when would we finally have a 360 Days Year on Earth in our **biblical human history future**.

A point to note is that the original understanding for the meaning of a **'day'** and the subsequent **'year'**, described and derived from the Bible as in Genesis Chapter 1, has somewhat been lost over time. This has been due to our own ever increasing and demanding requirements for more and more time measuring accuracy.

The biblical meaning for a **'day'** simply meant one period of light (sunshine) combined with one period of darkness or night time. This is without taking into consideration the changing periods of sunshine time and night time, during the course of the *Earth' Orbit* around the Sun – Gen 1:5 refers.

This combination of light and darkness, we do know now for certain, is the resultant mechanics of rotational motion of the Earth on it' axis on a daily basis, which describes the **'Biblical Day'** as per the description given to us through Gen 1:5.

A 'Biblical Year' is completed not only within a certain number of 'Biblical Days', but also more importantly, as the Earth experiences annually it' seasons - Gen 1:14 refers. It was because of the changing seasons that early man in his progress began to understand the first concepts of the year. Through their ongoing progress, I believe, they probably then began to eventually count the number of days that would actually incorporate all the seasons that made up a year and/or as it began it' repetitious cycle. This was probably in combination with their study of the heavens too. Quite naturally they must have come up with varying estimates; however, this was improved upon as the peoples of the world progressed through several progressive civilizations and cultures.

This if you understand it correctly, was actually in accordance to what the Bible had already established in regards to days, seasons and years - Gen 1:14 refers.

You also need to understand that GOD' WORD obviously takes precedence over man' later discovery of the days, seasons and years. This means that it was so, even before man had come to realize this was indeed the case. It probably then progressed until the Egyptians together with their annual sighting of particular stars, such as Sirius, began to provide us from then on with the more modern concept of the 365 Day Years.

Of course, as man began to advance even further and more rapidly and his requirements also were changing; it became eventually known in relatively recent times mind you, that the year was indeed obtained when the Earth completes each journey or orbit around the Sun and that it was the Earth together with the other Solar Planets that went around the Sun and not the other way round as had been believed to be so as in the past.

Therefore, in order for us to be able to resolve this 360 days year issue, we need to first get back to the **biblical reckoning for time.**

In further elucidation of the above, it was adequate to have time to be measured by purely natural means, incorporating three parameters only; day, season and year. The time value for a 'Biblical Day' was solely dictated by the Earth' rotation on it' axis, without having to consider the necessary adjustments for the now known many irregularities or variations during it' cycle. Similarly, a 'Biblical Year' was based on the Earth experiencing cyclically all it' seasons. As mentioned above, they too must have understood this as being that the **Sun** was going around the **Earth**, instead of the correct manner as known to us today.

This earlier 'error' did not seem to have caused any serious problems in regards to reading of the time per se but that the concept at the time that the Earth was indeed the centre of the Universe and of course of the Solar System too was naturally erroneous.

It did not matter also, during the very early primitive period of **'Human Skills'** progress; how many days were actually needed to complete a year. Obviously, however, these were not adequate as Man developed his agricultural and other skills and also increased his knowledge base of the heavens, the seasons and the more detail reading of time itself.

More so, by today' requirements and today' living standards, it would be definitely impossible to just confine ourselves to reading the time just as according to how it was done by early Man. This is besides the fact that evidently, this early method is still being used by some isolated and remote living tribes, even as presently.

However, having said this, the early biblical method is indeed a valid and an acceptable method for measuring time at any material time. This means even in today' context. More importantly, it is biblically legitimate, although indeed limited in critical accuracy, but as noted having been acceptable to GOD also. There is nothing wrong, if you wanted to read time as such, in the original biblical sense. However, you must recognize upfront, that it' application in today' context i.e. in our very rapidly advancing technological environments, it will be seriously very limiting to say the least.

So, the biblical reckoning of time measurements were commonly done in natural units as large as an **'Earth Day';** also following possibly the cyclic phases of the Moon; and even larger still, as a 'Seasonal' involving a **'Biblical Year'**.

This way of reckoning time was quite definitely adequate for the very early peoples. It was used by them for the sole purposes of measuring distances between places, when they moved nomadically from place to place, in search for food. Also, much later on, it was even used for the proper recording of their very own personal history and historical events. These were placed in their proper perspective, when it was referenced to the time and place that it had occurred such as planting & harvesting; famines and years of plenty; natural catastrophes like floods, earthquakes, volcanic eruptions; births & deaths; wars and even the reign of kings, etc.

However, as already mentioned, we all know this way of reckoning time does no longer meet all of our requirements today, as we have indeed progressed quite tremendously since the 'Creation Times' and in the process, fulfilling the Scriptures as in *Genesis 1:28*.

Besides the Biblical Day and Biblical Year, we also do have indeed a larger parcel of time, as indicated through the Scriptures of Daniel 9:24-27. These scriptures had actually mentioned the well known biblically famous; 'Seventy Weeks'.

Bible Chronologists on the whole do concur, this represents, a total of **490 years**. That means every day of the Daniel' 'Seventy Weeks', represents a year of time and that each year according to them was indeed **360 days** long.

I seriously beg to differ, once again, because the 360 day years have not happened as yet in our 'Human Biblical History'. However, from my understanding of these very Scriptures, '69 Weeks' could have already been fulfilled. Therefore, what I am willing to subscribe for a 360 days year with regards to Daniel' '70 Weeks', is limited to the final Week (last 7 years) of Daniel' prophesy. For through my own understanding of the scriptures, this 'final week' would happen sometime in the very distant future. **In fact, this 'final Week',** should be occurring right smack in the End Times, as I perceive it, from my personal study of the Book of Daniel and the Book of Revelation.

In other words having stated as above that possibly these '69 Weeks' have already been fulfilled this far; the last remaining single week according to my proposed understanding on this matter, seems to have been placed in some sort of suspended time zone or phase until the occurrence of the 'End Times'.

However, I am unable to follow through with this understanding, i.e. with regards to the Daniel' '70 Weeks'; simply because this book is not the forum for this discussion.

There are also a few more important **GOD appointed fixed 'time measurement periods'**, which are clearly expressed and also used as such in the Biblical Scriptures. Somehow, these were overlooked or not commonly quoted as often. These referenced 'time measured periods' are as follows:

a) for a season (Dan 7:12)

b) forever; even forever; ever (these three in Dan 7:18 and also in Dan 12:3) And

c) **a time (Dan 7:26, 12:7, Rev 12:14).**

We will however at this juncture and for our purposes, focus on **'a time'**. This parcel of 'a time', has in itself a time value, which is even much bigger than a year!!! However, in this stage of my book, I am still investigating this 'time measurement value' to find out what amount of time does it really represent. I am quite confident that I will somehow discover this and it will become known to you sometime later in the book.

In the above Scriptural example as described in (c), where this value of 'a time' was used; it was actually mentioned quite clearly in a time measurement combination as follows:

'a time and times and half a time'

Although, Bible Scholars will again quickly point out, this equals to **1,260 days**, a period of time, which is also mentioned in Rev 12:6, besides being mentioned in the Book of Daniel as indicated in the previous page; I wish to reserve comment at this very juncture. This is because I do have a notion this unique combination does indeed have a different computation which would give a different result and outcome to the above suggested and accepted thinking on this matter as to-date. So wait and see for a little while longer, as you progress forward in this book what this notion could possibly turn out to be. Of course, it will be still left entirely up to you whether to concur with this or not.

Based on my previous proposition and understanding; I should be able now to formulate for you several equation statements, which read as follows:

1) One Earth-Axis Rotation = One Biblical Day = One Earth Day

2) One Earth' Orbit around the Sun = One Biblical Year

3) **One Biblical Year** = The **number** of Earth Days needed for the Earth to complete One Orbit around the Sun.

4) **One Earth Orbit around the Sun, also = One Solar Year**

5) One Solar Year = The **number** of Solar Days (fractions of a Solar Day are taken into consideration) which are needed to complete One Orbit.

6) One Solar Day = The **time taken** for the Earth to complete one full rotation on it' own axis + a specific duration of variable additional time to be added to this. This additional time is actually the time required to bring the Sun back to the meridian (noon time), from the time the EAR was actually completed. This is to compensate or rather to make the necessary correction for the travel motion of the Earth in it' orbit during the two periods, i.e. between the two transits of the Sun at the meridian. Therefore, it is to be noted that in the process of getting the Sun back to the meridian, it naturally, also goes several minutes beyond the EAR Period at any material time to compensate for this Earth orbital travel motion.

This simply means that the Earth must complete more than a whole axis revolution (EAR), to bring the Sun back to the meridian (noon time) each time during it' orbit.

> 7) Therefore, we need to take careful note that it does not mean, One Solar Day can be equally interchanged for One Earth Day, although it still needs the Earth to rotate on it' very axis to provide most of it' time content.

Also:

8a) One Solar Day represents an interval of time, which according to scientists, changes over time.

8b) One Earth Day represents one complete rotation of the Earth on it' very own axis and therefore, is completely independent of the time taken for it' completion.

This makes the Earth Day to be completely independent of the corresponding changing intervals of time taken to accomplish the rotation. In other words, it does not matter in terms of an Earth Day, of how long it would take or even if it takes differing times to complete each at different locations of the Earth' annual orbit around the Sun.

This is the very key difference that separates my interpretation, which has been derived from my key understanding of the Scriptures - **Genesis 1:5, 14** refers. This had also been based on the basic Solar Planetary Cosmic data, as already mentioned previously and which is mentioned again as below.

> This for us establishes our **'Fourth Milestone Achievement'**.

Now, to that discovery as upheld by Science Scholarship regarding the slowing down of the Earth' rotation on it' axial axis, i.e. **1/1000 second every 100 years** (which is attributed to 'tidal friction' besides other planetary factors); I am totally grateful for this discovery. This subsequently produces for us longer days resulting in longer years over time. This will indeed continue as such, I believe, until the **slowing down** is possibly reversed, which I am assuming it would eventually be the case, as per my findings in this book. This very understanding for the possible reversal to this is also absolutely necessary for the successful outcome to be obtained as such in this book, which also in a way further supports this very conclusion. In other words, it is interdependent with each other. That is the slowing down of the EAR Period and then the required increasing of the EAR Period once again, is also directly interdependent to the generation of this 'Cosmic Construction' of the 'number' of the beast and vice versa.

> It also should be carefully noted: Although, human events and also our very specific time measuring requirements, scientific or otherwise, have by requirement been 'speeded' up greatly; **local celestial pace** i.e. pertaining to our Solar System, is still going on as usual, from the very time that it had become operative as such.

Therefore, the initial biblical based time reckoning is still very valid today, as the Solar System is still found to be in testimony of it.

> However, as was previously stated, it was adequate to meet the needs of the very ancient peoples and probably some tribes even living as of today. However, generally this was until the Sumerians; the Babylonians; Egyptians; the Maya; Greeks and eventually the Romans had come along to set the change in respective stages for the modernization of time reckoning, as they began to progressively understand the '**Celestial Mechanisms'**, which were set into motion by our LORD GOD ALMIGHTY for the measurement of time better.

I believe GOD' celestial designed time mechanisms were tailored in such a manner to suit the progress of man. This was primarily based on our intellectual capacity and creativity being the engine of growth, for the very important consequential technological advancements, that would subsequently follow accordingly, as we ourselves progress on to understanding **'time'** better from those very early primitive days of our ancestors.

It was **Albert Einstein** not too long ago in the earlier part of the last century in the previous millennium who had indeed, been deeply involved with the understanding of 'Time'. He provided us with an even deeper understanding to what 'Time' was and actually is and perhaps even possibly to be. Especially, the concept that time is not an **absolute entity** but depended on gravity, motion and where you are located in relation to the event happening or the object in Space. Probably, this continuing unravelling of the **'secrets'** of time, could be the very yardstick to further gauge our own human progress and success as being Mankind in this Universe.

Understanding **'Time'** even better than what we know of it as presently, would probably reveal more about us, our progress, our history, our future and would also result in furthering our technological advancement in our many Space exploration programs and other cosmic activities. This is besides our progress in the ongoing understanding of the Universe; atomic particles; sub atomic particles; sub sub atomic particles and etc., than we could ever imagine possible before.

Incidentally, 'Scientific Time' is now based on the **atomic second** and no more on the natural timed second. In fact this has been going on for some time now. The atomic second is even independent of the celestial motions and it gives us an easier definable accuracy, than these celestial motions can provide for our advancing time requirement purposes. This is also mainly due to the many frequent irregularities in the celestial motions, which causes immense difficulties to measure minute quantities of time in the immediate, that we do now critically require for various purposes.

From the above mentioned development of the atomic second, we have now the Terrestrial Dynamical Time (TDT), which being therefore, independent of the variable rotation of the Earth and which actually has replaced the previous Ephemeris Time (ET) since 1976, by the International Astronomical Union.

According to the definition in Wikipedia – the free encyclopaedia, TDT is actually a theoretical ideal, which real clocks can only approximate. The unit of TDT is the SI second, which according to Wikipedia is also currently based on the caesium atomic clock. Yet TDT is not itself defined by these atomic clocks. It is primarily used for time-measurements of astronomical observations made from the **surface of the Earth**. However, in 1991 it was renamed as Terrestrial Time (TT). This can also be referenced in Duffet Smith' Ephemeris Time and Terrestrial Dynamical Time, 1992, pg 22-23.

However, this does not mean that GOD' Cosmic Design was in any way faulty. For it was purposefully designed into it as such, to accommodate the numerous delicate complexities of the Universe at large and to integrate the relevant ones into the local complexities as operating in our 'Milky Way', right down to our own immediate Solar System. This is to keep it' entirety in perfect 'Cosmic Equilibrium'. For any of these 'delicate' complexities could possibly set off serious chain reactions, resulting in a universal catastrophe. Unless it is by the HAND OF GOD continually being re-compensated cosmically, elsewhere and everywhere.

Otherwise, this could possibly remove the entire Universe, as we know of it today from it' very existence in Space, and perhaps to even disintegrate it back into 'nothingness'. This was how it had all first begun from 'nothingness', having been revealed to us as such through Genesis Chapter One.

If you are able to recall or to remember my references made to Sir Martin Rees' Book much earlier, 'Just Six Numbers'; you will certainly realise this is highly possible and so the above is not of my own thinking on the matter.

For LORD GOD ALMIGHTY in the very beginning created the Universe from **ex-nihilo**; a Latin word meaning from nothing or nothingness. In some older Bible translations, you will find this word 'ex-nihilo' in the very beginning of Genesis, being used in regards to how GOD created the heavens and the earth. This is again somewhat similarly echoed in Hebrews 11:3 which states:

> **By faith we understand that the worlds were framed by the word of God, so that the things which are seen were not made of things which are visible.**

In fact surprisingly, Science today has also come to the scientific theoretical conclusions, that 'Space Entities' such as Black Holes, have their eventual demise too, i.e. they would finally vaporize into **'nothingness'**!!!

This also according to them in turn, is what would happen eventually to whole galaxies and which in multiplicity, also would happen to the entire Universe i.e. into ....nothingness!!! This is indeed a very refreshing 'scientific thinking', that impacts the very fundamental concepts of what would eventually happen to the Universe.

Isn't this just remarkable??? For the Bible had in fact revealed to us that it was our LORD GOD ALMIGHTY, WHO had created the entire Universe from 'nothingness' in the very first place – Gen 1:1 confirms.

It is only recently of now that Science seems to be proposing the very same thing, although in exact reverse, and sadly without giving the due acknowledgement to it' Creator as yet. Yet, it evidently seems to exactly impact, what our Bible, as per the Old Testament', had been stating for thousands of years in written form and long before that also in the traditional oral form!!!

Just for your information, it has also been known that the first time ever that the 'hour' was mentioned in the Bible, was already late in our Biblical History in the time of Daniel – Dan 3:6; 3:15; 4:19; 4:33; 5:5 refers (Authorized King James Version). This was the period when the Jews were already taken away to Babylon, during which time; I believe they had come to know about the **'hours of a day'** measurement of time and the calendar system as used by the Babylonians. According to Bible Scholars, this was sometime from the 6th Century BC.

Also, when I came to know about the time measuring accuracy of the Babylonians and the Egyptians, I realized that it was just really amazing of how they had derived their calculations and recorded their observations of the heavens in those very early days. This was achieved at a time, without any modern expertise or with modern technology aided means i.e. without any modern precision scientific equipment available to them. Most of their observations were achieved basically through the naked eye.

Biblical Scholarship has consistently proposed that there was a time in the Earth' past (before the Flood and during Daniel' '70 Weeks of Years') and there will be a time again in the future, when we will have 360 days (Solar) years again. Please do take note first and foremost, that all their references made to 'past time periods' are actually according to most of them being just a few thousand years ago. I humbly beg to differ as far as the Earth' cosmic and biblical human history is concerned and it is for this very reason that I am of the opinion their above Scholarship is indeed flawed. For I do accept and agree with what the Scientific Community have established with regards to the Earth having been around for Billions of Years. And further to this, I also base my acceptance on the 'Age of the Universe', which I had discovered through my studies of the Biblical Book of 2Esdras. All the evidences available are too overwhelming to deny this real situation than that as having been suggested by most Biblical Scholarship.

However, in support of Biblical Scholarship to a point, i.e. as far as most of our 'Biblical Human History' is concerned less the 'Cosmic Creation' part and the Pre-Adamic years, I would then subscribe to our human biblical time period existence, to have been only several thousands of years old. Projecting it in this manner does indeed soften the conflict to a certain extent with their teaching, and does narrow the time gap somewhat.

Also, I am in total agreement with any Bible Chronologists, who does agree, that there will come a time for the '360 Day Years' to occur in our future. However, as mentioned previously, there is a big difference between my proposal, calculations and understanding for when would the very **first 360 Earth Days Biblical Year** (ever since the beginning of our 'Biblical Human History') would take place in our distant future and their thinking on the similar issue.

Although, I did cover this somewhat in the 'Preview' at the beginning of this book, I will go through it once again to refresh your memory.

Firstly, let me point out again, there were **no past** occurrences of a 360 Days Solar Year or for that matter, an Earth Orbit around the Sun having 360 Earth Axis Rotations. This would be my stand as long as they insist that all of this had already taken place within our 'Biblical Human History'. I am not saying that it could not have occurred but what I am stating, **not within our Biblical Human History period**.

I hope that you have noticed that I have repeatedly and deliberately used this phrase of 'Biblical Human History'. It was done for a specific purpose, for I found this out and realised this for myself, only when I began writing the Addendum to this Part Two.

In other words, if the Earth at the very beginning had 36 hour long days or for that matter even 30 as an example, and it has been speeding up ever since until reaching the 24 Hour EAR Period i.e., which is also my proposed 'EARSS' Base (Earth Axis Rotation Speed Switchover Base), when it began slowing down at the similar rate of 1/1000th second every hundred years; then it is not time as yet for this 360 day years to have taken place. This is as far as this 'Biblical Human History' is concerned, derived from my very own understanding of the relevant 2Esdras biblical scriptures. However, it will surely take place, as I have already stressed this several times before.

Therefore, I sincerely believe my approach must then unashamedly actually claim the **singular distinction** of being able to substantiate for the very first time the 'Perfect Calendar Years'. These are also called in particular by many of us Christians as being the 'Prophetic Years'.

For through my approach, we can indeed achieve within the 'Celestial Solar System Laws' governing the Sun-Earth-Moon motions, to establish exactly when would we **first begin** to have indeed as biblically suggested; the **360 Earth Days Orbital Years.**

Also, please take note that the current year length, i.e. 365+ Days Solar Year was cosmically established in fact **several Billions of Years** ago!!! First discovered almost to it' accuracy by the Egyptians, who were the very first people to initially use a proper 365 Days Year Calendar System, several thousands of years ago.

They then improved it to 365.25 days by using their gathered data over the years on the star Sirius. This was later fine tuned even further, by the Greek astronomer, **Hipparchus** to 365.242. This was indeed accomplished by him, almost 2,200 years ago!!! This is extremely accurate even with regards to the present calculations of 365.242199 mean solar days per year.

Could it be said that Hipparchus was indeed as accurate as our present calculation is, in relation to his calculation for that time period 2,200 years ago. For we need to take into consideration the reduction rate of **1/1000th of a second every 100 years**. This then would have occurred consistently (22 times) over the last 2,200 years or so. Therefore, if we do compensate Hipparchus with these 22 times of adjustments; we then should probably reconsider the amazing accuracy of Hipparchus' calculation, as being as accurate in his 365.242 days year for that period and ours 365.242199 days year for our period.

What I am trying to point out here also, is that for thousands of years, the Solar Year has 'remained' as **365.X....X** days per year, even to our present day. This indeed reflects the really slow change rate of 1/1000th second every 100 years.

Of course, the above 365+ day year is gradually lengthening within this established scientifically known 'currently reducing rate' in the EAR Period.

That is as being experienced due to the **1/1000th second reduction in the EAR speed through every 100 years**. This would of course inevitably as per our scriptural supported proposition as explained previously **reduces** the number of **Earth Days** required for the Earth to complete an orbit around the Sun.

One Earth Day = One complete Earth rotation on it' axis

Therefore, it surely must be running into hundreds of millions of years, taking into account this very miniscule scientifically established consistent change rate, on which my calculations for the very first 360 Day Year in our biblical human history, also depends upon.

> It is then quite obvious from above, that we need to find out when we would have for the very first time, 360 Earth Axis Rotations in one Earth' orbit around the Sun. This is fundamental for our very purposes, as when this would occur, is also somehow intertwined with the 'Cosmic Construction' for the **'number'** of the beast. This I found out in the course of writing this book.

That is the reason why, I also cannot just confine myself to the Earth' revolution around the Sun i.e. Ephemeris time, although it is presented as being even more accurate than the Solar Time and the Sidereal Time.

Furthermore, although the day has been lengthening for a long time now, it is still called a 'Day' and is also dependent on the **duration** of an Earth Axis Rotation + a few minutes; which is variable during the year as it depends where exactly is the Earth in it' orbit around the Sun at that material time.

Therefore, in this specific sense, I still can consider the 360 Earth Axis Rotations (360 Earth Days), as being '360 Days' measure of time. Taking a 'Day' to simply mean one complete rotation of the Earth on it' axis, as currently being also observed, but obviously, bearing in mind that there is indeed that specific difference in time duration with a Solar Day.

360 Earth Days = '360 Days'

Let me give you a typical example to demonstrate this reduction in EAR. In this example, let us assume the 'EAR Period' is **reduced to** 24.22 hours long at some time in the distant future. This according to my calculations will then support:

364.96242775 Earth Axis Rotations (Earth Days), per Biblical Year.

Yes, you are right in noticing that the above number is indeed much less than the current 365.242199 days per year, although the fact remains that the

'Day & Year' has indeed become even much longer at that future time, then it is as currently.

Comparison Box:

Earth Days per Biblical Year: Solar Days per New Solar Year
364: 365.X.....X

This computation is correct, provided the speed of orbit and distance of orbit of the Earth around the Sun remains as constants throughout as it was possibly in the past. Otherwise, the changes, if any, have to be also taken into consideration. The calculated changes in the comparison box will take less than 6,679,000 years following the scientific proposed reduction change rate of 1/1000th second per every 100 years.

If instead, we are considering the mean solar day at that time then we need to add several more minutes to the EAR Period of 24.22. Since I do not have this exact data, the best that I can do here is to express it will occur, less than 6,679,000 years time. These years should then be added to the time period, when the Earth first acquired in the immediate past; 24.20144776 mean Solar Days/Year. This is because it is this length that was used to calculate our present Solar Year, which was also indeed established thousands of years ago as such. Then we can obtain when the above particular EAR change in reduction, would actually take place in the future.

As you can see, although the Day, as in this case, had lengthened from the present **24.20144776 hours** Day, by an additional 1 minute 6.788064 seconds; the corresponding Earth Axis Rotations needed in the same future orbit, through my understanding and interpretation, have indeed become even lesser then the present **365.242199 Solar Year.**

So, it is quite clear from this exercise of above, that if we continue to follow the present Calendar System, we will never be able to achieve a 360 Days Solar Year. So, going by the above comparison box, it appears to give us the possibility of eventually obtaining 360 Earth Day Years instead.

Therefore, in order to achieve a 360 Days Orbit, we have to first accept that a 'Day' is of course One complete Earth Axis Rotation Period and a 'Year' is the number of Earth Axis Rotations that are needed to complete One Earth' Orbit around the Sun. This acceptance was as such in the early biblical days.

Incorporating these two parameters together, which is actually also heavily influenced by the Moon' total interactions with the Sun and the Earth independently and also in combination with them, as a cosmic time controlling system; will celestially produce the 'Perfect Year'.

The calendar makers have used the mean Solar Day with the duration of 24.20144776 hours to calculate the length of the current and past years.

Also, we need to make reference to the imaginary celestial Vernal Equinox, where the Earth' Axis Rotation duration at this reference base, is taken to be 23.93447**222** hours. This is about 16 minutes less in duration than the mean Solar Day of 24.20144776 hours, which has been taken to compute the Solar Years.

In conclusion, the three relevant time controlling parameters must be taken into consideration. For we need to incorporate firstly, the long-term over time Earth Axis Rotational changes; secondly, the Earth' orbit around the Sun and thirdly the understanding of the Moon' part in all of this. It was the English Astronomer, H. Spencer Jones, who had in 1939 revealed that the rotational time based on the Earth' spin on it' axis varied noticeably. He had made these observations and based on his calculations he came to the conclusion that the Earth had sometimes rotated a little faster on it' axis than at other times. This phenomenon stretches the averaged 24 hours Earth-day, through a range of variations of slightly more than a quarter of an hour in duration; as the Earth journeys through the Solar Year.

This makes the **'value'** ascribed to the **second,** as not being entirely reliable due to these very variations. This is especially for scientific purposes where preciseness is most essential, especially for Space exploration; Astronomy; positioning of satellites in Space; the calculations which give us the position of specific stars; co-ordinating electrical power distribution across several complex networks; communications and transportation throughout the world; the latest GPS systems including the proposed US military plans with regards to their 'Star Wars Defence and Attack Systems'. These are some of the important examples, where time measuring accuracy and preciseness is extremely critical. There are obviously many others too.

This is the reason, why they have been for a long time in fact relying upon the **Atomic Clock** to tell time. For this is even independent of the axis rotation of the Earth. By means of this Atomic Clock, they are providing a 'value' ascribed to the second, which would be theoretically accurate to within one second in 300 million years. These are the cooled hydrogen maser clocks. This specific 'value' has been set since 1967, which is the duration of 9,192,631,770 periods (frequency) of the radiation corresponding to the transition between two hyperfine levels of the ground state of the cesium-133 atom. This transition varies by less than one part in 10 billion periods. This also expresses how tiny each of the graduations can be made to just one second of time. It is extremely important to have such tiny graduations when it is also connected or referring to very high speeds.

GPS is a classic example that needs this accuracy when tracking down any particular vehicle; whether it is in the sea, land or air to get its exact location at any time required. Therefore, these atomic clocks are also in fact employed in the GPS satellites. This is modern man's time achievement. Some of the facts as noted above regarding the Atomic Clock were actually mostly referenced from the Hutchinson Encyclopaedia.

Scientific scholarship has indicated, currently the Earth rotates once every **23 hours 56 minutes 4.1 seconds** (23.9344722 hours) of mean Solar time using the Vernal Equinox as it' reference base.

Now, if the EAR takes longer, then logically as explained previously based on my interpretation; it would mean that it would take even *less Earth Axis Rotations (also referred to as 'Earth Days'),* for the Earth to orbit the Sun in one complete circuit.

> However, you must also bear in mind that the overall time or speed of 8,839.39 hours per orbit, would remain the same, despite the lengthening of the day. Currently, we are also informed, this is taking **365.242199** days per orbit based on a 24.20144776 hours mean Solar Day.

The time variation in the Axis Rotation as mentioned in the previous page during any year, would be actually fluctuating between the shortest day length, which is currently 23.93447222 hours and the calculated mean Solar Day' length of 24.20144776 hours; as the Earth journeys through it' orbit around the Sun.

This directly means, fluctuating 16 minutes or more (accurately up to 16.0185324 minutes), from the Earth' Vernal Equinox referenced position. This time fluctuation can also be expressed in hours, as 0.26697554 hours.

Scientific Scholarship have also informed us that over the last 200 years, the rate of rotation within this fluctuating range has varied as much as 30 seconds, i.e. about 1 or 2 seconds per year.

Just for your added information, the above data would differ slightly from the similar data, as provided by the International Astronomic Union, which indeed provides for an even more accurate reading. For example, 365.242199 days will be in AU as 365.24219264. Our EAR as per our shortest day i.e. 23.93447222 hours will be in AU as 23.93447193 hours instead.

Now it is quite obvious that the current 365.242199 Days Solar Year was based on the mean Solar Day, which is 24.20144776 hours in duration.

'THE BIBLICAL 360 DAY YEARS'
The 360 Earth Days Orbital Years

BOOK ONE - PART TWO
Page 114

The Vernal Equinox is the name given to one of the imaginary celestial intersecting points, where the Earth' Equator and the Ecliptic, intersect. This Ecliptic is an annual Solar path, tracing points where the Sun' rays at noon every day strikes the Earth perpendicularly. The other intersecting point which is in fact opposite to the Vernal Equinox on the Ecliptic is called the Autumn Equinox. As the name suggests, indicates the annual beginning of the autumn season. The Vernal Equinox indicates the annual beginning of the spring season. Please refer to the following Equinoxes/Solstice Diagram as shown below.

The Equinoxes/Solstice Diagram

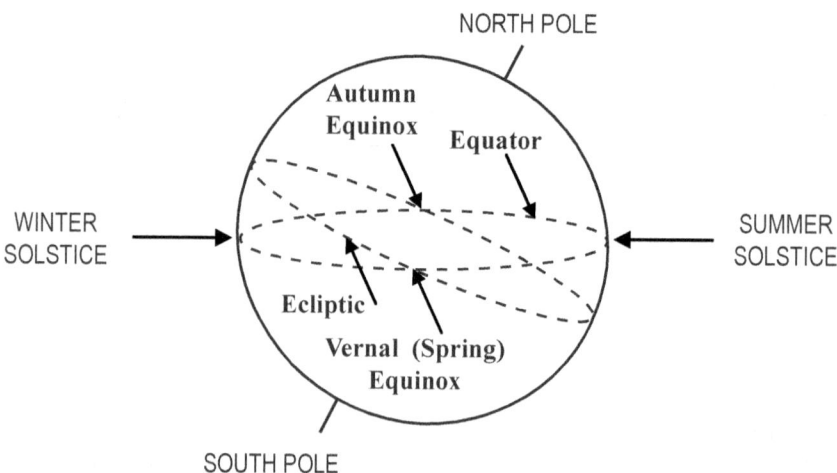

All of the above information, as provided for you, since obtaining the Fourth Milestone Achievement; is considered as actually being my *'Fifth Milestone Achievement'*.

Anyway, the orbiting distance for the time being, will be kept the same **583,400,000 miles,** together with the same orbiting speed of 66,000 miles per hour (106,194 Km/hr).

While you hold on to the above scientific Solar Planetary facts; for your information:

The metric system of measurement was actually first introduced and adopted by Law in France in the 1790's. This is according to the reference made in the Encarta '96 Encyclopaedia. This obviously was long after the Bible was written in it' complete form. Also, the Bible writers did not use miles in their measurement of lengths, but they actually made measurements in Rod, Pace, Cubit, etc. We do know however, that a Rod is 9 ft., a Pace is 3 ft and a Cubit is 1.5 ft. in length. This means that our mile being 5,280 ft. long and also equalling to 1,760 yards, would then similarly equate to 1,760 Paces. A mile also equals to 3,520 cubits. Cubits are a very common measurement in the Bible, whilst Pace was used only one single time, as found in 2Sam 6:13.

So, although we know that the Biblical writers were not measuring in miles, feet or even in yards; the fact is that it can be interchangeable with their measurements for lengths accurately reflecting the same result, maintains us on the right track. This is especially important in our continued pursuit for the 'Cosmic' based construction of the **'number'** totalling **666.**

This is important to note for the sum total **666** was Biblically revealed in the New Testament during much earlier times.

Now through Scientific Scholarship, we have been informed that the Earth' rotation on it' axis in the long term, would not be slowing down indefinitely. This is because as I understand, it is restricted or rather controlled by the gravitational forces of the Sun and the Moon, which operate together in a 'Cosmic Triune System' that includes the Earth; that directly affects amongst other contributing factors, the Axis Rotation of the Earth.

This current phase of slowing down, based according to this Part Two, proposes that it had begun from the very moment the Earth had acquired precisely the **24 Hours EAR Period.**

This became what I had previously termed as being the **Earth Axis Rotation Speed Switchover** base or **EARSS** for short. However, after ending Part Two, I found out in the Addendum of this Part, this statement would need to be further fine tuned to state the more correct EAR Period, for the above purposes. However, for the time being, we will continue using this RBP/EARSS of 24:00 as it is.

Scientists also tell us that the slowing down of the Earth' Axis Rotation is directly dependent on the winds on the surface of the Earth; the affects the Moon has on the daily tides, and the Sun' consistent gravitational affects on the Earth.

Also, the changing levels of the oceans, due to the melting Polar snows and the tidal actions (i.e. 'tidal friction') on the Earth' very sea surface; all contributes to this slowing down situation. We are also informed that the Moon is moving away from the Earth at a current rate of 1 foot every 30 years, which has direct implications amongst others on it' tidal effects on the Earth; which also contributes to the Earth' spin slowing down. We are also informed that with time, this rate of 1 foot every 30 years will slow down considerably, reaching it' slowest or weakest point of escape from it' orbit around the Earth. Then it will be reversed and begin to close in onto the Earth, once again.

We know all this through Scientific Scholarship and they also inform us, as just mentioned, this moving away of the Moon from the Earth is indeed not indefinite. This is because the Sun at **some future point,** would begin to **reverse** this moving away of the Moon, by pulling it back in and thereby once again speeding up the Earth' rotation on it' axis. So, we can conclude that the repeating of this cycle would go on, as long as the cosmic triune system, already described above is still operative.

Through my 'construction' progress for the **'number'** of the beast, I found out that the 'First Earth Axis Speed Changing Phase', occurred at the very beginning as the Earth first acquired a 24 Hours Period.

> This was in its natural course from a progressively faster EAR speed to the fastest rotation possible at its peak (i.e. 24 hours EAR). This then would switch over to a slower rotation phase. Ending at its slowest possible rotation as that would be allowed by the cosmic forces applicable, as already mentioned earlier. This is just as we are currently in, very slowly, but gradually progressing towards the ending of the progressively slowing down phase. Then at the ending, only to switch over once again to speeding up the axis rotation, towards the 24 Hour EAR speed.

Now, how did I come to the conclusion that the switchover base point was indeed at precisely when the Axis Rotation acquired the very first 24.00 Hours Period i.e., the very first time this was ever obtained and not any earlier or even much later as the case could be, at some other referenced base period???

You will find this out as you study through to PART THREE & FOUR, that it came about, as it was based directly on the cosmic construction of the 'number' of the second beast, which sum totalled 666.

With this in place, we will then be able to successfully construct the 'number' of the beast. This very understanding was one of the primary contributing factors amongst many others that led to this thinking of above. This is more than just a significant point to contend with here, because this possible occurring **cosmic phenomenon** is directly interlocked with the Holy Scriptures.

In other words, we are informed about this exact thing, through the unravelling of the cosmic mysteries held by the Holy Scriptures. In this particular case, the relevant Scripture begins for us in **Rev 13:18.**

This scriptural cosmic relationship, should further enhance our Christian belief that the Holy Bible, although, was written by mortal man, was indeed inspired by GOD, the Creator of the heavens and the Earth.

For only GOD knows about the very deep secret workings of the entire Cosmos in its entirety from the very beginning of it. However, now man, as he progresses, will probably discover to quite an impressive depth also too these natural cosmic workings. Also, GOD through HIS Word had shown us that He knows everything from the very beginning, not only from the perspective of time itself, as we have come to know it, but indeed before the very beginning, i.e. beyond the beginning and even after 'time' itself.

Beyond the beginning was the 'time period' when the Spiritual Heavens had only existed and similarly at the very end of it all will only be the one to exist, unless the physical world was also intended to exist together in somewhat a parallel sense.

In fact, GOD opens HIS Word in Genesis 1 & 2, with the detail revealing to us of HIS creating of the Universe step by step and everything in it. Our GOD did not hide this from us. GOD also had revealed to man through many biblical scriptural examples, which clearly had established, confirms and reconfirms, HIS complete control over all of the cosmic forces that are operating in the entire Universe. One such example, which would definitely inspire you to this very thinking, is when GOD ALMIGHTY helped Joshua to win the battle **as evident in** the Biblical Book Joshua, Chapter 10.

This particular cosmic solar planetary event, took place due to GOD' direct intervention at Joshua' personal request. This was so that he could have enough time to strike off the entire enemy (the five Amorite kings collectively) that he was facing at that particular time. This biblical event has indeed another outside 'witness' confirming this biblical event had indeed actually taken place. This other named outside 'witness' is indeed the 'Book of Jasher'.

According to the commentary notes of my Spirit Filled Life Bible, the Book of Jasher was an ancient classical book of poetry about Israel' heroes and exploits and it was referenced directly in the Bible in Joshua 10:13 and also in 2Samuel 1:18. Even in the Septuagint (LXX), which was the first Greek text of the Old Testament had made reference to it in 1Ki 8:53, refers and confirms.

Unfortunately, this particular 'witness', the Book of Jasher, had according to 'The Zondervan Pictorial Bible Dictionary' disappeared during the Hebrews Babylonian captivity.

We are also given another glimpse of GOD' awesome power and control over the Cosmic forces and the Earthly forces, through **Jesus Christ** (GOD THE SON in the GODHEAD and who had become a man to dwell amongst us) - Matt 8:26 refers and confirms.

We, have been allowed by GOD for some time now, to gradually over the centuries to rediscover these very biblical secrets. Yet, there are still probably many, many more secrets that are indeed still being held within GOD' written Word, as embedded within it, waiting for it to be properly understood by us. I hope that through my book, we are graciously allowed to discover even one and hope against hope perhaps even a few more; just as so many had done before, having been privileged and having successfully accomplished their mission. PRAISE BE TO GOD

This is indeed another big plus, which makes this book actually worthwhile reading, well at least from my perspective for the present day discovery of some of this age long kept 'secrets'. This in turn, I hope, would give us a better and deeper understanding through some aspects of GOD' Word and provide yet another wonderful and important testimony that it is absolutely and remarkably True.

Through this Scriptural relationship that it has with the Cosmos; I discovered that the *first EARSS* had to be exactly when the EAR of 24 hours was reached. (I must remind you once again, this will be further fine tuned, as you will find out after the ending of Part Two through it' Addendum.) The relevant Scriptures in Revelation, also in 2Esdras 14:9-12 and others, have also been equally responsible in channelling me directly to this later more accurate conclusion.

These Scriptures and the Cosmic **'number'** construction itself are the very check and balance that is keeping us on the right track.

This is the second valuable spin-off that has been discovered from these very quests. You will also understand this even more clearly, as you proceed on very carefully though, studying the details of the construction of this **'cosmic number'** of the second beast.

All of the above, since having established the 'Fifth Milestone Achievement', is to be considered as my *'Sixth Milestone Achievement'*.

This is definitely necessary to be established in our continued progress, in the construction of the **'number'** of the beast.

Coming back to our continuing progress: In fact as the Moon begins to be pulled back, as mentioned just awhile ago, into a closer orbit around the Earth, this would affect the very ocean tides and significantly at that too. This in turn would speed up the Earth' spin and the whole process would kick in again.

I also compute that the moving away of the Moon from the Earth, which has been happening for a long time now, and so based on this PART TWO, I would like to propose this had begun also at the switchover point of the 24 Hours EAR Period. This as you already know, has been termed by me, as the EARSS base point.

(This above statement too would be fine tuned accordingly, when I understand the relevant 'Cosmic Mechanisms', better in the Addendum).

The **Synodic Month** is the average interval between two mean conjunctions of the Sun and the Moon; when these bodies are near as possible, in the sky.

The Synodic Month of the Moon is longer than the Moon' Orbital Month around the Earth, for the same reasons that our mean Solar Day is longer than our Sidereal Day. The Synodic Month takes 29.53059 days as of currently. The AU however, provides currently 29.5305888844 days for a Synodic Month. This will continue to increase in minuscule amounts as per this 'construction' process, which is in turn fully based on the natural course of the cosmic process involved, which will cause this to take place.

Therefore, accordingly, Hipparchus' calculation for the Synodic Month at **29.53058 days,** which he had discovered and had calculated about 2,200 years ago, was closer to the correct answer for that time.

Based on this very understanding; I then concluded that the Synodic Month will be exactly 30 days long, when the Earth takes 360 Earth Days exactly to complete it' orbit around the Sun. This then has each calendar month to be 30 days long also. This is not just the Moon' eventual obtaining of a 30 Days period of motion consistently for a considerable large number of years thence on around the Earth, but it is also based on the very Scriptures, as found written in **Rev 11:2-3**.

This is another set of Scriptures, which do express clearly or rather does reveal GOD's direct and in-depth knowledge of the 'secret workings' of the Cosmos. Obviously and with certainty, the writer of these particular Scriptures attributed to as being the Apostle John, had no such pre-knowledge or prior knowledge of the Cosmos. This is quite conclusive due to his total lack of knowledge and education in these matters, as he was biblically confirmed as being just another ordinary Galilean fisherman. Therefore, due to this lack; we can safely conclude that he

was indeed divinely inspired to write these awesome revelations. **This in it' simplest and basic sense, is the further testimony that it was indeed divinely inspired writing.**

Even to have just the ability to write in those days for many would have been a tremendous feat already let alone to write in this scriptural and spiritual manner as expressed in the Gospels and elsewhere throughout the Holy Bible would be quite impossible to do so.

Rev 11:2, provides the total of **42 months,** for a particular Scriptural purpose; involving the Gentiles. Also, immediately in the Scripture verse that follows i.e., Rev 11:3; another 'measure of time' is given for another Scriptural purpose; amounting to **1,260 days**. More than coincidence, when we divide these 1,260 days by 42, we do obtain 30 days for each month. Although, this is common Bible Knowledge, it still prompts us to conclude that there will be a time when the month will also be 30 days long. However, for this to happen cosmically; the Synodic Month must also increase from it' present 29.53059 days, to reach the required maximum of 30 days to fulfil our cosmic construction needs of the number of the second beast, sum totalling 666.

The fact that Hipparchus had earlier calculated a slightly shorter Synodic Month about 2,200 years ago against the current calculations, indicates and suggests that the Synodic Month is in fact actually increasing over time.

In fact, it was actually **0.00001 day shorter,** during Hipparchus' time. This is indeed definitely possible, as it has already been established by Scientific Scholarship that the Moon is indeed moving away from the Earth. This would then cause the lengthening of the Synodic Month accordingly and this would continue over time, until the Earth' spin is once again speeded up by the Sun pulling the Moon back to the Earth. This once again would **shorten** the Synodic Month accordingly. This is another hint that the current slowing down of the EAR Period would also someday at some distant base point begin to once again to be speeding up.

Through the very understanding of the relevant scriptures, as indicated above, and according to my construction of the **'number'** of the beast; the 30 Days Synodic Month should occur simultaneously, as the Earth acquires my scriptural calculated **24.55 EAR Period.** This then can be truly called as the 'Perfect Year' or Calendar Year, which has also been called the 'Prophetic Years' by the early Biblical Scholars.

Scientific Scholarship inform us, that it would take about **5000 million years** for the Moon to be at 1½ times distance, as it is now with regards to the

Earth. This is it' maximum possible distance from the Earth, according to them, that the Sun' gravitational affects on it will allow; I suppose.

It is now, as we are informed, about 240,000 miles away from the Earth and it' orbital speed is about 2,300 mph. This would make it then, if my calculation is correct, to be **360,000** miles from the Earth at that future time, 5000 million years or so away.

This number 360,000 with it' back progressions such as 36,000, 3,600 and **360** are indeed very interesting. For you will see these often being referenced in our continued progress. It is also, significantly tied in somehow, in all of this complexity; especially in the construction of the beast' **'number'**.

It is also important to note that the estimated 5000 million years is the present estimated age of the Sun and that the next 5000 million years would be it' last, making this the final half of it' life cycle.

This was first proposed and calculated by the Astronomer, Gerard P. Kuiper of the University of Arizona, some thirty or more years ago. But a short article in the Encarta Encyclopaedia '96 on the Sun, indicated that the Sun is 4.5 billion years old and that it has enough hydrogen to last another 4.5 Billion years. It goes on to say that the Sun will then become a Red Giant Star. It will remain as such for about ½ a billion years. Then it will shrink to become a white dwarf star, about the size of the Earth and will slowly cool for several more billions of years.

Another report in the same encyclopaedia, on the subject of our Solar System, indicated that the Sun can go on for another 6 Billion Years more, shining just as bright as it is now.

From above, it can be concluded that the calculated period of 4.5 billion years would be the lowest and the 5,000 million years (5 Billion) and 6 billion years would be the highest estimated so far for the remaining sunshine period of our own Sun.

However, following my progress towards the very construction of the 'Cosmic' based **'number' sum** totalling **666**; I realised that **4,995 million years**, will be more precisely accurate for the time left for our Sun, before it eventually enters into it' 'expansion mode' and then finally becomes a white dwarf.

My scriptural derived figure of 4,995 million years (4.995 billion years) is just a mere 5 million years from that of Gerard Kuiper's scientifically derived 5,000 million years estimate. However, my calculation is scriptural dictated by the relevant Scriptures in 2Esdras and so it is not of my own doing. The only thing that I can be charged with regards to this 'time or age proposal' is that my understanding or my interpretation of these scriptures was wrong in the first place.

> In reconfirmation: This is indeed another daring statement and is concluded as such quite definitely, as developed by myself and that it had been totally derived from the very astounding Scriptures as found written in 2Esdras 14:9 - 12.

This indeed is really an awesome revelation. As you progress with me through this book, you will find out, how I actually arrived at this precise age of 4.995 Billion Years for the age or rather the second half-life of our Sun. You will find out, it was totally derived based on the revelation or the proper understanding of the 'embedded mysteries' in the relevant referenced 2Esdras Scriptures.

> This establishes for us, our very important **'Seventh Milestone Achievement'**.

You will appreciate the 'arguments' for this exact figure being the age of the Sun (i.e. it' progress through the second 1/2 of it' time period). This will become apparent as you proceed with me, in the construction of the 'cosmic number' of the second beast.

> Once again, we discover specific knowledge of the Cosmos, through the proper understanding of these relevant Scriptures without even looking up into the night sky!!!

It should also be noted, obviously, that due credit should be given to all the Scientists in the past, like Kuiper, who through their very own secular scientific methodology, were able to calculate the age of the Sun, with such accuracy too. Their result also provides me, with a scientifically supported validation. Their calculations were totally being secular based; and my calculation or offering is being mostly based on the relevant referenced scriptures.

Naturally, for the scientific mind and the 'free thinkers', secular facts and theories will be more appealing and easier to accept and to verify one way or the other. However, when more and more cosmic truths are found to be already established by GOD, as evident through the relevant Scriptures, and some of which are even revealed as such in this book; may motivate some to even study the Holy Bible with more scrutiny. Well I hope so too anyway, and I say this, without any conceitedness on my part.

Furthermore, the very in-depth involvement of the Deuterocanonical included 2ESDRAS, or to some this being referred to as an Apocryphal

Biblical Book; in the extensive manner in which it is involved in the establishing of many 'Cosmic Facts', is indeed truly very remarkable.

The Astronomers and relevant scientific community have also proposed a 4.5 Billion Years age for our Earth and a 10 to 17 Billion Years age for the Universe; overall.

As you can see, they have provided a very large range for the possible age of the Universe, which could provide you with the thinking with regards to their inability at this point in time, to be more specific and certain. Based on this, there should be some room by the scientific community to also accept and be able to also accommodate my Scriptural derived figure of **4.995 Billion Years left for our Sun.**

The proposed 4,995 million years left is also similar in period, to the time that has already been fulfilled by the Sun. This is naturally based on what scientific scholarship suggests; that the Sun is indeed in its second half of its life. This provides the Sun with an overall useful period of **9.99 Billion Years,** almost encompassing a perfect ten. You will understand my reasons for accepting this specific time period, more clearly, as you further progress with me in the construction of the **'cosmic number'** of the beast.

We have been informed through the already available scientific data, that the speed of the Earth around the Sun is **66,000 mph,** with an orbital distance to travel of **583,400,000 miles.** This speed of 66,000 mph seems to be also pointing us into the right direction. With this data we then can calculate **8,839.39 hours** for the Earth to orbit the Sun each time. It is to be also noted that the eccentricity of the Earth' orbit around the Sun is virtually a circle. This confirms that there would be only very slight changes to it' travelling speeds throughout the elliptical orbit. The Earth' average distance from the Sun is 92,956,000 miles (149,566,204 km), which varies by about 3,100,000 miles only, during the course of the year. This average total distance has been taken to represent 1 AU (One Astronomical Unit). However, the mean distance is 92,897,000 miles (149,471,273 km).

If we take a day to be typically 24.20144776 hours, as presently, we then can calculate that it would take the Earth, 365.242199 days to orbit the Sun. This is our current mean Solar Year in days.

With this in focus, it then becomes just simple arithmetic to find out when we would eventually have the 360-Earth Day Orbital Years. This is of course for the very first time in our biblical human future, as it had not occurred in our entire biblical human history to date.

This means, we are actually calculating, when our Earth will have exactly **360 Earth Axis Rotations,** with which it would complete an orbit around the Sun. This will also obviously constitute one complete year in time measurement, as the Earth would have completed exactly one full orbit around the Sun.

Therefore, the EAR Period of **24 hours 12 min** i.e. 24.20 hours being also a **Referenced Base Position (RBP)** (details of this RBP will follow)**;** we will find out that we need exactly another **21 minutes** to be added to this Earth' Axis Rotation Period. This when reached or obtained in the distant future (biblical human future), will be the beginning of the very first 360 Earth Days Orbital Year.

This means when our Earth' rotation has a period of exactly 24.55 Hours, we should begin to have for the very first time in our 'Biblical HUMAN History' or rather in our future; 360 Earth Days Orbital Years.

> Based on the available scientific data, that every 1/1000th second slowing down of the Earth' Axis Rotation takes a 100 years; then, this additional 21 minutes **(1,260 seconds)** lengthening of the day to 24.55 hrs, from the Referenced Base Position (RBP) 24:12, will take exactly **126,000,000 years** and I mean exactly.

I would eventually find out that the obtaining of this precise number and time period would be indeed a major milestone breakthrough in our continuing progress for the construction of the **'cosmic number'** of the beast.

> Therefore, this is indeed our *'Eight Milestone Achievement'*.

The workings for these 21 EAR minutes becoming to represent 126,000,000 years are as described below. However, before we proceed into this; let us first look at something very intriguing.

When I had converted the **21 minutes** into seconds, the number that had emerged was no other but the startling number **1,260**. Startling, because I had realized the number 1,260 was in fact first significantly mentioned in the very Book of Revelation 11:3; then mentioned again in Rev 12:6.

Remember, our construction of the **'cosmic number'** of the beast, although is designed 'Cosmically', yet it is revealed to us only through the Holy Scriptures of the Holy Bible.

This again definitely connects **'Cosmic Mechanisms'** directly together with the **'Cosmic Secrets' that** are cryptically embedded in the Holy Scriptures. This once again reveals and reconfirms GOD as being the sole and absolute Creator of all the Heavens and everything in it, according to its order, which includes all life in it too.

These **'Cosmic Connections'** that have been linked directly to the Holy Scriptures inevitably brings the final phase in my personal 'Christian Execution' of extinguishing secularly accepted concepts, such as that of Charles Darwin (Origin of Man & Evolution) and also that of Dr Stephen Hawking' model of the Universe. Not that their scientific efforts and brilliance are in anyway being suggested here to be without substance or accuracy, far from it; but that they had left out completely and in its entirety the 'Supreme and Divine Architect' for all of it, if I do understand it correctly. This being none other than our LORD GOD ALMIGHTY, from all of their brilliant equations and propositions!!!

I however do sincerely believe that the greatly honoured Dr Stephen Hawking - the world renown and well celebrated Scientist, Physicist, Cosmologist etc., may be slowly coming around to the very understanding and finality that there is indeed in the very first place, GOD, and that GOD is somehow involved in all of this; when he had exclaimed in an interview, that was also reprinted in our local newspapers: "That we need to now find out the **'Mind of God'**. This I believe was in the sole context to the workings of the Universe, especially of how it all had come about originally and the way it is now.

In fact Albert Einstein the former super genius had also repeatedly mentioned about this 'Mind of God'. As we are very fortunate to still have Dr Stephen Hawking with us at this time, despite the severity of his 'medical condition'; I do sincerely propose and of the opinion that it is GOD' very plan for Dr Steven Hawking to have been able to reveal the wonderful workings of the Universe to us. So it was also in the case of Charles Darwin and his Theory of Evolution and selectivity, well at least to a point, as is the case with Dr Stephen Hawking, as we bring these into biblical perspective, i.e. the scriptural version of these important happenings.

I do humbly consider myself really fortunate and also personally most privileged to have discovered some of these scriptural embedded **'Cosmic Secrets'**, in these present times. Well, this is what I do humbly do think. This is especially, when the Holy Bible had been so thoroughly studied and researched by such eminent scholars from many varied fields of academia, over the last several hundred years.

If what I had discovered is indeed found to be accurate; then it would be particularly sweet and rewarding, personally. I am also still confident that there are several more such 'secrets' to be still discovered in the Holy Scriptures.

This is why, the obtaining of this number and time period of 126,000,000 years is indeed very significant and not just a mere coincidence. As you will further learn later, that even other relevant numbers as also mentioned in Revelation, will find it' rightful place, not only in the **'Cosmic Mechanisms'**, but also progressively into the construction of the **'cosmic number'** of the beast, itself.

Furthermore, the time period **126,000,000** years, has in it' construction also, the number **1260**. This as mentioned previously is scriptural recorded and as shown above is directly responsible for the very generation of this number **126,000,000** in the very first place.

There are definite relationships with the above Scriptures that do indicate this number 1,260 and the other Scripture i.e. in **Rev 12:14.**

These referenced Scriptures - Rev 11:3, 12:6 and 12:14 do refer to the same scriptural subject of the particular **woman** who had a male **child** born to her.

> However, we need to take careful note that these scriptures, are describing in my opinion, another particular and specific measure of time, which is not just equalling to a mere 1,260 days as was proposed by others, but indeed going also far beyond. I do stand very firm with this understanding.

This is also similarly thought of as with regards to the other specific scriptural time measurement of:

'a time and times and half a time',

as found written in Dan 7:25. However, please do take note, I am not refuting that it does not equate or relate to as such i.e. 1260, but rather stating that these scriptures have also another perspective to describing a larger time dimension that could still be attributed to it.

In other words to my understanding, it does not just represent a time measurement, as commonly thought as presently:

360 + 720 + 180 = 1260 days

This particular scriptural time measurement of 'a time and times and half a time' was used for a different set of people: the saints. For in my recently acquired understanding of these relevant Scriptures, as already mentioned; this 'time measurement period' being first described in Dan 7:25, had also occurred in the period linked together with the 'woman', as described in the Revelation Scriptures which has already been mentioned on the previous page. The term 'Woman', as used here, was indeed the symbolic expression for Jerusalem. This is according to Biblical Scholarship.

> Although, all this fresh understanding may seem to be conjecture at first, but if you bear with me in patience, you will surely realise otherwise. For when we correctly combine the two numbers representing the 'time measurements' i.e. **1,260** and the particular time period which is represented by 'a time and times and half a time', i.e. by **multiplying** these two resultants together (based on my fresh understanding), **instead of equating** these numbers to each other, as is the only present accepted practice; we will then get the startling number and result: **126,000,000 years**!!!

How about that!!!

This practically blew my mind. Yes, this is totally amazing. To make this even clearer to you, study the following:

First place this multiplied number, in separate boxes, as shown below.

1260	00	00	0

The elements of the number 126,000,000

Then multiply the elements, as follows:

1260 x Time x Times x Half a Time

'Time' based on the above elements, as shown in the boxes above, carries obviously the intrinsic value: 10 x 10 = 100.

It follows then as I had discovered, that 'Times', is the repeating of the value of 'Time' once again, which = 100.

In this new perspective of these Scriptures, it does not mean that it is twice the value of 'Time' i.e., 200 years but being just 100 years.

With the above perspective in place; then 'Half a Time' = 10 Years. No there is no mistake here. For we need to take care to carefully note that the Scriptural time component of **'half a time'** does not directly mean it equals to 50 years. For it actually equals to only 10 years, as just expressed.

Therefore, in this context, **'half a time'** actually means **one equal part** of 'a time' value divided exactly into two, as shown and expressed above, i.e. 10 x 10. This means taking the **square root** of 100 years, where the **100 years** is indeed the year value that I had ascribed to the first Scriptural time component, i.e. to 'a time' as shown on the previous page.

These are all what I had indeed discovered in the construction process and it could very well be exactly as the scriptural attributed time values for the Scriptural time components of:

'A time' = 10 X 10 = 100 Years;

'Times' = repeating the value of 'a time' i.e. 100 Years for one more time.

'Half a time' = the square root of 'a time'. That is, square root of 100 years = 10 Years.

'a time and times and half a time'

This is found written, as already mentioned in the Holy Scriptures - Dan 7:25 and in Rev 12:14.

From the above analysis, this specific Scriptural time measurement combination is indeed further describing a total time period value of **100,000 Years**; if it is left to stand alone. However, in this construction process through my newly applied understanding; this time period value of 100,000 years is to be then **multiplied** by the other scriptural resultant number - 1,260. This is the number as already mentioned which is found written in Rev 11:3 & 12:6.

This then amazingly, gives us our required:

126,000,000 years

> This is incredibly the precise number of years being required for the Earth from the RBP 24:12, to finally acquire a 360 Earth-Days Axis Rotations per year, at the very distant future RBP 24:33, for the very first time in our biblical human history.

1,260 X 100 X 100 X 10 = 126,000,000 years

> This is indeed our *'Ninth Milestone Achievement'* in this intriguing scriptural and cosmic related process.

Now, for reasons of your own, if you are still not agreeable or rather still not convinced of the above multiplication procedural concept as just presented above; you still need to accept the generation of this resultant number, **126,000,000 to have some accuracy and credence.** This is in terms of the specific time measurement that it represents in years. For this is also based in the first place, in addition to the above proposed but secondary multiplication procedure; on the additional 21 'EAR Minutes', that are precisely needed, to be added to the Earth' Axis Rotation Period, as recorded from the RBP of

24:12. This is indeed critical for you to understand and to accept accordingly.

These 21 'EAR Minutes' are needed to be added to the Earth' Axis Rotation Period, that was precisely attained and recorded at the RBP 24:12. This would enable in the natural cosmic solar process for the 'day' to be lengthened accordingly and precisely, to meet the very much proposed needed future **24.55 Hours** Earth Axis Rotation Period. These 21 'EAR Minutes', followed the calculated rate, as provided by Scientific Scholarship.

This rate is 1/1000th second change to be added every 100 years to the overall EAR period.

For the Earth' Axis Rotation to progress eventually through the cosmic Solar Planetary processes, to finally provide us for the very first time in our biblical human history; a 360 'Days' Orbital Year, would take precisely an additional 21 EAR Minutes.

These 21 'EAR Minutes', converts accordingly into 'time in years', being our **126,000,000 Years** exactly.

I do sincerely hope that my secondary and as important multiplication Scriptural procedural concept would be also accepted by you. Based on this Scriptural procedural concept, I also had accordingly, concluded the 'time value', which must have been Biblically and divinely ascribed to this Scriptural Daniel time component; of **a time.** This is the value of 10^2 or written in it' full expanded form would be the important 100 years as already mentioned.

This is remarkably, the same time period that it would take for the Earth' Axis Rotation, to have a change of 1/1000th of a second. Also, as proposed by self, either in **increase** or in reduction as it could very well be.

Also, you can easily generate from this science calculated rate; that 1 second of similar change would take the Earth, **100,000 years**.

This is exactly equal to the time period of the Scriptural Daniel time components in the Scriptural combination of:

'a time and times and half a time'

This additional double discovery, in itself is quite remarkable. To make this connection, if I may say so, is also quite remarkable too. So, please do remember that 'half a time' is not expressing 50 years i.e. to be literally taken as being half of its value, but indeed it is actually the **square root** of it' full time value. Therefore, in conclusion, the 'time value' of 'half a time' is indeed 10^1 years or directly written as being only **10 years.**

So, we can actually progress this, in multiples of the order of ten. Also, you will discover that the application of the square root will be used again in this book later on.

To make things clearer, I have provided a few relevant equations to help you in understanding this even better. I have also taken the liberty to jump the gun a bit here, as I had equated 1 Year to 360 Days i.e. Biblical Days or Earth Days before actually proving it happening.

Half a 'Time' = 10 years   = 3,600 days   = 1 decade
'Time'   = 100 yrs   = 36,000 days   = 10 decades = 1 Century
Ten 'Times' = 1000 yrs = 360,000 days = 1 Millennium
100 'Times' = 10,000 yrs = 3,600,000 days = 10 Millennium
1000 'Times'= 100,000 yrs = 36,000,000days = 100 Millennium

And it progresses on accordingly. I also realised that if you multiply **360 by 4,** you will get the resultant 1,440. This number 1,440 is indeed a significant number for it is also indeed a hundredth part of another important scriptural number, which is of course the 144,000. This number is indeed the total of the 12 Tribes of Israel X 12,000 people from each tribe who will be sealed with the seal of the living GOD – REV 7: 1-8. This number 144,000 was first mentioned in Rev 7:4, then in Rev 14:1, 3. This number would also play a part in the construction of the **'cosmic generated number'** of the second beast; as you will find out a few paragraphs down.

With the above understanding, I have also been able to establish the following relationships between the two component numbers; **360 and 144,000** as follows.

360   X   4   =   1,440
360   X   40   =   14,400
360   X   400   =   144,000
360   X   4,000   =   1,440,000
360   X   40,000   =   14,400,000
360   X   400,000 =   144,000,000

According to the AU, a Sidereal Day has **1,440 minutes. Isn't this interesting to know in our context?** This number 1,440 is also the number as derived above, being 360 X 4, or being the hundredth part of the Scriptural number; 144,000.

Also, somehow, I had remembered reading in an article about the Maya Calendar System, which was indeed a complicated system for the initial scholars involved in that work to decipher and reveal to us, the very meaning of the ancient Maya hieroglyphs.

The reason that I had brought into this matter the Maya Calendar System, was to show you that even here, these component numbers **144,000** and **360** were **surprisingly**, also represented and used quite significantly!!! They represented specific periods of 'time measure', as used by the Maya.

The Maya used their method of time keeping, to primarily measure distances through travel-time and to record events in their history. They also used it for their religious or sacred events and even for their important agriculture. They in fact had developed three different types of calendars. Their sacred calendar, called the Tzolkin which followed a 260 day cycle. Their civil calendar called the Haab which followed a 365 days year having 18 months of 20 days each with an additional intercalary month of 5 days added at the end of it. Finally, they had a third type of calendar which is called as 'The Long Count Calendar' having just 360 days for each year. This is the one that I am particularly interested here for our intent and purposes.

This is also the same calendar type that is now causing some controversy with regards to many who do believe that it does indicate the end of the world, as it completes it' 'Long Cycle'. This we have been informed had first begun on **August 13, 3114 BCE** and will end it' very first 'Long Cycle' on **December 21, 22 or even Dec 23/24, in the year 2012**, which would also be providing us with the winter solstice for this coming year (2012). Their chronology revolved around a greater cycle of 13 Baktuns (about 5,128 Solar years time period), which is as read on their 'Long Count Calendar' began:

13.0.0.0.0 **4 Ahau 8 Cumku** which corresponds to our:

August 13, 3114 BCE.

The 4 Ahau is corresponding to their sacred calendar reading and the 8 Cumku is corresponding to their Civil Calendar reading. All of these three systems are running simultaneously together. The Long Count Calendar is a progressive five stage notational position reading calendar system which begins with a baktun.katun.tun.uinal.kin (reading from left to right). That is from the smaller to the larger. A Kin being the smallest measurement of Mayan time is just a day long.

> The ending of the current cycle, which is the time (possibly Dec 23, 2012) of which we have been also scholastically informed, would be when **our Solar Sun will align with the centre of the Milky Way Galaxy**. This galactic centre event is the event that many correlate with being possibly the end of the world!!!

Anyway, the Mayan method of time keeping was to record in an increasing order of a number of days, being grouped together, to represent higher orders of time. This is somewhat like what had been already shown to you previously, in those increasing order of ten '360 Equation Series' but then again, not exactly similar, as they follow a base of 20. This is called the vigesimal system, which also includes the **concept of zero**, long before the Europeans had any knowledge of it.

For your better understanding and convenience, the following is provided for you, as found in the Encyclopaedia Britannica.

The Maya used the word **kin** to represent a single day. **Uinal (a Mayan month)** was the measurement of 20 days or 20 kins. **Tun (being a Mayan year)** was 18 Uinals or **360 days**. **Katun** was 20 Tuns or 7,200 days. **Baktun** (which means cycle) was 20 Katuns or **144,000 days.** So for this 'Long Count Calendar' system, we have at best 5 notational positions.

> **As you can read, the Maya time measurement 'Tun' represents 360 days and the immediate following time measurement which is Baktun, represents 144,000 days!!!**

For some specific reason, the Maya changed or decided to down the value for a Tun of time measure, from being 20 Uinals to only 18 Uinals. This gives a total of 360 Days, whilst the former multiplying by 20, would have given a value of 400 Days instead. However, from my perspective, this quite obviously does not follow a 'Calendar Year' or rather a 'Prophetic Year'; as the 360 day years have yet to happen in our own 'Human Biblical History'.

However, with regards to their equating of a 'Tun' to being just only 18 Uinals, convinced me that it was not a mistake, but had been done deliberately with a specific design in mind. This design, I believe is cosmically dictated and therefore they had somehow planned out their calendar of 360 days based on this accordingly.

They then provided a time measure of a Katun = 20 Tuns; followed by **20 Katuns = One Baktun**. One Baktun is equivalent to **144,000 days**, following their gradual upward increasing higher order scale.

> You will discover later on, in Book Two that the number 144,000 in the Holy Bible, could also be taken to represent 144,000 years. This is yet another discovery that I had made, whilst, in the midst of writing this book.

Also, if you were to equate these 144,000 years to 360 days for each year, you will get indeed a total of **51,840,000 days.** Hold this resultant number in your mind for a while, as I continue on to reveal something amazing to you.

Although, the 'Long Count Calendar' system is at best a five stage calendar system, which follows a greater cycle of 13 Baktuns only; I am going to reveal to you something very interesting here. So please do follow me, carefully.

Now, as I was studying the resultant numbers or rather totals in days for each of the above Maya specific time measurement periods; I found out the following:

a) Let us provide the next two increasing orders after a Baktun. We already know that One Baktun = 20 Katuns.

Since at this very stage in the development of this book, I am not aware as yet of any higher orders of time in this 'Long Count Calendar' system, I need to postulate the next two higher imaginary orders just for my intent and purposes, to show you something very interesting. Let us simply call the first imaginary postulated higher order of time in this calendar system as MX and the other as MY.

Let us modify the value of MX to be **18 Baktuns instead of 20**, just like the Maya did when they established the value for a Tun, as being **18 Uinals** instead of it being 20 Uinals, if the time sequence pattern was to be followed. Following the above method, we will then get 2,592,000 days.

This number **2,592,000** is also actually found in a very different culture from that of the MAYA, which also expresses this as being a specific time measure and it is found exactingly in the **'Indian/Hindu Cosmological Time Cycles'**.

Here it is found as expressing 2,592,000 **'First Mean Motions'** of the Sun, which when understood correctly, will also surprisingly express similarly; **2,592,000 days** as produced by **7,200 Earth Years 360 days each**. Of course this time period would exceed the Maya greater cycle long count of 13 Baktuns, which equates to only 5,128 Solar Years only.

I am of the opinion that the MAYA may have also based their Long Count Calendar System with this cosmic understanding of following a 20, 18, 20 micro time cycle pattern within it' greater longer cycle. This perhaps will make it in synch with the other ancient time systems.

Isn't this just amazing to have such similarity, even in such diverse cultures that had never been in contact with one another or possibly even knew of the other' existence at that time. Despite this, these yet were able to produce such similar results; both measuring and expressing such large time periods in their own innovative ways. The references made to the 'Indian/Hindu Cosmological Time Cycles' can be referenced in this book, being represented in a special Sexagesimal Modified Chart. Please refer to the Appendices for the referring page.

b) Getting back to the Maya calendar; this means that 'MY' has to equal to 20 MX. This is because through my **applied understanding** of the Maya 'Long Count Calendar' system, which I am of the opinion, follows a definite pattern of **20, 18, and 20….**

Therefore, I presume this should progress on accordingly, in the increasing scale time measurements of my projected and extended Maya Calendar System. In fact the Maya word Baktun, means cycle which further indicates to me that this cycle, **20, 18, 20** would begin its repeating pattern from here onwards in their Calendar system.

Accordingly, I deduced, we could possibly keep on repeating this similarly as **20, 18, and 20** as long as we need to. I will show you the cycle **20, 18, 20** repeating once again in the equations below.

Now, I may be wrong in assuming this cycle was incorporated by the Maya into their amazing 'Long Count Calendar' System. However, coincidentally if I may say so, when we multiply out the value in days for 1 MY; we will surprisingly get **51,840,000 days!!!**

Yes, this is the same total of days being represented by our Biblical 144,000 (years), when we equate each of these years to a 360 days year too!!! This number of days is similarly also found in the 'Indian/Hindu Cosmological Time Cycles'.

For a clearer understanding, I have provided the following for you.

1 Day	= 1 Kin	= 1 day
20 Kins	= 1 Uinal (a Mayan month)	= 20 days
18 Uinals	= 1 Tun (One Mayan year)	= 360 days
20 Tuns	= 1 Katun	= 7,200 days

The First Cycle has been completed. Second Cycle of 20, 18, and 20 as per my applied understanding should begin right now.

20 Katuns	= 1 Baktun	= 144,000 days
18 Baktuns	= 1 MX	= 2,592,000 days
20 MX	= 1 MY	= 51,840,000 days

Second cycle of 20, 18, and 20 is now also completed as above cycle

Third cycle should begin now, if we so wish to continue applying it to the Maya time calendar system as per my applied understanding.

Based on the above revelations, please study below, the remarkable similarity in these two equations. One was derived from within the Maya 'Long Count Calendar' System and the other was directly derived from the Holy Scriptures of the Holy Bible.

20 MX = 20 X 2,592,000 = 1 MY = 51,840,000 Days
144,000 Years X 360 Days = 51,840,000 Days

Sometime after establishing the above concepts, I had the opportunity to access some Mayan data from an internet website - 'The Classic Maya Calendar and Day Numbering System', which was explaining some details about the Maya Calendar. Through this, I also discovered that the Maya had provided for larger Maya time measurements even after a Baktun time period. This was named as a Pictun and then which progressed to a Calabtun and finally a Kinchiltun.

This means that our proposed MX could possibly be replaced by a Pictun and our proposed MY, could possibly be replaced accordingly by a Calabtun and followed lastly by a Kinchiltun.

This internet article did not follow the system of 20, 18, 20 micro cycle as I had done through my **applied understanding,** but equated 1 Pictun to be 20 Katuns; 1 Calabtun to be 20 Pictuns and 1 Kinchiltun to be 20 Calabtuns.

However, by employing my **applied understanding** with regards to the Maya 'Long Count Calendar' system, I have decided to maintain it as such in the 20, 18, 20 time sequence pattern.

Therefore, below follows accordingly, just as a **projection**, to be able to observe some remarkable time relationships, if my version could be the case indeed:

At the end of the first cycle, we obtain:

20 Kins	= 1 Uinal (a Mayan month)	= 20 days
18 Uinals	= 1 Tun (One Mayan year)	= 360 days
20 Tuns	**= 1 Katun**	**= 7,200 days**

At the end of the second cycle, we obtain:

20 Katuns	= 1 Baktun	= 144,000 days
18 Baktuns	= 1 Pictun	= 2,592,000 days
20 Pictuns	**= 1 Calabtun**	**= 51,840,000 days**

And in the third cycle, this would continue as:

20 Calabtuns	= 1 Kinchiltun	= 1,036,800,000 days
18 Kinchiltuns	= ? = 18,662,400,000 days	= 51,840,000 years
20?	**= 373,248,000,000 days**	**= 1,036,800,000 years**

All these results can be tracked in my 360 Equations Series; The Indian/Hindu Cosmological Cycles and even the Babylonian Time Systems.

Coming back into focus:

The calculations for the 21 EAR Minutes (1,260 seconds) are as follows:

- As scientifically established the $1/1000^{th}$ second reduction (and I also compute similarly for the possible increase) in the Earth' Axis Rotation takes 100 years.

- This means, for 1 second reduction/increase in the Earth' Axis Rotation, as the situation may be based upon, would take accordingly 100,000 years to fulfil.

- 1 minute change (60 seconds) will take 6,000,000 years.

- 12 minutes would accordingly take, **72,000,000 years.**

- As already explained the 21 EAR minutes change i.e. **1,260 seconds** to the Earth' Axis Rotational Speed, will indeed take **126,000,000 years** to fulfil.

24 minutes i.e. 1,440 seconds takes **144,000,000** years. This number 144,000,000 has in it' construction, the previous mentioned Scriptural number **144,000** which is clearly seen as above.

This means, we can also deduce from this understanding that 1.44 seconds in EAR Period change will take 144,000 years to fulfil.

Also, you will be able to read in Rev 21:17 that the **NEW JERUSALEM** will be a city built in a perfect cube scale of dimension 144 cubits, according to the measure of a man, that is, **of an angel**. This is somewhat similar in the construction of another perfect cube as in 1 Kings 6:20. This was the inner sanctuary of the first Lord's Temple, which was built by king Solomon, son of king David. This was measured to the scale of 20 cubits, in which the Ark of the Covenant was to be set. You will also learn soon, how I used this 144,000 in the 'Cosmic Construction' of the 'number' of the second beast.

As I had established much earlier, that we needed exactly 24.55 Hours (i.e. 24 hours 33 minutes), to be the Earth' Axis Rotational Period, in order for us to have exactly 360 Earth Days/Orbital Years; let us check this out and see whether this is so, by simple arithmetic as follows:

1. $\dfrac{\text{Hours, Earth to Orbit Sun}}{\text{No. of Earth Days in a Year}}$ = Duration of Day (EAR) in Hours

2. $\dfrac{\text{Hours, Earth to Orbit Sun}}{\text{Duration of the Day (EAR) in Hours}}$ = No. of Earth Days in a Year

So in case (1) above:

What we want to achieve is to obtain the duration of the day that has been calculated earlier, as being **24.55 Hours**.

The time taken for the Earth to orbit the Sun, at a speed of 66,000 miles per hour, covering a distance of 583,400,000 miles, would be **8,839.39 hours**. The required number of Earth Days in this Orbital Year is of course our required **360 Days**.

$\dfrac{8,839.39}{360}$ = 24.5538611 hrs (This _ means, repeating)

From above, it is clearly seen that our earlier calculated and required duration (Earth Axis Rotation Period) of **exactly 24.55 hours**, does not equal to the answer produced in Case 1, as shown above. This is obvious, as there is a time remainder. This exceeds our very precise limit for the duration of the day, which is precisely required for achieving a 360 Earth Days/Orbital Year. This remainder, **0.0038611 hours** which equals to **13.89996 seconds** in Earth Axis Rotation Period time, means that it will take another additional 1,389,996 years approximately, to be further added to our already precisely calculated **126,000,000 years** (the period of time as required to achieve a 24.55 hours EAR).

Obviously, this additional 1,389,996 years totally defeats our every effort this far, to achieving and obtaining a 360 Earth Days Year at that pre-calculated future precise time.

This means, based on the above Case 1, we just cannot have a 24.55 Hours EAR period precisely on the 126,000,000th year, as computed from the RBP 24:12. This is indeed so very vital to our progress, not only to achieve the 360 Days Year, but to also ultimately determine the 'number' of the beast, itself.

We just cannot ignore this by trying to go around it or by evading it completely, without having to fulfil this extremely critical requirement. This is evidently quite obvious, due to it' definite relationship with the relevant Scriptures as in Revelation and also it' subsequent link up with the other relevant Scriptures as in 2Esdras and also in the Book of Daniel. Therefore, this situation is not good at all.

Is this the end to my very quests???

Let' take a look at another earlier example again, as follows:

Hours, Earth To Orbit The Sun = Hours/Solar Day
Number of Solar Days in the Current Year

$$\frac{8839.39}{365.242199 \text{ days}} = 24.20144776 \text{ hours/day}$$

The time taken in hours for the Earth to orbit the Sun (8,839.39 hours), was calculated, using these two scientific data as provided below:

1. Speed of Earth, with which it orbits the Sun, being approximately **66,000 mph**.

2. The elliptic travel distance of the Earth, as it travels around the Sun, as being approximately **583,400,000 miles**.

It is quite obvious that these figures are rounded off figures for our easier 'handling'. Well anyway, I will still use these same facts, as provided by Scientific Scholarship for this calculation and also in Case 1 and subsequently also in Case 2.

The Hours/Solar Day and the 'Number of Solar Days' in a current year is also provided for us through Scientific Scholarship.

The reason, I provided this particular example, is to show you that the result or quotient of the division, in the equation above, must equal precisely to the scientifically established length in hours of the current Solar Day. This as you can see, is indeed the case here, as confirmed in this equation. This is in direct contrast to the critical problem that we are now currently facing, as in our above Case 1.

Here, the quotient does not agree precisely with my calculated length of the Earth Day i.e. 24.55 hours, which is also the Earth' Axis Rotation Period at that future time; 126,000,000 years away.

Knowing quite well that I was now dug deep in grave predicament, I could either chicken out now or persevere on to find out the possible solution to this mountain of a problem; if there is one. And yes, I decided to find out the solution, as I felt it in my very bones that there would be certainly an answer to this difficulty, for the relevant Scriptures involved in these quests cannot be wrong. This was the scriptural confidence with which drove me on relentlessly despite this setback.

So, I began doing some more searching, and surprisingly found out something interesting with regards to Orbits; Johannes Kepler; Albert Einstein and *Perturbation*

I discovered, from my reading of a short article on Orbits, as found in the Encarta Encyclopaedia '96; that an orbit is **perturbed** when the forces are more complex than those between two spherical bodies. It goes on to state that **Kepler'** Laws are exact, only for unperturbed orbits.

Therefore, if I understand it correctly amongst the other factors that are possibly also involved in this perturbation: The attracting or limiting forces that do exist between Planets due to gravity and these all interacting simultaneously together with the 'forces' exerted by their controlling Star, as in our case, the Sun, could cause their elliptical planetary orbits to change with time, and possibly cyclically at that.

When I read the article, I thought, could it be possible that the Earth' elliptical orbit around the Sun could also be subject to this possibility of 'perturbation'. This could effectively cause the required changes in the Earth' Orbit that could possibly shave off these excess 13.89996 seconds from the EAR Period as obtained in Case 1. This we precisely do need in order to accomplish our present quest and more importantly to fulfill the Holy Scriptures.

Also, just like the Moon moving away from the Earth, as scientifically discovered and which is happening currently, thereby increasing it' orbital travel distance around the Earth; could the Earth also be similarly slowly moving over time from the Sun and then later at a predetermined period of time close in back once again to it' closest possible orbit around the Sun within a well defined and predictable orbiting range cycle.

This range would obviously be dictated by the various gravitational forces of the orbiting Solar Planetary Bodies and the Earth' Moon and the Sun interacting all together, to somehow, limit the size of the elliptic changes; whether in expansion or in contraction.

I am also quite inclined to believe, if this is indeed possible, then these effective changes possibly caused by perturbation, must be indeed so infinitesimal and accordingly spread over a really long period of time and being cyclic at that as the very concept above suggests in expansion or in contraction, to comply and fulfill the relevant connected scriptures.

Anyway, the hypothesis of the 'astral body' being offered as a proposition theory for the change in the Earth' orbit and due to this it had subsequently responsible for the causing of the Noah' Flood to have become that as suggested by them; globally devastating was already mentioned very early on in this book.

However, less I forget, I think it is appropriate for me to mention here again about that single 'Astral Body' proposed phenomenon, that if it had actually occurred then it needed to have caused these three major affects on the Earth.

1) It' gravitational effects on the Planet Earth had immediately caused the Earth' very Orbit to be increased substantially by a massive **5¼ days** from it' supposed to have been originally 360 days annual orbit to 365¼ days.

2) This in turn caused the Noah' Flood, which coincidentally occurred almost simultaneously, with the close passing of this particular 'Astral Body', to become globally devastating in magnitude.

3) This then in turn caused the Earth to be noticeably and quite immediately at that, to massively tilt **23½ degrees** off it' axial axis. This astral body causing tilt then directly resulted in the commencement of Planet Earth having seasons.

This then would be somewhat indeed contrary to how God had caused it to first begin, as clearly confirmed in Genesis 1:14. This I believe was the tilt itself that GOD had initially naturally designed into it for us to experience the four seasons on an annual basis from then on without the interference of the Noah' Flood.

Besides the above, the 'Astral Body Theory' is also defeated by my proposed and required cyclic occurrence, which is indeed particularly important to us. This means that it must also at some point, once again, through the similar mode or some other means, reverse this increase of 5¼ days to the Earth' orbit, to re-establish their original 360 Day Years orbit. Only with this taking place, they could eventually fulfill the several scriptures that profess to these 'Biblical 360 Day Years'.

This very understanding being presented here for the proper switching back to the 360 day years is crucial to uphold their theory, and even that of mine. In other words it must provide a proper basis for this to be carried out by the Cosmos and the Solar Planetary bodies of the Sun, the Earth and the Moon. How are all of these going to be working together to bring about this reversal and regularly at that through a cyclic process over and over again unless there is something more to this.

As already explained very early on in this book, I do not subscribe to their suggestion as being the evidential answer supporting their globally devastating Noah' Flood, rather than that which was confined to a more local 'Biblical involving territories' flood at best. This is my view on the matter.

Therefore, I am proposing, the very possibility of engaging 'perturbation' or some other cosmic phenomenon affecting the Earth' Orbit. This would be cosmically cyclic in it' occurrence, so that we could eventually have a **360 day years cycle** and then back to it' **original orbit of 365¼ day years** and then repeating this cycle, as long as permitted, by the relevant cosmic forces. This is the only way that I could think off, currently, that could execute these necessary changes, so that our Planet Earth could experience these orbital changes as the Holy Scriptures in the Holy Bible professes to us. Perhaps you may have other suggestions and if so, I will be most happy to be informed of these too. Who knows it may end up being the correct solution after all. Yet, the fact of the matter is that there has to be a cosmic explanation for this happening. Also, far as I am concerned with regards to the relevant scriptures; it is indeed happening as suggested by the Scriptures. There is no doubt about it whatsoever in my mind.

It is this very requirement that our previous mentioned Gordon Lindsay had completely failed to accomplish in his book, 'God's Plan of the Ages', although he had linked the changes or the switching of one cycle of 360 day years to another cycle of 365¼ day years to biblical events and secular events of significant importance. This switching then after some period of time is once again reversed back to 360 day years only to repeat these two cycles over and over again through **39 times** in total as far as his propositions are concerned.

Besides these event linkages, there is no other explanation given of how is this going to be carried out in the cosmos, i.e. in our Solar Planetary System, in particular our Planet Earth. What cosmic or Solar Planetary forces would make our Planet Earth' orbit around the Sun, able to go through all of these switching back and forth??? How is it accomplished??? How does 5¼ days of Earth orbit around the Sun simply disappear with such suddenness practically overnight in these proposals???

Linking of these events is one thing, but how is this then translated to be affecting the very orbit of the Earth around the Sun to periodically change it from 360 day years to 365¼ day years??? These are question that need to be answered by those who are in support of his proposition in his book sometime ago i.e., 'God's Plan of the Ages'.

What I had also read in other sources was that the distance of the Earth' travel around the Sun and the speed with which it did this, **remains the same**, despite the slowing down of the Earth' rotation on it' very own axis. This has been scientifically established as already mentioned before. I also came upon some facts that were reported under the topic, 'Orbit – Perturbation Theory' over the internet; that the planets which primarily **perturb** the Earth' orbit are Venus, Jupiter and Saturn. All of these three Planets, together with the Sun, also do perturb the Moon' orbit around the Earth.

Now I am not certain to what extent is the Earth' orbit perturbed but the very fact that it does happen gives me an opportunity to further explore it in this direction, whether this perturbation could cause sufficient effective changes in our Earth' Orbit, which would in turn shave off these additional and problematic 13.89996 seconds gradually through the 126,000,000 years cyclic period till that future EAR Period 24.55 hours is obtained. This is to be precisely accomplished by the time the 126,000,000 years have exactly transpired i.e. at that RBP 24:33.

This science based 'perturbation', may be a better alternative to be engaged here than that of the 'Astral Body' phenomenon because:

1) It does not cause sudden and abrupt changes to the Earth' Orbit.

2) It does not cause any changes to the tilt of the Planet. For I had previously mentioned that the 'Planetary Tilts' are a common characteristic of the Solar Planets and who knows one day soon, Science will discover the same in other newly discovered Planets belonging to other Star Systems; other than those of our own Sun. This would further fortify what I am stating here now. In other words, the Earth had this tilt from some point in its evolving, as GOD had designed into it as such, so that we could have the four seasons as we have it today. And so it was not due to the direct result of the Noah' Flood; even if it was indeed a globally devastating flood as they had claimed.

3) Perturbation affected changes to the Earth' Orbit, as what we would require, would be indeed so infinitesimal and occurring of course, cyclically, spread over very relatively large periods of time.

4) Furthermore, 'perturbation' is scientific based and also is a Solar Planetary factual happening. This is besides the evidential existence of tilts in other Solar Planets, having long been confirmed by Astronomy, which I had brought up in refuting further their Noah' global devastation. It would

be quite erroneous, if we allow this 'astral body close passing theory', to be similarly applied to these other Solar Planets, causing their axis' to tilt also accordingly. Now wouldn't this be so?

However, with the accepted scientific discovery that **the gravitational attraction between Planets causes their elliptical orbits to change with time,** makes me then to think that by invoking this, I could indeed shave off this additional problematic time period of **13.8996 seconds slack** . This obviously needs to be removed in my present quest, to achieve the desired end result that we so desperately need.

All of these scientific related facts cemented by the relevant Scriptural truths made me to realise that it may be very possible, that the speed with which and the elliptical distance of the Earth orbiting the Sun, may also be subject to **some minor changes** through this **'perturbation'**.

Whether this could happen for my proposal at the end of the day, needs to be scientifically verified, but at the least, it has a scientific basis in support of my hypothesis for this to happen, i.e. the perturbation of the Earth' orbit.

Other new and more recent Solar System related findings, is that we do have a tenth 'Planet' orbiting the Sun, instead of the original nine. This may actually shatter the long standing astronomically supported 'Nine Planets Solar System', which was established way back in 1930, with the then discovery of Pluto, by Clyde Tombaugh.

The tenth Planet, named Sedna, after an Inuit goddess of the ocean, was discovered on November 14, 2003 by a NASA team led by Dr. Mike Brown of the California Institute of Technology. It is also still being scientifically debated; whether to classify Sedna as a true Planet of the Solar System and the other on-going debate to in fact declassify Pluto as being a true Planet. The reason I brought this up, was to impress you that even within the restricted context of our own Solar System, there is still a lot more out there, that we do not know or comprehend as yet. This article with regards to 'Planet' Sedna, was contributed by Mark Henderson and printed in 'The Times', USA. This was then reprinted in our own local 'New Sunday Times' newspaper under it' section of Astronomy, dated April 11, 2004; from which I had extracted the above data and made these references to prove a point.

Therefore, based on our progress this far and keeping in view the overall supporting evidences of the relevant Scriptures supporting the 360 Day Years at some point in our human biblical future; we could suggest that the **'constants'** i.e. the speed with which and the elliptical distance that the Earth travels during it' orbit around the Sun, may also be subject to this cosmic **'perturbation attraction between the Solar Planets'.** This could then cause the necessary, correspondingly expected and needed changes over time, which would then produce for us, our Scriptural supported 360 Day Years.

> It was also revealed in the same article, that Albert Einstein had previously explained of an obvious perturbation in the **perihelion** of the Planet Mercury.

Furthermore, we are informed that the Sun perturbs the lunar orbit by several thousand kilometers.

> Atmospheric drag causes the orbit of an Earth Satellite, to shrink.

We are informed by scientific scholarship that the oblate shape of our Planet Earth also causes the direction of it' Node and Perigee to change regularly.

Armed with all of these added possibilities, I then thought could it be that the Earth does indeed have an extremely slow but cyclic change after all, with regards to it' elliptical orbit around the Sun over time. This also causing a corresponding change to it' speed of travel around the Sun; then by applying all of this basic understanding with regards to the perturbation possibility, I realised, that we may very well achieve our very results finally.

By having the elliptical orbit to be perturbed from the approximate 583,400,000 miles, by just a minuscule amount of 3,620 miles only, we will then be able to achieve the required elliptical orbit of **583,396,380 miles** at that particular period of time in the future. This is absolutely necessary, for us to achieve our 360 Day Years precisely, as and when the EAR obtains its 24:55 hours EAR speed.

The time taken to progress from position (RBP) 24:12 to RBP 24:33, would remain as exactly 126,000,000 years.

The above minuscule changes as proposed would be continuously accumulating, until the overall required change of 3,620 miles is finally realised, and occurring precisely in the very beginning of the **126,000,000th year.** This produces for us the required elliptical distance of exactly **583,396,380 miles** at that precise time period.

Due to these slight changes to the elliptical orbit, the Earth would then be brought just that little bit closer to the Sun without affecting life on Earth. So, based on this effect of perturbation, the speed of the Earth' travel around the Sun should also increase gradually from 66,000 mph to the speed requirement of **66,010 mph** exactly, as the Earth reaches Reference Base Position **24:33**.

This means, there has to be an **upward speed change** of very infinitesimally accumulated speed increase changes, as the Earth gets a little closer to the Sun each passing year through the 126,000,000 years.

Also, precisely on the **126,000,000th year**, our required speed increase would have been reached i.e. at precisely 66,010 mph. Again this speed change once obtained will then once again begin to reverse to it' original 66,000 mph.

These consistent speed changes will also produce reciprocating Earth Orbiting duration changes and vice versa. These accumulating Orbit duration changes, precisely ending on the **126,000,000th year**, would then give the Earth, as we hope and above all need, the precise required Orbit duration of 8,838 hours.

This 8,838 hours orbiting duration, would result in an overall accumulated reduction of **83.4 minutes** in the Earth' elliptical/orbit travelling time spread over 126,000,000 years. This reduction difference is calculated from the time that Earth' orbit duration around the Sun, began taking **8,839.39 hours.**

Take note, as previously explained, the elliptical journey during this duration would have been reduced from the current 583,400,000 miles to 583,396,380 miles; an overall reduction of 3,620 miles. Therefore, this reduction of 83.4 minutes is also accumulated in very small increments over a period of 126,000,000 years as just mentioned.

Based on these three parameters, i.e. the required Earth speed of 66,010 mph; the elliptical orbit distance of 583,396,380 miles, which produces for us the orbiting duration of 8,838 hours and all these three being collectively reached precisely on the 126,000,000th year period; we will then for the very first time in our Earth' Human Biblical History have the beginning era of 360 Day (Earth Day) Years.

> All of the above is finally my *'Tenth Milestone Achievement'*, which is needed to be established for our continuing progress, in the construction of the **'number'** of the second beast.

With an 8,838 Hours Orbiting Time, we will finally have our 360 Days Biblical Year, based upon a 24.55 Hours Earth Axis Rotation Period, or simply written as, 24.55 Hours Earth Day.

Hours to Orbit the Sun = No. of Earth Days in a year
Earth Day in Hours

> **8,838/24.55 = 360 Earth Days in a Year**

We commonly call these as being the 'Prophetic Years'. Yes, the Earth will finally have it' 360 Day Years after all, as first announced to us by the relevant

Scriptures, in the Books of Daniel and Revelation. Even if the perturbation theory being applied here does not become a reality, then there must be another solar cosmic mechanism that would propel the Earth or steer the Earth to an eventual 360 day years. This then building up again, progressively, to the **original** 365¼ day years without ever effecting the very inherent axial tilt of the Earth except for it' inherent variations within it' limiting range that already exists with it as such.

Through this PART TWO of my book, I have actually attempted to provide a Non-Biblical, Non-Scriptural approach to also be obtaining these very key results. However, taking note that, it has yet to occur in our Biblical Human History.

Now that we have established these 'TEN Milestone Achievements'; I have laid the very foundation just right for us to embark next on to our second quest, i.e. to continue our progress in the actual construction of the **'number'** of the second beast, sum totalling **666**. The successful obtaining of the 'number' of the beast, will also offer further support and proof, whether our conclusions in regards to the 360 Days/Year is indeed accurate or not. This is because these both situations are linked to each other, intricately and also being scriptural verified.

This is the **first serious attempt** in establishing the '360 Day Years', both Scriptural and also to be offering some possibilities for the very important science-wise verification needed to uphold this hypothesis by Scientists who may be interested to proving this to be correct after all; as it has definitely astronomical significance to being doing so.

So, by establishing these 360 Day Years, we could probably lend further support for the already well known reasons, in the shifting of ancient recorded eclipses. This having been verified through modern scientific calculations seems to have shifted hundreds of miles to the east of where they should have appeared. It was because of this actual evidential shifting; that scientist assumed that the day must be lengthening by some 10 to 15 microseconds per year.

I found this data written in an article, which was printed in a book, titled 'Time'. This was printed some thirty years ago though or even more; by Time-Life International (Nederland) NV, page 107. In this article, it was stated that since eclipses depend on orbital motions of the Sun, Moon and Earth, they 'run' on orbital time. But their areas of visibility, which depend on what part of the rotating Earth' surface is in the right position for seeing the eclipse, are governed by rotational time. Therefore, if the area of visibility was not where it should have been; it then follows that **rotational time** was out of step with **orbital time**.

Anyway, my evidences for the above Solar Planetary Earth Cosmic changes will be established even more firmly, as you will see in the next PARTS - THREE AND FOUR in BOOK TWO. However, the 'Addendum' which was actually prepared very much later, although attached immediately after this, changes some of the necessary fundamentals that I had already established in this present PART of this book. Hopefully, this would be considered as being a positive and necessary correction.

So, perturbation coupled with the EAR slowing down at the scientific calculated rate of $1/1000^{th}$ second per every 100 years will eventually get us our 360 EARs at the precise appointed time of the 126,000,000 years time interval; as I had calculated it from the RBP24:12 to RBP24:33.

360 EARs X 24.55 Hours (Mean EAR Period) = 8,838 Hours

If we calculate, how many hours are there in the present Solar Year of 365.242199 days, we should arrive at the result of about 8,839.39 hours.

365.242199 Solar Days X 24.20144776 Hours = 8,839.39 Hours

We then can clearly see that there is indeed only about 83.4 minutes time difference, from the present 365.242199 Solar Day Years and our future 360 Biblical Earth Day Years in terms of the Earth' orbital time around the Sun. This is just an hour and 23 minutes 24 seconds in total time difference. Surprisingly, really not a big difference in time value after all, despite a big drop of about five and a ¼ days from the Annual Calendar. This then may not be of such significance or any significance at all, in terms of causing any serious disruption to the climate prevailing at any material time.

END OF PART TWO

PRAISE BE TO GOD

E : gcf@globalchristianfamily.com

ADDENDUM OF PART TWO & BRIDGE TO BOOK TWO

Now, I had thought that I had successfully completed my earlier assignment in obtaining the most important sought after 360 Earth Day Years per orbit of the Earth around the Sun. Also, through this effort similarly obtained for the other subsequent 361; 362; 363; 364 and 365 EARs Earth Day Years per orbit too. Yet, there was still this nagging uneasy feeling inside me. It was like something was indeed amiss, that was not sitting quite right with this completion.

So, after many months of studying or attempting to come up with other possibilities in establishing the 360 days year, using other pathways, I finally did come around once again to accepting that the 360 Biblical Earth Days orbit is to be generated by the 360 EARs per orbit. This is also the case with the other 361 – 365 Earth Day Years being generated by their respective EARs/ orbit too. This was what I had already established earlier in PART TWO.

Despite having reestablished or having reconfirmed the above, I did finally come to realize, much later though, what was it that was indeed causing this nagging uneasiness (I would prefer to calling this now, the promptings of the Holy Spirit; you will understand why yourself as you proceed on), which I was just mentioning as above. It was that without even ever realizing it, I had actually in the process, had simultaneously resolved the ***360 Solar Days Years issue too***!!!

Now, please do allow me the opportunity to elucidate this to you more clearly and most definitively. We may not have fully appreciated or realized this earlier that each EAR Period will produce accordingly one Solar Day; well almost anyway. In other words, all the 365 EARs down to the 360 EARs and then up again through this range respectively, are also the specific contributors to having their respective number of Solar Days too; if you do think about it carefully!!! This has been in fact the case ever since we had the mighty Sun shining upon the Earth. Of course, the problem materializes as already mentioned before, when the Solar Day begins to get longer and longer than the EAR Period itself, which is as currently taking longer to complete as time goes by.

In other words as the EAR Period is **slowing** down as the case is presently, this having been established through scientific scholarship, happening at a rate of 1 second every 100,000 years; the Solar Day is then indeed getting longer accordingly. And also possibly, through my developed Oscillation EAR Model (OEARM), the Solar Day in the far future after the slowing down phase of this EAR Period range, to be even shorter and shorter than an EAR Period at that material time, when the EAR Period range becomes to gradually **increase** at the same rate as above. This as I seriously compute would materialize as indicated so that the underpinning premise for this thinking which is based on the Scriptural fact that the Earth would eventually have it' 360 Day Years, which I do envisage through this very understanding would be established by the Solar System itself. This is specifically through the Sun, Earth and Moon working together to bring this Earth event to come about.

However, now trying to use this same OEARM (you will come to know about the OEARM later in the Addendum) with the Solar Day as above, as I had done similarly with the EARs; I would find out soon in the next few paragraphs below, this cannot be used as such directly, for there is indeed a big twist to be added to it.

As you very well know, a Solar Day is indeed only completed with some additional help through the travel motion of the Earth. This is the additional time needed as it' orbits the Sun, to bring the Sun back to the **meridian,** which is used to compute the end/begin of each Solar Day. This is where the problem also is because of this requirement to have the Sun back to it' meridian at any particular location an observer is located with reference to it.

To make it easier for you to understand and also for me too with regards to this meridian, I have taken an extract from the Wikipedia - the free encyclopedia, with a few grammatical additions for further clarity by me to help us as follows:

Let us consider that the Sun is directly overhead (this is termed as at it' zenith) at a point on the equator, location; latitude 0°. You being the observer are also standing at this very same point which is termed as the geographical point of the Sun. If you were to measure the height of the Sun above the horizon i.e. the skyline (please check Wikipedia for Horizon, to better understand what this is) with a sextant (and also this, if you are not too sure), you would find out that the altitude of the Sun is 90°. By subtracting this figure from 90°, you will find the zenith distance of the Sun, which in this case would be 0°. This would be the same with your own latitude. So in a way it would locate where you are too i.e. as observed in direct relation to the zenith of the Sun which occurs at 12 noon each day to establish the beginning and/or the ending of a Solar Day. This too would be the very beginning of the next immediate Solar Day at this very same 12 noon.

Zenith of the Sun actually means, that the altitude of the Sun being at it' highest point from the observer. That is being perpendicular to the observer in relation to the horizon. It is this requirement that has made the Solar Day to be currently exceeding the very length of the particular EAR Period at this material time. I hope this is clear to you. If you still have difficulty in understanding this, then do kindly read about the Sun' meridian in any other internet provided article on this matter.

This indeed had created the important problem in the first place, which had channeled me then to proceed to establishing exactly the '360 Earth Days' in a year instead.

However, together with the above new proposition, I have just begun to realize myself, that if we take for example, the fast 365 EAR Period years, well at least it was exactly that at RBP18:24:12(A). This is an Earth Axis Rotation Speed Switchover (EARSS) Base, located at about 500,000 years ago at the very beginning of the 18th EAR Oscillation Cycle. All of this too will be known to you later in this Addendum. Since then, this EAR Period has been slowing down continually, and this in turn directly causes the Solar Day itself to be getting longer and longer.

This simply meaning, the Solar Day would be taking more and more time to have the Sun back to it' meridian (at noon) each day from the observed location. This in turn would be producing for us longer Solar Days, which in turn would produce longer Solar years. However, having stated this, where is the limit to be drawn with regards to how long can the Solar Day really become within this 365 EARs/orbit. The reason that I bring this up is because the EAR Period is moving, according to this OEARM, to it' next lower level being the 364 EARs/orbit. Obviously, the Solar Day cannot be extending on it' very own without the limiting factor of the number of EARs at any level, as it directly determines the number of Solar Days too, accordingly.

This became quite evident to me, because the Solar Day is indeed currently already more than a **quarter** of a day longer than the 365 EARs/orbit as currently. And we have just moved only about **500,000 years** or so ago from the very RBP18:24:12(A), which began for us in the first place this current 365 EARs/orbit.

You will come to know that it will take **25.2 million years** for the EAR Period movement to the next level of EARs/orbit each time. In this particular case, it would be from 365 EARs down to 364 EARs/orbit. So from this perspective, the Solar Day cannot be continuing to becoming longer and longer with practically no ending to it until probably 25.2 million years later.

Thereby, this was the very reason that I began to realize that the Solar Day must than have it' own 'Oscillation Cycle or even Cycles'. This being within and around any particular EAR Period Level, as the Earth travels through this long 25.2 million years journey, which reduces the EARs/orbit from being 365 EARs/orbit to 364 EARs/orbits as in this particular phase.

This then would provide the possibility for it at times to be longer than the particular EAR Period and at times possibly to be even shorter than the

'THE BIBLICAL 360 DAY YEARS & THE SCRIPTURAL COSMIC 666'
ADDENDUM & BRIDGE

particular EAR Period in each EAR Period level. This would then be happening several times during this journey of 25.2 million years.

This understanding then gives the very possibility, that at several locations and time, during this long journey between the changing of the EARs Period from one level to the next level; the Solar Day would be exactly that of the same duration with the particular EAR Period at that material time. This would similarly be happening, with regularity, as the EAR Period keeps on **reducing** in it' speed of rotation through the other respective EAR Period Levels of 364; 363; 362; 361; 360. And then back again in the **increasing** EAR Period mode from here, through the similar range of levels though through different space-time locations to be obtaining again the fast 365 EARs/orbit.

So, all during this journey, the Solar Day, according to this thinking would mesh regularly within it' own oscillation cycles with the EAR EARTH DAY as the Earth moves from one EAR Period Level to another.

In other words, as a typical example for the above to be happening, the Solar Day must be oscillating forth in **lengthening mode** from the RBP, which had first established the **365 EARs/Solar Days**. This meaning at the very beginning of every EAR Period level, the number of Solar Days per orbit is identical with it' counterpart; the Earth Day. As the EAR begins to proceed to it' next lower 364 EARs per year orbit around the Sun in a **reducing speed mode**, as is currently the case, the Solar Day for reasons already explained would be **lengthening** in it' duration. However, this would be continuing as a hypothesis, until the Solar Days oscillation cycle reverses this lengthening trend to becoming shorter instead. This would then at some stage in the Solar Day oscillation cycle, coincide the Solar Day again, with the Earth Day' duration exactly.

This I envisage would be happening in the mid-way of this oscillation cycle. From here the Solar Day due to this Solar Cosmic Oscillation Cycle mechanism in play would continue becoming shorter and shorter until it is reigned in again towards the mid way once again but in lengthening mode. This will continue until reaching the mid way again of this oscillation cycle where once again, time permitting, it would reverse into shortening mode and begin a new oscillation cycle all over again.

So this constant oscillating cycles would consistently have the Solar Day to be in exact duration as the EAR Period itself, occurring in each three times and thereby several times throughout this journey depending on the number of repeating cycles until reaching the next level. At this new level, the Solar Day begins to once again **lengthen** in duration, as the EAR Period continues to reduce further, but this time around within it' new **364 Solar Days** year orbit duration. The oscillation cycles then continue accordingly throughout the entire range of EAR Period level changes.

So, in conclusion, when we had the 365 EARs/orbit beginning at the beginning of the 18th EAR Oscillation, we would have had also at that time, 365 Solar Days/orbit too. This would be similar for all the other EARs Period Levels including the 360 EARs/orbit, in which I am particularly concerned with for the intents and purposes of this book.

> This then establishes for us at the very beginning of the 360 EARs Period Level, *360 Solar Days too* and possibly at even some other locations in it' oscillation cycles, similarly.

Then when the EARs begin to **increase** in it' speed of rotation from one EAR Period Level to the next, as an example, from 360 EARs to the next higher level of 361 EARs, the Solar Days oscillation cycle would first be in the **reducing** mode. This is the only difference from the earlier set of Solar Day oscillation cycles, which always begin in the **lengthening** mode.

> So, according to this OEARM, the Earth would also have it' 360 Solar Days per year after all. This would be at the very beginning of the 360 EARs Period orbits which would be occurring as per this OEARM, **126 million years away exactly**, as computed from when the EARS were 365 Earth Days/365 Solar days too.

This meaning that the 360 Earth Days would actually be also the same 360 Solar Days too.

Having established this theoretically, at least, the challenging question that still remains glaringly staring at us, is how is this Solar Cosmic mechanism of Solar Day oscillation cycles actually will come about to make these effective changes accordingly to establish all of this for us.

We know for sure that the EAR Period in reduction or in increasing is a definite contributor. We also know of the other definite contributor. This being the Earth's travel motion in it' orbit around the Sun. We also know of the third parameter, which is actually in conjunction with these two that actually brings the Sun each time back to the meridian.

However, all of the above parameters do not cause the Solar Day oscillation cycles to be in such operation as already explained and presented as such to you as in the previous paragraphs.

So, there must be another cosmic contributing source to this overall Solar Cosmic Mechanism which would make this to be possible. So after some thought having been put into it, I developed a hunch that it has possibly something to do with the Sun and Earth working in another possible combination that possibly causes the switching back and forth in an definitive oscillation cycle of the Meridian of the Sun at it' zenith. In other words, if the Meridian for some reason begins to oscillate as suggested, this then could have that contributing criteria which would in turn cause the Solar Day to be also directly oscillating within this very specific range to eventually establish for us the 360 Solar Days too as being the very same with the 360 EARs which produces for us the 360 Earth Days/orbit.

This also similarly will be the case with the 365 Solar Day Years; 364 Solar Day Years; 363 Solar Day Years; 362 Solar Day Years; 361 Solar Day Years; 360 Solar Day Year and then up again through this range from here to the 365 Solar Day Years again; a total journey of 252,000,000 Years. This journey length will also be explained to you clearly how it was obtained within this Addendum too.

How exactly this Solar Cosmic Mechanism proposition with the switching forth and back the Meridian in full oscillation cycles in the workings of the Sun and the Earth in combination would be taking place is not known to me currently.

So I leave this very possibility of it to be taking place, to the scientist of our day to figure this out; if this is indeed the case or not. Or even perhaps, hope against hope, to come out with their own propositions too. This would be great too.

Yet, this too would not have been known in the very first place, if I had not pursued the concept of the EAR Period being reduced or increased (increasing as per my proposal) as per the scientific established $1/1000^{th}$ second every 100 years, which in fact would cause eventually the 'number of Earth Days' in a Year to indeed be reduced or increased accordingly as the situation may be.

So, the very idea for the Earth to be eventually obtaining 360 Days in a year had in fact come about originally, even before my very concept was derived for this **undiscovered as yet cosmic event,** from the relevant referenced Holy Scriptures. Driven by this singular mindedness, that we will eventually have these Biblically declared 360 Day Years, had urged me on to investigate further and eventually come up with this concept of reading 'time' the original biblical way, based solely on the daily EAR Period. This led one thing to another, which successfully obtained for us, the '360 Earth Days Year' and now just as above, even the 360 Solar Day Years too.

This has also made me to realize somehow (through the further Holy Spirit promptings), that the 'time' with which we would be obtaining the very **next** '360 Days', would some mysterious way help us to actually construct the very **'number'** of the second beast!!! Incredible isn't it.

I will be achieving this very objective to some extent as just mentioned, in this 'Addendum', as you learn more about our Planet Earth' **'Oscillation Cycles'**. These are different from the above suggested oscillation cycles of the Solar Days/orbits.

Yes, this is also something very new being now introduced here for you to assimilate. It is not the same as to what Gordon Lindsay was projecting in his book, GOD's Plan of the Ages, but it is indeed also oscillating but independently to secular events but quite definitely connected still to some prophetic proclaimed scriptural events that have to be still played out in our Biblical History/Future. Through these Solar Cosmic Planetary established **'Oscillation Cycles'** for the Planet Earth, I will in turn be establishing or rather finding out together with you, the many times that we possibly already had the '360 Day Years'. Yes, I did say **had** despite having said throughout so far in this Book that we are yet to have our very first 360 Day Years. So, let me qualify this statement here, so that we all are standing on the same common understanding this far.

> Yes, we did actually have previously 360 Day Years too, but these were outside the well defined biblical period of our biblical human history.

This actually means that our Planet Earth was indeed experiencing the 365¼ day years and the 360 day years cycles long before man had even walked on this Earth. So, it was not something that had happened overnight, as such, but was and still is an inherent characteristic of our Planet Earth' orbiting of the Sun through its 'Oscillation Cycles' of 365¼ day years and the 360 day years. This cyclic phenomenon occurs regularly over large consistent period lengths of time.

In this respect, I must point out that I was indeed being very consistent in expressing in writing that it never had taken place, but was very careful to point out each time, if you do remember, **not** in our biblical human history. This then in no way means that they who had earlier proposed for a Pre-Noah' Flood 360 day years Earth orbit of the Sun being also as they had thought was the original orbit of the Earth were indeed accurate and correct. Far from it, as you will further find out here, and as already mentioned over and over again, **not** to have occurred in our biblical human history. This of course, also includes the Noah' Flood too.

So, their proposition still stands erroneous, if I dare say this, from the point of view as expressed in this book, and hopefully, you too will concur with me by the time you have finished reading.

Also, based on the findings as written in this 'Addendum', I will also be correcting some previous data or stated facts, as incorrectly established earlier in PART TWO of Book One. In actual fact, these 'Oscillation Cycles' were also already evident in PART TWO, but I did not see it until now.

So, you will learn that the 360 Solar Day Years, according to this Oscillation Earth Axis Rotation Model (OEARM) being proposed newly here, would indeed be at the very mid-base of each and every 'EAR Oscillation Cycle' covering 252,000,000 years in total.

> It is also at the very beginning of every **mid-base** EAR Oscillation Cycle (EAROC) that the speed of the EAR Period would begin to consistently increase once again, until it completes the second half of the EAROC. Then it will begin to consistently slow down accordingly, each time, to the very next mid-base, when it would once again speed up as before. This is the hypothesis.

This means there are in fact two dominant EARSS (Earth Axis Rotation Speed Switchover) bases in the entire Oscillation Cycle. This is where each time we will have a 'reverse change' in the speed of the EAR. The 'timing' of which is indeed controlled directly by the solar & planetary cosmic forces affecting it, and also indirectly, such as the effects on the tides and on the winds of the Earth. This in turn also contributes to this 'timing'. There could be also other contributing cosmic forces from outside of the Solar System, affecting it too. This is the hypothesis.

So, we have one at the very beginning of the EAROC i.e. when it begins to slow down from the 365 EARs, at a consistent rate day by day. This continues until it obtains it' minimum cosmic allowable axial axis rotational speed of 360 EARs per orbit at the mid-base.

Also, another one at the very beginning of the mid-base, as the EAR begins to increase with this same consistent rate that it had earlier slowed down with. This again is the hypothesis. It then finally reaches the end of the EAROC, as it obtains it' maximum cosmically allowable speed of 365 EARs per orbit.

This as per this hypothesis has being going on through these 'EAROCs' that have already been completed in the past and will continue as such even the one that is ongoing as currently and through those that are still yet to come in the Earth' near & far distant future.

> For your further realization, this very present Oscillation Cycle Phase, that even we ourselves are currently in, has indeed also already incorporated our **entire ancient biblical human historical events & accounts.**

This directly means, firstly: **Less** the Universe Biblical Creation Accounts that were encompassed or rather embedded, locked away within the most sparingly few divinely expressed 'perfect ten' biblical words, yet being so definably expressible once understood correctly as such.

Incidentally, these 'perfect ten words' as shown below (NKJV), make up the very first scriptural verse in the Holy Bible. This is of course Genesis 1:1.

In the beginning GOD created the heavens and the earth.

What a magnificent beginning for the Universe and for the opening in the Holy Bible!!! So awesome in just using ten words and yet so powerfully packed. It was so simplistic in it' description of the most complicated matter that anyone, anywhere, at anytime, could ever probably think about in their entire lifetime through scientific proposals/theories or otherwise; of how GOD ALMIGHTY had indeed created all of this with such magnificence at that. So majestically announcing **their** very joint divine 'agreement' originating for us the creation of the Universe and the Earth out of nothingness i.e. ex-nihilo. This is a Latin word describing the creation to have been created 'out of nothingness'. **Hebrews 11:3** also confirms this biblical derived/deduced scriptural truth, 'out of nothingness', which was first expressed and implied through GEN 1:1.

> HEB 11:3 By faith we understand that the worlds were **framed** by the **WORD OF GOD**, so that the things which are seen were **not** made of things which are visible.

The word **'framed'** as used here, is describing in meaning what Strong's #2675 was informing us as follows:

framed, katartizo in Greek: To arrange, set in order, equip, adjust, complete what is lacking, make fully ready, repair, prepare.

You could take the above variously provided meanings and use it as follows from my perspective of these:

To arrange by the **WORD of GOD** for the Universe as such in it' primeval state so that it will emerge exactly as we have it now with all the stars, galaxies, planets, and etc., as intended by the Creator, GOD ALMIGHTY.

Set it in order by the **WORD of GOD** so that it will emerge as it is now as being discovered through all the physics, mathematics, astronomy and cosmology being presently available and presented to us as such. The knowledge of which having been accumulated over hundreds of years through contributions made by eminent scientific minds in the past and still as of now by others and will continue as such into our future until we have acquired all the understanding necessary in order for us to fully comprehend how the Universe was indeed put together and to evidently exist as such.

This was so clearly though very briefly proclaimed to us as such by our GOD ALMIGHTY as in Gen 1:1 and then sometime later into our biblical history, having been elucidated in much more further detail possible, by the accompanying scripture in Heb 11:3 and the like.

To equip by the **WORD of GOD** from my perspective meaning to provide every possible 'whatever', which will make it possible for the Universe to finally emerge and be sustainable as it is over such large periods of time past and will remain as such until the very end of the Ages. This has been clearly foretold by our GOD ALMIGHTY from the very beginning of creation as in the Biblical Book, 'The First Book of Moses' which being commonly referred to as Genesis. And for the 'End of the Ages' as having been foretold too in the very last arranged Biblical Book, which being 'THE REVELATION OF JESUS CHRIST'.

> This 'whatever' will be more clearly defined for you a few pages down though it being my personal proposal or attempted contribution towards this 'awesome creation mystery' that still boggles the scientific minds despite centuries of engagement.

To adjust; complete what is lacking; make fully ready; repair and prepare by the **WORD OF GOD** is from my perspective as being described in it' entirety through this encompassing scripture Heb 11:3, was indeed possibly the relating of it to the *'Preparation & Development'* (P & D) of the Earth itself. This is yet another new suggested proposition of mine perhaps going against the very grain of doctrinal teaching on the subject of the duration of creation and the mode of creation itself. Yet I will attempt to do this though with much caution due to the above teaching a few pages down.

There are several biblical and scriptural truths in this scripture overall that need us to take it section by section to fully grasp and appreciate the very understanding that this scripture is professing to us and so eloquently at that too. One plausible way to understanding this scripture (HEB 11:3) from my perspective besides the above descriptions, is in its reconfirming of the commonly accepted understanding of the GOD ALMIGHTY Universe creation i.e. 'out of nothingness' it was created by the WORD of GOD. In other words GOD ALMIGHTY had indeed spoken it into existence and by HIS WILL it is sustained as such; meaning it exists just as the whole of GENESIS Chapter One professes in particular GEN 1:1; GEN 1:3; GEN 1:14 – 18.; also, Rev 4:11 in addition to the Heb 11:3, describes and confirms to us. This is accepted at least by Christians all over the world and the like-minded, as duly derived at from the reading and understanding of the above scriptures though not limiting to these only as the evidences for it are far from being exhaustive to say the least. And in continuation of it this particular scripture HEB 11:3 was in fact describing to us the **second stage** of this understanding, 'out of nothingness' creation.

This then being that GOD had created the **'whatever'** which is the invisible for the specific purpose to create the Universe 'out of nothingness' simultaneously or as the scripture puts it very clearly, *not made of things which are visible*. This evidently is pertaining to the Universe which was created 'out of nothingness' which now we can see it as evidently possible due to a transformation of some of the invisible 'whatever' created in the 'large complex processes' of the 'GOD ALMIGHTY CREATION' to become eventually the visible Universe.

So the Universe was made of things that were **not** visible in the first place as testified by Heb 11:3. This was the invisible 'whatever' which I had just introduced here in my attempt to explain this part of the scripture. This then had eventually caused the very **emergence** due to some GODLY induced process (which scientist would probably be able to discover in due time, I hope) to cause the transformation **of it** into the matter that now exists as the visible Universe just as our GOD ALMIGHTY had wanted it to be. Of course as just mentioned the unraveling of how this complex process did take place has to fall to our most eminent scientific minds of the present and of those who are yet to come onto the scene, to eventually unfold for us this 'process or processes', so that many of us could understand the science of it too.

Now scientific scholarship pertaining to Cosmology and matters relating to the Universe has mostly done away with the Holy Scriptures as expressed within the Holy Bible. This is due to their myopic requirement of it to being tested and verifiable through the evidences for the event/s as described by the Holy Scriptures within it as to be underpinning this Universe creation scriptural truth. However, in my ongoing opinion their requirement is just one part of the same parallel dimension of getting to the truth of the matter. For there is yet another and this is through 'FAITH'. Anyway, it is totally to their tremendous loss even from a scientific perspective of requirements, for the Holy Scriptures does indeed offers even the scientific mind many leads to scientific discovery and thought. It is indeed a Holy Book of provable and workable super scientific ideas if you put away your prejudices and earnestly look for it. I on the other hand have no problem to incorporating what science progressively informs us as scientific discoveries and theories are tested; verified; established and accepted by the discerning scientific community, to be blended with my understanding of the relevant scriptures concerned without any daunting to my Christian belief in our GOD ALMIGHTY.

As Galileo so aptly put it as follows:

"I DO NOT FEEL OBLIGED TO BELIEVE THAT THE SAME GOD WHO HAS ENDOWED US WITH SENSE, REASON AND INTELLECT HAS INTENDED US TO FORGO THEIR USE"

GALILEO GALILEI, 1564-1642

No problem at all because, I am of the opinion that all that science is paradoxically doing is further informing us of how all this had indeed come about with regards to the Universe to a great extent, together with all the life which is here to a greater extent; both of which GOD ALMIGHTY had intended it to be as exactly as such.

To a great or greater extent, meaning, many a time science will be riddled with 'missing parts' to their theories and proposals whenever it also involves what the Holy Scriptures were also revealing about the same thing too. In these circumstances, they will not be able to build up the whole entire picture. This is when and where with the appropriate understanding together with the proper application of the relevant Holy Scriptures, we would be able to eliminate these 'missing parts' and come to a better scriptural based scientific linked conclusion.

If for some reason, science had got it wrong, then all we need to do is to throw out this science and possibly wait till they get it right, so that we would eventually get the full picture too. The beauty of science is that it is always being challenged by fellow scientists to further fine tune it' accuracy and if found lacking, the once accepted scientific fact is then exposed to be not acceptable anymore. Therefore, whilst we are waiting for these revisions and amendments; the Holy Scriptures would remain as they were in the Holy Bible unscathed by this scientific linked generated setback. However, it would be not so easy to dispense away with, if it was instead, found to be lacking the other way round.

> As an example: Without the proper scriptural understanding of the 'Resurrection of our LORD and SAVIOUR JESUS CHRIST', there cannot be any Christianity and this could even lead us to think and perhaps even to know and to accept that there is indeed **no GOD** from this mistaken perspective. Such would be the possible implications and outcomes based on the connected 'Biblical TRUTHS' of the Holy Scriptures, if such interpretational errors were established with regards to these as an example and were to be propagated and accepted as such.

Even if lesser events, relatively speaking, as compared to the above 'Resurrection' was also found to be suspect and worse still to be in gross error not in its interpretation but in the 'Biblical Truth' itself, then this too would be quite disastrous, if we are unable to defend rightly the position.

So, as I understand it, the relevant scriptures do inform us through the reading of it that the Universe was indeed created ex-nihilo which when linked to Heb 11:3 and others similar like it, establishes to my understanding how this was or possibly could have been executed by our Creator as I deduce following the scriptural path. First the 'whatever' being the possible beginning of the

Universe to be, was created 'out of nothingness' as GOD ALMIGHTY spoke it into existence through the CREATION POWER of HIS WORD. This then progressed on as GOD ALMIGHY had intended it to emerge the Universe proper within the time frame as GODLY accorded to it. In a way, we can look at it as being one continuous process with a two stage development being unfolded for us for our benefit, to understand this entire creation better and the majesty of our CREATOR.

Now Science may be on the very verge of discovering to **almost** how this is indeed possible quite soon without the very understanding and/or acceptance of the scriptural testament of the 'out of nothingness' creation. For as I had mentioned earlier, they will establish their theories but there will still be some important missing parts which only the Holy Scriptures do hold the correct pieces to fit into this entire mystery. I am scripturally confident that they will indeed be able to do so and hopefully it will also include the 'whatever' ingredient as having been mentioned here.

> Thereby, having said all of the above, I have indeed a strong notion or intuition if I could call it that, the best candidate for this **'whatever'** which was not visible obviously not to us anyway as HEB 11:3 had clearly revealed that it was so, could be just **'pure energy'**.

> As many of you would know through our school science that energy cannot be created nor can it be destroyed by man anyway. It points then to our GOD ALMIGHTY, WHO through HIS HOLY WORD we know, can create this energy and if it is possible through my understanding of it to be pegged to being the 'whatever'. This is because there is nothing impossible with GOD. This is amongst our first premises for our belief in GOD ALMIGHTY, that there is nothing impossible with GOD.

Further to this, my Christian belief though which may not be supported by the scientific trained mind as already having been mentioned previously, is anchored in the absolute scriptural accuracy of the Holy Scriptures. It is on this very premise that dictates to me, the 'whatever' could just be this pure energy, which man cannot create nor destroy. This could be what GOD ALMIGHTY had created in the very first place being somewhat described through Heb 11:3, as my sincere interpretation view of it, for the sole purposes of creating the Universe 'out of nothingness' that we currently do have visibly evident all around us.

Besides creating this 'whatever' – it possibly being this pure energy that I am suggesting here, if this was indeed the case, then according to the scriptures, GOD ALMIGHTY had even measured out the 'SPACE' required for the Universe. This by default has become the 'Universe Space' in the larger SPACE that does surround it and the Universe was put into it.

This larger 'Space' obviously had already existed prior to the creating of the Universe. And it is quite possible, as a theoretical proposition, this measured Universe Space has the allocated expanding capacity or feature that though encapsulating the Universe at every stage of it' expansion, in turn maintains by some 'physics' the homogeneous expansion of the Universe itself from whatever size it was at the very beginning. In other words, the Universe Space could be itself responsible for the controlled and accelerating rate in the overall expansion of the expanding Universe and thereby plays it' part in this expansion. This eventually ensuring that the Universe does not expand beyond this 'Universe Space', as it reaches it' own outermost limits as divinely designed by our GOD ALMIGHTY within the **time frame (UET) as GOD had allocated to it** from the very beginning.

In other words when the pure energy of the early Universe was first created ex-nihilo, it was placed in this containment of Universe Space i.e. it' expandable SPACE, which kept this pure energy, homogeneously expanding throughout within it. This may offer us a possible reasoning why the Universe is as such homogeneously uniform though expanding throughout the Universe Space. This too, could be the very reason, for the Universe' elliptical shape, of which, we have been informed as such by the current scientific evidences.

In other words from my theoretical proposition, the containment itself does have some of it' own 'physics' written into it by our GOD ALMIGHTY that had kept this energy homogenous within it' expanding self. This has been going on if this was indeed the case, all through the journey of creation and the aftermath of it i.e. the 'Big Bang' and the inflation stage too, as the 'pure energy' through GODLY design began transforming some of itself due to the 'physics' into the pre-matter and eventually matter itself. This as it progressed expanding eventually became the visible Universe after the 'Big Bang and the inflation stage. All of this was due to the 'physics' existing within it at that time. The rest becoming what scientist have been describing to us as being 'Dark Matter' and 'Dark Energy' and all the time doing this in a uniform homogeneous manner.

The 'how part' i.e. the 'physics' for this to be possibly happening in the way that it is described as above, some of which is already known to scientific scholarship, can only be revealed to us by our eminent scientific minds. I however, had linked it to our Holy Scriptures accordingly, with a few additions of mine chipped in too.

The above attempt could probably explain the very beginnings of the Universe to the very end of it, which is indeed the underpinning amongst other things too of the wonderful scriptures as written in Rev 1:8 and also Rev 22:13 as shown below.

> **"I AM THE ALPHA AND THE OMEGA, THE BEGINNING AND THE END, THE FIRST AND THE LAST."**

In conclusion, in my attempt to explain the creation of the GOD created Universe, one could picture the Universe itself as being a gigantic ATOM with all of it' 'Atomic structure constituents' being held together within this GOD measured UNIVERSE SPACE. Whether there are other such 'UNIVERSE ATOMS' other than our own 'UNIATOM', is left for the scientific minds to explore, as they continue providing us with MultiVerse theories and other cosmological theories and etc.

Anyway, GOD ALMIGHTY provides us with these continuing hints for the creation 'out of nothingness', in the quantum understanding of how particles exists and do come into existence, which could possibly be an exact copy of how GOD ALMIGHTY had put this entire gigantic **UNIATOM** together.

All of the science that we do currently have of how this could be possible has actually been provided to us by our relevant eminent scientific minds so that the rest of us could learn how all of this GOD Creation was indeed put together. This could possibly be good so that they who are unable to believe in GOD ALMIGHTY with just their hearts could eventually do so also with their discerning minds and then proceed through intellectual evangelizing themselves to reach out to the scientific educated global populace that is ever growing in numbers worldwide.

This growing group is from my perspective another 'Nation' to itself, cutting across all borders if you do think of it, and thereby needs to be also 'reached' and preached the 'WORD OF GOD' accordingly, less they do perish which is not pleasing or acceptable to our GOD ALMIGHTY.

Also, I did mention earlier, this 'pure energy' possibly being the 'whatever' had in fact emerged the matter or rather the precursor of the matter. This idea of energy transforming into matter was actually borrowed from current scientific scholarship and scientists have informed us, this pre-matter, could be in the plasma state at that time due to the very high temperatures possibly existing in that early miniature environment which they have suggested with regards to the 'Big Bang' and the aftermath of it through the inflation stage. This could be the similar case in the Pre-Big Bang Universe. Well any way this is better left to our scientific minds to reveal to us accordingly.

One such person who comes to my mind at this moment would be Monsignor Georges Lemaitre who had been the first to propose in his time, the 'primeval atom/s', which suggested the 'pre-matter state' at the time of the 'Big Bang'. He had also suggested that the Universe was indeed expanding and not in a static state which Einstein was indeed proposing at the time.

Eventually, after some time had passed, Einstein too was convinced that the Universe was also indeed expanding and was not static, anyway, at his current time.

Monsignor Lemaitre was in fact the very first learned individual although being a 'man of the cloth' (a Jesuit Priest), who had provided us with the very first scientific understandings for the origin of the Universe.

> This sometime later became the established and accepted 'Big Bang' theory for it. Unfortunately, all the glory and credit had bypassed him as he was not fully and properly credited with it at the time. Thereby, others like Edwin Hubble who had in 1929 able to take up and complete the science and the mathematics of Monsignor which in turn was established by Stephen Hawking' own science to be the 'Big Bang' origin of the Universe.

This 'pure energy' emerging the 'pre-matter', as being proposed by our scientists now, is trying to capture this very event happening i.e. **energy becoming matter.** This they are trying to do through the accelerating particle experiment using the HADRON ACCELERATOR COLLIDER that is located in CERN, Switzerland. Einstein had actually established this theoretically in reverse as suggested in his famous equation:

$$E = Mc^2$$

> Yet as of the present, Scientist are still **not able** to provide us with any substantial explanation of how all the **'matter'** which does make up the Universe to be the Universe had been present in that very dense state as they had suggested had existed 'Pre-Big Bang' in the very first place.

> In other words, though the origin of the Universe as scientifically suggested was in that dense state (Pre-Big Bang), it was also through their very scientifically calculated suggestion, that it had encompassed or encapsulated all of the matter i.e. including every particle or anti-particle in any form that the scientific mind could possibly perceive or has yet to perceive could be accounted for, had existed in that extremely dense state. This extremely high crushing pressure and unthinkable high temperatures present in this dense state then became proceeding paramount at some stage for the 'Big Bang' to have occurred.

> If at all they had attempted as I had understood from a lecture given at M.I.T. by Professor Dr Alan Guth, titled 'The Universe and 3 Examples' dated 22/May/2009 having been also recorded and placed on YouTube, which I was fortunate to stumble upon only recently in April 2012; was that it was already there. **Existing as it was from the very beginning, meaning, including the Pre-Big Bang beginning!!!**

> This in some essence is also being very 'scientifically truthful', although, without being able to offer any scientific reasoning to explain for it' very existence as such, which as they state, then became the unfathomable gigantic Universe after the Big Bang.

I am attempting through my understanding of the relevant scriptures to be providing the reason or reasons of how all that matter or rather 'pre-matter' had been present before the 'Big Bang' had indeed taken place. This in turn I do sincerely hope perhaps naively though could provide us with a much clearer picture of a GOD created Universe from ex-nihilo from a scriptural based scientific linked perspective. This meaning in the 'Pre-Big Bang' state, which scientist simply are unable to explain because they had started their thinking from the other end of things for they did not in the first place rely upon what our GOD ALMIGHTY had so generously informed us in Gen 1:1 and which I had linked it to Heb 11:3.

My understanding of the 'Pre-Big Bang' GOD created status of the Universe to be, does not necessary deny or discard with the 'Big Bang' Theory or for that matter the 'Inflation Theory' that had proceeded as suggested by Professor Dr Alan Guth immediately from the 'Big Bang' event. Of course my understanding is also totally dependent on what scientists are informing us about this currently as scientific scholarship progresses on. So my understanding with regards their 'Big Bang-Inflation Theory', and etc., will be based on what they are continuing to propose and scientifically establish as time and science progresses on.

Yet, scientist too have also informed us that they still do not know what this 'Big Bang' really was indeed and that they only know of the **aftermath** possible effects of the 'Big Bang'. And this was when the expanding Universe was about 380,000 years or so at best after the 'Big Bang' had supposedly occurred. Although, according to them, it still does imply of a 'Big Bang' having occurred, yet there is nothing that is known of the 'Big Bang' itself. They then go on to inform us that it could have been also possible that no Bang had actually or was necessary to have occurred in the very first place. Anyway, the Inflation Theory has been introduced to scientifically explain to us what exactly could have taken place, or had indeed taken place, if I understand it correctly, at the instant of the Big Bang occurrence.

Prior to the Inflation Theory, scientists were only able to go as deep as 380,000 years from the 'Big Bang' supposedly occurrence. This is as far back that they can possibly see into the 'Cosmic Background Microwave Radiation' data as provided by the COBE EXPLORER Satellite. Further back than this, remains as theories and hypotheses. Of course my opinion here would not amount to much or probably even zilch, as I do not have any academic credentials to back me up except that I am a Theist. However, what I am unfolding here is through my scriptural perspective of the relevant Holy Scriptures, as I reveal and do support it' scientific implications or influences. For I do propose besides all the other aspects of it i.e. the theological, the literal, the allegorical and the historical; that it is indeed a really wonderful source of scientific facts and **'Biblical Technologies'**. These are present as such in the Holy Scriptures indeed for us to be able to scientifically copy, to a certain extent, for the overall benefit of mankind.

> Anyway, coming back to my proposal: It is like to say that the 'whatever' or rather 'pure energy' which I am envisaging could possibly be the invisible part that Heb 11:3 was describing to us, in the creation of the Universe ex-nihilo, could very well be the very 'stem cells' of the Universe. That is if I could put it to you in this biological manner.

This is the 'pure energy' to emerge the primeval atomic structures of the Pre-Universe.

We are informed by Professor Dr Alan Guth of the possible existence of precursor matter at the very beginning, if I understand it correctly from the lecture as mentioned above. He is also the brilliant originator of the 'Inflation Theory'.

They have also evidently assumed for not having any firm theory of it, that all the matter that does exist today, had existed in that very dense state which was given a scientific based calculated size. Now through the 'Inflation Theory', this has further been reduced to as per the revised calculation to being just a **speck** before the 'Big Bang' had occurred. This inflation stage of the 'Big Bang' according to Dr Alan Guth lasted 10^{-37} seconds for each phase of the inflation stage as it expanded exponentially through these phases of such similar brief periods of time. And if I understand it correctly from his lecture, there were about **18** such phases before the matter emerged as large as a marble Universe.

However, as already mentioned, they are unable as yet to suggest anything of how all the matter got there in the very first place though which they have suggested had been compressed into just a **speck** at the very beginning of the 'Big Bang'. This is where my suggested scriptural perspective, comes in to close the loop through this only **GOD created possibility** of the GOD created 'pure energy' being a good candidate to being the 'whatever'. This is what I am proposing here as being offered in it' transition to emerge all of this pre-matter which later became the visible matter that we can see and that which we still cannot see being the invisible dark matter, including that of the invisible dark energy. This also we cannot see but know scientifically that all of these are present as definite constituents of the gigantic Universe that we now have as such.

> So it was indeed a **building up** to the possible critical time of the 'Big Bang' which would then be including the 'Inflation Stage' occurrence. Thereby, my scriptural based perspective offering was indeed not a compression as being suggested by the current accumulated scientific scholarship.

> I must be out of my mind to be offering such a Universe model against these great minds but the driving force behind this is quite apparent being the relevant Holy Scriptures and hopefully my correct interpretation of it accordingly. This will provide the very elusive answer of how all of this 'matter' had existed 'Pre-Big Bang Pre-Inflation Stage'. This is an answer that scientist will not be able to provide us with despite their combined genius and combined joint effort in attempting to do so unless they find a way to couple it to the relevant Holy Scriptures as having been mentioned here.

> This 'Dark Energy' and 'Dark Matter' could probably in turn give us a lead for the possible existence of this 'pure energy' in the 'Pre-Big Bang Pre-Inflation Theory Stage' for the origin of the Universe being created ex-nihilo.

> Perhaps, this was what the larger portion of the 'pure energy' got transformed into and until scientists do discover what this is all about, we can only be on the sidelines, to wait and see what would their eventual outcome findings turn out to be.

This 'pure energy' exact quantity as **framed** by GOD ALMIGHTY in the evidential scriptural description as provided us in Heb 11:3 was GODLY blueprinted just to specifically emerge this 4.6% type visible matter that we have in the visible Universe and the remaining invisible to become what scientist currently refer to being as Dark Matter (about 22%) and the rest as being Dark Energy (about 73%). This is the total scientifically computed possible mass for the entire Universe. This seems to be inevitably describing probably the same ratios in our ability as currently to utilize our Brain power or Brain Matter (only about 3 – 5% of the entire mass in our thinking process). The rest probably controlling and monitoring our entire body functions in order to keep us alive and well.

As mentioned, these percentages breakdown was provided to us by the wonderful and amazing scientific minds that our GOD ALMIGHTY had provided for us who had measured or rather weighed the Universe through their mathematics and the science for it.

As mentioned previously also, it was Dr Alan Guth who had proposed, if I understand it correctly, that it could have begun or started when the Universe or rather the Pre-Universe was just a mere speck. This speck being about **a billionth in size of a single proton particle,** until it had finally emerged as marble size before continuing on in it' normalized expansionary phase which scientists say is still continuing even as currently. All of this initial exponential expansion i.e. the initial inflation phases (**18** phases in all, if I understand it correctly); each had lasted for just a mere 10^{-37} seconds!!!

This science is simply amazing and there is still more yet to come, I understand. Anyway, I want you to just remember this very short time distance of the inflation period phases, each being 10^{-37} seconds. Also do remember that the Universe, as I had earlier proposed, had in the very beginning of its creation, begun in the **building up** and **not** in the compressing of all that matter into an extremely dense state, as having been presented by scientific scholarship, including that of Professor Dr Alan Guth.

Now just another piece of very interesting science as provided to us by none other than the extraordinary super genius Einstein, who had through his theory and stupendous world acclaimed equation, $E = Mc^2$, provided us amongst other things with the understanding for the conservation of energy. That **Energy cannot be created** meaning essentially not by any circumstance whatsoever then what is already available and present. I want to add to this thinking, the scriptural perspective, i.e. **not by man**, to make the explicit distinction that this obvious Einstein limitation was not pertaining to GOD ALMIGHTY even if it did not cross his mind or was of any relevance to him at the time when he proposed this to us. The second thing that Einstein informed us was that Energy neither **could be destroyed** by any circumstance though it could be changed to another type or level of energy. Again I would want to include the scriptural perspective, i.e. **not by man**, to make the same distinction that GOD ALMIGHTY definitely could.

For as Einstein had put it and which is accepted the world over especially with the scientific community; **Energy cannot be created nor destroyed.** This could be the very reason to point this scientific established fact directly to a GOD ALMIGHTY created ex-nihilo Universe.

Einstein' theory however, does not offer us any explanation of the more philosophical and metaphysical question: "Where did all the energy that exists as it does in the first place had come from???"

> We cannot claim that it was just there as it was, since the Universe is scientifically accepted also now as being finite. This meaning, that it would have an eventual ending and thereby must have a beginning too. This is the exact reasoning that can be derived through the Holy Scriptures which was proclaiming to us this exact conclusion very loudly as in Gen 1:1. This as a scientific theoretical fact was indeed established somewhat recently through the Arvind Borde/ Alexander Vilenkin / Alan Guth Theorem.

This theorem directly informs us that for any cosmological modal of our currently known expanding Universe or that of the MultiVerses which are being currently proposed too, all of these too, must have a beginning and have an ending. This makes the Universe to be a **finite** creation just as the Biblical Scriptures have foretold to us accurately so long ago. For it will eventually have an end too.

> This is a clear example of the 'missing parts' that I was mentioning a little earlier with regards to the scientific reasoning leading to discovery and theories when it also involves what the Holy Scriptures do tell us of the same events that are scientifically being researched.

So, this proposed 'pure energy' having been created by GOD ALMIGHTY as per my proposition being the 'Universe in transition' i.e. before transforming some of itself into the visible matter, would then of course be at all times keeping in line with the Einstein offering for the conservation of energy.

> Therefore, **HEB 11:3** was distinctively correct (Science-wise though in the 'ROOT FORM') from my scriptural perspective of it, in revealing to us that the things which are **seen** were **not** made of things which are visible.

> HEB 11:3 **By faith** we understand that the worlds were framed by the **word of GOD**, so that the things which are **seen** were **not** made of things which are visible.

> This then had emerged into the Universe proper eventually and that we can only understand how this **phenomena** of emerging the 'invisible' into the visible Universe that we can see and observe as such, is **by faith**. However, coupling this together with the relevant science that are being currently used in attempting to discover this exact thing happening, would hopefully reveal this exact process eventually to us someday soon I hope.

And before someone out there shouts, "What is Faith"; Heb 11:1 as appended below explains to us this exact thing of what Faith is as follows:

> Heb 11:1 Now **faith** is the substance of things hoped for, the **evidence** of things not seen.

The Universe that we now have in this Universe Space and time is indeed still possibly going through its 'Big Bang' aftermath paces, i.e. being in this expansionary phase, though as scientist have informed us being very much slower than the inflation stage phases. This expansion or moving away from us as per my understanding of the relevant scriptures would quite possibly culminate when the Universe finally occupies all of it' pre-measured 'Universe Space' as provided for it by none other than our CREATOR GOD ALMIGHTY. And then who knows it probably could become a 'Static Universe' at that future time, exactly as Einstein had thought that the Universe was in his time though i.e. Static, not expanding away.

It was Monsignor Georges Lemaitre who was in fact proposing to Einstein the very opposite, that it was dynamic and expanding. We now know that it is as what Monsignor Lemaitre was informing us as such in his time as later confirmed by Edwin Hubble and then through the 'Big Bang' theory as established by Stephen Hawking and now further substantiated and followed by Alan Guth through his 'Theory of Inflation' being the latest piece to be added to the commonly accepted cosmological model presently.

> And it had to first take a 'Priest of Science' to tell this other eminent scientist, Einstein, the way that it all actually is and to point him too in the right direction!!!

> Heb 11:1 Now **faith** is the substance of things hoped for, the **evidence** of things not seen.

Although the Universe was not actually the thing that we had hoped for, for it had pre-existed before us ever coming into being, however, this then brings into proper perspective the biblical scripture that was as mentioned in my previous pages being Heb 11:3. This is pertaining to our understanding with regards to how the Universe was possibly indeed created and had come into it' very existence through the underpinning of 'what faith' actually is capable of doing for us besides making every GOD generated mystery understandable and acceptable as such. In fact it would be good for us to further understand and explore with our mind, 'what faith is', by reading the entire biblical book of Hebrews. It could become a new firm science or is it already, besides the theological aspect of it. For GOD HIMSELF (JESUS CHRIST) had described it (I am paraphrasing here) that if you have the faith as **large** as a mustard seed, you could tell the mountain to move!!! The exact scripture is as follows:

Mathew 17:20 So Jesus said to them, "Because of your unbelief; for assuredly, I say to you, if you have faith as a mustard seed, you will say to this mountain, 'Move from here to there,' and it will move; and nothing will be impossible for you.

In one Sunday Service Sermon, which I had the opportunity to attend, the Pastor preaching delivered a startling revelation which I had never heard preached as such before with regards to this exact scripture. He revealed through his teaching, if I understood it correctly, that the 'Mustard Seed Faith' which JESUS CHRIST was talking and referring to here was not about our GOD given measure of faith (Rom 12:3 refers to this gracious provision). It was indeed JESUS CHRIST FAITH through HIM indwelling in us being our anointing and our witness when we have truly become such **believers** and having such **faith** in our LORD JESUS CHRIST. In this aspect, we would then be able to do any remarkable thing necessary as required and as needed by us. And I would like to propose to this here, as and when it is qualified by the GOD condition - according to **HIS WILL** and thereby, acted upon by **HIS FAITH** which was required only in such mustard seed size faith, but nevertheless, just the same which was working through us at the time. This is all that you and I will ever need.

This is something for you to spend a little time to think about, whether you are able to agree to this revelation or otherwise. Please do let me know either way. I would be most happy to share it with the pastor concerned.

There was another interesting and unique use of the mustard seed analogy or parable by JESUS CHRIST that in my understanding of it actually further cements what the Pastor had preached on that Sunday. It is as appended below with some background to it given to you for JESUS needing to use this mustard seed analogy again.

When JESUS was teaching in one of the synagogues on the Sabbath an incident took place when HE took it upon HIMSELF to heal there and there a woman who had been inflicted with an infirmity for **18** years. She could not raise herself up. In other words she had possibly a severe crooked or fused spine as suggested in the commentary which made this impossible for her.

This compassion shown by JESUS CHRIST on the Sabbath was immediately shot down by a ruler of the synagogue who protested JESUS' action on such a day as the Sabbath. You can read how JESUS rebuked this ruler.....in the continuation of Luke 13:15-17. And it was here that JESUS had revealed something very profound in the following scripture of Luke 13:18-19 as follows:

18 Then HE said, "What is the Kingdom of GOD like? And to what shall I compare it?

JESUS then goes on to answer these very questions as follows:

19 "**It is like a mustard seed**, which a man took and put in his garden; and it grew and became a large tree, and the birds of the air nested in its branches."

Through this parable, JESUS CHRIST was comparing the Kingdom of GOD to being like a mustard seed which was planted, I envisage on good soil, and as a normal consequence of this resulted in such magnificent growth to attract life all around to it. This reveals to me was indeed JESUS CHRIST GOD the SON in fact referring to HIMSELF being planted through faith in HIM by any individual through the consequence of the individual' open willingness to accept **JESUS CHRIST** indwelling as he totally accepts though gradually perhaps at first GOD ALMIGHTY in a born again Christian experience. This acceptance and surrender then continuing growing from strength to strength on the promises of our LORD and SAVIOUR JESUS CHRIST, as we move through HIS blessings in spiritual prosperity, as each one of us then ultimately acquiring through GODLY grace the freely GOD given Salvation as our justified reward and inheritance in and through **CHRIST JESUS**. Amen

So the Kingdom of GOD is similar to the 'MUSTARD SEED FAITH' mentioned in Mathew 17:20. JESUS CHRIST is indeed the 'Kingdom of GOD' which indwells in us when we accept HIM as our LORD and SAVIOUR.

> The scripture in Luke 17:21, describes this exact understanding as follows: "nor will they say, 'See here!' or 'See there!' For indeed, the **Kingdom of GOD is within you**."

This is simply amazing!!!

It is not referring to a heavenly place; a kingship or even to a destination, but to JESUS CHRIST GOD the SON HIMSELF will be abiding in you at first as small as a spiritual mustard seed with the potential of immense and profitable growth as you continue relying upon HIM more and more each day with every breath you take and every step you make!!! Alleluia, PRAISE BE TO HIS HOLY NAME. Amen

With this very understanding of the Holy Scriptures, it is quite alright, I propose, for Cosmologist/Physicist Dr Alan Guth in his 'Inflation Theory' to project and describe through his brilliant calculations, that the Universe to be was just a **speck** (i.e. a billionth part of a single proton particle) before inflation had been initialized at the very beginning of the 'Big Bang'.

Also, evidently, based on this very understanding 'out of nothingness', had indeed divinely authenticated from the very beginning, their divine authorship of the Holy Scriptures and the Universe at large. Science will eventually come around to proving this to be true too, scientifically; well I hope so anyway within my lifetime.

Secondly, from my perspective of the relevant scriptures: **'In the beginning'** also describes the very time period before the very clearly accentuated 'Preparation & Development' (P & D) accounts period, which have been incorrectly though popularly referred to traditionally as being the **'Creation Week'** by most of Christendom i.e. across all Denominations.

This is not only in name that we do so, but that we actually do profess that the 'Creation Week' describes the very creation time of the Universe and of course the Earth inclusive within the Six Days. This was our Catechism and Sunday schooling then. Perhaps in these well known scientific times, this may or may not have been modified too.

However, according to this 'brand new thinking' that I had developed as of recently in this Book with regards to the P & D accounts of the Earth as having been presented and introduced to you; the traditional concepts and understanding for the 'Creation Week' is quite obviously not possible to be accommodated anymore as such. For the 'P & D' accounts being referenced here, are with regards to the making of the **Earth** habitable for plant, animal, bird, fish, every creeping creature, etc., and above all the ultimate purpose being for human life for GOD's GLORY to be manifested in us. All of this P & D activity has been well covered through the biblical 'Day One to Day Six' inclusive. This then actually describes as per this new thinking, which as you can see only incorporates the P & D of the Earth. For the fact of the matter is that by that time the Universe and the Earth had already existed, as it had been, as described by the very first verse of Gen 1:1.

In the beginning **GOD created the heavens** *and* **the earth.**

This scripture was not describing the process as such but of the time period in which this was GODLY accomplished i.e. being within this time frame of **'In the beginning'**.

> This 'P & D' of the Earth is in fact expressed in greater detail, as we find out in the immediate and subsequent scriptures of Genesis 1:2-25. This covers the 'P & D' accounts of the Earth, as described in Day One until much of the Sixth Day. The 'Seventh Day' was not a Day for the 'P & D', but a 'Day' of rest.

The final introduction of 'people' came in the very Sixth Day, as described in the 'P & D' accounts of the Earth, together with the land animals. Genesis 1:24-31 confirms.

Genesis 2:7-25, further expounded this to even greater creation detail. We find this out firstly, with regards to the special creation of the man; Adam.

Then secondly, we also find out about the special preparation and development of the 'garden', eastward in Eden.

Then finally, we find out about the amazing and remarkable special creation of the woman; Eve.

GOD had by then completed making the Earth most perfectly hospitable, going even far beyond than merely making it just humanly habitable. As easily observable, it is so majestically beautiful from every angle that you may think or be able to conceive it in your mind better still do open your eyes and see...............

Sometime during the Sixth Day period, Adam was created in that very special manner, that we have all come to know through Genesis 2:7. He was then literally physically placed in this special GOD prepared 'Eden Garden'. Just before the Sixth Day had actually come to an end, our LORD GOD ALMIGTHY even went to the extent at some point in this same 'Day', to providing an appropriate companion, to be a helper, to perfectly accommodate Adam in this new and special garden environment.

> This alone provides us with the clear understanding that each of the 'SIX DAYS' were not to be as we had always thought these to be, as being merely 24 Earth Hour Days. Rather quite apparently a very much longer period of time, possibly running into the millions of years or more. It could be for many that our Christian teaching is possibly also in line with this too now.

Eve was created to cater to all of Adam' wants and needs and of course for the very divine and higher purpose and that was to bring into this world together with Adam, the biblical generations to come. Genesis 2:8-25 confirms.

'Helper' does not mean being a maid of sorts but to help in every aspect possible. This including, making this team of **a** man and **a** woman; companion and friend; husband and wife; father and mother to being a GODLY ordained partnership through the blessed sacrament of matrimony.

Also, Eve' own GOD provided contributing constitution in this matrimonial partnership, is divinely expressed and written within this one word of being a 'helper', is simply amazing and yet truly complex indeed. This has been however, unfortunately misunderstood and abused to the maximum in many nations and still is even to this day. Eve' position is indeed biblically and scripturally a very respectable and awesome position within the matrimonial partnership team as mentioned.

Adam (man, male) has his own divinely constituted position being very well consolidated appropriately within this context of 'partnership living' to the part that Eve (woman, female) has to play too within this GODLY ordained relationship for life. In other words 'Eve' can never usurp the position of 'Adam' in the eyes of GOD and which for all intents and purposes should also be rightly in the eyes of this world. Yet Satan has been working night and day to reverse this as much as possible or to upset this status quo in order to destroy GOD' overall divine plan. And the reality of the matter is that Satan seems to be succeeding in most families today as what we see of how society is changing and becoming more dysfunctional every day. Yet I am totally confident this GOD established Family Unit would still prosper despite this destructive action.

Well anyway all of this comes through with this 'new revelation', which I had simply termed as being the 'P & D' accounts of the Earth, being biblically expressed accordingly from Gen 1:2 onwards.

This had then catapulted Homo sapiens or rather 'Human Beings' into this particular and important 'Oscillation Cycle Phase', that we (i.e. you and I) also find ourselves in, even as of today. It is the one and the same 'Oscillation Cycle' in which the Biblical Adam & the Biblical Eve had also been in, as they walked on this Earth during their time!!!

All of the above was to establish this particular fact in this book that is being written, which was the basic fundamental reason that had made me to go into and to have continued for a while the further expounding of the Genesis Chapters, 1 & 2. I sincerely hope that it will be found acceptable at least to some extent.

This was done to drive home these important & relevant points in my further efforts to correctly realize my very quests too.

I am of the very understanding that with regards to this important but indeed extremely brief divine summary, as we have it in Genesis 1:1; it is in definite regards to the creation of the entire Universe and of our Earth.

Now, this does not imply nor is contrary to what scientists are evidently proving and having shown us with regards to the 'newer developments' that are currently still progressing on in the Universe.

With regards to this continued progressing, it is what the scripture expresses to us too; that is everything which was needed for it to exists, expand and to develop into the Universe, as we had it then and will have it in the future, was indeed finished and available in the biblical time frame of **'In the beginning'**. This very 'expression' in my opinion is further expounded and re-emphasized in Genesis 2:1 & 2:4.

In other words, in our own local cosmic context, the Sun and the rest of the Solar Planetary System, which includes the Earth had come into planetary existence sometime very much later after much of the Universe proper was brought into it' very own existence. Here too in the scripture of GEN 1:1, this continued progress is quite evident.

You will have more detail explanation of this as indicated below.

However, before advancing there, this further defines that the 'Universe Creation', which does include the ongoing **development** of the Universe and the continuous maintaining of it' universal equilibrium in all aspects pertaining to its existing, is also indeed a progressing one. For we have been informed of new galaxies being established and new stars being born, of course many of these having happened hundreds of light years ago or even more; others dying or already have become black holes long ago. Even new planetary systems evolving has being picked up and relayed to us even as currently by the Hubble telescope and also by other sophisticated scientific equipment.

> In fact, we will learn in Part Three, from the relevant scriptures as found in 2Esdras (an Apocryphal Biblical Book), what this time frame **'in the beginning'** actually amounts to. Yes, we will find this out with scriptural certainty. Not only this, but right here in this Addendum, we will also discover, when our Planet Earth had most probably come into it' own existence too through biblical calculation parameters!!!

Yes, this may come as a very big surprise to you and even perhaps to your utter amazement, that GOD had indeed revealed to us scripturally, even all of this. Unfortunately, all of this had been missed out much earlier, even though it had been very highly scrutinised and had been engaged in extremely detailed biblical study, scholarship and discourse of our biblical past and future. Roman Catholicism, Protestantism and even through the vast Evangelical biblical scholarship had not provided us quite exactly, what this measure of time 'in the beginning' really amounted to nor have they even started to explore this.

Then came the second part of Genesis 1:1.......
And the earth.

This informs us of the additional ongoing development or rather coming on stream of the Earth into the Universe' Solar Planetary grouping being the third planet distanced from the Sun. This is from my understanding of the scriptures as it also provides us with the real sense of having a large time gap in the ongoing developments of the Universe and then later of the Earth itself when it came on stream too.

The biblical use of the word **'and'** immediately followed by **'the earth'**, in this extremely brief divine summary of the Universe and it' future Solar (our Sun) and it' Planets, was another foundation that had generated this 'new revelation', i.e. with regarding to the 'P & D' accounts of the Earth.

> The scriptural word **'and'** as used in this very context, you would soon be finding out, actually separates the creation of the Universe by several billions of years from the subsequent entry or formation of the Solar Planetary System in the Milky Way Galaxy. This is indeed one such galaxy amongst the billions out there as scientifically substantiated!!! This is simply awesome to say the least.

> This is indeed a completely new understanding for the 'creation accounts', which have indeed just come through, as it is, in these few days since Easter of April 2004.

This could give you a hint of how long this book is taking me to complete, since I had first started writing it several years or so, ago.

This also eventually had led me into this newly discovered direction of the **Earth' Oscillation Cycles**, which actually directly follows the consistent reduction/increase i.e. reversal speed changes operating in the EAR. This EAR speed changes have already been explained to you in Part Two in greater detail. These changes are indeed stretched over considerably long periods of time, following a constant rate. This is not to be mistaken for those being of the 'immediate variations' in the EAR, which occurs throughout the year during it' orbit around the Sun.

Now, the First Day of 'P & D' until the Sixth Day of 'P & D' inclusive were all pertaining to the way GOD was indeed uniquely preparing & developing the emergence of the Planet Earth, from it' 'cocoon like pre-state' (although being quite violent in nature) to metamorphosis into a beautiful, dynamic and vibrant life sustaining Planet Earth. This obviously, without any doubt had set it with specific divine intention apart from the rest of the Universe Creation. Unmatchable from every aspect, to what we now have called it somewhat amazingly and affectionately, as being **'the big blue marble'**.

You must take notice now and irrefutably realise that the Earth was indeed *already in existence*, even before **'P & D' Day One** had actually begun it' 'time' ticking. For the 'P & D' Day One, to my understanding of these Scriptures, came after the biblical time frame of **'in the beginning'** had been completed. It explicitly describes scripturally the actual **'pre-condition'** state of the Earth as first being completely immersed in water, at that point in time, before it too was 'reborn' through the Six Days of 'P & D' into what we have it now.

Genesis 1:2 confirms.

To think of it, every human birth, can be somewhat likened to that of the Pre-Earth, as it also is completely immersed in 'water' i.e. amniotic fluids, before being actually born into this natural world of sunshine, air, water and land.

Most scientific based descriptions of the 'Pre-Earth', informs us that there were indeed no 'life forms' of any kind whatsoever that you may think of or may have come to know of now, that had existed on Planet Earth at that pre-state period. It was completely and absolutely lifeless, not even the most primitive and simplest of life forms had existed. Zilch. This completely agrees with the Scriptures. No conflict here. Then scientists go on to inform us that the atmosphere was mostly made up of methane and hydrogen sulphide with very little oxygen. No problem here either. They also go on to further describing huge volcanoes, which were in continuous eruptions; gigantic earthquakes; gigantic tsunamis and other gigantic natural catastrophes and so forth.

Yet still their description based on what information they could gather through science and scientific hypotheses are still not enough. For it lacks that added dimension, or perspective that only the Holy Scriptures can provide us with such clarity though being brief in it' details. As an example, even before the methane and hydrogen sulphide atmosphere were present on the Earth, the Scriptures do reveal to us that the Earth was indeed first completely immersed in liquid water and that it was gripped in indescribable darkness.

Further to the above, their scientific based description of the various massive land masses which existed in the Cambrian period, such as that of Africa; South America; Antarctica; India and Australia, were according to them indeed under one huge land mass, which they called or named as 'Gondwanaland'. This is indeed biblically very interesting. The others were Angara and Euramerica. All this they say may have happened 500 million years ago and about 300 million years ago, these huge land masses or continents, all had become joined together as one giant continent, called Pangaea. This was referenced from the book, 'Chronicle of the World', jointly published by Longman Group UK & Chronicle Communications Ltd.

> More importantly, all of this actually reflects, what the Scriptures had already revealed to us as in Genesis 1:9-10.

What science had done or discovered was to elaborate and define even more clearly to us, this scriptural briefness in this divine given summary, much more vividly and much more in-depth.

GOD ALMIGHTY called the dry land, Earth. This as a matter of course eventually became the name of the Planet, and it still stands today. All the other planets and stars and other entities in the universe, have been named by us. GOD ALMIGHTY also gave us the name of the waters that he had made to be gathered together in one place, as he was also allowing the dry land to appear. The name as divinely given was 'seas' and in some other translations even as 'oceans'; but we do get the point.

All this had taken place on the Earth, when GOD ALMIGHTY had actually selected it from amongst the millions, or rather billions of planets out there. Once this 'divine selection' had been made, we are also informed through the very scriptures about it' magnificent transformation.

This was only achievable, by the further and direct intervention of our LORD GOD ALMIGHTY. We are clearly informed about this transformation through it' 'Six P & D Day' process, as described in the first two chapters of Genesis and even in John 1:1-3 and 1:10.

You will also notice in your individual and careful study of the Scriptures especially that of the Old Testament, our LORD GOD ALMIGHTY had repeatedly made all kinds of 'selections', as revealed to us. This also means throughout time and space and even amongst those spiritual beings in the spiritual realm, that have been with GOD before 'time' and 'space' was created and had been set into motion. This is indeed a deduced assumption on my part, in the overall sense, but one could easily be inclined to understand as such, when you read through the scriptures yourselves.

Take some time to rethink through all of this, if you do need to.

So, this 'divine selection' of the Planet Earth, and to have it transformed into the only habitable planet as we know it through the scriptures, making it the singularly unique planet in the entire universe, should not come as an arguable surprise to you at all. Of course this depends, if you do accept my proposition, with regards to the 'selection' issue.

Why do we generally perceive or suggested to perceive that we are rather second best with regards to the scientific hypotheses which has been so popularised by the movies and through television that there are other or rather could be more intellectual sophisticated 'civilizations' out there i.e. alien life forms which are more advanced than us???

Why can't we just accept GOD' biblical revelation that we are actually the only living beings in the entire Universe and that someday, we will be the future space colonists perhaps populating 'habitable planets' as having been discovered by us? It is probably time for them who continue making such suggestions to come to terms that our LORD GOD ALMIGHTY only created us human beings in their image, as testified by the evidential Holy Scriptures. This acceptance should clearly end this hopeless and futile confusion and direct our energies and monies in more fruitful challenges ahead.

So far, the Holy Scriptures have yet to be found wanting or failing, in any of it' biblical revelations. No modern scientific discovery from any scientific discipline has ever overturned any truth or of any evidence that the Holy Scriptures have revealed or stated within it. Please do consider this carefully. Whether it is concerning Archaeology, Cosmology, all aspects and avenues of history or even our own physical nature in reference to other living things, which the Holy Scriptures has maintained that we are i.e. our flesh is different from the flesh of the animals - the flesh of the birds - and that of the fish. Nothing has ever been overturned by the sciences including the differing DNA (deoxyribonucleic acid) between us and the rest. This too has withstood the exploits of the 'evolution theory' and to date of the latest advancement in the most recent DNA discoveries related to our genetic code, genes and through the deciphering of our entire Genome.

However, having said all of this, I know, this is not going to change anything, but I needed to say it anyway. On second thoughts, perhaps we do need these very quests to inspire us and to seriously motivate us in continuing searching for any life forms on another planet or on any other cosmic constituent. This is so, that it may lead us to someday, eventually, even populate those that are possibly to be found humanly habitable. Either way it seems that it would serve to meet our very own human special interest to continue these scientific expeditions into inner and outer space explorations. In that sense, I am totally for it, to be exploring other planets and to even settle some of them in due time, if at all this is possible. Perhaps to think of it our future survival may also eventually depend on it.

Well anyway once this 'divine selection' had been made, the Planet Earth, obviously needed more further reconstruction and appropriate renovation, for the very grander divine purposes that GOD had intended it for. This warranted **their** direct intervention **in agreement**, to emerge it as the ultimate and singularly unique planet in the entire Universe.

> This **'P & D'** of the Earth was for the very purposes to ultimately accommodate **'life'**, as we know of it only here on Earth and in such abundance at that. Everything that was done was for the sole purpose of providing for our survival as a people.

> The very logical, necessary and well planned sequences of the creation as clearly defined in the Genesis Chapters; also exhibits and exposes this very divine intention. This in itself informs us the very necessity for the P & D days.

Now before someone argues that I am suggesting that there were some serious imperfections in **their** joint divine creation of the Universe in the first place and was it not possible for GOD to have done this right at the very beginning, so that the Earth would have turned up the way they wanted it to be from the very beginning; let me attempt to explain this matter to you. Not that I know the very 'Mind of GOD', far from it, but that it is my appropriate drawn conclusion that I had arrived at after studying the 'WORD' over and over again, throughout these many years.

From my personal study of the Holy Scriptures throughout the entire Holy Bible, in summary, the following describes the divine way that GOD seems to have chosen to operate.

OUT OF **CHAOS**; TO BRING PERFECT ORDER
(In fact the chaos was indeed a controlled chaos)
OUT OF **TURMOIL AND STRIFE**; TO BRING COMPLETE PEACE
OUT OF **SUFFERING**; TO BRING ABSOLUTE HEALING AND REST
OUT OF **FAMINE**; INTO YEARS OF PLENTY
OUT OF **LACK**; INTO ABUNDANTLY OVERFLOWING
OUT OF **SLAVERY**; INTO FREEDOM
OUT OF **SIN**; INTO ABSOLUTE FORGIVENESS
OUT OF **POVERTY**; INTO OVERFLOWING RICHES
OUT OF **DESPERATION**; INTO HAVING EVERY HOPE IN GOD ALMIGHTY
OUT OF **CURSES**; INTO HIS BLESSINGS AND FAVOUR
OUT OF **'BLINDNESS'**; TO SEE THE 'LIGHT'
OUT OF THE **SAVIOUR' CRUCIFIXION**; SALVATION FOR ALL MANKIND
OUT OF **DEATH**; INTO ETERNAL LIFE
AND SO FORTH........

So, it is not that GOD could not have created the Earth in the first place as it is now and not having to transform it later through those 'SIX P & D DAYS'; but it is the very way that GOD had chosen to operate. This is what I came to realise from the reading of the Holy Scriptures. There is just no 'why' to this it seems. It is just the way it was as GOD had probably meant it to be, and is, and probably will be in repetition in the future. This does not discount in anyway, the 'GOD FACTOR' in the creation. Hope this agrees with you too.

Also, if it was not the case, then to think of it, we also should not be here. No chance at all, for this to have happened i.e. you and I, to be here if that was not the case indeed. This is, if we understand that GOD is omniscient i.e. all knowing: past, present and of the future, and even beyond these in or out of 'time & space' dimensions. Therefore, GOD would have known even before ever creating us what would happen. No argument possible here!!! Especially, that which would have eventually taken place in the very 'Garden of Eden' that would consequently rob mankind of our future and indeed set aside GOD' own plans for mankind. Yet even despite having the divine omniscient knowledge of even this outcome, our LORD GOD ALMIGHTY, went on with the ORIGINAL DIVINE plans accordingly.

Do you seriously think, even according to our **mere human thinking, logic and philosophy**; GOD would have created us, just so that Satan and his cohorts could have this immense victory over the CREATOR, to further mock GOD, after having fallen much earlier from GOD' GRACE ??? Was it not painful enough already, from whichever way you want to think of it, for our LORD GOD ALMIGHTY to have the most acclaimed and celebrated Archangel, yes, Lucifer (since then – the fall – becoming Satan) turn against GOD. Also whereby, the Heavenly Kingdom had lost about 1/3 of the angels, simultaneously together with Lucifer' downfall. These too had joined Lucifer i.e. Satan' evil ways. As you may very well know whenever we make reference to Lucifer now it is actually to his downfallen status, Satan, as it refers to the same individual. Lucifer was Lucifer the Archangel and after the fall became the Satan who has relentlessly waged war after war against the heavenly places, though indirectly, by attacking the image of GOD; yes, us human beings from the very beginning of our creation. Adam and Eve being the very first victims.

All of them following Lucifer were 'sent out' of the spiritual heavenly realm, as they too were of Lucifer' cohort agreeing in their shockingly evil desires. They had also followed Lucifer in his futile & foolish attempt of taking over the Heavenly Kingdom. All of this shockingly evil desires orchestrated right in the very centre of the Heavenlies, had indeed taken place before the Earth, as we know of it now, had even come into it' very existence. This event was even before the creation of the early Universe.

> Yet, even in this, GOD has been more than gracious to be revealing to us this spiritually devastating 'Heavenly Crisis' too. This GOD had done through HIS written word by the divinely inspired Scripture writer.

Our GOD is indeed GOD who chooses, selects and elects – John 15:16 refers. Yet, you are still **free** to make your own freewill choices, despite this divine selection, if you are fortunate enough to be amongst the very chosen. Lucifer and his followers are a classic example for the case in point in the heavenly realm. Peter the Apostle in the earthly realm, denied Christ three times even though being divinely appointed and being a strong follower of Jesus Christ. Jonah at the beginning had refused to obey. Moses had doubts and even on one occasion did not follow the divine instruction 100%. And there were many others who had to struggle somewhat when they had been chosen.

> My further and personal observation to all of this, through GOD' divinely inspired written word, is that; it is absolutely true that GOD is omniscient. However, GOD through THEIR own volition i.e. by their own will, allow things to progress through 'freewill and circumstances', even allowing time and space to take it' own course too within it' measured allocation, knowing very well that the final outcome would be agreeable totally to their original plans. Amen

Obviously, many of the biblical scriptural events currently ongoing and those to be taking place and even that of which is happening in our own Christian lives in the areas of our influence, progresses on beyond our very own limited physical life spans. This makes it impossible for us to be able to observe any of this very agreeable GOD ordained outcomes and may make some to become somewhat dismayed in the present and some even perhaps to lose hope and faith in our LORD and SAVIOUR JESUS CHRIST. However, this too will be witnessed by our descendant generations to come in the near and distant future. They will clearly realize all of this with the evidential unchanging biblical scriptural knowledge of it' prophesies, as written in it accordingly, and the present work that many Christians had begun in the areas of their influence by having stayed on the course. **Praise be to GOD.**

Through scriptural historical fact, the Lucifer case is indeed a good example. Also, the several classic examples as given in the Holy Scriptures as when Jesus Christ had walked on this Earth amongst us, being GOD and MAN at the same time during his 33 years. This including, that of HIS very own scriptural prophesied crucifixion.

GOD had employed and observably continues to do so, engaging those specific 'circumstances' that do come our way, through the natural process and even at times, through spiritual intervention as clearly supported in the

Holy Scriptures as such. GOD also uses other people to help us to change our mind, our ways, our 'lifestyles' yet not interfering with our freewill though, but to help us to somehow fit ourselves accordingly into this 'divine selection'.

FOR IT IS QUITE OBVIOUS THAT IT IS NOT EASY TO CARRY THE PART OF THE ONE WHO HAS BEEN 'SELECTED' OR 'CHOSEN'. JUST AS ABRAM HAD DEMONSTRATED AND EVEN MOSES HAD DEMONSTRATED TOO, WHEN AT FIRST HAVING BEEN 'CHOSEN'. YET GOD WOULD ENABLE US TO DO SO WHEN THE TIME COMES THE VERY MOMENT WE STEP OUT AND STEP UP IN FAITH TO DO THE VERY THING ASKED OF US IN OUR CALLING.

Yes, GOD does have a will and it is not 'free' like our own which was divinely given to all of us. For **HIS WILL** is not under any subjection by any entity, to be given the release status of being 'free'. For there is no entity, that exists in the physical, nor in the spiritual realm, through any dimension that has any authority over HIM or over HIS 'WILL'. If you did not know this in the very first place that GOD ALMIGHTY also has a 'WILL' of HIS own, then turn to the Gospels and you will find JESUS CHRIST himself, pointing this out so definably to us, as in the garden of Gethsemane - Matthew 26:39, 42 confirms and yet again in John 5:30.

And of course, how can we miss out the Scripture that provide us with the wonderful LORD' prayer where it states: **'YOUR WILL be done'**.

There are many more scriptures confirming that GOD has a will of HIS own. In fact all the spiritual beings in the spirit realm with HIM have indeed their own freewill too. How do I know this? As explained in the previous pages, it comes through their own will fully rebellious acts, referring of course to Lucifer and his fallen angels. If they had not their own 'freewill' and the capacity to exercise it as such, they would not have fallen, now would they???

> I am of the opinion also for all that it is worth, that when we reach 'eternal life status', we too will still retain our freewill through eternity too. The test of allegiance to our LORD GOD ALMIGHTY does not just end here on earth, but is a constant acceptance of our LORD GOD ALMIGHTY, as always, through our own unfettered freewill. **GOD; I do propose will not have it any other way.**

This is what I personally had deduced from all that 'Lucifer evil desires' happening in the spiritual heavenly realm.

Again, I am not saying that I do know how GOD thinks and acts, but if we do agree that the Holy Scriptures are indeed from our LORD GOD ALMIGHTY; then it is these Holy Scriptures that brings me to this appropriate obvious observation. Furthermore, you can check this out by studying the Holy Scriptures yourself.

Alright, coming back into focus here: The 'early earth' needed further 'divine attention & intervention' to become this unique singular 'big blue marble' in the ocean of the Universe. It was not by chance or by close association or by environmental necessity that it had occurred over time. This is the very reason why, there is none other like it, in the entire Universe, unless GOD had chosen or will choose to repeat this exact thing.

It is also somewhat in the similar manner that we may be able to draw a scriptural parallel to this, that is in the way GOD deals with those of us, who have accepted Jesus Christ as being our personal LORD and Saviour. The continuing process - as GOD breaks us, remoulds us and refines us into becoming sons and daughters of GOD is the parallel. Amen.

It is scripturally evident as you read below, that no part of the Universe including that of the Earth creation ever took place on the first 'P & D' day. What was divinely accomplished though, on this first day of 'P & D' of the Earth was the divine pronouncement of the 'light':

GEN 1:2   The earth was without form, and void; and darkness was on the face of the deep. And the Spirit of GOD was hovering over the face of the waters.

GEN 1:3   Then GOD said, "Let there be light"; and there was light.

GEN 1:4   And GOD saw the light, that it was good; and GOD divided the light from the darkness.

GEN 1:5   GOD called the light Day, and the darkness HE called Night. So the evening and the morning were the first day.

This was the 'FIRST DAY' in the 'P & D' account of the Earth. There was night and day from then onwards. But what 'light' was this??? Do you know???

This setting apart, of the Earth in such manner, in turn sets this particular 'Solar Planetary System' apart from the other possibly millions of planetary systems already existing and some even still in the cosmic process of emerging from their star dust/gaseous clouds etc, in this very 'Milky Way Galaxy' and also beyond. Also, ultimately having even this galaxy set uniquely apart from the billions, yes billions out there, in the Universe at large. We have been reliably informed through scientific scholarship that there are more than **100 billion galaxies**. They go on to inform us that there are 400 billion stars alone in our own Milky Way Galaxy and that our Sun being a star itself is indeed **150 trillion miles** from it' very centre!!!

Does this give you, for those of us, who have not been too interested in matters such as these, some understanding to the expanse of the Universe??? This entire expanding expanse of the Universe, is indeed GOD' creation of the heavens (Universe), in the biblical time frame as expressed in Gen 1:1 - **'In the beginning'**.

This brief summary is also further expounded or further emphasised, as I had explained it earlier, in Gen 2:1 & Gen 2:3-4. Here you will see in Gen 2:1, another divine summary with regards to the creation, which reads:

> Thus the heavens, the earth and all the host of them, were finished.

Here the scriptural term 'host', meant that the other 'heavenly bodies' together with these, such as the Milky Way; Solar System; other galaxies; etc, etc, were also finished. GOD announced the completion of the creation of the Universe and everything in it with such an insignificant but powerful exclamation through the inspired writer:
......were finished.

No bells and whistles here to celebrate this GODLY achievement and accomplishment; just the simple divinely spoken words .....were finished.

The words 'were finished' to my understanding was also making or rather linking this specific 'time' reference to the 'biblical time frame' i.e. **'In the beginning'** - Genesis 1:1 refers. All of these were created, including that of the Earth, even before Genesis 2:4-5 puts it to us in a clearer scriptural perspective for our better understanding as to when the 'creation' had actually taken place, as follows:

GEN 2:4 This is the **history** of the heavens and the earth when they were created, in the day (i.e. literally making reference to the biblical time frame of **'IN THE BEGINNING'**) that the Lord God made the earth and the heavens.

The reference was inserted to denote biblical similarity to the 'time frame' i.e. **'in the day'** referring to **'in the beginning'**.

GEN 2:5 before any plant of the field was in the earth and before any herb of the field had grown. For the Lord God had not caused it to rain on the earth, and there was no man to till the ground;

These however were then emerged as how the 'P & D' of Genesis 1 had described them in their sequence of coming on-stream. This making the Planet Earth to become uniquely positioned in the Universe, in the Milky Way Galaxy and in our Solar Planetary System, as we see and experience it even as of now, with our expanded knowledge of the greater expanse of the entire universe.

We do have yet another brief scriptural encounter, which does pertain to the creation of the Universe, in fact to be more exact to it' most significant galaxy, being 'The Milky Way', i.e. at least from our point of view.

This is the very galaxy that we find our Solar System also nicely embedded in. We catch this 'Milky Way' and some more purposeful made references to the Solar System, such as to the Sun and Moon, being well presented here, but in typical brief divine summary descriptive terms, as found in Genesis 1:14-18.

The clincher that proved this was of the 'Milky Way', as a whole or overview if you like is found in the very last sentence of Genesis 1:16, which is:

He made the stars also.

Of course, this is not only pertaining to the stars of the Milky Way, but in our very context, when we look up into the night sky, the only stars that you and I will ever be able to see with our naked eyes, are those that belong to none other than that of the Milky Way Galaxy. So it was in this very context, that I was claiming the clincher, as such.

So, we have in the first two chapters of Genesis:

(1) An overall creation descriptive divine view of the Universe.

(2) A somewhat closer view of the Milky Way, together with it' integrated Solar Planetary System, though briefly.

(3) In greatest detail possible but in divine summary, the remarkable metamorphosis of Planet Earth, to becoming habitable & hospitable, ultimately for the likes of us human beings. Yet we are now so desperately though unintentionally so, trying to kill off with our consistent destruction of the overall environment through the 'progress' that comes to us directly which generally we all seek after as sole individuals and indirectly which is spurned by the mega giant corporations to propel nations forward above the others, constantly.

All of this divine description was indeed clearly and in a way ridiculously smart as it was encompassed in amazing narrative through just the first two chapters of Genesis!!! Remarkable isn't it.

The rest of the creation account i.e. the second part of Genesis 1:1, and then continuing from Gen 1:2 until the end of the Sixth Day of 'P & D' i.e. Gen 1:2-31 and Gen 2:1-25 are mostly about the Earth and about all 'life' on the Earth as already been defined. It also gives some details of the other main players in the Solar System i.e. the Sun of course and the Earth' single Moon all of which are within the Milky Way. This too, has been described in these very scriptures, though very briefly as well.

The reason all of the above was brought up was to mainly drive home to you that the **'Oscillation Cycles'** in our very context of interest, are pertaining only to that of the Earth. The Earth, as you may very well know, came in pretty late, relatively speaking of course, into the overall cosmic developments.

Therefore, this evidently makes this particular 'Oscillation Cycle' in our very context, the singular most significant of all past and yet to come of such Oscillations. It is for this very reason; I will from now on take it for all intents and purposes, that the '360 Day Years' have yet to happen in our 'Biblical Human History'. Although in reality, these 'Earth Oscillation Cycles' have already occurred several times before in our Earth' Cosmic History, suggesting also, that we have had previously these '360 Day Years' too accordingly. However, these '360 Day Years', **have not occurred as yet** in our 'Biblical Human History'. This is according to this Oscillating Earth Axis Rotation Model (OEARM), for man had at the time yet to walk on this Earth, prior to this very present and still ongoing Oscillation Cycle.

Then in our context and dimension, the previous occurrences of these '360 Day Years' are indeed not that important after all, for obvious reasons, except for the very next one which has yet to occur.

This will happen evidently, according to our discovered 'scriptural schedule'. This is the **126,000,000 years** scriptural schedule, which in fact began this very present oscillation cycle. This period is also the very **mid-base point** for the cycle and according to this scriptural schedule would be located at the Reference Base Position, RBP 24:33.

> Could this singularly important oscillation cycle, be the very 'time duration' i.e. which was described or referred to as, "this generation will not pass away", which the New Testament was always making such references to as Jesus Christ himself did, in the very Gospel of Matthew??? Matt 24:34 refers.

> In fact the entire Chapter of Matthew 24 and even Matthew 25 are indeed very significant here, as it does incorporate many revelations of the last arranged Biblical Book, "The Book of Revelation of Jesus Christ" as follows:

1) 'THE BEGINNING OF SORROWS'
2) 'THE GREAT TRIBULATION'
3) 'THE RAPTURE'
4) 'THE SECOND COMING OF THE SON OF MAN'
   AND
5) 'THE FINAL JUDGMENT' – **SHEEPS ON THE RIGHT HAND AND THE GOATS ON THE LEFT**

> Through my personal study of these relevant Holy Scriptures, including that of Genesis (first two chapters), the Book of Revelation; 2Esdras; Daniel; and also based on the outcome of these two books as presently being written, all have taken place or will be taking place, as the events may very well be, within this **present** 'Oscillation Cycle'. This is my very observation and understanding that leads me to this very biblical derived conclusion.

These Matthew chapters are indeed very significant because it also incorporates the divine message & divine warning as given to us directly by none other than **'Jesus Christ The Messiah'** HIMSELF. This also includes HIS foretelling to us of **HIS second coming.** And this time, JESUS CHRIST will come again not as a SAVIOUR being sacrificed as the 'LAMB OF GOD', having been brutally crucified on the cross for the sins of all mankind, but as **'KING IN JUDGMENT'**. In fact, as the 'KING of Kings and the LORD of Lords' - Rev 19:11-16 refers and confirms.

Chapter 24, also includes 'the rapture' and chapter 25 closes with the *separation* of the righteous (the sheep on his right hand) into 'eternal life' and the goats (the cursed, on his left hand) into everlasting punishment, into everlasting fire. This having been *first* prepared for the devil and his fallen angels. **This means essentially, it was never meant to be for us.** Yet all that had changed as you very well may know, how. And yet this may still come as a big surprise to many:

> **THAT HELL WAS NOT MEANT FOR US AT ALL EVER, IN THE VERY FIRST PLACE!!! AMEN**

This phase of the Oscillation Cycle that we are currently in, also quite evidently, does include the Noah' Flood. In fact, Matthew Chapter 24 also makes reference of the Noah' Flood directly through JESUS CHRIST, HIMSELF.

> This inclusion of the Noah' Flood in this very phase of this Oscillation Cycle, further compounds my personal conviction and biblical understanding, that the Noah' Flood was not responsible in anyway whatsoever, to the tilting of the Earth' axial axis.

The 'tilt' had evidently taken place or rather it had been incorporated into it' very infrastructure in the formative years as it began to emerge and operate as being a Planet. This evidently, is just being like the very tilts of the other Solar Planets too. However, all having been incorporated with their very own axial angled signature tilt. This being due to some other cosmic based forces, which was somewhat common evidently and instrumental to having all these planets to similarly be operating i.e. existing with their very own signature tilts. I am positive minded, that our relevant scientist are on the verge of proving this too, going by a recent news article. It also somehow involves Einstein' theory of Relativity, I think, according to this article. Also, not to say the least or forgetting that it is due to this very tilt that we have the seasons; just as we have it even now evidentially.

This Oscillation Phase (i.e. till the mid-point) covers a time period of exactly 126,000,000 years. Therefore, it is **252,000,000 years** in total for every full Earth' Oscillation Cycle to be completed.

Strangely, this previously calculated 126,000,000 years, somehow comes to play in another important and significant role here and that is to set the specific time period, which would lead us to a full Oscillation Cycle. This is remarkable indeed.

So, now we know in multiplicity, that every oscillation cycle takes exactly 126,000,000 years to mid-point and therefore **252,000,000 years** from beginning to end. This is indeed a very significant conclusion and it was also because of this, I had to restudy in-depth and expound the first two chapters of the Book of Genesis. This consequently also led to the new and revolutionary expounding, if I may so, if I am allowed to put it this way. This was needed to establish, how many oscillation cycles had indeed been completed and passed since the Earth had been created??? This also inevitably led me to discover, what number we are currently in at this moment and possibly how much of this too has also indeed already expired!!!

SOMETIME EARLIER, I HAD IN FACT GIVEN A HINT TO THIS DISCOVERY, WHEN I INDICATED THAT WE ARE STILL IN THE SAME OSCILLATION CYCLE IN WHICH ADAM & EVE WERE IN AT THAT TIME SO LONG AGO!!!

How much of the **'P & D Sixth Day'** account were actually contained in this phase of the present oscillation cycle is indeed anybody's guess???

However, the obtaining of some of the answers for such questions would not have been made possible, without having this 'new expounding' of the Genesis Chapters 1 & 2. In fact this may cause some controversy amongst the conservatives, because it does not completely support what had been taught to us this far with regards to the creation accounts, by eminent biblical scholarship and the traditional theological accepted teaching. This is scary indeed.

With the help of all of the above and more, I have concluded that every oscillation cycle is indeed 252,000,000 years in duration. It obviously covers the few thousand years biblical time period, which Bible Chronologists have consistently proposed for the entire Old & New Testament. However, as already explained with my understanding on the matter, it does not include the entire creation week or rather all of the P & D Accounts.

However, it does cover or incorporates the scientific view of about 100,000 years ago, that Homo sapiens (human beings), had begun to become more and more prominent for the first time on this planet.

This also accordingly confirms as per my 'OEARM', that prior, during and even after the Noah' Flood, the Earth had already indeed acquired the 365+ days per year. Also, the very first 360 Solar Days Year is yet to happen in this Oscillation Cycle; for we have yet to reach it' mid-point.

You will learn that we are still very far from it, even at this present stage in time of our Biblical Human History.

Now that we have established the time period for these 'EAR Oscillation Cycles', we can actually calculate in which number we are in presently and further to this calculate even the possible age of the Earth. We can do this based on the facts as derived scripturally through which we have established these, as you will read in the following page.

1) That about 500,000 years have indeed passed since the beginning of this present 'EAR Oscillation Cycle' as previously mentioned, which had begun from RBP 24:12.

2) Scientists have informed us that the Earth has been estimated as being 4,500,000,000 years old.

However, we cannot use this estimated age in our 'OEARM' for the simple fact that, when we use this period of 4.5 Billion Years, it will take us even pass our future RBP 24:33. This I found out by dividing 4.5 Billion Years by our Scriptural calculated and derived length for each 'EAR Oscillation Cycle', i.e. 252,000,000 years. The result that we get i.e. 17.8571428571 possible cycles tells me, based on the scientific estimated age of the Earth i.e. 4.5 Billion Years, that we have indeed completed 17 'EAR Oscillation Cycles', and that we are currently into more than 85% of the 18th ongoing 'EAR Oscillation Cycle'. This calculates out to be about 216,000,000 years into it.

As you already know, I have calculated that our RBP 24:33 also being the very mid-point of this present 'EAR Oscillation Cycle', is 126,000,000 years away from its very beginning at RBP 24:12. This obviously then, will unmistakably overshoot it' mid-point by 90 million years, taking us very much past our own future. So this cannot be the case following my 'OEARM'.

We also need to check whether this time period i.e. 17 past EAR Oscillation Cycles (i.e. 4.284 Billion Years), does fit into our 'OEARM', in the very first place or not.

This is quite easily concluded based on the fact that our Sun, as I had calculated in Part Two, was 4.995 Billion Years old at the RBP 24:12. This means that the Earth has to be much younger than the age of the Sun, as at that RBP 24:12. So, taking another look at the 17 EAR Oscillation Cycles as was initially based on the scientific proposed age of the Earth, which I had taken following my 'OEARM' being completed as such at RBP 24:12, does seem to be able to accommodate an age of 4,284,000,000 years. This is also well within the scientific estimated age of the Sun being 4.5 Billion Years old.

As the problem, which we have already seen above, is when we use the full age of the Earth as currently estimated by scientific scholarship, we will quite definitely overshoot the mid-point of this 18th EAR Oscillation Cycle (18 EAROC). So this tells me that we need to have an estimated age of the Earth, which is 4.284 Billion Years + a period of years which is less than 126,000,000 Million Years.

I have actually already calculated prior to even writing this very section, as in 'Part Three' of this book, that we have indeed passed this RBP 24:12, by about 500,000+ years. Based on the very fact that we are currently using a mean of 24.20144776 Hours for a Solar Day, thereby, the total length of our current Solar Year calculates out to be 365.242199 Solar Days with the current orbiting duration of 8839.39 Hours.

The EAR Period as at RBP18EAROC:24:12 is calculated as being 24.20 Hours. As the Solar Day is in fact even a bit longer than an 'EAR Period', we can conclude according to the findings of this 'OEARM', that we have indeed passed about 500,000+ years, since then. This is based on the 'rate of change' in the EAR speed, since then to now based on the already available scientific data of 1/1000th second change every 100 years.

So with this information, all we need to do it seems is to add another 500,000+ years or so to the 4.284 Billion Years as shown above to satisfy all the data parameters in my calculation of the Earth' age, according to this 'OEARM'. So, the age of the Earth should be as per this OEARM - **4,284,500,000+ Years**.

Interestingly, this takes us into the **18th OC** being only about 215.5 million years off the scientific based calculation of 4.5 Billion Years, which is less than 5% difference overall.

However, what is there to stop it, from being even younger than the OEARM 4.2845 Billion Years? Well for one, it will take us further and further from the scientific based estimate of 4.5 Billion Years.

Another question comes up then: Could we increase this newly calculated age by say another 100,000 years or so? What is it that would eventually stop us from doing this on an estimation trial and error basis, as long as we do not cross the mid-point of this EAR Oscillation Cycle restriction? Well for one is the very fact that we have already calculated that we cannot exceed the time that had already indeed passed us by (i.e. about 500,000+ years) since the RBP18EAROC:24:12(A) being the very beginning of the 18th EAR Oscillation Cycle.

So, it does not really give us very much room, for proposing the age of the Earth based on this OEARM, due to these 'restricting parameters', which have become well known to us as above. Lastly, although it is not apparent right now, this actual cosmic construction of the second beast' number, which sum totals 666, actually dictates exactly that:

1) The Earth' Oscillation Cycle that will be and is the most significant would be this **18th** Oscillation Cycle. This somehow points us also to the **18th** verse of the 13th Chapter of Revelation. The same that I am currently engaged in to deciphering and to understanding. Though this being somewhat speculative, it is this **18th** verse that had actually set me on this journey in the quest for the number of the second beast, in the very first place.

2) I have also discovered that an Oscillation Cycle will begin whenever the EAR does obtain a 24.20 hours EAR period and that the Oscillation Cycle' mid-point will be precisely 126,000,000 years away. This means the mid-point being exactly located 21 EAR minutes away (at RBP 24:33), generating an EAR period of 24.55 hours. As mentioned, these 126,000,000 years will take exactly 21 EAR minutes to be added to the beginning EAR period of 24.20 hours i.e. bringing it to be 24.55 hours EAR period at that future time. These '21 EAR Minutes' or '1260 EAR Seconds' has it' number **1260** also in the Scriptures!!! This is found in REV 11:3. Also a full oscillation of 42 EAR Minutes in total has its number of **42** also found written in the holy scriptures as in REV 11:2 and REV 13:5!!!

3) Could all of this just be purely speculative or just mere coincidences, or if we seriously think about it, could this be indeed having a specific divine

purpose and design, leading us to the discovery of the number of the second beast?

Well anyway:

4) 17 full Oscillation Cycles have already passed us by since the Earth had been created within the Biblical Time Frame of 'In the beginning'. However, these 17 'EAR Oscillation Cycles', being timed or calculated here are definitely an integral part of the 'Six Days' that do make up the 'P & D' Accounts of the Earth after the 'beginning'.

5) As per my OEARM, we are also indeed currently in the 18th EAR Oscillation Cycle.

> A part of the 18th EAR Oscillation Cycle can be equated to a portion of the 'Sixth Day', which through this OEARM falls into this particular 'Oscillation Cycle'.

We do know based on the Scriptures, that it was sometime during this 'Sixth Day', that Adam was created. Then at some point in time our LORD GOD ALMIGHTY had then placed him in a specially prepared location, which the Scriptures refer to as a 'garden'. This 'garden' was aligned eastward in a much larger territory, that was referred to by it' name being Eden in the Scriptures.

This is another valid reason, why our 500,000+ years, as added onto the time period as at RBP18EAROC:24:12 was to accommodate the very entry of these very special 'Human Beings' - Adam and Eve. This would give them enough time to procreate and spread their descendant generations, through Africa, Europe, Asia and the Americas. Therefore, in this very context, this can be taken to be quite an accurate model too with regards to our overall estimating of the age of the Earth, as being 4,284,500,000 years. This follows the 'OEARM' (Oscillating Earth Axis Rotation Model).

According to the footnote in my 'Spirit Filled Life Bible (NKJV) page 7: Eastward in Eden indicated that the area of Eden lay east of present-day Israel, somewhere in Mesopotamia or Arabia. This is indeed very interesting.

Just like the overall 'Preparation & Development' of the Earth, this 'garden' was also specially prepared and developed as per GOD' own directives, Gen 2:8-24 refers. In fact, Adam was also assigned by our LORD GOD to 'tend and keep it', as the Scriptures inform us in Gen 2:15.

This special 'garden' (through divine selection of a particular land area of the earth), is indeed extra special in terms of the rest of the prepared and developed Earth. In fact this 'garden' in Eden, was indeed prime land by any standards, as it was served by a river, which had an abundance supply of water. It was definitely a fertile region. This we know from the Scriptures, for it also was fed by four large tributaries.

This land within Eden was obviously highly fertile land. It was also indeed a very large territory, for here also, GOD had formed every beast of the field, however through a more 'selective process', than the previous accounts of creating the animals as in Genesis Chapter 1. For there were no more Dinosaurs and other such animals to speak of as such in the 'garden', as they had all died out long before the 'garden' events.

For by this time, when Adam was created and placed in the 'garden', the Dinosaurs had already died out, having come on-stream on this Planet in the 17th 'Oscillation Cycle'. This is according to my 'OEARM', which also happens to be in line with the time period that science had also suggested the same.

> The Dinosaurs were on the Earth about 200 million years ago, before they finally had died out too. None of them had survived into the current 18th Oscillation Cycle.

This could also possibly be the reason why there were no huge Dinosaurs included in the Noah' Ark. Also, there were no reason to speak about fish, perhaps, because the river passing through, must have carried with it fish. Every bird in the air may not necessarily mean every type of bird there were existing at the time globally, but probably a selection too as limited to the local area as created for Adam.

Also, a final point with regards to the Noah' Flood being a localised flood from my perspective and thereby being confined in a specific territory (meaning not being global), provides us with the understanding that due to this there was no necessity at all for having every pair of every animal that were existing globally, to be brought into the Ark per se.

This understanding could probably help all of those who were and possibly still are wondering their socks off; how would it be possible for the Ark to accommodate every type of animal in pairs mind you into that confined space of just one ARK??? This would then otherwise make it more of a fantasy than it actually being the word of GOD.

This in my humble opinion would be really pushing our 'religious fortune', so to speak, to explain this to anyone who is really curious to know how is this possible to avoid bringing our entire Faith into ridicule just because this was what that had been taught us by our 'Religious Knowledge' teachers who were similarly taught by their own teachers too!!!

I hope that you would be able to relate to this understanding, positively, with an open mind, as we need to move on. If you are not in agreement to this, just remain in your status quo and let us move on too.

The Scripture, Genesis 2:18 continues: I will make him a helper comparable to him. We should be careful to note, it was not that GOD had somehow fallen short of HIS vision to provide a helper comparable to Adam when he had created the animals for the Garden of Eden, rather that Genesis 2:18 must be understood in two parts.

The first part was that our LORD GOD had clearly declared that it was not good that man should be alone.

Here you will see that God introduces/created these selected animals and birds for Adam so that in principle, he would not be alone in the Garden of Eden. This in my understanding fulfilled the first part of GEN 2:18. That he was now not alone per se. Now comes the understanding for the second part of the Gen 2:18 Scripture, which reads:

> But for Adam there was not found a helper comparable to him.

Now this may easily lead anyone reading Gen 2:18, when they without considering it in two separate parts; to actually think that GOD having made all the animals somehow had fallen short of having one of these created animals to be made comparable to Adam and for it to be the helper to him. It is quite obvious to us that no animal could have become a helper comparable to him for that was not GOD's intention anyway. Therefore, as just mentioned to my understanding this was not the divine intention or purpose of the first part of Gen 2:18. It was the divine intention of the second part.

So in other words, once all the animals were created for the Garden of Eden and for Adam; the writer informs us through obviously an 'inspired effort': ....But for Adam there was not found a helper comparable to him - Gen 2:20 confirms. It is now that GOD puts HIS second part of Gen 2:18 into action i.e. to create Eve to fulfil this divine intention and in multiplicity enable the producing of the 'Adam & Eve Generations'.

You can take note also, that it was very divinely specific indeed: **One Eve and not two, three, four or more.** This drills down to us too by divine example in the creation of only one Eve, meaning: One wife only for any of us, at any one time. Here also, it is good to take note that GOD had brought Eve to Adam.

Well one other important factor that separates the rest of the Earth from this special singularly unique 'garden territory', is the fact that it is only here and no place else in this entire physical world, that the 'tree of life' and the 'tree of knowledge of good and evil' could be found at that time.

THIS IS ANOTHER ACT OF DIVINE SELECTION.

Since the 'fall' both have been lost to the world. The 'tree of knowledge of good and evil may not be of any consequence to us now, as we do know now much about the good and also much about the evil. However, the 'tree of life' had not perished, but it is still available in the very midst of the 'Paradise of God' - Rev 2:7 confirms.

> This could have only meant one thing according to my basic understanding on this matter that it was consequentially at some early point after the 'fall' totally removed from Eden. This was due to the obvious, that GOD had to remove it before it too was compromised by the cunning works of Satan.

As an afterthought, if I am allowed to make this comparison, Jesus Christ has now become our very 'tree of life' linking us to the ever blissful eternal life through salvation as underpinned in the scriptures found in John 14:6 as follows:

> Jesus said to him, "I am the way, the truth, and the life. No one comes to the Father except through Me.

Also, read John 15: 1 – 8 ... "I am the true vine.....

We have also another interesting reference made of it in Rev 22:1-2.

It had suddenly come into my view though, that Adam and later Eve were actually not barred from eating fruit of the 'tree of life'. Please check it out for yourself. It was only the fruit of the 'tree of knowledge' i.e. of good and evil, that they were banned from eating. This was not even a tree of total and complete knowledge per se, but only that knowledge pertaining to **good and evil** that they were not supposed to have taken and eaten. If you are discerning enough here, you will clearly become aware that this knowledge did not cover as an example of it' lack, the knowledge of Truth, neither did it cover the knowledge of knowing GOD – just as John 16:13 and 2 Cor 4:14 expresses respectively.

This in turn may prompt us to query, "Why did Satan not choose the fruit of the 'tree of life', instead???" This would also be interesting to know. My perspective to this query is simply that Satan had intended to kill both Adam and Eve so it was quite pointless for Satan to direct them to choose the 'tree of life' instead, as it would have obviously defeated his evil intention. This is particularly important because Satan knew that their act of disobedience to follow, first by Eve & then subsequently by Adam too, was to rob them of their very life as what GOD had related to them would happen in GEN 2:16-17, refers.

Anyway, as we already know very well from the Scriptures after the 'fall', GOD had quickly removed Adam & Eve from the Garden of Eden. This was done as being their banishment punishment and also before they took the opportunity to take of the 'tree of life' too - Gen 3:22-24 refers.

Anyway to highlight another biblical point that it was also sometime later, after Adam was first created, that Eve was then created. Also, something interesting here to note is that when Eve was indeed created, she was in fact created right there in that 'garden territory' as found in Eden. Adam was in fact created outside of it. Something that was not highlighted before and which is not in conflict with Genesis 1:27 either and it could be of some biblical significance too, if any.

In fact Gen 2:21-25 was indeed expounding the very creation of Eve. Eve was indeed the **only** Eden 'baby' of that time and the only one that it would unfortunately have for all time; if I stand correct in this understanding. This is an important singular distinction that we cannot deny her for any reason whatsoever. So, in a way, it was Eve who was truly the singular native 'born' citizen of the Garden in Eden; while Adam was given his citizenship by GOD.

Now, coming back, if you do remember in Part Two/Book One, I had mentioned earlier that Dr Arthur Beiser had suggested, that after a period of 5,000 million years, we will have 36 hour long Solar Days. This is based on the $1/1000^{th}$ second rate of reduction change, as presently is occurring in the EAR every 100 years. The key or fundamental question that I would like to raise here is that:

"Would this currently 'reduction rate change', be cosmically allowed to continue long enough in this direction, to cause this very pronounced impact, as suggested by Dr Arthur Beiser???"

That is, "Would this currently 'reduction change rate' actually be allowed to continue for over such a long period of time, by the very operating planetary forces in conjunction with that as contributed by the Earth itself".

Now, if we simply follow what Dr Arthur Beiser had stated, that the present reduction change rate in the Earth' Axis Rotation, when continuing for 5,000 million years (the specific time period that was referenced by him to explain the significant impact this minuscule reduction change rate would have over the long term), then we would probably have to accept for the time being what he goes on to inform us:

> That it would indeed produce 36 hour long days, after this period of time.

It is not too difficult to imagine, what such long periods of Days and Years would have on our climate around the world, as we go through the daily eighteen hour long hot days and equally long cold nights, depending where you are living at the time. In fact, Dr Arthur Beiser himself on the same page informs us that the affect this would have on the atmosphere such as the producing of gigantic tornadoes and extremely severe tropical hurricanes may well be catastrophic.

This must mean to say, it would have extremely dire consequences on the very delicately balanced ecosystems that support the very fragile 'life' on Earth, which is so clearly visible as such, even as presently.

Even a small change in one ecosystem seems to have a snowballing damaging affect on many other existing interdependent natural ecosystems. This evidently exhibits serious life threatening parameters not only upon each other, but can directly affect eventually, our very own survival as well. This has been scientifically well measured and documented, even as of today, when Earth conditions are still well within it' life supporting parameters, despite the presently known fast depletion of the Ozone layer; all types of pollution; rampant deforestation; population explosions everywhere; climatic changes ongoing everywhere, and etc. Then how much more worse off would we be at that future time, when compounded with all of these present ongoing environmental damaging effects coupled with such long periods of day and night as suggested by Dr Beiser.

This would create such an unprecedented atmospheric havoc which leaves very little to the imagination. Therefore, I realised after quite awhile though, this very concept of longer days producing longer years, although is scientifically sound hypothesis, but yet in my OEARM view this is indeed up to a point, as far as the present 'Solar System Operatives' are indeed being effectively in force. In other words, this present 'Solar System', I found out soon enough, as based on my 'OEARM' of the Planet Earth eventually acquiring 360 Solar Day Years, in no way will allow us to have 36 hour long days.

In fact, I will also find out based on this 'OEARM' (Oscillating Earth Axis Rotation Model), neither could we have 30 hour long days nor even just a mere 25 hour long day.

Also take note that the Earth had begun this very present *'Oscillation Cycle'*, when it had acquired a 24.20 Hours EAR Period. This establishes our RBP24:12 (Reference Base Position). In fact all 'Oscillation Cycles' based on this 'OEARM', will commence when the Earth acquires every time a mean <u>24.20 Hours EAR Period</u>.

> This in turn establishes the 'OEARM' generated fact; that the 'Oscillation Cycles' begin in the 365+ Solar Day Years Phase and not in the 360+ Solar Day Years Phase.

I will also name this RBP24:12, as being the Earth' Axis Rotation Speed Switchover Base Point (A), which actually begins this present 'Oscillation Cycle', with a reducing Earth Axis Rotation Period. Just before this happening, the EAR was indeed speeding up as per this 'OEARM'.

If you do recall in Part Two, I had actually used the RBP of 24:00 to be this EARSS base point.

> However, now according to this new 'OEARM', we need to correct this error or rather fine tune it further by shifting the **EARSS** to the new RBP of 24:12 (A).

This is indeed when the Earth had acquired each time the 'Mean EAR Period' of 24.20 Hours. This means not only in this particular 'EAR Oscillation Cycle', but for every past 'EAR Oscillation Cycle' and the future ones to follow too.

Currently, the mean Solar Day is taken to be 24.20144776 hours. This means that we have already passed this RBP24:12 (A). Currently, these 24.20144776 mean Solar Days are indeed producing 365.242199 Solar Days in a Solar Year. This obviously comes about through the consistent reduction in the current phase of the 'EAR Oscillation Cycles'.

The above understanding has also some definite basis to depend upon, which fundamentally is derived from within the relevant Scriptures of the Holy Bible and through basic cosmic data pertaining to our Earth. Not forgetting of course, this also according to my renewed understanding with regards to the 'Oscillation Cycles'.

First of all the Holy Bible indicates through appropriate interpretation of relevant Scriptures, as found in the Biblical Books - Daniel & Revelation, that 'Years' in the future will indeed be very much shorter than as presently. This meaning that these scriptures suggest that we will eventually have 'Years' being only 360 Days long. I also found out through my OEARM, this would be for a specific period of time only before reverting back to its original 365+ long days once again to commence the next Oscillation Cycle.

It does not indicate any shorter years than this, although there were previous civilizations using even shorter days/year for their time reckoning calendars such as 354, 346 and even 254 days, if I am not mistaken. Yet all of these were their correctional attempts to accommodate the changing seasons and seasonal or annual flooding of their rivers, etc., which actually became out of sync over time with these corrections.

Secondly, there must be a limit on how fast the Earth can be allowed to rotate on it' axis without having all of us flying off into space, despite the effects of gravity. Also, how slow it can rotate too without making our movements to become more laborious and without changing the climate too adversely that we just cannot survive under those conditions. For these speeds subsequently could also affect the very composition and conditions of the atmosphere; our climate; and ultimately even the volume of the waters that are available to maintain that vital equilibrium to sustain all types of 'life' here.

Based on these available Scriptural evidences and our own Earth' limitations imposed upon it, by the cosmic operatives in our Solar System and at large in the Universe; I compute that these 360 Solar Day Years, (which also incorporates the 360 Earth Day Years), must be the shortest possible years that the Earth could ever experience in terms of the **'number of days'** in a year.

The reason that I had highlighted the **'number of days'** in a year, as above, is because you will find out later that despite the big drop of five days+ from the annual calendar; the **'number of hours'** in any particular year, is not that much different from that having 365+ days in a year. In fact surprisingly, there is also **no difference** in the orbiting hours as you will learn later, except for the possibility that which is caused by the affects of **perturbation**. We have already discussed this perturbation in BOOK ONE, Part Two.

To further qualify this statement: It is as far as the 'number of days' or rather the number of Earth Axis Rotations that are possible to be reduced, but yet, to still constitute a year and in this sense, a Solar and/or Biblical Year.

Although, the Bible is also somewhat silent in the aspect of how long 'years' could actually be, this is indeed overcome by the very fact that we do have as currently, which brings me to this point 365+ days long years.

> This I will firmly propose based on this OEARM cannot **progress** any further i.e. to reach the **366th day**.

Therefore, based on my proposed OEARM, this sets or fixes the first part or rather the 'immovable parameter' of the Oscillation Cycle' construction, which I am currently proposing here to you.

This is indeed an important breakthrough in my quest to establishing the 360 Solar Day Years although it is hypothetical at the moment.

So, a typical 'Earth Axis Oscillation Cycle' (EAROC) begins at the very ending of a fast EAR Period of 24 hours 12 minutes (i.e. 24.20 hours) of the previous OC. This then begins from here the slowing phase once again in the EAR Period. This is in the reducing speed phase of the OC. The Earth in this OC phase then proceeds onwards to it' mid-base, as it gradually reduces in it' EAR Period, until reaching it as located at RBP24:33. This is where a second EARSS takes place from a reduction in EAR speed to an increasing phase of the EAROC. At this mid-base, the EAR is exactly 24 hours 33 minutes slow (i.e. 24.55 hours). It is also at this very mid-base of the EAROC, that we will have the 360 days years for a specific period of time. This second EARSS base will be located at precisely 21 EAR minutes later, as calculated from the very beginning of the OC at RBP24:12(A).

Finally, the EAROC will be exiting at the other end of the OC, located precisely at RBP24:12(B). This will be precisely located at another **'21 EAR minutes'** later (i.e. when the EAR will be once again acquiring the **24 hours 12 minutes fast EAR Period**) as calculated from it' mid-base as located at RBP 24:33.

Also, simultaneously obtaining at this ending RBP location, i.e., at the RBP 24:12(B), for a specific period of time, the **365+ day years**. This would then be the beginning of the next EAROC.

We could also consider, if we so wish, to having this ending **RBP24:12(B)** of as being it' **third EARSS** base. However, take note, that here, it would also be at the very same time, the very **first** EARSS for the next immediate EAROC.

So, you can see from this, there is no possibility of the Earth even reaching the 25th hour in the day. This also means that each oscillation cycle, takes up exactly '42 EAR Minutes change', in total. That is during the reduction phase of the OC, 21 EAR minutes is gradually added to the EAR Period and then in the increasing EAR Period phase, 21 EAR minutes is gradually taken away. This brings the EAR Period back to its status quo after exactly **42 EAR minutes change**.

These EAR Period Changes operate within a very definable change rate of 1/1000th second every 100 years.

> This causes an EAR Oscillation Cycle to span across or cover a total duration of exactly **252,000,000 years**, as previously established.

I found out as previously mentioned in Book One, that as the day began to lengthen due to this reduction change rate currently happening in the Earth' Axis Rotation; the Earth is also actually experiencing a corresponding and definite reduction in the number of Earth Axis Rotations (EAR) it needs to complete the annual orbit around the Sun. This reducing phase will continue, until a specific 'number of rotations' is finally obtained over time as the Earth reaches the very **mid-base of the EAROC**. Here, the reversal in the speed of the EAR Period occurs, as it progresses on to complete the 'Oscillation Cycle' in a gradually increasing EAR Period phase. This is the other immovable parameter in these 'EAR Oscillation Cycles'. This reversal will occur and establishes the mid-base of the 'Oscillation Cycle'. This is due to the relevant cosmic forces acting upon the Earth' Axis Rotation, which would eventually cause an increasing trend in the EAR Period from this mid-base of the 'Oscillation Cycles'.

All that has been described above is of course still theory until proven to be the case. However, all these changes would be following the same consistent and constant change rate of $1/1000^{th}$ second per every 100 years throughout the EAROC. You will see this more clearly, when I show you the basic computation, supporting all of these above results.

Therefore, based on all of these data as above, I have indeed come to the scriptural revelation conclusion that the length of the years would constantly oscillate between the 365+ Solar Days/Year **maximum** and the 360 Solar Days short years **minimum**.

Biblically speaking in Biblical time reading terms, these years will be oscillating between 365 Earth Days down to 360 Earth Days and then up again to 365 Earth Days only to repeat the cycle once again. This would be the complete loop or complete oscillating cycle.

> Scientific Scholarship having become singly concerned only with the length of the day, from my understanding, with it' subsequent affect on the duration of the year, thereby had missed somehow, the significance of the small slow but incrementally consistent and definitely gradually changing **number of Earth-Axis Rotations** to complete one orbit over time.

'Time' here, will be discovered to be over several millions of years before any single change to the number i.e. pertaining to fully completed EARS would be actually possible. For example, from 365 down to 364 EARS; 364 down to 363 EARS; 363 down to 362; 362 down to 361 and finally 361 down to 360 EARS. Then from the mid-base of a typical 'EAR Oscillation Cycle' this very change would then be increasing from the 360 EARS up to 361 EARS; 361 up to 362; 362 up to 363; 363 up to 364; 364 back to 365 EARS. This would indeed eventually after a very long period of time complete each 'Oscillation Cycle' from the time it had first begun.

> Based on these very findings, hopefully you will also come to the similar conclusion that it is not possible to have in the future, 36 hour long days, let alone 25 hour long days as concluded and proposed through this OEARM.

This I had already established quite clearly by following my renewed and fortified understanding of the Scriptural based projections. This to my understanding irrefutably confirms that it is not cosmically possible for the Earth to have even a full hour to be added to its EAR.

So, according to my previous suggestion and proposal, the length of the Solar Year would be oscillating between 365+ Solar Days down to 360 Solar Days and then up again to 365+ Solar Days. Once this is obtained then it is the beginning of another 'EAR Oscillation Cycle'. Similarly, the corresponding Earth Axis Rotations would be oscillating from 365 down to 360 and then up again from 360 to 365. The transition from 365 Earth Axis Rotations down to 360 EARS and then up again to 365, is indicated just below for a typical EAR oscillation. This will continue as such, as long as it is allowed to, by the natural cosmic forces and the overall galactic and universe cosmic forces affecting it as such, if any.

Slowing Down Phase in the EAR speed as in a typical EAR Oscillation Cycle:

RBP 24:12(A)	adds 21 EAR minutes	until **RBP 24:33**
Beginning of OC		Mid-base of OC
365 EARs		**360 EARs**
24hrs 12mins EAR		24hrs 33mins EAR
(24.20 hours/day)		**(24.55 hours/day)**

Increasing Phase in the EAR speed as in a typical EAR Oscillation Cycle:

RBP 24:33	reduction of 21 EAR minutes	until **RBP24:12(B)**
Mid-base of OC		Ends a 42 minutes OC
360 EARs		**365 EARs**
24hrs 33mins EAR		24hrs 12mins EAR
(24.55 hours/day)		**(24.20 hours/day)**
		Begins next OC

You will find out as above, this is precisely indeed not more than **21 EAR minutes** either way. That is 24.20 Hours plus the 21 'EAR Minutes' to provide us with the 24.55 Hours/Day and then 24.55 Hours minus the 21 'EAR Minutes' to provide us with the 24.20 Hours/Day

You can clearly see from all of the above presentation and calculation using the scientific established change rate to the EAR period, that we just cannot have an increase from 365.242199 days, say to 366 Solar Days/Year sometime in our Earth' future. This is despite the EAR is indeed slowing down at present and we see the corresponding Solar Year is indeed increasing in it' length for it too as it' own oscillation cycle within this EAR Period range. This in turn would limit it' lengthening and if occurring then it' shortening too, perhaps even to being shorter than the EAR Period. Therefore, in conclusion to this before it can lengthen to say 366 Solar Days/Year, it is stopped in it' track, so to speak, by that **'self-regulating solar cosmic mechanism'** kicking in as per this proposed OEARM. This having already been mentioned earlier will once again start increasing but from a day lower. That is 364+ Solar Days/Year as you can study from the above. So, it is simply not possible for us to have a 366 Days Year in our Solar Calendar.

For as the **EAR reduces further** in it' speed of rotation on it' axis over time, but yet continues in orbit around the Sun with an unchanging speed, and the distance of orbit is as currently except for the accommodation of the possible 'perturbation effect'; this will in fact cause the number of EARs per Orbit, to indeed reduce from it' present 365 EARS i.e. eventually down to the next level being the 364 EARS per Orbit. This is due to the **'self-regulating solar cosmic mechanism'**, that I was highlighting to you earlier. This also pulls down the number of Solar Days that would make up the Solar Year. For obviously, a completed EAR, is still directly responsible to contributing much of the time that makes up for every Solar Day that we would have and in multiplicity in a Solar Year. Of course, to complete a Solar Day, we need to take into account besides the time taken to complete an EAR, the additional travel time motion of the Sun to be back at it' meridian each day.

So, here you do see, that if we observe only EARs as our time keeping system, which is indeed the initial Biblical System intended for keeping time by the early people; we will have indeed our **360 'Earth Days' Years**.

This by simply applying the already proven and accepted scientific discovery, that the EAR period is indeed reducing in it' speed currently, I am able through this proposed OEARM approach, show you the obtaining of the '360 Earth Day Years'. Of course, I have also already established that these would be also the 360 Solar days too, having exactly the same time period of 24 hours and 33 minutes for both day types.

> This is indeed our **'11th Milestone Achievement'** having been necessary for us to obtain it in order to continue our ongoing progress.

> One Earth Orbit takes 8,839.39 hours with a speed of 66,000 miles per hour or rather 105,600 km per hour typically.

'THE BIBLICAL 360 DAY YEARS & THE SCRIPTURAL COSMIC 666'
ADDENDUM & BRIDGE

EAR speed switchover from faster to slower occurs regularly at RBP 24:12(A) or rather at the beginning of every oscillation. As in this particular case the 18th Oscillation Cycle, it will occur at RBP18:24:12(A).

EAR slowing or when increasing, as the case maybe, at the time during the different phases of the OC changes at a consistent rate of 1/1000 sec per 100 years.

EARTH' 18th Oscillation Cycle begins now at RBP18:24:12(A)

EAR Period Begins at 24.20 HOURS AT RBP18:24:12(A)
24hrs 12mins : **365.264049586 Earth days/orbit**

24.20144776 mean Solar day duration i.e. 24 hours 12 minutes 5.211936 seconds, establishes the current 365.242199047 Solar days/orbit

EAR Period 24.21666666
24hrs 13mins : **365.012663455 Earth days/orbit**

EAR Period 24.23333333
24hrs 14mins : **364.761623109 Earth days/orbit**

EAR Period 24.25 (RBP 18:15)
24hrs 15 mins : **364.510927835 Earth days/orbit**

EAR Period 24.26666666
24hrs 16 mins : **364.260576924 Earth days/orbit**

EAR Period 24.28333333
24hrs 17mins : **364.010569664 Earth days/orbit**

EAR Period 24.30 (RBP 18:18)
24hrs 18mins : **363.760905349 Earth days/orbit**

EAR Period 24.31666666
24hrs 19mins : **363.511583277 Earth days/orbit**

EAR Period 24.33333333
24hrs 20mins : **363.26260274 Earth days/orbit**

EAR Period 24.35 (RBP 18:21)
24hrs 21mins : **363.013963039 Earth days/orbit**

EAR Period 24.36666666
24hrs 22mins : **362.765663475 Earth days/orbit**

EAR Period 24.38333333
24hrs 23mins   : **362.517703349 Earth days/orbit**

EAR Period 24.40 (RBP 18:24)
24hrs 24mins   : **362.270081967 Earth days/orbit**

EAR Period 24.41666666
24hrs 25mins   : **362.022798635 Earth days/orbit**

EAR Period 24.43333333
24hrs 26mins   : **361.77585266 Earth days/orbit**

EAR Period 24.45   (RBP 18:27)
24hrs 27mins   : **361.529243353 Earth days/orbit**

EAR Period 24.46666666
24hrs 28mins   : **361.282970028 Earth days/orbit**

EAR Period 24.48333333
24hrs 29mins   : **361.037031995 Earth days/orbit**

EAR Period 24.50   (RBP 18:30)
24hrs 30mins   : **360.791428571 Earth days/orbit**

EAR Period 24.51666666
24hrs 31mins   : **360.546159076 Earth days/orbit**

EAR Period 24.53333333
24hrs 32mins   : **360.301222826 Earth days/orbit**

EAR Period 24.55 (RBP 18:33) THE MID-BASE OF THE OC
24hrs 33mins   : **360.056619144 Earth days/orbit**

EARTH has now reached the important mid-base of it' 18th Oscillation Cycle at RBP18:24:33 with an EAR Period now of 24.55 (i.e. 24 hours 33 minutes). This is possibly it' slowest possible EAR Period.

> It is also quite clearly evident from the above that we did not achieve the desired result of obtaining exactly the 360 Earth days/Orbit, which as per the scripturally derived calculation should be taking place in the Biblical Human History/ future for the very first time at the precisely appointed 126,000,000th year.

You have already been informed this precise period of time had commenced from the RBP18:24:12(A) and which would culminate in the far future at the future RBP 18:24:33. However, you must certainly realise from this, that we did achieve the **360**.056619144 EARs at RBP18:24:33. This is quite close indeed to our expected objective but yet for all our intents and purposes, this is still not acceptable.

The reason why we did not achieve the ideally required result of 360 Earth Days/Orbit precisely as it should have been is because we did not take into consideration as yet the probable affects if any of the **perturbation of the Earth**. If it does as this OEARM proposes which is also based on the scientifically confirmed fact that the Planets - Venus, Jupiter and Saturn do perturb the Earth' orbit and also based on the relevant supporting scriptures to this 360 days year happening; then we may have the EARTH' orbit shortened that little bit and may be even it' speed of orbit. Anyway, this would have to be verified by the relevant scientific minds.

On my part it exists as a proposal and a hypothesis based on my understanding of the very relevant and supporting scriptures. This perturbation as per my proposal would need to alter the Earth' orbit to a time period of **8,838 hours** as required for this intent and purpose. By using this orbital time duration instead of the currently accepted **8839.39 hours orbit,** we will achieve our expected objective at the RBP18:24:33 precisely.

Well, I really do hope that there is such a perturbation effect or some other reason that has not been explored as yet for this OEARM hypothesis to become a real possibility after all.

With the possible or rather probable accumulated perturbation affects taken into consideration throughout the 126,000,000 years, then:

360 EARs X 24.55 Hours   = 8,838 Orbit Hours
(Mean future EAR Period)

Also, if we calculate, how many hours are there in the present Solar Year of 365.242199 days; we would arrive at the result of about 8,839.39 hours.

365.242199 Solar Days X 24.20144776 Hours = 8,839.39 Solar Orbit Hours

This also concludes once again, that the Noah' Flood was not responsible in anyway whatsoever, for the Earth to have acquired a 365¼ days year, as is evidently occurring as presently. It also concludes for that matter, that the Noah' Flood was not responsible to have been the cause to have changed it from their supposed to be original, i.e. 360 days year, as they had so proclaimed, to the present occurring 365¼ days year.

> However, the '360 Day Years' are indeed an integral part of this Planet' 'EAR Oscillation Cycles'. If this holds then these **'EAR Oscillation Cycles'**, could be possibly accepted, as being another significant and important cyclic motion to be added to the already eight cyclic motions that the Planet Earth goes through; bringing this total to possibly **nine** in the accepted future.

> If this should become the case, then it must be a '**big miss'** surely for scientific scholarship or am I just being simply atrociously ignorant.

Most of us only know of the two most common motions of the Earth. The first one is of course it' daily rotation on it' axial axis that gives us our days. And the second, is it' annual journey or orbit around the Sun, which gives us our years and the annual seasons with regularity due to the Earth' off-centre axis being inclined at 23°26'15".

So in conclusion, if the hypothesis turns out to be correct, then the 360 days year is indeed solely an Earth Solar Planetary Cosmic event, as demonstrated by all of the above description and as much detail explanation that I could present as such based on my understanding of the relevant referenced scriptures. I will also later discover these 360 days years would be factored into the cosmic construction of the **'number'** of the second beast, sum totalling 666.

> This is indeed my **12th Milestone Achievement'** which being absolutely necessary for us to continue on our progress onwards.

Could this change in the 'number of days' per orbit, also be a common occurrence in any or all of the other Solar Planets for somewhat similar reasons based on their own possible cyclic motions, if any, with the effects of perturbation???

Below, you will find more interesting facts pertaining to these 'EAR Oscillation Cycles'.

> You may have also come to realize regarding the Earth' Axis Rotation that it does first begin slowing down at the very beginning of each and every 'EAR Oscillation Cycle', as the Earth acquires each time a 24.20 EAR Period.

Now this differs from what I had actually proposed very much earlier with regards to the '360 Earth Day Years' as in Book One. These 'EAR Oscillation Cycles' have indeed fine tuned my very thinking on practically many things that I had proposed back in Book One, including, where should the **EARSS** bases be actually located. This now actually occurs first at the very beginning of each and every EAR Oscillation Cycle, whenever the Earth acquires an EAR Period of 24.20 hours. And then the EARSS would once again occur at the very mid-base distance of the particular EAROC when the EAR begins to increase in it' EAR Period. This gradual increase continues right till the very end of each EAROC, which at the very end of it, also begins the very next immediately following EAROC, similarly, and which gradually begins reducing once again in it' EAR Period. This repeating reducing phase will continue as such until it' own respective mid-base distance is reached at precisely 126,000,000 years. Here once again it begins to gradually increase in it' EAR Period.

In this similar manner the EAROCs have been going on from the very beginning EAROC as the EAR Period acquires the EAR Period of 24.20 hours. And probably will continue as such indefinitely until the relevant cosmic mechanism forces cease exerting it' effects on the Earth in such manner.

However, I will not change anything in Book One, pertaining to the '360 Earth Day Years', because it was from that platform, I am now able to actually understand how we can obtain the '360 Solar Day Years' too, as explained in this Addendum. This accomplishes successfully as far as I am concerned the original and first quest, as set out in the very beginning of this Book One.

So, according to this new 'Oscillation EAR Model' (OEARM), we do not have an EARSS base at 24:00. We now have it located at RBP24:12(A) i.e. when the EAR acquires the 24.20 Hours Period at the very beginning of every 'EAR Oscillation Cycle'. Then another, when the Earth acquires the 24.55 hours EAR Period at RBP 24:33, which is at the mid-base distance of every 'EAR Oscillation Cycle'. And of course at the end of the EAROC at RBP 24:12(B) when the EAR returns to it' original 24.20 EAR Period. This is also the beginning of the next EAROC.

So, 24.20 mean Solar Days are actually produced from the very beginning of each and every 'EAR Oscillation Cycle'.

This is more than just a successful conclusion although being just hypothetically generated through this proposed OEARM. For it is another significant point to contend with here. This is because this **cosmic phenomenon** is directly interlocked with the Holy Scriptures, to further contribute in revealing to us, the mind-boggling cosmic construction of the 'number of the beast' sum totalling to 666.

So, in conclusion the Addendum findings here, actually fine tunes our 'discoveries' and revelations in Book One, to an even greater degree of accuracy and clarity.

So, recapping the main changes that we need to observe since Book One is as follows:

a) It is not a case of having just one single very long period of EARs in the increasing mode, followed by just one single equally very long period of EARs in the reduction mode, until the Sun literally stops providing it' 'life' sustaining sunshine. This was my fundamental understanding in Book One, as I also had followed at that time to a certain extent Dr Arthur Beiser' proposal of 36 hour long days.

However, in this Addendum, I had discovered that we have indeed several shorter 'EAR Oscillating Cycles', relatively speaking, within which, each having a consistent and equal reduction and also similarly in equal increase when this is the case, in the period speed of the EAR.

> These EAROCs follows the scientific established 'change rate' with regards to the gradual changes in the Period speed of the EARs. This makes the EAR to first keep on reducing until mid-base and then from this mid-base to be increasing once again until the very ending of the particular ongoing 'Oscillation Cycle'. All of this is according to this same science backed 'change rate', which I had employed throughout as such in the EAROCs as developed according to this OEARM hypothesis.

All of this has already been described and explained in detail to you earlier in this Addendum.

b) The first Earth Axis Rotation Speed Switchover (EARSS) did not begin at RBP24:00, as projected previously in Book One. For through this Addendum, I have now come to realize that all these EAROCs do actually begin when each time the **EAR Period of 24.20 hours** (i.e. 24 hours and 12 Minutes) is obtained. This then would be the beginning RBP24:12(A) for the particular EAROC.

In the same manner following the above understanding, when each time the **EAR of 24.55 hours** (i.e. 24 hours and 33 minutes) is obtained, this would be at the EAROC' mid-base.

Finally, when the EAR Period returns to it' original daily Period of 24.20 hours i.e. another 21 EAR minutes later, this will then indeed end every 'EAR Oscillation Cycle' accordingly at it' respective ending RBP.

This means as an example, for the 18th EAROC, this particular EAROC would have begun at it' own respective **RBP 18:24:12(A)**. Then it' mid-point would be at **RBP 18:24:33** with it' own ending at **RBP 18:24:12(B)**. This ending RBP would then become the beginning RBP (A) for the subsequent 19th EAROC as follows:

'THE BIBLICAL 360 DAY YEARS & THE SCRIPTURAL COSMIC 666'
ADDENDUM & BRIDGE

RBP 19:24:12(A) (EAR Period: 24 hours 12 minutes); followed by it' mid-point at **RBP 19:24:33** (EAR Period: 24 hours 33 minutes) and ending at RBP **19:24:12(B)** (EAR Period: 24 hours 12 minutes).

This was the case from the very first EAROC i.e., from the RBP **01**:24:12(A) – **01**:24:33 – **01**:24:12(B) and will continue as such into the very future. Please do take note, that all the RBPs although seem to be referring and to be in the very same positions are indeed at different locations each in the Universe Space as the Solar System indeed travels around the Milky Way Galaxy. Astronomical Scholarship informs us that the journey around the Milky Way Galaxy takes the Sun about **220,000,000** years to complete. This is indeed getting quite close to my EAROC of 252 million years for each to be completed. This means that for each EAROC to be completed, as the Sun travels around the Galaxy, it would take an additional 32 million years for it to be completed too. How accurate is the calculation for the 220,000,000 years journey is not known to me at this point but if it could be a little lower around **216,000,000 years**, the numbers would seem to become very familiar to us. First of all, this would cause an exact additional **36,000,000** years for an EAROC to be completed after the Sun has completed it' journey around the Galaxy. This is somewhat like the necessity for the EAR to further rotate after it had completed it' daily axial axis rotation to bring the Sun back to it' meridian which actually constitutes a Solar Day being around 4 minutes longer than a Sidereal day which is correspondingly exactly to an EAR Period.

Secondly, as a quick observation the number 216,000,000 when halved would result in the amazing Babylonian time keeping number of 108,000,000. As you read through the next segment of this Book, 'More Ancient and Modern Civilization 'Time Sequence' Relationships', you will come to know that the Babylonian Hour is indeed divided into exactly **1080** time divisions at the first level; each measuring about 3.3 seconds each!!! Who knows this could be another definite connection amongst the other possible reasons for the Babylonian to do so, as it seems to be related in the overall context with the time that it takes the Sun, Earth and the rest of the Solar System to travel around the Milky Way Galaxy. These numbers are also found in the 'Ancient Indian/Hindu Cosmological Time Cycles' which you will come familiar with in the next immediate segment after the Addendum as just mentioned above. Coincidence you may say but then again it may not be so, but having a more purposeful time keeping GOD design factored into it.

The Sun as it orbits around the centre of our Galaxy, which Astronomical Scholarship informs us, is about 150 trillion miles from us, bobs up and down as in an **oscillation cycle**, which according to them takes 64 million years to complete. However, if they had computed it as being exactly **63 million years** instead then it would be exactly a ¼ of my proposed EAROC duration of 252,000,000 million years each. So the time taken for every four completions of the Sun's Oscillation Cycle in it' orbit around the Galactic Centre would equate to the time for one EAROC to be completed if this is the actual case!!!

The Milky Way Galaxy is **100,000 light-years** across, but only **1000 light-years** thick. So during the course of the 64 million year cycle (63 million years perhaps) the Sun rises above the galactic plane 500 light-years, passes down through the galactic plane until it is 500 light-years below and then comes back up again level with the galactic plane to complete this oscillation cycle. There will come a time however, when the Sun would pass directly through the Galactic disk centre causing a perfect Galactic alignment between the Sun, it' planets and the centre of the Galaxy. This is the intriguing **'Galactic Alignment'** which is abuzz around the world today, for Scientist projects it to be happening this very 2012 December 21-23 time period. Some are even suggesting that it could be **'Dooms Day'**; the end of the world as we have it now.

The above Astronomical facts can be referenced from several websites; however, the one that I had referenced was from 'Universe Today'.

Coming back to our recapping: These location changing RBPs as the Earth travels together with the rest of the Solar System around the Milky Way Galaxy can be appreciated or identified by the changing number of the EAROC from one, two, three and so on.

We are now as mentioned and as established previously, currently in the **18th EAROC**. In fact we have moved from it' own respective beginning RBP i.e. **RBP18:24:12(A)** some **500,000 years** or so ago. Since then it has been moving gradually towards it' mid-base position which would be 126,000,000 years into the future (less the 500K years) as computed from it' beginning RBP.

c) There will be no such possibility for us to be having 36 hour long days here on Earth, which was suggested by Dr Arthur Beiser sometime ago or for that matter even 30 or 25 hour long days following this OEARM proposal. The 'days in the year', will however still have it' quarter of an hour variations though, as it is happening now, during every Solar Orbit.

d) I also found out as I was studying this, that the EAR Periods according to this OEARM, will not allow the number of mean Solar Days per year, to increase say from it' present 365.242199 days to the very next day being the 366th, nor will allow it to reduce to any lower than 360 Earth Day Years. This is all due to the **'Self-Regulating Solar Cosmic Mechanism Forces'**, that I was informing you as previously.

Finally, just to remind you once again, that we are actually currently in the **18th EAR Oscillation Cycle**. The very same that **Adam and Eve** were also in at the time, when they were created through very special and unique means by our LORD GOD ALMIGHTY.

PRAISE BE TO GOD ALMIGHTY

Contact me if the need arises:
E: gcf@globalchristianfamily.com

More Ancient and Modern Civilization 'TIME SEQUENCE' Relationships

Through further research, mainly pertaining to the contents of Book One, I came upon several more very closely related time sequences and equation relationships in the way ancient civilizations observed time to that as generated and expressed in it. These are not only with the **Maya,** a South American People Group of Guatemala whom also had extended all across right to Mexico, but also with the **Babylonians** and with the **Indians of India** in their respective ways of keeping time. This even includes our modern time-keeping ways.

I will also be making several specific references to my **Indian 'brothers' of India,** especially to some of their own Hindu Sacred Vedic Books and some Indian astronomical based literature. Amongst these of course is their important SuryaSiddhanta, as translated by Burgess. This is actually pertaining to the development of their Indian/Hindu Cosmological Time Cycles. This section is going to be very interesting.

There are some time periods that were established in these Hindu sacred books that also uncannily share some common ground in the way some time periods are also developed in my Book One & even in my Book Two. These time periods which I had developed in these two Books of mine were actually developed through the application of my very own understanding of the relevant Scriptures, as found primarily written in the Biblical Book, 2Esdras.

This 'common sharing' as mentioned above, is quite strange to have come about, in considering of the major differences that exists according to the religious aspect, that both do not generate similar spiritual understanding & worship of the One LORD GOD ALMIGHTY, that we Christians have come to know as being Jehovah or Yahweh; but yes, this is yet the very case with respect to time.

All of these time systems or rather the time period measurements have been developed through specific **'time scales'.** I discovered through my Book One, that we can link up with any of these time systems by the simple application of a bridging time-scale, which these time sequence equation relationships in the following pages will clearly demonstrate.

If you do recall in Book One/Part Two, I had indicated a series of 'time equations', with increasing powers of 10; one of which began with:

$$360 \times 4 = 1,440$$

This result **1,440** as mentioned also earlier is a 100th part in 'time value' of the Scriptural number, 144,000. Following this, I realised that we can obtain other sets of equations in progression, as developed from these following beginning equations; 360 X 1; 360 X 2; 360 X 3; 360 X 4 and so on. To make this even much more clearer to you, let me lead you through some examples of these 'equations', as shown on the next page.

Before we begin, I also realised as previously mentioned, if we divide our modern averaged 24 hours day of 86,400 seconds by 60, this will also produce the result **1,440** (minutes). The similar number as indicated above.

Therefore, again I repeat that all the time systems seem to me, to be tied together somehow, except for each following their different **concepts,** scales and divisions of time. This further tells me, all of these 'time systems', point to a common source of reference for its development, invention and realization. And I most certainly propose it is quite obviously **'Cosmic'** related. The very same that our LORD GOD ALMIGHTY had created and inculcated into it a system of time measuring, which is evidently also synchronous with their own respective time keeping system.

360 Equation Series 1
360 x 1 = 360
360 x 10 = 3,600
360 x 100 = 36,000
360 x 1,000 = 360,000
360 x 10,000 = 3,600,000
360 x 100,000 = 36,000,000

360 Equation Series 2
360 x 2 = 720
360 x 20 = 7,200
360 x 200 = 72,000
360 x 2,000 = 720,000
360 x 20,000 = 7,200,000
360 x 200,000 = 72,000,000

360 Equation Series 3
360 x 3 = 1,080
360 x 30 = 10,800
360 x 300 = 108,000
360 x 3,000 = 1,080,000
360 x 30,000 = 10,800,000
360 x 300,000 = 108,000,000

360 Equation Series 4
360 x 4 = 1,440
360 x 40 = 14,400
360 x 400 = 144,000
360 x 4,000 = 1,440,000
360 x 40,000 = 14,400,000
360 x 400,000 = 144,000,000

'THE BIBLICAL 360 DAY YEARS & THE SCRIPTURAL COSMIC 666'
More Ancient and Modern Civilization 'TIME SEQUENCE' Relationships

> The above '360 Equation Series', to my very understanding, as you will also find out later in this book, do continue progressively on, as long as it is applicable and is relevant, I believe, such as: Equation Series 5; 6; ....100.....1,000.....10,000 and so forth.....

The numbers **360, 7,200 and 144,000** are all found quite surprisingly in the Maya calendar time system too and represents, as already made known to you, in this Maya Calendar an equivalent number of days.

The number 1080 as found in the beginning of Equation Series 3 is the exact number of Divisions, which is quite surprising again, which the Babylonians had actually divided their hour into.

To make this connection, is indeed just amazing!!! Don't you think so too???

When I first came to know, that the Babylonians had actually divided their hour into 1080 divisions of time measurement, I just could not understand the life of me, why???

Why did they need to divide the hour into 1080 divisions especially in those very early times??? What were the driving purposes or their concerns to having done so with such precision at that???

Why not into 60 or 120 just to stretch our own imagination to accommodate the Babylonians. Now that I have seen the above equation emerge as it is, i.e. as shown here being the **360 x 3 = 1080**; it provides me at least with an emerging logic that would later become even more strongly established: "Why they had done so".

This may not however to you, be the exact reason why, but it does give us something to grasp onto now, to comprehend their very rationale in actually doing so. Sometime in Book Two, I will be able to further demonstrate the Babylonian' other valid reasons that I envisage for them to be doing this specific number of 'divisions'. It was definitely not done i.e. divided as such by just mere accident or by just sheer coincidence, but through a systematic and most evidently a purposeful design. Also, if you do remember towards the very ending of the 'Addendum', I had indicated a linkage of this to the total time that it takes the Sun to travel around the Milky Way Galaxy.

I also found out through an Internet article, as written by Duncan Watson, though it is already of common knowledge, that a Zodiacal Period equates to about 2,160 years and that the entire Zodiacal Cycle constitutes a total time period of 25,868 years, is indeed tied to the very precessions of the Equinoxes.

> Precession here means slow movement of the longitudinal axis of the Earth, which when plotted against the ecliptic, exhibits the earlier occurrences of the Equinoxes in each successive Sidereal Year. This is indeed another important and relevant motion of the Earth which is recognised amongst the already known existing eight.

For example, according to Duncan Watson, when we say that we are in the 'Age of Aquarius', this means that it is the Zodiacal star sign of Aquarius rising on the horizon at the equinox in the Northern Hemisphere. It will continue to do so for about 2,160 years (30 degrees, or 1/12th of the sky); then another zodiacal star sign will be rising to occupy it for another 2,160 years.

Also, according to Duncan' internet article report, this Zodiacal Cycle period was well known to the Sumerians (a very early civilization being the non-Semitic element of ancient Babylonia). In fact, the Zodiacal signs and names for all of the constellations with which we are familiar with in the sky were first designated by them. Isn't this simply incredible!!! That a people group, living in those very ancient times so long ago, were yet so knowledgeable and accurate with regards to their knowledge of the night sky, to be able to know this despite the separation between each Zodiac Cycle by a massive 2,160 years!!!

Yet I do wonder, did they also know that the 'Precession of the Equinoxes', as expressed by their Zodiacal Cycle was indeed the direct result of the 'slow gyrating motion' of the rotating Earth' axis caused by the gravity of the Sun and the Moon working together in unison on the Earth' equatorial bulge??? But then again, whether they indeed knew about this or not is nothing compared to the fact that they were able to see this 'movement' i.e. the 'precession of the Equinoxes in the heavens. This is simply amazing if you do realise, in repetition, that the Sumerians were according to 'The Oxford Concise Dictionary', the early and non-Semitic element people in the civilisation of ancient Babylonia. Also, from another source of reference, there were other ancient peoples belonging in this group from Sumer, whom were also present at the time being the Akkadians. Some of their i.e. the Sumerians and the Akkadians cities were Nippur, Adab, Lagash, Umma, Larsa, Erech, Ur (Ur being the very birth place of Abram who was later renamed by our LORD GOD to be Abraham). Interesting to know isn't it.

These people groups were indeed a very vibrant civilization, located somewhere along or near the Euphrates, even before we heard of the Egyptians being the great 'People of the Pyramids' having built these more than 5,000 years ago. You can further check this out for yourself. Also, there is ample information in books and the Internet on this very topic of the 'Precessions'.

The reason for bringing all of this up, was to show you that the time value for each Zodiacal Star Sign Period being 2,160 years, is again found in my beginning **6th 360 Equation Series**; as I had progressed it accordingly as follows:

$$360 \times 6 = 2{,}160$$

It also equates to 1080 x 2 = 2,160. This 6th 360 Equation Series, also inevitably ties or rather offers a vital link to the Sumerian Time System, with our ongoing establishing of the scriptural based time system. Our scriptural based time system, through this study, will also eventually establish for us the **'Mother of all Time Systems'** being the Universe Expansion Time (UET); as you will find out in the course of this book.

The numbers, as found in the corresponding '360 Equation Series' of above being **3,600, 72,000,000, 1,440 and 144,000** can also be taken, as referring to our modern day Earth Time System. For our hour is divided into 3,600 seconds. In Book Two, you will find out, that the number **72,000,000** which is expressed in Equation Series 2, has a real significance of how 'Earth Time', is related to the overall time of the Universe Expansion Time (UET). This UET is yet another original concept that I had developed and discovered during the process of writing this book. Since this is quite complex for now, we will leave this for until later. Also, of course 1,440 relates to the number of minutes in our averaged 24 hours day.

The number 144,000 as found in our 4th '360 Equation Series' is also found in the Holy Scriptures and you will find out that the number 360 can also be Biblically derived. You will also soon discover this 144,000 is also representing a particular time period in years, in the 'Indian/Hindu Cosmological Time Cycles'.

It is clearly evident, the common number linkage, in all of the above time equations, is none other than the versatile number, 360.

Also take note, for some reason, I needed to progress each of these equations i.e. the '360 Equation Series', to only their **sixth progression** level each and no further. Why this is so is yet to be known by me except that it is only relevant to this final 6th level. Now as an example, let us take all the 6th endings of the first six series of equations as follows:

1) 36,000,000
2) 72,000,000
3) 108,000,000
4) 144,000,000
5) 180,000,000
6) 216,000,000

This exposes a definite pattern of a constant and fixed increase from one series ending to the next, by a value of **36,000,000**. This is realised by taking each series to it' very sixth progression equation level and then comparing each at that particular 6th level, as these above equation examples exhibit.

For some reason, I also think that the limiting of these very '360 Equation Series' to only it' 'sixth level progression', has got to do with GOD limiting the 'Preparation & Development' of the Earth to also only 'Six Days' which also had completed HIS work for the Universe. Now this may seem to be very farfetched but the progression and subsequently the usefulness of these equations abruptly stop at their sixth level progression.

Another way of looking at these '360 Equation Series', is to link all the **beginnings** instead of the endings together. Following this way, we will get one continuous sequential running '360 Equation Series', beginning from 360 X 1; 360 X 2; 360 X 3; 360 X 4; 360 X 5; 360 X 6; 360 X 7; 360 X 8;....360 X 120;......360 X 144;.....360 X 1110 and beyond.

We will see later that there is some connection with this continuous running sequence and the way the Indian/Hindu formulated through an astronomical based construction their Indian/Hindu Cosmological Time Cycles. Although, being an ancient civilisation too, it still has many of it' roots still intact, even visible clearly as of today.

All of these numbers (endings) have obviously in their construction, the common linkage building block number; which is **360**. If we progress these '360 Equation Series', to the **120th** 360 Equation Series set, we will get surprisingly, the value at it' 6th progression level the ending; **4,320,000,000**. Let us take this to be referring to **4,320,000,000 years**.

120th '360 Equation Series'

360 X 120	= 43,200
360 X 1,200	= 432,000
360 X 12,000	= 4,320,000
360 X 120,000	= 43,200,000
360 X 1,200,000	= 432,000,000
360 X 12,000,000	**= 4,320,000,000 = 4.32 Billion**

> You will find out later that these 4.32 Billion Years, is exactly the age of the Universe as it began it' **12th Period** of Universe expansion. You will understand better about these **'12 Periods'** that I had just mentioned here, as you properly graduate to Book Two. For what I am saying here prematurely though, you need to continue reading it in Book Two, in order to fully grasp this, for it being another original conceptual understanding of mine. I had the humble and gracious privilege of discovering these '12 Periods of Universe Expansion', through the relevant understanding and appropriate application of the 2Esdras Scriptures. However, for now, it would suffice for you to know, that the beginning of the 12th Period of Universe Expansion, was when the Universe was **just 4.32 Billion Years old**, at that time.

This result or discovery was achieved and developed through the direct application of those relevant scriptural verses, which will be mentioned in the beginning of Part Three, as found in the Biblical Book, 2ESDRAS. It was through which I had first discovered the scriptural embedded mysteries, amazingly describing our entire 'World (Universe) History Time'. However, to appease your 'need to know now', the scriptures that will be referenced are found in Chapters 13:57 - 58 and 14:9 – 12 in the Biblical Book 2Esdras. If you are having a NKJV of the Holy Bible or similar you will unfortunately not find this biblical book in it. This Biblical Book, 2ESDRAS, is a Deuterocanonical Biblical Book in the Holy Bible translation as used presently, predominantly by the Roman Catholic Christian World. All that the word Deuterocanonical means is that a further series of Biblical Books, other than the 66, which were already also canonized earlier, were canonized later in the 'Second Canon' by the 'Holy Fathers'.

These Second Canon Biblical Books unfortunately are left entirely out in the mainstream of the other Holy Bible translations, as currently being used by those Christians other than the Roman Catholic. This in my most humble opinion is definitely a terrible loss to them. Now, I am no authority at any level on whether these Books should be included or not, but I am of the opinion that if the (Roman Catholic Authority) Biblical Scholars and Theologians deemed it fitting in the Second Canon to include these Books which the Holy Fathers having approved these, then I personally do accept them as such. It is as simple as that because I do not have any sort of politico-religious motivation or any other ultravires motive not to be doing so.

Furthermore, this book that I am currently writing, also owes its possible continuation into Part Three, on one of these series, which is of course the Biblical Book, 2ESDRAS, which was included in this Second Canon. Without it, there would not have been any possible solution and conclusion to the construction of the 'number of the second beast' in this book. It is an irrevocable integral part to solving this divine mystery. This further has led me to believe that these Books, in particular including the 2ESDRAS, are scripturally justified to be belonging to this divinely inspired deuterocanonical group of biblically accepted books at least by the major segment of Christianity – The Roman Catholics.

Now for the Protestants out there, who do come across my book; for your information the 'Protestant World' was using the full translation of the Holy Bible as per se, as used by the Roman Catholic, even after their separating from this 'Christ Body', for a period of about **274 years since then**. That is for more than a quarter of a millennium!!!

In fact, it was only in 1885, that the then Archbishop of Canterbury (Edward White Benson), the Head of the Church of England (Anglican Church), who had ordered these series of Biblical Books to be taken out. This eventually led to the entire 'Protestant World' unfortunately in my opinion, following suit as being evident today.

This was indeed another unfortunate and gigantic break-up within the Christian World. Why did Anglican Archbishop Edward White Benson had supported this move in the very first place, which he may or probably should have known would inevitably separate the 'Protestant World' even further apart from the Roman Catholic Church???" Could it have been intentionally done with this purposeful design in mind? I may be completely and absurdly wrong for to be even suggesting it being religiously-politico motivated. However, even not being so, this inevitable separation would finally identify 'The Protestant' as a completely different 'Christian Body', even having their very own bible translation. In my observation, this would thereby cut all roots and ties with the Roman Catholic Church and it' religious papal authority over the Christian world.

This from my point of view besides the above had indeed generated the intended spin off based on their very contention that these Deuterocanonical Books do not share the similar 'Divine Input - inspired' of our God Almighty.

Even the Pentecostal, Evangelical, Charismatic, who basically consider themselves to being 'born again' Christians according to the scriptural term that is used in John 3:3, such as those connected to the Assemblies of GOD (A.O.G) and various other well known Church groups, also do not include the second canon biblical books. This has caused many to be thinking or rather having been influenced to think and thereby accepting that it is entirely a doubtful text, when presented as such, by their 'Church Authority'.

However, I am sure; there are many Christians like myself out there, who would be very comfortable in using either translation. I personally read the Roman Catholic translation when I need to refer to the Deuterocanonical and the first Bible that I read from cover to cover was indeed the Good News Bible (a Roman Catholic Bible). However, for most of the time now, I do keep for my personal daily use the Spirit Filled Life Bible, published by Thomas Nelson Publishers, which is the New King James Version. I will continue using this, unless some serious faults are found with it. So far so good, no problems encountered as yet. I also do refer, time to time, to the 'Authorised King James' (AKJ) translation, when I do specifically need to get an even clearer 'root' English translation of a particular scriptural verse of the 'Word'.

With this conclusion, I have only one thing further to say on this matter and that is, before you do make your final decision regarding the Deuterocanonical Books, which the Protestant mostly prefer to refer to these as the Apocrypha; first read them and find out for yourself, whether you would consider having them included or not. You sincerely do owe it to yourself to have as much of GOD' canonised Word, that has also for several centuries been recognised as such, being the 'Holy Word' of our LORD GOD ALMIGHTY; even at one time by the very Protestant. It also reportedly bridges the missing 400 years or so of scriptural history between the Old Testament and the New Testament. Furthermore, this had been already established, approved and accepted as such, by many imminent Biblical Scholars and Theologians so very long ago, even before there were any, who were called 'Protestant' or the today' version of the 'born again' Christian.

Also, take very careful note, that there is indeed a very big difference between the Apocrypha Books and the Pseudepigrapha (i.e. commonly referred to as being the spurious writings which claimants claim to be scriptural) categorised books. Many may have confused themselves somewhat with regards to these two separate and different categories of books; the Apocrypha and the Pseudepigrapha books as being one and the same!!! This misconception could be also the major part of their problem, one way or the other, in not being able to accept the actual Deuterocanonical Books which are also called the Apocrypha.

Besides this very real confusion, there are many Christians out there who have not heard about the Apocrypha Books and the Pseudepigrapha spurious writings in the first place. Therefore, they are even easier to be duped and to be led astray from their faith in JESUS CHRIST being GOD and Man at the same time and to succumb to those Pseudepigrapha stories that Jesus Christ was indeed married and that he had children like the rest of us. His lover or wife as they seem to proclaim was indeed Mary Magdalene; etc., etc.

Do some investigative research yourself and find out what is the difference between the Apocrypha Biblical Books and the Pseudepigrapha spurious writings category of books. It may even change your mind, to accept that the Apocrypha Books should remain after all within the 'Library of Biblical Books' that make up the Holy Bible; despite your past learning and teaching.

For your added information the Roman Catholic Church quite obviously takes a strong stand against those spurious writings i.e. the Pseudepigrapha books, which many have used to attempt manipulating our Faith into disrepute and possible destruction.

I believe that these are spread by unscrupulous 'terrorists' who are against our very 'Faith' and even directly against our LORD GOD ALMIGHTY, as they are definitely driven by satanic impetus. They have caused these very writings (Pseudepigrapha books) to be readily floating around; attempting and threatening to ridicule and destroy the established Word of God, as contained in the recognised and approved Holy Bible from time to time through every generation. Their ultimate purpose is to draw away as many Christians from their faith, especially those having little knowledge of these Pseudepigrapha books as time goes on. These Pseudepigrapha books will be continuously from time to time used and brought up just as in the past, to attack the very foundations of our 'Faith'. From this you can see the sinister hand of Satan behind the scenes orchestrating such people to cause confusion in those who are not well learned in their Christian belief. Therefore, we must remain strongly grounded in the WORD at all times teaching also the generations to come.

These next few sentences have just now been included here (21/July/ 2006). These are referring to the infamous book in our context, "The Da Vinci Code", and the making of the movie with the similar name.

This is a classic example of these unscrupulous 'terrorists' being referenced as such, being at it again. In my opinion this was not just about making money or the human ability of good intriguing storytelling, but a well planned, well orchestrated and a very well attempted character assassination, if I could say so, of our Lord and Saviour Jesus Christ. This is my opinion for what it is worth and I do hope that there are many out there who would join me similarly in this opinion.

I did say well attempted, because this attempt unlike those before was indeed more potent due to the now available international media, especially global television, which reaches across all borders and across all religions and cultures. And more importantly or rather more damagingly, it reaches a lot of new Christians who may not have the necessary background or rather the in-depth knowledge of these Pseudepigrapha books and could become somewhat confused or shaken in their new belief, which is further compounded due to this well orchestrated attempt. I am also inclined to believe that many seasoned and well grounded Christians may also have fallen to this argument or presentation as such. This could be also partly because these Pseudepigrapha books have been purged and kept out from the hands of the common Christian i.e. the lay person. There is just very little Christian teaching to the lay Christian across all borders with regards to these spurious books. However, despite all of this renewed effort by these **'terrorists'**, it is quite obvious this attempt on the whole too, has indeed failed, because the 'wise amongst us' have shown up its weaknesses.

However, on a more positive note, looking at it from another perspective, the author Dan Brown surely has initiated unintentionally perhaps yet another wave of what we can refer to as the wake-up call for many of us. This is to educate Christians through all levels possible of these still existing Pseudepigrapha Books, the reasons why these have been justifiably removed so long ago, by the then 'fathers' of our Christianity to thereby close any such loopholes for future 'terrorists' attacks.

Let us now move on, with the matter at hand. I also realised, as we continue these '360 Equation Series' further, i.e. just up another 24 Series from the 120th; we would eventually also be able to obtain the familiar number, **51,840,000**. This result **51,840,000** would appear as mentioned in the **144th** '360 Equation Series'. Yes, even this '360 Equation Series', the **144th**, seems to be familiarly connected with the important Scriptural number; 144,000.

For your convenience, this Equation Set is as follows:

144th '360 Equation Series'

360 X	144	= 51,840
360 X	1,440	= 518,400
360 X	14,400	= 5,184,000
360 X	**144,000**	**= 51,840,000**
360 X	1,440,000	= 518,400,000
360 X	14,400,000	= 5,184,000,000

This was as also previously explained, firstly obtainable both by multiplying 360 days which represents our 'number of days' at the Mid-Base of our 'EAR Oscillation Cycles', with the Biblical and Scriptural derived 144,000 (years).

Thirdly, the 'number of days' as indicated in the Maya Calendar System i.e. for One Calabtun time period represents **51,840,000** days.

Is all of this making some sense to you now? Well, I sincerely do hope so. However, if it doesn't, do not worry, but just keep on reading.

Also, according to a very interesting exegesis, as placed on the Internet, the established thousands of years old time system i.e. the 'Indian/Hindu

Cosmological Time Cycles' through Dwight William Johnson, I learnt that the Indian/Hindu 'Great Ages' are based on the Kalpas and Yugas. A Kalpa is a great period of **4,320,000,000 years (4.32 Billion Years).** Once again this information is of common knowledge to those who are familiar with the 'Indian/Hindu Cosmological Time Cycles', though I was first introduced to it through Dwight Johnson' internet article. Thanks would be in order.

> **You can clearly see my own independently calculated 4.32 Billion Years which being the possible age for the Universe at the beginning of the 12th Period of Universe expansion, is also amazingly used to represent a Kalpa; being a specific time period as derived by the ancient Indian/Hindu for their own cosmological time system!!!**

According to Dwight' well presented exegesis the very **'Indian/Hindu Cosmological Time Cycles'** represent numerically the **'life' of our Solar System** and is a very comprehensive system of time measurement, based upon the sexagesimal number system. This **'Indian/Hindu Cosmological Time Cycles'** has time units as small as $1/216,000^{th}$ of a day (this refers to a 0.4 seconds time measurement) and as large as 3.1104×10^{14} years.

I learnt from his exegesis and others like it, that their 'time cycles' for a day, had been at the very beginning of the Indian/Hindu progress to their later establishing even greater and more advanced cosmological time cycles, interestingly were measured through the **breathing rates** of the great meditating sages of that time. These also similarly followed the sexagesimal number system, as follows:

10 long syllables (gurvakshara)	= 1 respiration (prana)
6 respirations	= 1 vinadi
60 vinadis	= 1 nadi
60 nadis	= 1 day

This different system of time segmenting of a day is truly just amazing to say the least. The Indians of India came up with this fantastic ingenuity of using their natural observation of the breathing rates of their wise priest men, trained in the breathing regiment skills of Pranayama. With this awesome disciplined ability in Pranayama, they went on to devise an original time keeping system, as described above. This is testimony to the fact that they had no knowledge at the time of the hour, minute and seconds being as divisions of time per day.

This is of course unlike the Babylonians, who had used a segment of time of a day, which is the hour and divided the same into 1080 Divisions and also into smaller sub-divisions of time, which as you may already know, astonishingly measured even hundredths of a second.

This from my perspective and understanding suggests that the Indian/Hindu system of time measurement was indeed totally original in concept, in comparison to the Babylonian time system. This is quite obvious due to it' somewhat 'primitive though natural based methodology' and I use this term with the greatest respect to their ingenuity, which had differed greatly from that of the Babylonian sophisticated time keeping system. There are also other supporting reasons for establishing this fact in favour of the Indians.

The point that I am attempting to make here is that they had developed their time system, through the use of their very own cosmological/astronomical concepts and understanding, without any being borrowed from the outside of their empire and/or influence.

For you can see from this simple comparison, the Indian/Hindu' time keeping was a gradual building up time system; 1 respiration, 1 vinadi, 1 nadi, 1 day. Whereas, the Babylonian' was indeed a breaking down of time. That is a measured segment of time in a day = 1 hour; then 1 hour into 1,080 Divisions; then each of these into 76 subdivisions each. Of course, there are several other ways to amplify the differences between these two time keeping systems. As an example, one was based on astronomy whilst the other had masterfully linked astronomy to our biological rhythm of breathing; which is indeed the very essence for us to be able to live.

Through another internet article by Glenn R. Smith (Durgadass), I came to learn that the number of respirations that are made in a day (i.e. Sidereal Day), by the breath control technique called Pranayama, is 21,600 pranas (respiration). This means in one 24 hour period or between 2 consecutive sunrises, a person practising Pranayama takes an average of 21,600 breaths. Each of these trained breaths would be about 4 seconds long.

Therefore, 21,600 breaths = 60 Nadis/day = 3,600 vinadis = 21,600 pranas, as shown in the table on the previous page. All this time measurement is following the sexagesimal system.

1 Sidereal Day	= 23 hours 56 minutes 3.4446 seconds
60 Nadis	= 23 hours 56 minutes 3.4446 seconds
1 Nadi	= 23 minutes 56.06 seconds
1 vinadi	= 23.93 seconds
1 Prana	= 3.99 seconds

The Indians also came up with an innovative understanding which is indeed observable; that the Sun has three mean motions.

This they had achieved through their own innovation and amazing astronomical knowledge and perception in that early time long before western scientist and others had discovered these facts about our Sun. In fact they developed the three mean motions of the Sun by separating out the 'three components' that make up a Sidereal Year. As you may know, a Sidereal Year is equalled to 366.2563795 diurnal revolutions of the Earth, as per their calculations. So, what they did to establish the concept of the three mean motions of the Sun, was to take these 366.2563795 diurnal revolutions of the Earth and separate them as follows:

One Sidereal Year =	360	(First Mean Motion of the Sun)
	6	(Second Mean Motion of the Sun)
	0.2563795	(3rd Mean Motion of the Sun)
	366.2563795	diurnal revolutions of the Earth

A Sidereal Day is in fact about 4 minutes shorter than a Solar Day. Also, as the number of diurnal revolutions of the Earth in a Sidereal Year is one greater than the number of mean Solar Days,

Therefore,

1 Sidereal Year = 365.2563795 mean Solar Days.

All of the above could be another strong supporting fact or evidence to be offered, for the benefit of the ancient Indian scholars, sages, etc; that the development of their 'Indian/Hindu Cosmological Time Cycles' were indeed completely independent from outside influences, such as the 'implicated influences' that their critics claim, were imputed by the invading Persians. Implicated influences, simply means here, that they were influenced by these Persians or even by the Greeks in the development of their Cosmological Time Cycles. This suggested that the Indian/Hindu had not developed this understanding through their very own developed original ideas; concepts; astronomical knowledge, perception and thinking.

Anyway, according to Dwight' exegesis, the three mean motions of the Sun as shown above are used in the construction of the 'Indian/Hindu Cosmological Time Cycles'.

He goes on to say (to think of it), that the three mean motions of the Sun as expressed by them, are somewhat similar in concept to the hour, minute and second hands of a clock measuring time. This directly means, as their individual cycles are completed, although all of which are indeed running together, but yet they are each counted separately.

He concludes by saying, that by using these three mean motions, the ancients developed a system of time reckoning that put the day, year, and longer time intervals into exact correspondence with each other.

Just a short note here: With regards to Dwight' presentation of the Indian/Hindu larger amount of time i.e. 3.1104×10^{14}, where another report, prepared by Duncan Watson states: This large amount of time just mentioned here, should actually be 3.14159×10^{14} years. Also, Duncan indicates to us that the smallest time unit measured by them could have been as small as 0.16 second (Dwight indicated 0.4 second).

This 0.16 second is equivalent to a wink of an eye, which the ancient sages also knew about and I think, they could have probably used this also, as a precise basis, to initiate the day 'time cycles' just as they had done with their trained respiration rates. You may quite easily calculate that **25 eye-winks** would also equate to 4 seconds. This is indeed the precise time taken by each trained human respiration as achieved consistently, through the Indian/Hindu technique of Pranayama.

I will be referring to Duncan' report again from time to time, but for now we will continue with Dwight. I do not know whether you find all this interesting or not, but it is included here for a specific purpose.

Dwight' exegesis was mainly based amongst others, on the very ancient Hindu Sanskrit Literature Astronomical text, the SuryaSiddhanta. He informed us that he had used the translation of this text as translated by Ebenezer Burgess, which was published in 1860, in the Journal of the American Oriental Society, Volume 6, New Haven, USA. Dwight' exegesis, can be accessed through his web site if it is still available,

http://www.aaronsrod.com/time-cycles/index.html

I also had found out from Duncan, that 'The Great Ages' are similarly mentioned often in the sacred Hindu text of the Mahabharata and also in other Hindu Literature, such as the Srimad Bhagavatam.

Unfortunately, as websites are here today and gone tomorrow, I have decided to explain to you here, as clearly as I can, what I learnt from both Dwight and Duncan and through other similar reports, with regards to the Kalpas and the Yugas and how these time periods do relate to their **Hindu deity Brahma and our own Solar System**.

I am following through with this because it provides some further confirmation that my totally independent, scriptural based establishing for the age of the Universe and for the age of our Solar System has indeed yet another source of supporting reference to some extent, which was indeed also established several thousands of years ago. It provides me with the avenue to beef up even more strongly, what I had stated much earlier, that there are definite linkages between different time systems as developed by the ancient civilizations. I do also propose or of the opinion that all of these should be able to be linked back to the mother of all 'time systems', as expressed in the embedded Scriptural mysteries of the complete Holy Bible (i.e. which includes the Deuterocanonical). Some of these 'embedded Scriptural mysteries' are being unfolded for you and for me, right now in this inaugural book of mine, which is actually indeed a combination of two books; 'The Biblical 360 Day Years & The Scriptural Cosmic 666'.

From these both exegesis, I began to realise and also could deduce from it that Brahma, a Hindu deity/god, was and still is being considered to be the deity or god of the Solar System and also having been it' very creator. This is a deity having been **established** by the religious system of Hinduism and whom the Hindus worship, as such. Some relatively recent Hindu Scholars have even attempted in their zealousness, to even stretch this philosophy, this mythogenesis and/or mystic belief, to include the entire Universe. It is not surprising relatively speaking, that the more recent religious Hindu Scholars, wanted to connect their deity Brahma, as being the creator of the entire Universe and not just limiting to our Solar System. If I had understood this wrongly, then my ignorance has indeed defeated me again, needless to say. So if this is not the case then I stand corrected and extend a thousand apologies to all my Indian/Hindu population out there.

We are also informed that Brahma lives only for a **hundred years** in each cycle, but these are **'Brahma Years'** not earthly years. From their exegesis and somewhat similar reports of others, I came to the conclusion that although these 'Brahma Years' as considered by the Hindu religious system were 'divine years', but in actual fact, I had also found out that these 'Brahma divine years' are even **greater** in time value then their 'ordinary divine years'. Yes, I had come to know that there are indeed two types of 'divine years' in the Indian/Hindu religious system.

> Furthermore, we are informed that, after these 100 special (Brahma) divine years are completed in each cycle, it is followed by a **rest period** or interval equivalent to this period.

> After which time, Brahma is reincarnated together with the whole Solar System (which incidentally, also ends with the 100 years period, each time); and the whole cycle begins once again.

Subsequently, I also had come to know, that **One Kalpa** coincides with **one single special 'divine' day** (daylight only) of Brahma' life. And when the one single 'divine' night (Brahma' night only) comes, our Universe ('Universe', here is referring to the Solar System, since Brahma is considered by the ancient Hindus as being their god of the Solar System) will be reabsorbed (Pralaya) in his divine sleep.

This exegesis amongst many other similar studies, research and reports that are out there; informs us, that One Kalpa Period equates to **4,320,000,000** Earthly years. It takes two Kalpas, as evident from the above; one to fulfil 'one day' in Brahma' life and the other to fulfil 'one night' in Brahma' life.

Now, "How did they come to this very conclusion, in reference to their equating of One Kalpa Period (4.32 billion years) to one single 'Day' in the life of Brahma or for that matter, concluding that Brahma lives for 100 Brahma Years???"

If I am allowed to present the possible reasoning here for this, then it could be as follows:

That it was probably based on their cosmogony and also based on their ancient Hindu science of astronomy. Both of these had always been tied very closely together to be directly influencing and the shaping of the emerging Hinduism religious beliefs and philosophy, which were developed and brought into the fabric of their ancient society, through their very own local ancient mystics and sages.

> For I do personally observe, otherwise, that it should have been a **'received knowledge'** or revelation i.e. through the process of being inspired directly by their very deity, Brahma, or from the others of their gods. Worse still scenario, as suggested by some; from even an earlier people than the Indians themselves, which I do not particularly want to subscribe to and deny the Indians of their ingenuity in this area.

> Now, there is nowhere to my personal knowledge, where it had been stated as such, that Brahma had **informed** any of the Hindu Scholars, or the Sadhus (Hindu priesthood) or even their Gurus or to anyone for that matter with regard to the above i.e. it was realised through **'divine' revelation**.

> Since this was not the case, unless I could be corrected from my present perception to this concept, then it has been well known in fact that Brahma himself is indeed a **created deity by them,** (i.e. through their most early Indian astronomers/sages).

This human creation for having such a deity was indeed a needed substitution to relate and to record their astronomical discoveries for posterity, which were nicely fitted into the overall developing Hindu mythology. This then could be easily assimilated and accepted by the masses of their population, being ignorant and lacking the very critical understanding and more importantly the necessary tolerance to this higher knowledge of science at that time as accumulated by their astronomers. If their astronomy and cosmogony were not presented as such, they possibly knew that they could even have been killed quite easily, as this was beyond the understanding and acceptance of the general public and their immediate rulers at that time. In other words, it would have been too difficult to accept in relation to any existing 'belief' system of theirs at that early time.

Note: This is based on my own but brief understanding of their Hinduism. I will stand corrected, if this is actually not the case. However, we do have from one important aspect, supporting proof to my very understanding as such, as found within Duncan' report. His report provides us with the precise manner in which the 'Divine Age', equivalent for a 'day' of Brahma' life was indeed established. Yes indeed!!!

It was simply based on **attributing** two time periods which were calculated by them, based on their cosmogony amounting to 12,000 years each. One 'period of time' being the 'age of darkness' and the other being the 'age of light' or enlightenment.

They also attributed to these two time periods the **'sacred distinction'** of being conferred the status of being **'divine years'**. The age of darkness is over and according to them, we are now presently well into the age of enlightenment. They also inform us that each divine year can be equated to it' human or earth year, by multiplying it by the factor **360**.

As mentioned above, all of this was in fact tied together, with their ancient cosmogony and their astronomy which amongst others informs us that the entire Solar System rotates around another Star System in our galaxy. The brightest of which and in fact the controller of this great rotating journey of the Solar System is Alcyone. This star is actually in the Pleiades cluster of stars as found in the Taurus Constellation.

> **Coincidentally, of all the constellations or cluster of stars that are out there in the heavens; they (the Hindu ancients) had chosen the very same Pleiades as we know of it in the Holy Bible!!!**

> **I emphasise this 'coincidentally', because this Pleiades Constellation or cluster is also mentioned three times in our very own Holy Scriptures!!!**

How about that!!! **It is found in Job 9:9; Job 38:31 and in Amos 5:8.** We are also informed in the very brief commentary that I have in my Bible, with regards to this Pleiades cluster, that it consists of seven stars and is located near another Constellation; the Orion.

Also, in the same Scriptures, we have this above Orion Constellation, similarly mentioned. This has three bright stars in an almost straight line and is commonly called as the Orion Belt and is located as seen from the Equator. It is these very same three stars that the three Great Pyramids at Giza in Egypt, near Cairo are exactly aligned to as clearly evident even of today. Isn't this just remarkable and quite definitely something to ponder about with regards to it' inclusion into our own Holy Scriptures?

I had the wonderful opportunity about a decade or so ago, to have seen these 'Great Pyramids' with my very own eyes at Giza. It was simply amazing to see these structures rising towards the very skies, and that too to realise these Pyramids were built more than 5000 years ago and in that great size, but yet with that incredible accuracy in design and alignment to the Orion Belt. The very same Orion Constellation that was as mentioned in our Holy Scriptures.

There is also another Constellation as mentioned in the Holy Bible which is the Bear. This is actually located as seen from the North Pole. I don't think anyone has yet made any Scriptural or secular connection that could be of some relevance to our efforts here, in this book. However, it is still good to note that it is also mentioned in our Scriptures and therefore, I do propose, that it should have some special significance for it to be mentioned here too.

> Now, modern day astronomy concurs, that the Sun indeed travels in orbit around the centre of the Milky Way Galaxy. Universe Today in the Internet refers. However, I am as to date not privy to data with regards to whether modern day astronomers do or do not concur with the ancient Indian/Hindu astronomers, that it is indeed around the Star Alcyone. Nevertheless, this in itself does bestow some further degree of credibility, to the originality of the 'astronomy' of the ancient Indian/Hindu Scholars.

It is also right here that the ancient mythogenesis process takes over as evidently reported by Duncan, that in the ancient Hindu literature such as the **Laws of Manu**, the total period of the cycle or orbit around Alcyone was given a period of 24,000 divine years.

To recap, this period was made up of two great sub-cycles, as already mentioned previously, being the 12,000 divine years each.

This comprises of Maha -Yugas, an ancient Indian time period:
Maha = Great, Yuga = Age

> One sub-cycle of 12,000 divine years into darkness; the other sub-cycle in similar time length, emerging out again into a period of enlightenment.

They tell us that the Star Alcyone emanates a strong energy system (suggesting a photon belt or we may today relate this phenomenon somewhat to the 'disturbances' caused by the regular cycle of Sun Spots), that directly and mysteriously affects us as the Solar System orbits closer to Alcyone.

This energy emanates some mystique powers that have an effect on our very consciousness. This has moved us into an 'age of enlightenment', which underpins as presently being experienced by us quite evidently, through all the discoveries and inventions that have been going on for several hundred or rather for thousands of years in the global sense, according to them.

> With these periods of 'time' in focus, we are also informed through Hindu literature and their sacred texts, that there are even larger periods of time, than the journey of the Solar System around Alcyone. One such period is the **Kalpa Period** and others are also that 'time' to which the Kalpa Periods were indeed connected to or equated to, which were then attributed appropriately to their deity/god, Brahma.

It has become quite clear to me through this exegesis and other similar reports that they have attributed and indeed have calculated out this precise period of **4,320,000,000 Earth Years or Human Years** by following the above 'Alcyone Connection'. This they actually had accomplished by incorporating the appropriate number of 'Solar Alcyone Orbits', which they must have deemed necessary for some specific astronomical reasoning and simultaneously equated this period to being One Kalpa Period.

Knowing this was more than sufficient for me, to inculcate their findings into my book, although it is steeped in mythology. For who knows, this was the only possible way for them to express their understanding of their astronomy to the people at large. To also connect their own royalty, priests, events and etc., to the mysteries of the heavens. This I envisaged they had accomplished by creating this 'mythology of the Hindu deities', together with their own attributing to these deities with such divine powers and relating all of these to their self-created sacred events. These were achieved through the very complex process of mythogenesis, which was stretched over a really long Indian/Hindu historical period. As mentioned, all of these coupled together of course with their underpinning astronomy and cosmogony, which had triggered the creation of their deities, in the very first place, for easy public consumption by their populace.

It is also interesting to note here, that their deity Brahma has indeed a fixed period to live each time, although relatively speaking, this period, covers a very large span of Earth Time/human time. And although, after an interval of time, Brahma is once again **reincarnated** to become **Brahma again**, unlike other Hindu reincarnations, (which must move up or down the wheel of life), Brahma together with the whole Solar System being reincarnated also; he still has a **fixed period** to live each time in the same Hindu divine capacity.

Here again, we see very clearly that the learned ancients had indeed associated Brahma with a definite astronomically calculated period of time, which must be associated with their cosmogony of the heavens or rather the Solar System as in this case. This is clearly evident by them also limiting his (Brahma') creation activities to the **Solar System only** for a **fixed period** of time and which therefore not encompassing the entire Universe. However, the more zealous Hindu Scholars in more modern times want to establish this as such.

In a quick but rather unfair comparison to the above, our LORD GOD ALMIGHTY tells us, through the Holy Bible, that HE is indeed the Alpha and the Omega (Rev 1:8 and Rev 22:13 confirms).

This means in plain English that our GOD, is the beginning and also is the end, **not of GOD** though but of all that had been created by GOD; such as the entire Universe, which includes of course our tiny Solar System, being indeed just a speck in it (relatively speaking with regards to the vastness of Space & it' Universe) and every living thing in it, as was purposed by GOD.

This is so, because GOD has no beginning and has no end and therefore has no interval of not **being** at any time when so ever, whether transient or otherwise. How do we know this: It is because Genesis 1:1 in the Holy Bible begins the testimony of it for us and it is reinforced throughout the Holy Scriptures over and over again of the supreme power of GOD's sovereign authority over everything on Earth, in the Universe and in the Heavenlies, which also includes though not limiting to GOD's omniscience; GOD's omnipotence and GOD's omnipresence. Not limiting only in written form but also the obvious evidences surrounding us all on this Earth and the Universe. And further more in our very own lives and every living thing that share this Earth with us whether plant, animal, etc.

For according to ALMIGHTY GOD as revealed to us through the Holy Scriptures REV 1:8 as follows:

"I am the Alpha and the Omega, the Beginning and the End," says the Lord, "who is and who was and who is to come, the Almighty."

This directly means besides what has already been explained above; even before time had begun and even after 'time' as we have come to know of it, has come to an end; **our LORD GOD ALMIGHTY will always still be.**

In other words, after their created Hindu deity, Brahma, has ended their fixing of 'his created period of living', which occurs each time in his cycle; **our LORD GOD ALMIGHTY, will still be.** Amen.

Also, when their created deity Brahma is reincarnated through their created mythology, as documented in their 'sacred texts', which makes it sacred of course in the mythological sense; **our GOD will still be.** Amen.

> This is really indeed very refreshing to take note of, particularly, if you are a believer in Christ Jesus. That is our LORD GOD ALMIGHTY is not a created being having been created through our very own humanly frail 'figment of our imagination'. For our LORD GOD ALMIGHTY is way above all of this human conception and of every living thing and of every 'dead' matter, that had existed; or is currently existing; and/or will exist in the near and very far future with GOD's permission whether visible or otherwise.

This also clearly exhibits and explains of how the cleverly constructed and progressively developed creation through the amazing ancient Indian/Hindu human imagination going through the purposeful process of the 'philosophical-mythogenesis factoring', resulting in the establishing of the colourful existence of their varied and many Hindu deities that are quite well known in the present Hindu society.

There are in fact probably more than a **million** at least Hindu deities being worshipped and recognised by the Hindus, as such, on the whole in one form or the other.

> This is simply amazing that something that was first invented by man to be a god, to be a deity and eventually believed as such by thousands of millions through every generation past and is still ongoing strongly in the very present times within the Hindu society is just mindboggling.

You may have already possibly realised by now, that their equating of **4,320,000,000 years** to a Kalpa Period, is indeed the same precise number of years that I had used for my own scriptural based proposal for the precise age of the entire Universe, as it had begun it' **12th Period** of Universe Expansion.

It was also in this same Period, although very, very much later into it, that the Solar System came into it' own; first beginning with it' Sun and then followed closely by it' Planets too. Perhaps the Indian/Hindu astronomer/priest was indeed trying to explain this very same thing with regards to the

Universe, when they had established the Kalpa Period of 4,320,000,000 years. You will rediscover this in greater detail, as you follow through into my Book Two.

Also, having already revealed to you much earlier that two Kalpas equates to one 'complete day' in the life of Brahma, however, Duncan informs us, that a grave 'error' was indeed committed when they did the arithmetic to convert to Earth Years the '100 Brahma Years'. This had inevitably caused the very result to become 360 times more than what it should have been in the very first place. This was discovered very much later, when it began to cause 'difficulties' to their ongoing astronomical observations and calculations.

> So instead of Brahma' age being 3.14159×10^{14}; it should have been calculated as being only 864,000,000,000 years, according to Duncan' report.

Also, having studied Duncan' report regarding this '360 multiplication error', I must admit that I could not see where the error was actually made, except to conclude myself that could it have been possible that Brahma' fixed life span, was not as that translated or understood in the first place as being '100 Brahma Years', but indeed should have been just **'100 Brahma Days'** instead.

These **'100 Brahma Days'** being my suggestion, when converted into Human Time, would unmistakably also result in Duncan' proposed correction amendment of being **864,000,000,000** Earth Years as the corrected Brahma' age.

This according to my understanding is what the translation work of Ebenezer Burgess, in the First Chapter of SuryaSiddhanta, Item 21, seems to be suggesting to me as follows:

21) His (i.e. Brahma') extreme age is a hundred, **according to the valuation of a day and a night**. The half of his life is past; of the remainder, this is the first Kalpa.

This is indeed really amazing, just to have another somewhat related reference for this exact number of years, **4.32 Billion Years,** which I also had similarly obtained through my own independent studies, without having any foreknowledge then, of the above Hindu Kalpa Period. And the workings or the footprints of my independent studies, as a testimony to this fact, are written down in my continued research for the cosmic based construction of the **'number'** of the beast in my Book Two. You will as already mentioned earlier, discover later in this book of the amazing connection that these 4.32 Billion Years have with regards to the age of the Universe, as calculated in this book.

Also, you may be able to observe some uncanny resemblance with regards to the **choice of words** describing a very relevant cosmogony concept, as used in the Ebenezer Burgess' translation of Item 21 of the First Chapter in the SuryaSiddhanta with that of the Biblical Holy Scriptures. It was through the appropriate understanding of this Biblical Holy Scriptures which I had used to establish the very age of the Universe i.e. from the Biblical Book, **2ESDRAS**. Of course it could be purely by coincidence that some of the key words seem to be similar in nature but what about the matter it was referring to.

Making this connection of the SuryaSiddantha to our 2ESDRAS though it is limited to the Item 21 at the moment, is somewhat like the linking or rather the attempt of linking the Gilgamesh Epic to the Noah' Flood event!!! Anyway, I leave this for others to follow through to make more concrete connections or disconnection, if that may be the case too. For your convenience, below, you will find the very verses as highlighted in both the SuryaSiddantha and our 2ESDRAS, to which I was specifically referring to having the somewhat similar **choice of words**.

14:10   The world is no longer young; it is rapidly approaching old age.

14:11   The whole history of the world is divided into twelve periods, and the tenth period has already arrived

14:12   and it is half over; only two and a half parts remain

<u>SuryaSiddantha</u>

21) His (i.e. Brahma') extreme age is a hundred, **according to the valuation of a day and a night**. The half of his life is past; of the remainder, this is the first Kalpa.

Of course, I am only presenting this comparison in the 'choice of words' and some shadow of similarity in the time concept as highlighted above here, because I did not know of this SuryaSiddhanta literature before actually discovering the Universe' age as it was in the 12th Universe expansion phase. And also because this **4,320,000,000 years Universe Age** as computed by me to be at the very beginning of the 12th Period, also as an afterthought, exactly equates to One Kalpa Period of time. Also, for me their reference to 'Brahma' is probably their way to be referring to the Solar System through the Sun.

Anyway, see what you can make of it.

Here below, I will now try to attempt explaining, based on Dwight' exegesis, how the ancient Hindu astronomers developed this Kalpa Period to be equated to the 4,320,000,000 years. This exegesis identifies these years to be Sidereal Years.

For your information, 'Sidereal Time' is often used in Astronomy and a Sidereal Year equals to 366.2422 Sidereal Days, which over the course of one year, as evident in it' length becomes one full day longer than our tropical year of 365.2422 solar days. This is so, because a Sidereal Day is the period between 2 passages of a star across the meridian at the vernal equinox, being 23 hours 56 minutes 4.10 seconds. Whilst the mean Solar Day, is the time between 2 passages of our Sun across the meridian, being 24 hours 3 minutes 56.55 seconds. These accumulated daily additional differences between these two time systems, through the course of a full Sidereal Year, causes the Sidereal Year to be one full Sidereal Day longer then our Solar Year.

According to Dwight' exegesis:
12,000 divine years have been denominated or called as a Caturyuga Period. I have already explained to you as previously, how they had developed this particular time period of 12,000 divine years, through the 'Alcyone Connection'. I also had found out through other reports, this period is also called as the MahaYuga Period.

> Also, take note that we are informed through Dwight' exegesis, that 1 Divine Year = 360 Sidereal Years.

This Caturyuga Period, can be further sub-divided into 4 major sub-periods, called Yugapadas or Ages; of varying periods of years.

Every Kalpa is a total Period of 1000 cycles of all of these four Yugapadas, which is equivalent as already mentioned previously, to only 'One Day' of the Hindu deity Brahma' life.

The four Yugapadas, according to their divine years (pre-conversion stage to Sidereal Years) are equated and represented as follows:

Krtayuga Period relates to	4,800 Divine Years
Tretayuga Period relates to	3,600 Divine Years
Dvaparayuga Period relates to	2,400 Divine Years
Kaliyuga Period relates to	1,200 Divine Years
=	**12,000 Divine Years** **One Caturyuga Period**

===================

Each of the Yugapada time periods are actually made up of two other specific time period components. The first is called the Dawn Periods and the ending is called the Twilight Periods. So, the above can now be rewritten, as follows:

Dawn	400	Divine Years
Krtayuga	4,000	Divine Years
Twilight	400	Divine Years
Dawn	300	Divine Years
Tretayuga	3,000	Divine Years
Twilight	300	Divine Years
Dawn	200	Divine Years
Dvaparayuga	2,000	Divine Years
Twilight	200	Divine Years
Dawn	100	Divine Years
Kaliyuga	1,000	Divine Years
Twilight	100	Divine Years
	12,000	Divine Years

Now, according to my continued understanding of this exegesis; this above Caturyuga or MahaYuga Period of 12,000 Divine Years, when converting to it' Earthly Years or Human Years, needs to be multiplied by 360. We need to multiply by 360 because this is according to the Indian/Hindu Cosmological Time Cycles requirements which are based on their cosmogony of the heavens.

> One Divine Year = 360 Sidereal Years.

Here, we see yet again, our common factor of 360 being used. However yet again, the question arises in my mind, "How did they come to know about this above 'equation' in the first place???"

The answer to this question as previously answered, which had been based on my understanding, was obviously that their 'cosmogony and astronomy' were indeed made to be connected to their mythogenesis of deities and their own generating of the accompanying sacred events and through their science had established that there are fundamentally two 'types of time' out there. These they simply called as **'Divine Years'** and **'Human Years or Earth Years'**, if I do comprehend the 'Indian/Hindu Cosmological Time Cycles' correctly.

To me if my understanding is correct on this matter, these two distinct time periods or types of time available to us as mentioned just above, in particular, their 'Divine Years' could be their way of referring to the Universal Expansion Time which I had discovered (UET) and the other (Human Years) being of course our own Earth time. You will understand better when you progress into my second book what this is all about.

Well anyway:

**12,000 Divine Years x 360 = 4,320,000 Sidereal Years
= One Chaturyuga Period**

Therefore, One Chaturyuga Period now equates to the four Yugapadas, as follows:

1. The first is Krtayuga, and now has a time period of 1,728,000 sidereal years.
2. The second as above is Tretayuga, and now has a time period of 1,296,000 years.
3. The third as above is Dvaparayuga, and now has a time period of 864,000 years.
4. The fourth is Kaliyuga, and now having a time period of 432,000 years.

Please do take note, that all of the above, which totals to **4,320,000 years** still falls way below of what 'One Kalpa Period' and subsequently what 'One Day' of Brahma, actually equates to in terms of Earth Years.

Now taking a short break from Dwight and Duncan, let' move on to another very interesting and relevant internet researched article. This was very well written by James Q Jacobs, which he titles, The Aryabhatiya of Aryabhata. This makes reference to an English language translation of a Sanskrit work of Aryabhata (an Indian Mathematician and Astronomer - born 476 died 550), by William Eugene Clark.

Jacobs found written in this translated work, the following:

> "In a yuga the revolutions of the Sun are **4,320,000**; of the Moon 57,753,336; of the Earth eastward 1,582,237,500; of Saturn 146,564; of Jupiter 364,224; of Mars 2,296,824;......." (page 9).

Now, if we just focus on the very first part of this translation i.e. "In a yuga the revolutions of the Sun are 4,320,000......:

This immediately gives me the very understanding, that these 'revolutions' of the Sun that Aryabhata was indicating here, were actually what had been thought as formerly for quite a long time until the famous Galileo Galilei (1564-1642) an Italian Physicist, Mathematician and Astronomer had informed us that it was the Earth that actually went around the Sun and not the other way round. In fact it was Copernicus (1473-1543), a Polish Astronomer who was also connected (to some holy order) to the Church, who had started this new thinking. This was later championed with proclaimed evidence through Galileo.

So, based on the above analysis, a 'yuga' here, is one MahaYuga Period or called by it' other name, a Chaturyuga Period.

This ancient Indian/Hindu Cosmological Time Period Cycle being a Chaturyayuga Period representing a period of 4,320,000 years, was the same period in years that Aryabatha had concluded that the Sun (which actually should have been the Earth in it' orbit around the Sun) does make one revolution per year. This was as Aryabhata understood it at that time, that it was the Sun orbiting around the Earth and therefore in total; 4,320,000 revolutions in a 'yuga' or rather in a Chaturyayuga Period. This actually rewrites the confirmation and attestation for the accuracy of the ancient Indian astronomers belonging to the Indian/Hindu Cosmological Time Period too.

Also, if I understood the above translated Sanskrit report of our Aryabhatha' astronomical/mathematical work into English correctly; I think the number of revolutions that the Earth makes eastward, which he had calculated it as being 1,582,237,500; must have been calculated by multiplying the number of 'revolutions' that the Sun makes in a 'yuga', i.e. 4,320,000 by the number of diurnal revolutions per Sidereal Year, that the Earth in turn makes on it' axis.

Now I do not know whether this was indeed the way that he had actually calculated this out, but the result that I had obtained through this very multiplication, i.e. 4,320,000 X **366.2563795** (the bold is the current number of diurnal revolutions that the Earth makes in a Sidereal Year) = 1,582,227,559 revolutions.

This indeed quite evidently falls short by exactly 9941 diurnal revolutions (i.e. 9941 Sidereal days) or rather more than 27 Sidereal Years shortfall. However, in comparison to his calculations and his astronomical observations; this does indicate interestingly to me, some possibility of him actually having done so.

> With this in view, I then decided with the above thinking in place, could we actually factor in a compensation to take into account for the 'rate of change' in the speed of the Earth' rotation on it' own axis, at the time when Aryabhatha was making his calculations and observations.

Now I do not know whether my calculation in reference to the compensation used is accurate for that time based on the scientific reduction rate of 1/1000 second every 100 years; but if we do multiply 4,320,000 X **366.258680555** (the bold being the possible diurnal revolutions which Aryabhatha may have used being also hopefully the actual compensated diurnal revolutions that the

Earth was making at that time in a Sidereal Year), we will indeed get the result that Aryabhatha obtained exactly.

> **That is 1,582,237,500 revolutions that the Earth would have made or will be making eastwards or anti-clockwise if you do prefer in a yuga.**

I am also of the opinion that Aryabhatha did not know at the time that the Earth' speed of rotation on it' axis is indeed slowing down at that specific scientific calculated rate of 1/1000 second every 100 years. So all of his calculations as shown above, as far as the Earth is concerned and perhaps even concerning the other planets, may have not taken this into consideration over the full time period of a yuga although it' impact may not be too significant within the short Chaturyayuga time limiting factor.

Also, if you had noticed that the **366.25868055** diurnal revolutions is indeed that little bit more than our current **366.2563795** which does keep in line with a slowing down in the Earth' Axis Rotation. This too then is indeed scientifically compliant, if it was calculated correctly.

> However, my proposition does indeed point us in the right direction and definitely has some basis to be taken note of too. Well I do sincerely hope so.

Now, if we restudy the first part of this English language translation, it actually states: 'In a yuga'...., the Sun according to Aryabhatha, would be making 4,320,000 revolutions. As far as this understanding is concerned, it is absolutely accurate, despite the erroneous fact as held at the time, that he and everyone else thought that the Sun was indeed orbiting (revolving) around the Earth, instead of the reverse. It also establishes another solar planetary fact, that despite the changes in the number of revolutions that the Earth makes on it' axis eastwards per sidereal year over time, the number of revolutions that the Sun (in fact of the Earth going around the Sun) will not change in any yuga or for that matter in any period.

This further establishes that the speed, with which the Earth orbits the Sun, and the distance it needs to travel to complete this orbit each year, also does not vary unless it is possibly affected by **perturbation**.

This has already been discussed in detail accordingly in PART TWO.

Further to my possible discovery of how did Aryabhatha may have worked out his calculations, I also discovered something very remarkable and indeed significant.

> If we take the number of revolutions that the Sun (actually, that of the Earth makes around the Sun in an annual orbit) makes in a yuga i.e. 4,320,000 to be instead the number of revolutions that the Sun itself makes rotating around it' own centre and then multiplying it by 25 (days) i.e. the period that it would take for the Sun to completely rotate once at it' centre each time; we will remarkably get the result of **108,000,000 days**.

Now studying this resultant number of **108,000,000**, we may probably be able to understand better, why the **Babylonian** may have divided their basic time scale of **one hour into 1080 divisions**; if we scale the 108,000,000 rotations down properly.

> They may have developed their time system based on this very fact of the Sun rotating at it' centre every 25 days and who knows even used this specific period of time of 4,320,000 which produces their possible time scale at the upper most end of 108,000,000 days cycle. This infers, that they most probably had the astronomical knowledge at that ancient time; that the Sun completes one rotation at it' centre every 25 days and even more remarkable, then went on, to possibly use a similar period of 'time' being the 4,320,000 years to establish their own time system.

This is indeed quite remarkable indeed, if it turns out to be correct, because relatively speaking, this phenomenon regarding the Sun was only discovered by us in the modern era, probably in the last few centuries or so. Therefore, for the ancient Babylonian to progress on to possibly as I had suggested, develop a time system based on this knowledge, would be simply amazing. This is indeed another remarkable discovery to be added to the very understanding for the Babylonian to actually divide an hour of a day into 1080 divisions. Hopefully, by the time I finish writing this book, I will be more certain of why or how they did come up with the idea of dividing an hour of time into a precise 1080 divisions besides the one that I am proposing now as above.

The other important thing that I had discovered based on this was that the period of time i.e. 108,000,000 days is indeed the number value that I had obtained in the 6th **ending** of the 3rd 360 Equation Series.

This is:

$$360 \times 300,000 = 108,000,000.$$

This is the same set of Equations, that we also find the value of a Babylonian' hour being divided into. This is:

$$360 \times 3 = 1080 \text{ 'Divisions'}$$

This actually begins this 3rd 360 Equation Series progression. This is indeed very interesting to find out too.

This time period of 4,320,000 years, which the ancient Indian/Hindu had used in developing their Cosmological Time Cycles, and which Aryabatha had similarly used to establish his calculations, has also a more than significant connection to the development of Ezra' World (Universe) History Time, as described in the biblical book - 2Esdras. This I must state was first discovered and first developed accordingly, in this very book, which I am currently trying to complete.

Also, according to Jacobs' research, another Indian mathematician/Astronomer, **Pusila**, is also credited together with Aryabhata, by G. R. Kay in his appendices.

From this Jacobs article, I understood that Jacobs was in fact trying to highlight to us the extremely accurate Aryabhata ratio finding, which when divided as follows:

1,582,237,500/57,753,336 gives us the amazing result, **27.3964693572.** This is the number of rotations per lunar orbit.

Now Jacobs is credited with finding out when these 27.3964693572 rotations per lunar orbit actually had occurred. According to Jacobs, it had occurred in **1604 BC**. Assuming this to be accurate, here is my personal congratulation to Jacobs.

Please do check out his website, for further information and reference to the bibliography, which is located at as shown below, if it is still in operation:

www.geocities.com/athens/olympus/4844/aryabhata.html
I also understand it has been migrated to:

http://www.jqjacobs.net/astro/aryabhata.html

This is what I was afraid of, when referencing information through the internet. One day it is there and then the next, it could be gone into oblivion; removed.

Now coming back to Dwight' referenced Internet article:

Every Kalpa Period relates to 1000 cycles of the four (sub) Yugas in total or rather to 1000 cycles of the Caturyugas.

$$4,320,000 \times 1000 = 4,320,000,000 \text{ years}$$

> Therefore, One Kalpa = 1000 cycles of the entire combined four Yuga's (and similarly, to 1000 Mahayugas/Caturyugas) = 4.32 Billion Years.

What caught my serious attention was the 4.32 Billion Years for a Kalpa period. This is actually as previously mentioned, the value in years of the age of the Universe, when it had begun it' 12th period of Universe expansion, as I had calculated it, based mainly on the Deuterocanonical Book, 2Esdras. Also, we will discover later in Book Two, that the Universe will be **39.96 Billion Years** at the very end of these 12 Scriptural Universe Expansion Periods of Ezra' World History time as I had developed it through my understanding of the relevant scriptures in 2ESDRAS. Also, remarkably, there are exactly 9.25 Kalpa Period Cycles in this age of the Universe that I had calculated, through my applied understanding, of the relevant scriptures as found written in 2ESDRAS. You will also discover in Book Two, that I had developed a very unique ratio i.e. **1:9.25** and/or **9.25:1**, through Scriptural means (that was made solely through 2ESDRAS), which bridges the gap even that much closer between their 'Time Cycles' and my discoveries

Ezra' Age of the Universe = 39.96 Billion Years
= 9.25 Kalpa Periods

I also personally had discovered, that in the Indian/Hindu system, each Period in the 'Yugapadas' when it is converted into human years, is in fact reduced by exactly **432,000 years** between each Yugapada, until the Kaliyuga Period, which indeed itself constitutes a period of 432,000 years. It exposes a definite design for a definite purpose, although it is recognised also as being astronomical derived.

I had earlier indicated to you, that my '360 Equation Series', were increasing between each other, by a specific **36,000,000 years,** from one equation' 6th ending to the next immediate equation' 6th ending and which continues as such, accordingly and perhaps possibly even indefinitely to a certain extent.

As we see in each of the four Yugapadas, a fixed reducing rate of 432,000 years from one Yugapada level to the next, and in our '360 Equation Series', an increasing rate of 36,000,000 years, however, both of these specific fixed rates in years are linked together by the common denominator, **360.**

This 432,000 years separating period, is also indeed a $10,000^{th}$ part of the age of the Universe, as it entered into it' 12th Period of expansion. You may be able to see a related connection between these two systems, just like in regards to the other time systems. At the most appropriate time, I will also show you yet another interesting and most amazing relationship that the Indian/Hindu Cosmological Time Cycles have, not only with our '360 Equation Series', but also with the Babylonian system of time keeping.

We are also informed about the already known information through Duncan' internet article that: Each Kalpa Period is divided into 14 Manvatara Periods. These are also referred to as the 14 Manu Periods, which follows the Laws of Manu. Each Manu is attributed to a specific time period in the overall Kalpa Period, which according to the Laws of Manu is presided by a Manu.

Now, I am not personally sure what is a Manu, but Duncan points us to the reference **(i.e. The Monier-Monier Williams, Sanskrit-English dictionary)** for it' explanation or description.

Each Manu/Manvatara Period lasts for exactly 71 Caturyuga/Mahayuga cycles. However, to have a total of 1000 Mahayugas, (which in total equates to One Kalpa, as previously mentioned), the remaining Mahayugas are divided accordingly among the remaining Six Periods, i.e. each will have 72 Mahayuga cycles each instead of 71. Remember also, that 4,320,000 Years = One Mahayuga/Caturyuga.

Also, I had personally discovered when this Indian/Hindu derived 432,000 years that separates each Yuga, as previously shown, is multiplied by 120 or even the value of One Mahayuga in human years i.e. 4,320,000 years is multiplied by itself 12 times projecting 12 Mahayuga Cycles; it amazingly results to **51,840,000.**

12 Mahayugas or 12 Caturyuga Cycles = 51,840,000 years.

Of course, we also get this number when multiplying the original time period which was calculated as being 12,000 Divine Years by 4,320. This means the 'Indian/Hindu Cosmological Time Cycles' has the in-built potential to achieving this result too. In fact you can achieve this result by multiplying each of the Yugapadas by these following numbers, which are arranged in an ascending order:

Krtayuga (1,728,000 X 30)   = 51,840,000 years
Tetrayuga (1,296,000 X 40)   = 51,840,000 years
Dvaparayuga (864,000 X 60)   = 51,840,000 years
And Kaliyuga (432,000 X 120)   = 51,840,000 years

In other words:

30   Cycles of the Krtayuga Period   = 51,840,000 years
40   Cycles of the Tetrayuga Period   = 51,840,000 years
60   Cycles of the Dvaparayuga Period   = 51,840,000 years
120 Cycles of the Kaliyuga Period   = 51,840,000 years

Suddenly, we have here an explosion of the unique linking number, which I first had discovered through the projected Maya Calendar System i.e. 51,840,000!!!

For once again, we see a remarkable similarity that bridges all of the various 'time systems' somewhat together, so far as mentioned in this book and as shown again below:

a) One Calabtun time period in the Mayan Calendar System, which I had modified for a specific purpose, backed with the appropriate reasoning for doing it is taken to be equating to,

51,840,000 days.

b) The Biblical 144,000 years X 360 days   = **51,840,000 days**

c) Our 144th Equation Series also carries this **number** :   **51,840,000**

d) 12 Caturyuga Cycles (Indian/Hindu Cosmological Time Cycles) as just shown above 12,000 X 4,320 = **51,840,000 years**

We will establish the Babylonian Time system to be similarly linked sometime later, as I need to settle a few more details pertaining to this matter.

To finally recap on this Indian/Hindu Cosmological Time Cycles:

Remember, Dwight had informed us that 1 Divine Year = 360 Sidereal Years. This equation in fact was established through the Laws of Manu, which also gave us the 14 Manu Periods in a Kalpa and which was also responsible for establishing that the Solar System completes one rotation or cycle around Alcyone every 24,000 Divine Years. This was based on the 'Laws of Manu', as described by Swami Sri Yukteswar, the Guru of Paramahansa Yogananda, in his book "The Holy Science", according to the internet article, which was written by Duncan Watson.

According to Sri Yukteswa, Alcyone is the brightest Star in the Pleiades constellation.

Surprisingly, through yet another internet article which I had stumbled upon, that is according to Shaun' Research on the Jehovah' Witnesses (Watchtower Society); he presents to us an investigative article written by B. J. Kotwall, which states: That for **62 years** (1891-1953), the Watchtower Society taught their followers, that God resided on this star, Alcyone!!! This belief was taught since 1891 to 1953 and appeared evidently as disclosed by him as written in their Volume 3 (1891) of their 'Studies in the Scriptures'. Now, if this was indeed the case, can you just imagine as a matter of opinion, such absurd nonsense as this, by a group proclaiming to be professing our God Almighty. It is not surprising to me that with such thinking, the WTS forms no part in the global family of Christianity, which makes up the Body of Christ on Earth.

Returning to Duncan Watson:

We further find out as previously mentioned, in which Swami Sri Yukteswar explains that the emanations of this Star Alcyone, affects the very consciousness of humans on this planet. Also, we have already been in an age of darkness and have now moved into an age of enlightenment. This cycle of darkness and light is completed in 24,000 Divine Years i.e. 12,000 Divine Years each way. You can refer to these as being the 'ordinary divine years', that I had mentioned very much earlier.

Now do you see again, how these 12,000 ordinary 'divine' years came about in the first place? It began first through their Indian Astronomy that devised a Kalpa Period, and ended up in the mythogenesis process through the formulation which when doubled equated to 'One Divine Day' for their Lord Brahma; a Hindu deity created particularly through this mythogenesis process.

It is quite obvious as evidently established that the 'Indian/Hindu Cosmological Time Cycles' did develop into a measurable 'Time System'. Perhaps as mentioned previously this was their way of explaining astronomical findings to people who had no 'science' backgrounds or knowledge of the cosmos. For this was a time when superstition and mystical beliefs were more easily accepted by the general population of that nation and at that time even elsewhere in the world; when many were steeped in these from time immemorial. This is quite apparent as it seems to be fortunate for us, even as of today, for it becomes quite obvious as you tour the length and breadth of India. I hope that I have stated this correctly.

To make it all clear to you, let me unfold it to you once again.

We have been informed that these 12,000 Divine Years = One Mahayuga Period or One Caturyuga Period. And according to their sacred books such as, 'The Mahabharata': 1000 Cycles of this Period = One Kalpa Period.

Therefore,   12,000 ordinary 'Divine' Years X 1,000 cycles
       =   12,000,000 ordinary 'Divine' Years.

These now need to be converted to human or earth years by multiplying it by 360, because 1 divine year = 360 sidereal years.

Therefore:

12,000,000 X 360 = 4,320,000,000 Earth Years
= (One Kalpa Period)

Now, as we have already been also informed, that One Kalpa = One 'day' in Brahma' life and similarly One Kalpa = One 'night' in Brahma' life, and as all of this is being represented in Earth Years, then the following is correct:

4,320,000,000 X 2 = 8,640,000,000 years

This now constitutes quite obviously one full 'Day' in Brahma' life.

You can see here, quite immediately, that there is a definite relationship between this total and the number of seconds in our day.

24 hours X 60 X 60 = **86,400 seconds**

Can you see the scaled time relationship???

It also establishes, the equation, that 'One Second' in Brahma' 'life' (full day), takes 100,000 Earth Years to be completed.

Strangely, this is the exact time period that scientists have informed us that the Earth is indeed slowing down as currently at a rate of: One Second every 100,000 Years. We are also informed that Brahma lives for '100 Brahma Years' each time, and then he rests for a similar period before being reincarnated.

Therefore, 8,640,000,000 Earth Years (1 Full Day in Brahma' life) X **360** days in a divine year X 100 Brahma Years = **311,040,000,000,000 years** = 3.11040×10^{14}

This in my understanding should now be referred to as being the other type of divine years that I was mentioning quite earlier on. These probably should be understood as being **more divine** than the ordinary divine years, as they are directly attributed to Brahma' 100 years. Yet more importantly, this also differentiates the value of 'time' for an ordinary divine year and these special Brahma 'divine years'.

The Mayan; The Babylonian; The Egyptian; The Indian/Hindu; The Biblical Universe Expansion Time (UET) which I had developed according to 2ESDRAS (which will be further proven to you in Book Two); our present day modern time measurements and I also believe even the 'Chinese Time System', (the study of which has not been included here) are all firmly bridged together by a common numerical linkage value. This is no other than the number, 360.

In fact, you could scale upwards or downwards and still maintain these common linkages.

For example, you could move upwards to 720 or progress on to 3,600 and beyond or even scale downwards to 36; 3.6 and so on.

Also, following through with my '360 Equation Series' to it' 1,110th Equation Series, we can actually obtain the age of the Universe, as it is calculated in this book in Part Two, i.e. **39.96 Billion Years.** This would be the age when the Universe reaches the end of the 12th Period of Universe Expansion, which is currently still in progress.

Now this may seem **not to be in line** with the latest scientific pegging of the age of the Universe, if we make reference to NASA's Wilkinson Microwave Anisotrophy Probe during their sweeping 12-month observation of the entire sky. They indicated that the age of the Universe can be precisely pegged at being **13.7 Billion Years**. Also, that the first generation of stars to shine in the Universe, first ignited just 200 million years after the Big Bang. This was reported in a local daily Newspaper, the Sun, dated Feb 13/2003.

Please do not quit on me as yet, but do follow through to the end of Book Two and then make up your own mind. So, please stay with me on course through this book and see what you will eventually and finally find out at the end of it. Thank you.

As I had mentioned above, we can also obtain our scriptural derived age for the Universe as it completes the 12th level expansion through my '360 Equation Series' as is shown below:

1,110th '360 Equation Series' and specifically referring to it' Sixth Level ending as follows:

360 X 111,000,000 = 39,960,000,000 years.

I am certain, that a few of you out there could even show us many more common linkages with the other time systems.

I only continued to present all of the above, just to reaffirm to you that even the previous civilizations, in some uncanny way, though separated by time and distance, language and culture, etc., used their knowledge of the Cosmos, to develop their time systems that were somehow linked in several specific ways to each other. This also includes our modern era civilization.

We also cannot forget the specific and overall Scriptural linkages not only pertaining to the 'Biblical TIME', but also 'Biblical Time' to the time systems of the ancient civilizations.

To finally round this stage up, let me present here the following chart. This in a somewhat simpler form had also been used by Dwight in his exegesis and also by others. I have also taken the liberty to include some personal observations, together with some relevant and important inclusions in addition to their own presentation. This was done not to just further modify it, but so that it could also demonstrate how it links directly to my very own '360 Equation Series', in particular to the **beginnings** of each series. Secondly, through these modifications, I had actually transformed or rather changed the entire character of the original Chart to even accommodate the Divine Years.

So, you may realise, this new enhanced modified chart is not only exhibiting a Sexagesimal Number System as it was originally intended, but also now includes other possible applications from another perspective, if you know how to read it correctly.

PRESENTATION OF THE SEXAGESIMAL NUMBER SYSTEM IN IT' ENHANCED VERSION AS DESIGNED AND AMENDED APPROPRIATELY FOR THE PURPOSE OF THIS BOOK BY CHARLES ALPHONSO

According to the Sexagesimal Number System, a count of six for every 360 count is equivalent to one for every 60. Also, this is the basic counting principle behind the **six** Indian seasons.

The Chart goes on to demonstrate to us that by counting six days per year being the **'Second Mean Motion'** of the Sun, as it completes a cycle of 360 days, which is the **'First Mean Motion'** of the Sun (being also the number of degrees in a circle); actually occurs also after exactly a 60 year count.

Also, according to this Chart, this 60 year count represents the **Babylonian Sossos** (being a specific Babylonian time period) and it also, further goes on to demonstrate the other Babylonian time periods of **Neros** (600 years) and **Saros** (3,600 years).

Here we clearly see the possible linkages with the Babylonian Time System, which in my opinion was developed as such, not by intention but because there is a common overall controlling factor or source that inevitably links all the different 'Time Systems' together. This has been mentioned to you as previously being the Cosmos' precise GOD created time structured design of the heavens.

You will also see the number **1080**, which is the Babylonian' exact number of time divisions in an hour of time, being associated through the **'First Mean Motion'** of the Sun, which in itself, is a totally Indian/Hindu Cosmological Time Cycle' concept.

Besides this, even the sum total number of the second beast of Revelation, **666**, is clearly defined and generated here. This is exhibited or expressed through the **Second Mean Motion** of the Sun, as the Sun times through **111** Sidereal Years and simultaneously completes the **39,960 First Mean Motion** of the Sun.

These 111 years time period, is in itself, a **360** millionth part of the entire age of the Universe as at the end of it' 12th Universe expansion period; as calculated through the **Scriptures**, being **39.96 billion years**.

Also, as clearly can be seen that the corresponding **39,960 First Mean Motion** of the Sun is precisely a millionth part of this Universe' age when it is at the end of it' 12th Phase Level expansion, as just mentioned above. This is simply amazing to say the least.

You will learn later in Book Two that this number **111** has indeed a significant relationship of producing the sum total of 666, when it is arranged in a particular pattern through the numbers of 1 to 36. However, this is not the number pattern that we are pursuing but it does however link us up appropriately in the right direction. This number pattern will be shown to you later.

So to have three major components such as the 111, 39,960 and 666, all in the same timeline projections, as is shown on the Chart below is just simply remarkable.

This further confirms to me or rather gives us a stronger hint that the number which would sum total to 666 is indeed a particular **Time Period** in a **particular Time System**.

As the Sun completes 111 Sidereal years, the 'First Mean Motion' of the Sun clocks 39,960 motions or cycles, according to the 'Indian/Hindu Cosmological Time Cycles'. Simultaneously, as this is being accomplished, the 'Second Mean Motion' of the Sun has also indeed completed **666** Motions or cycles. These motions can be described as being just similar as to the 'hands' in our time-clocks. These follow each other proportionately and accordingly, to enable us to read the time, as it is occurring in real time terms accurately, within a particular time breakdown required, as the case may be.

Also, a point to note here in astounding similarity is that, just as the 666 motions is associated to the '**Second** Mean Motion**'** of the Sun, the same sum total **666** is attributed to the **second** beast. This is scriptural.

As you study this modified Chart carefully, in which I have also included my own '360 Equation Series' (specifically the beginnings of each series), you will notice that you could also take the Sidereal Years Column i.e. 1, 2, 3....... and so on, as also actually being their **'Divine Years' Column** too, as was established through their 'Indian/Hindu Cosmological Time Cycles'. This can be achieved when you attach it as such to the second column, which I had taken the liberty of introducing here too.

This is indeed very interesting, for then the **'First Mean Motion'** of the Sun Column, does actually represent not only it' number of Mean Motions that it makes directly corresponding to the appropriate number of Sidereal Years, but also simultaneously, representing in the same column, the converted 'Divine Years' into it' Earth Years.

> As an example: 111 divine years can now be taken to actually convert to **39,960 Earth Years**.

Furthermore, this particular **39,960 First Mean Motion** of the Sun produces coincidentally or surprisingly, as the case in point is even to me, **666** as per it' directly corresponding **Second Mean Motion**. This is truly amazing to discover, that through an ancient Indian/Hindu time system, we are able to realise the sum total of the second beast as revealed to us in our Holy Scriptures in REV 13:18.

> This seriously brings a sobering to everything that I am trying to accomplish here and quite definitely encourages me that I am certainly not on a wild goose chase after all!!! In other words, there is some sanity in this entire maze of new proposals that I had made, including through new concepts and new ideas that have not been explored before until now. This is a first, as I claim it to be so; unless proven otherwise.

Let us now take a look at the Sexagesimal Chart, which the Indian/Hindu Cosmological Time Cycles were based on, as shown in the following pages.

Notes: The **'First Mean Motion'** of the Sun together with the **'Second Mean Motion'** of the Sun describes the total number of completed diurnal (in this case, referring to the daytime only) revolutions or Sidereal Days in a Sidereal Year. Also, all of my '360 Equation Series' are being represented here by their **beginning equations** only for each series, and therefore, are seen here in a running sequence.

Surprisingly, this running 360 Equation Series sequence totals are identical to the 'First Mean Motion' of the Sun for every corresponding Sidereal Year as described and as used in the Indian/Hindu Cosmological Time Cycles. I had not the foggiest idea, that when I had first introduced these 360 Equation

Series, in this book, that it would lead to this linkage and in such remarkable manner, in my wildest of dreams.

Finally, in the first column, we are also able to convert each 'divine year' to an Earth Year equivalent by multiplying it by the required 360 and it' result is as shown in the column under the 360 Equation Series.

You may also remember from previously, that we indeed have a **3rd Mean Motion** of the Sun which describes the remaining or remnant part of a diurnal revolution. However, for this Chart it is not necessary to be included but for continuity sake, here are the 3 Mean Motions of the Sun, as shown below:

1 Sidereal Year =	360	(First Mean Motion of the Sun)
	6	(Second Mean Motion of the Sun)
	0.2563795	(3rd Mean Motion)
	366.2563795	diurnal revolutions of the Earth

SIDEREAL YEARS AND THE DIVINE YEARS	MY 360 EQUATION RUNNING SEQUENCE SERIES; FIRST MEAN MOTION OF THE SUN; AND THE CORRESPONDING EARTH YEARS TO THE ORDINARY DIVINE YEARS	SIDEREAL YEARS SECOND MEAN MOTION OF THE SUN	SIDEREAL DAYS (daytime) Diurnal REVOLUTIONS
1	X 360 = 360	+ 6	366
2	X 360 = 720	+ 12	732
3	X 360 = 1080	+ 18	1,098
4	X 360 = 1440	+ 24	1,464
5	X 360 = 1800	+ 30	1,830
6	X 360 = 2160	+ 36	2,196
.	.	.	.
10	X 360 = 3,600	+ 60	3,660
.	.	.	.
60 (Sossos)	X 360 = 21,600	+ 360	21,960
.	.	.	.
111	X 360 = 39,960	+ 666	40,626
.	.	.	.

'THE BIBLICAL 360 DAY YEARS & THE SCRIPTURAL COSMIC 666'
More Ancient and Modern Civilization 'TIME SEQUENCE' Relationships

120	X 360 = 43,200	+ 720	43,920
144	X 360 = 51,840	+ 864	52,704
180	X 360 = 64,800	+ 1,080	65,880
240	X 360 = 86,400	+ 1,440	87,840
300	X 360 = 108,000	+ 1,800	109,800
360	X 360 = 129,600	+ 2,160	131,760
400	x 360 = 144,000	+ 2,400	146,400
420	X 360 = 151,200	+ 2,520	153,720
480	X 360 = 172,800	+ 2,880	175,680
540	X 360 = 194,400	+ 3,240	197,640
600 (Neros)	X 360 = 216,000	+ 3600	219,600
720	X 360 = 259,200	+ 4,320	263,520
840	X 360 = 302,400	+ 5,040	307,440
960	X 360 = 345,600	+ 5,760	351,360
1080	X 360 = 388,800	+ 6,480	395,280
1110	X 360 = 399,600	+ 6,660	406,260
1200 (Kaliyuga)	X 360 = 432,000	+ 7,200	439,200
2400 (Dvaparayuga)	X 360 = 864,000	+ 14,400	878,400
3600 (Saros) (Tetrayuga)	X 360 = 1,296,000	+ 21,600	1,317,600

The Basic Chart seems to stop here from the Internet Article, but I decided to continue it further, just to show you something quite interesting and very relevant.

4800 (Krtayuga)   X 360 = 1,728,000   + 28,800   1,756,800

By just including the ordinary divine year, 4,800 as above; you will notice that together with the three earlier entries, these do represent in sequence the Four Yugapadas that make up a Mahayuga or Chaturyuga Period, totaling **4,320,000 years**, through the 'conversion' process.

Let us continue this Chart even further, to extend until the Kalpa Period as follows:

7200	X 360 = 2,592,000	+ 43,200	2,635,200
11,100	X 360 = 3,996,000	+ 66,600	4,062,600
72,000	X 360 = 25,920,000	+ 432,000	26,352,000
144,000	X 360 = 51,840,000	+ 864,000	52,704,000
11,100,000	X 360 = 3,996,000,000	+ 66,600,000	4,062,600,000
12,000,000 (One Kalpa)	X 360 = 4,320,000,000	+ 72,000,000	4,392,000,000
24,000,000 (Two Kalpa)	X 360 = 8,640,000,000	+ 144,000,000	8,784,000,000

Two Kalpa time periods = One Complete Day in Brahma' Life. And he lives for 100 Brahma Years and then after another similarly fixed period, Brahma is once again reincarnated to live in another cycle of 100 Brahma Years. This mythogenesis would seem to be continuing or to be valid according to it' concept, probably as long as the Solar System is still in operation.

Now for the Big One:
The age of the Universe as at the end of the 12th AUET/12th Ezra' PERIOD of WHT-WFT, would be covering a time span of:

666,000,000 million years per PART of a PERIOD

60 PARTS in total, divided into 5 Groups in each PERIOD, as derived from my understanding of the relevant referenced Scriptures in 2ESDRAS, will generate the future age of the Universe as follows:

```
        111,000,000  X  360  =  39,960,000,000
                            +     666,000,000
                            =  40,626,000,000
```

Now here are some comments, which were as attached to the previous chart version in Dwight' exegesis. This also now includes my interpretation of the same and thereby modifying it, besides adding other important observations to some of the newer entries that I had also made to make this amended Sexagesimal Chart even much more clearer to you.

In an interval of a Sossos (i.e. a 60 years 'Babylonian Time Period'), the 'First Mean Motion' of the Sun, according to the 'Indian/Hindu Cosmological Time Cycles' completes a cycle count of 21,600 = 60 × 360. This cycle count of 21,600 can be taken to represent the number and the count of the **arc minutes** in a circle. That means there are 21,600 arc minutes in a circle.

A count of the **nadis (refer to the notes below),** each is equivalent to 1/60th of a day, would then total in this Sossos interval for the 'First Mean Motion' of the Sun, as being 1,296,000 nadis. This 1,296,000 nadis cycle count of the 'First Mean Motion' of the Sun is indeed exactly the number of **arc seconds** in a circle. A count of the nadis in this same interval of '60 years' for the 'Second Mean Motion' of the Sun, would then accordingly be; 21,600. This again is the number of arc minutes in a circle.

Likewise, a count of the 'First Mean Motion' of the Sun, in a period of 600 years' time interval i.e., a Babylonian 'Neros' period, would be 216,000 cycles. This is indeed the number of long syllables i.e. **Gurvaksharas** in a day (refer below).

A count of the 'Second Mean Motion' of the Sun, in this similar interval of 600 years, according to the 'Indian/Hindu Cosmological Time Cycles', would then be 3,600 cycles. This is indeed the number of **vinadis** (refer below) in a day.

After 3,600 years (i.e. a Babylonian 'Saros' period of time in years), the 'First Mean Motion' of the Sun would have completed a cycle count of 1,296,000. This is indeed the number of seconds in a circle. In the same interval, the 'Second Mean Motion' of the Sun, would have completed 21,600 cycles. This is indeed the number of minutes in a circle.

Notes:

As previously mentioned, according to the ancient Hindu sages, the trained number of breaths (Pranayama) each about 4 seconds in duration taken each day, can be translated to measure the time of a day. Therefore,

10 long syllables (gurvakshara)	= 1 respiration (1 prana)
6 respirations	= 1 Vinadi
therefore, 60 gurvaksharas	= 1 Vinadi
60 Vinadis	= 1 Nadi
Therefore, 3,600 gurvaksharas	= 1 Nadi
1 Nadi	= 1/60th of a Day
60 Nadis	= 1 Day
therefore, 216,000 gurvaksharas	= 1 Day
and 3,600 Vinadis	= 1 Day

One of the observations of my enhanced Chart that you could easily make is that our number 144,000 X 360, as previously shown to you i.e. 51,840,000 can also be found in this Chart under the 'First Mean Motion' of the Sun. This is the similar number of days as found in my proposed Maya Calendar system.

In all of these 'Motions' of the Sun, the 'Second Mean Motion' is obviously, very much slower than the 'First Mean Motion' and of course the 'Third Mean Motion' of the Sun, which has not been included here, is definitely even very much more slower than the 'Second Mean Motion' of the Sun. This is unlike the 'hands' of our clock, where the Second Mean Motion i.e. the 'Minute Hand' is indeed running faster than the First Mean Motion i.e. the 'Hour Hand' and the Third Mean Motion i.e. the 'Second Hand' is even very much faster than the 'Minute Hand'. In fact here, it is the exact reverse.

I am quite certain you would be able to find more connections to the other time systems.

Now, I had discovered purely on my own (without any conceitedness being implied here), something really amazing. In fact perhaps, I was actually merely joining all the dots together, to inevitably come to an expected and if I may say so, quite a surprised discovery.

Could it be possible, just like the great Indian Sages of India in the ancient past, who had cleverly used breathing rhythms and even the winks of an eye, to establish an accurate time system; that we could also use some other human body natural rhythm to also establish another connection to our GOD given time keeper, i.e. our 'Cosmic Clock', which is none other than our very own Sun. Of course, we now do know that it also works in tandem with the Moon and also the Earth itself to give us our time together with the affects that our Milky Way Galaxy and the Universe at large do impose on it too; but the principal player in this trinity is quite obviously, the Sun.

> I personally then realised or came to discover that our very own **heartbeat**, which through medical science, we have been informed beats at **72 beats per minute** regularly for most of us. Could it be I wondered then, that we could use this very heartbeat regularity, to establish another time keeping connection with our ultimate 'Cosmic Clock'?

> This was indeed the very case, as I had discovered, for when you multiply 72 heartbeats by 60 minutes, you will get exactly **4,320 heartbeats per hour**.

Now, this may not give you a clue as yet, i.e. what connection does this have with our 'Cosmic Clock'? Yet, a closer look may prompt you to recognise that the number **4,320** is indeed somewhat familiar to you by now.

> So, when you go on to rhythmically establish that it takes exactly **four heartbeats** on the average to beat out 3.3$\underline{3}$ seconds, then these very same 4,320 regular heartbeats, amazingly establishes for us, precisely **1080 divisions** of time in an hour. This is the similar number of time divisions remarkably too, that was clocked in a Babylonian hour!!! Isn't this simply amazing to discover that our own heartbeats, beating inside each one of us, have a relevance to how our time can be measured too!!!

> Also, I once again amazingly realised that the number of heartbeats averaging in an hour i.e. **4,320 heartbeats,** have in fact, a direct connection with our **very own Sun** and in turn with the Milky Way Galaxy and in the overall sense even with the **Universe** at large!!!

If we once again study the Aryabhatiya of Aryabatha' calculation, pertaining to a Yuga, you will discover that the Sun rotates **4,320,000 times in a Yuga**. A familiar looking number indeed, although, it is obviously a thousand times in number value, yet can establish a direct relation to the **'number of heartbeats'** that we have in an hour on a regular basis.

> Not only that, but scientists have also informed us, that the Sun actually completes one rotation once every **25 days** at its own equator or centre. If this is the case, then 25 days equates to 600 hours of time duration. Deducing from this, then for each 100 hours, our hearts would have beaten on the average, **432,000** times. And for the entire duration of 600 hours - it would have beaten **2,592,000** times exactly.

So, for every 100 hours, that makes up being part of the Sun' rotation duration (i.e. 1/6th rotation) at it' own centre, the average heart is beating in relation to it, 432,000 heartbeats and for the full duration of 600 hours (i.e. the time required for the Sun to fully rotate once at it' centre every 25 days) it would have beaten **2,592,000 times**. This highlighted number is also exactly as it is found in the Indian/Hindu Cosmological Time Cycles in a double Saros (7200 years i.e. 3,600 X 2) Babylonian Time Period, as depicted in my enhanced **SEXAGESIMAL** Chart in the previous pages.

Another interesting and relevant fact that I had come to realise or had discovered, which I had made some mention of it as previously, was that the **4,320,000** years time period of a 'yuga', is indeed **1/9,250th** part of the expanded age of the Universe which is **39.96 billion years,** being as per my calculations based on the Holy Scriptures at the end of its 12th Period of Universe expansion!!! This ratio can also be somewhat similarly applied to the number of our heartbeats in a 100 hours time period being 432,000 or in just one hour i.e. 4,320 to the expanded Universe at large. This is also simply amazing to say the least. Therefore, these 'number of heartbeats' per every 100 hours and per every 600 hours, with regards to the fully expanded age of the Universe according to the 2Esdras Scriptures is as follows respectively. 1/925,000th and 1/92,500th part of the Universe' age at the end of its 12th Period of expansion.

I had also discovered that one Kalpa period (i.e. 4,320,000,000 years) is indeed 1/9.25 times of this Universe expanded age as at the end of the 12th AUET/12th Ezra' Period. In fact, I had used such a ratio i.e. **1:9.25** to calculate out the expansion of the Universe per 2ESDRAS, until it' 12th Period of expansion, even before coming to know anything about the Indian/Hindu Cosmological Time Cycles or the relation that our heartbeats could probably have with our Sun and the Universe at large.

Just for your information, this chapter which is relating to the **'More Ancient Civilization 'TIME SEQUENCE' Relationships'**, was only inserted sometime after the fact, when I had first finished Part Three and perhaps even Part Four to a certain extent.

With all of this in focus, it may be very possible to finally conclude, that the Sun, Earth, and even perhaps also the Moon, the Milky Way Galaxy and even the Universe at large; all together have a direct affect on the very number and way our heart beats every minute, as being possibly purposefully designed into us by our GOD ALMIGHTY from the very beginning. This truly, directly connects us to the stars. In particular, one star, in direct contention i.e. our Solar System' single star being of course our Sun.

Also, it is common knowledge that the Moon does indeed control when the tides will occur and it has also been established that sometimes even our mood swings too. Also, it has something to do with the monthly menstruation in women, etc. So, it is not entirely surprising or even farfetched to propose and to even accept that the Cosmos has indeed some purposefully GOD designed control on the very number of heartbeats, we humans have per minute. It is not some arbitrary beating of the heart, left entirely on it' own, but that it is also fine tuned to the Sun' own rotation at it' centre; which also ultimately rhythms to a rhythmic Universe Pulsing System, as exhibited by the relationship in turn to it' own expansion.

> GOD ALMIGTHY placed the very pulse of the Universe or should I rather say in downsizing my reference, the pulse of the Solar System, as orchestrated by the Solar Sun directly scaled down into each of our hearts. This probably dictates the regularity in our very 72 heart beats per minute besides other biological and other anatomical possible reasons.

> **The pulse of the Solar Sun is also in our very hearts!!! Incredible, to just think about it, but highly possible too, as we have just found out as shown above.**

So, it could very well be that our own independent individual heartbeat, may not be so independent after all, well at least in it' design. Therefore, it is not surprising that when two pulsing heartbeat cells from a frog as an example are brought together into contact with each other, though at first beating with a different pace, eventually within a very short period of time, begins to beat rhythmically synchronised with one similar pulsing pace.

When GOD had set the Universe into the 'time keeping system motion', it had also affected the very pulsing of our own life, as we individually do come onto the scene, one by one, according to the Universe GOD initialised human beings queue. Something to definitely consider and to explore further in more detail, don't you think so? Anyway, you will get to know more of this later and perhaps there could possibly be a few more body rhythms to be discovered that can be used to measure 'Time'. Any takers???

PRAISE BE TO GOD ALMIGHTY

Please do keep in touch, if you have any queries and/or comments to make.

E: gcf@globalchristianfamily.com

'THE SCRIPTURAL COSMIC 666'

BOOK TWO

Some Interesting Self-Discovered Facts

If we divide the age of the Universe that had been scripturally computed through this effort, being **39.96 Billion Years** at the end of the 'World History Time – World Future Time', as presented and derived by me through the appropriate understanding of the Apocryphal or more commonly referred to as the Deuterocanonical Biblical Book, 2ESDRAS, by the number of times the word **beast** has been used in the entire Biblical Book of Revelation, i.e. by 37; we will remarkably get the result, **1,080**,000,000.

As you already had been informed, the **1080** as shown above, is indeed the number of Divisions that a Babylonian Hour is actually divided into. This is simply amazing to discover now!!! This then reveals the possibility for us to finally realize from this relationship alone, perhaps the engaging logic behind the possible design of this ancient time system which has such great accuracy not so much of linking it to the Biblical Book of Revelation but by directly linking it somewhat to their possible knowledge or perhaps realization that the Universe on the whole is indeed expanding. Of course this is somewhat speculating on this possibility, but nevertheless, it does point us to a cosmic solution for the Babylonian to have done so with regards to their remarkable time keeping design. You may remember being informed earlier that the Babylonian had designed their time system to obtain the 1080 Divisions in an hour of time (each reading 3.3$\underline{3}$ seconds), which does equate similarly to the same 3,600 seconds as present in our hour of time too. This in itself is simply remarkable, to say the least!!!

> Also, it then follows that there are exactly **60 million 666 year cycles** of time, in the fully expanded age of the Universe, as at the end of the 2ESDRAS' WHT-WFT, which culminates for us in the **39.96 billionth years**.

> It is as if I am now possibly discovering the time that had been allocated to us from the very beginning till the very completion of the history of the 'world' that has already been predetermined by none other than our GOD ALMIGHTY. This is from when GOD had decided to first create the Universe from ex-nihilo to it' very ending according to the 12th Ezra' Period of WHT-WFT. This indeed closes the very 'loop of time' to this phase of GOD' creation or rather the created, which through the Holy Bible we find out that it also includes the plans that GOD had and has for us.

> **This entire thinking and logic was extracted or derived through my very understanding of the relevant referenced 2ESDRAS Holy Scriptures and it expresses and indeed possibly exposes the greatest ever 'Grand Master Conductor' of all time in all of this, as found described in Revelation 1:8 and Rev 4:11, as follows:**

REV 1:8
"I am the Alpha and the Omega,
the Beginning and the End,"
says the LORD,
"who is and who was and who is to come, the Almighty."

REV 4:11
"You are worthy, O LORD, to receive glory and honour and power;
For You created all things,
And by Your will they exist and were created."

Also somewhat amazing is that the sum total 666, which has been residing for most of us in a quite mundane or innate state in REV 13:18, has now been possibly revealed through this effort, as being indeed a divinely predetermined Universe Time Cycle. That is this 666 years time cycle, 60 million of these to be exact, do exist as time cyclic periods until the very end of the ages. This I had the gracious privilege to have discovered, as I had derived it, from within the relevant referenced Holy Scriptures as described in 2ESDRAS!!! Praise be to GOD.

PART THREE

The Cosmic Based Construction, Leading to the 'Number' of 'The Beast'

According to one of the **Apocryphal** Biblical Books, **2ESDRAS**, these also being referred to as the **Deuterocanonical** as found included in some Bible translations, describes the important **'Seventh Vision'** in it' Scriptures of Chapter 14:1-13 as shown below. However, before we do go there, let us also read 2ESDRAS Chapter 13:57-58, which gives us some important and very relevant background, which also sets the stage for my fresh and new understanding of these very scripture revelations, as revealed to me in 2ESDRAS Chapter 14:1-13.

13:57 I went for a walk in the field, worshipping and praising GOD Most High for the miracles HE performs in HIS own good time.
13:58 For HE controls the ages and what happens in them. I remained there for three days.
14:1 On the third day, while I was sitting under an oak tree,:
14:2 suddenly a VOICE came out of a bush near me and called, "Ezra! Ezra!" I stood up and answered, "Here I am, LORD."
14:3 The VOICE continued, "I revealed MYSELF from a bush and spoke to Moses when MY people were slaves in Egypt.
14:4 I sent him to lead them out of Egypt, and I brought them to Mount Sinai. I kept Moses with ME there on the mountain for a long time,
14:5 while I told him the **secrets** about the **ages and the end of time.** I told
14:6 what to make public and what to keep secret.
14:7 Now I command you
14:8 to memorize the signs, visions, and interpretations that I have given you.
14:9 **You** will be taken out of this world into the **heavenly world** where you and **others like you** will live with MY SON until the end of time.
14:10 The world is no longer young; it is rapidly approaching old age.
14:11 The whole history of the world is divided into twelve periods, and the tenth period has already arrived
14:12 and it is half over; only two and a half parts remain
14:13 So set your house in order, warn your people, comfort those who are humble, and teach those who are wise. Then say goodbye to this mortal life.

When we come to understand the above Scriptures in it' proper perspective, you may come to realise that GOD had indeed revealed to us the single largest time measurement period that had covered our past, also operating as currently in our present and will continue as such into our future; all being directly relevant to us.

Thereby, you also need to first discover, as I had understood it, the hidden or the not expressed 'time structures' which the above 2ESDRAS scriptures had revealed to me through the very brief statements and that also only in summary.

This I had discovered is a typical 'pattern of writing' or 'pattern of revelation' that most of the inspired scripture writers were inspired to write in and it is quite obvious from this very 'pattern' that they themselves did not know the very details or rather the nitty gritties, as they were not writing off their own accord, ability, knowledge and foresight; but were given to write what GOD had wanted to be expressed in such manner. In other words, it was not through their own knowledge accumulation or thinking per se, but what knowledge that was given to them or accorded to them by the ALMIGHTY, in a divinely and intentionally 'limited yet inspired' manner.

This is important for you to understand as such and to acknowledge it being as such, for if not there is no reason for the divinely inspired scripture writers to write or to give us the revelation evidences in such a brief and/or summarised manner. This we can quite easily see is the evidential case throughout most of the entire range of Biblical Books with regards to the 'mysteries' and biblical events that exists in it, as expressed by them. This is right from the Book of Genesis to the Book of Revelation.

They simply did not know the very intricate details to explain these 'mysteries' clearly to us, unless **GOD** had wanted to reveal it to us and thereby, appropriate explanations were at times given to us accordingly.

This **lack** in itself is in further support of their receiving it as being inspired in a divinely intended **'limited' manner**. This had been GOD intended as such, to my conclusion, so that none of them could claim that they were indeed writing on or off their own accord. Exceptions to this were quite obvious when they were also the key eye witnesses to the event or events as such which is quite clear in several cases throughout the Gospels of the NEW TESTAMENT; The Biblical Book Of ACTS; and similarly in some of the other biblical books too, just to mention a few.

Also, we should rightly acknowledge and accept that there were many and still are as currently and also possibly will be similarly in the future, though not having been counted amongst the biblical inspired writers themselves, but have been given the GODLY opportunity after the fact to further discover and to further explore, to even interpret the 'hidden' and/or the 'limited given' divine messages, as we have it assembled as such in the Holy Bible.

In repetition:

> Many of these too in my humble opinion could have been and possibly still are, through the passing of the generations one by one, in which some having been divinely enabled to extract from within these scriptural texts and make such to become more clearly understood by the rest of us who are interested and willing to be taught regarding these GODLY provisions as found in the Holy Bible.

In fact, as mentioned above, you must surely be aware too that the study and the interpretation of the Holy Bible Scriptures are still continuing even in our most recent and current times. This making many also an integral part together with those divinely inspired biblical writers of the Holy Scriptures, as time and space progresses us on, as a people of this Earth. And in the same light, if by some remotest of possibilities, I am to be most fortunate enough to have found any degree of favour through GOD' grace, GOD' love and HIS unending mercy, despite my own weaknesses and failings, I am in any way found to be contributing towards this global human continuing effort, would simply be amazing; so help me GOD ALMIGHTY, I PRAY. THANK YOU LORD and SAVIOUR JESUS CHRIST. THANK YOU, GOD THE HOLY SPIRIT

At first study of these Scriptures, I thought that these Scriptures were indeed describing **12 PERIODS of World History only.** However, after very careful analysis, I found out that it was not the limiting case as such. However, it did strongly point me in that direction, that there were indeed '12 specific Periods of WHT (World History Time)' according to 2ESDRAS. Further to this acceptance, I also had discovered that there was yet more hidden scriptural **'time structures'**, even behind these 12 specific Periods of WHT. Am I confusing you too much? Don't worry; it will all come clearer to you, as you do proceed on.

After going through many different types of 'time constructions' through several months and having come to realise at the end of it that there were indeed **12 specific Periods of Ezra' WHT,** many of which were involved with the past leading right to the present times and having in fact also discovered that these were indeed encompassing the very **future WHT** that has yet to come upon us; I came to these additional final conclusions.

> It was that these very Scriptures were through my scriptural deduction, indicating, that we are currently in the 12th Phase Level of World History Time or rather more specifically in the **12th Phase Level** of our Universe' continuing expansion. This is ever since the 'Big Bang' had been reportedly established through scientific scholarship, as having occurred aeons and aeons ago at the very beginning of this Universe expansion.

> Also, all of the other expired 11 Phase Levels of Universe expansion were indeed responsible, obviously, to get us to this final era, so to speak. This inadvertently does link in this particular **12th Phase Level** of the Universe' expansion directly to the **12 PERIODS of Ezra' WHT-WFT**.

You may want to ask, "What are these 12 Phase Levels of Universe expansion that are suddenly being introduced here?"

> Well the answer is that from my understanding, as based on my scriptural perspective of the 2ESDRAS' referenced scriptures; I had deduced that there are indeed 12 Phases or Levels of Universe expansion to the end of the **2ESDRAS WHT-WFT**. Also, from my study of the referenced scriptures, we are currently in the final 12th Phase Level. This meaning directly, this particular **12th Phase Level**, is to be taken as being **the one and the same** to be encompassing the important divinely revealed **12 Periods of Ezra' WHT**.

In fact I came to realise, there isn't any 2ESDRAS' WHT to talk about in the other 11 Phase Levels except for the supportive history or historical cosmic record for the Universe' expansion being self-evident in it' own existence as it is today.

Therefore, in this deeper sense, the **2ESDRAS' WHT** which directly pertains to the 12th Phase Level of Universe expansion only is indeed very significant indeed, as you will find out very shortly.

These 12 Phase Levels are directly pertaining to our physical world, which is the expanding Universe in Space and Time, and as important, it' relationship to the 'Heavenly World', which GOD was revealing somewhat to Ezra. So before this there was the ageless Heavenly World only. This was subsequently joined by the eventual GOD creation of the physical world, which has definite scriptural time duration to complete as per GOD's plans for it. I am of the understanding that Science also does currently concur now in some shape and form to this time limitation for the continued existence of this universe and in turn for the Sun controlled Solar System too.

So, the above Scriptures to my understanding of it were indeed describing in some greater detail, this particular 2ESDRAS WHT-WFT which I have through scriptural deduction incorporated it entirely into the **12th Phase Level** of Universe expansion.

In fact through this scriptural deduction again, I came to decisively conclude that the 2ESDRAS WHT-WFT begins with the beginning of the 12th Phase Level and ends with the ending of this 12th Phase Level of Universe expansion. Thereby, dividing this particular 12th Phase Level of Universe expansion as being the one and the same as with the 2ESDRAS' 12 WHT-WFT Periods accordingly, as per the expansion rate of the Universe expansion per se.

> In other words, the 2ESDRAS' 12 WHT-WFT Periods follows progressively, one by one, as it takes up or uses up WHT more and more as per the exponentially increasing expansion of the Universe that was, is and will be as in the future - 2ESDRAS 14:11 refers.

Another way of putting it is as follows: This also meaning that both the 12 Periods of 2ESDRAS WHT-WFT and the 12 Periods of the 12th Phase Level of Universe expansion are indeed totally interrelated and inter-dependant to each other. Thereby, the 2ESDRAS' 12 Periods of WHT-WFT must each follow progressively the similar rate of each Period of Universe expansion in this 12th Phase Level.

> Following this conclusion as above, the scriptural verse 2ESDRAS 14:11 would then mean accordingly, that the **Tenth Period** of 2ESDRAS' WHT is actually the **10th Period** in this 12th Phase Level of Universe expansion.

Also, following through with these relevant 2ESDRAS' 14:11-12 Scriptures and the understanding that I have derived from it; this 10th Period is to be understood as having already **ended**. Therefore, regarding these scriptures, we are currently running through the **11th Period** which is indeed **half over**.

14:10   The world is no longer young; it is rapidly approaching old age.

14:11   **The whole history of the world is divided into twelve periods, and the tenth period has already arrived**

14:12   **and it is half over; only two and a half parts remain**

The scripture 14:11 indicates to me that the 10th PERIOD is indeed in the past. Now before you go on a rampage against my understanding, allow me to explain something to you.

It is like this. If you had gone on a holiday to a far off destination and when you finally come to the end of your journey, you may express or declare aloud that you have already arrived.

This is the crux to my understanding regarding the 2ESDRAS 14:11 scripture was indeed revealing that the 10th Period had indeed already ended and that we have progressed ½ the way through the next Period which as mentioned above would be the 11th Period. However, when you read off the WHT-WFT time that had expired, you will be naturally reading it as being 10 and a ½ PERIOD have already ended.

The 2ESDRAS 14:12 scriptural verse also very clearly informs us that only **2 and a ½ PARTS of it remains** to be filled i.e. with WHT-WFT accordingly.

This scriptural statement revealing that the Period is indeed **half over** and that only **2 and a ½ PARTS remain,** directly reveals to me by my taking the liberty in making a scriptural based assumption here, that each 2ESDRAS' WHT Period is indeed sub-divided into **FIVE PARTS** of WHT-WFT just as each Phase Level is also similarly divided into 12 PERIODS each.

> So, in multiplicity, if this is indeed the case, then we will have in a Phase Level, 60 such 'time' PARTS.

> We must not forget at this stage the other 11 Phase Levels of Universe expansion that had brought the Universe right to the doorstep, so to speak, to this 12th Phase Level era which also incorporates the 2ESDRAS' 12 PERIODS of WHT-WFT.

You must also by now have become familiar that each succeeding Phase Level from the very first one will take up an ever-increasing amount of Universe expansion. Also you need to take careful note that through this scriptural deduction as derived from the relevant 2ESDRAS scriptures, I had realised that all of these prior 11 Phase Levels of Universe expansion were indeed **void** of Ezra' **WH(T).**

It is as if our 2ESDRAS' Biblical World History only became significant or rather had begun as the Universe began it' 12th Phase Level of expansion ever since the 'Big Bang' had been scientifically reported as having occurred at the very beginning of the Universe expansion. This I had located as such at the very beginning of the First Phase level of our Universe expansion. Therefore, repeating it again, 2ESDRAS' WHT-WFT was, is and will be in its entirety subscribed totally in this 12th Phase Level of Universe expansion only.

With this Universe expansion in view, we must also understand that all of these 12 Phase Levels have each actually progressed (i.e. the previous 11) with the still current 12th, also progressing accordingly to the divinely initiated Universe expansion plan, as scientifically endorsed to have begun with the 'Big Bang'. The Universe is reportedly in expansion continuously and also **increasingly,** as informed by the scientific community, and is as described somewhat in my Chart E similarly. No conflict here. The reference page for this is found in the Appendix towards the end of this book.

In order not to get confused with the 12 Periods of Ezra's WHT with the **12 Phase Levels** of Universe expansion, which I have taken to being part of the 'hidden' time structure that I had derived from the understanding of the relevant

2ESDRAS scriptures; I have now taken the liberty, if you would allow me this discretion, to call these 12 Phase Levels as being the Alphonso' 12 Phase Levels of Universe Expansion Time. In the shorten version, simply as the **'12 AUET Phases'**.

> Also, this currently ongoing Alphonso' 12th Phase Level, incorporates quite obviously the birth of the Solar System, and also the entire future of our Planet Earth and our Solar System, as the Universe continues to expand into 'Universe Space and Time' in this Phase Level. From the scriptures, we can clearly learn that there is still more Earth Time and thereby more 'World History' to be written and to be experienced by us or rather by those who would be living in the future material time in progress.

I also had deduced that in this Alphonso' 12th Phase Level, each of the 12 Ezra Periods of WHT-WFT, is also time phased into **12 sub-periods** of WHT-WFT each. In other words, this would reveal that there is another level of the 'hidden' time structure, behind each Period of WHT-WFT.

> So, in total there are **144** such sub-periods in this Alphonso' 12th Phase Level. Can you see the familiar number unit of **144**, which is also seen in the Revelation Scriptures as the **144**,000?

> In total, despite these additional sub-periods time structures being introduced here, there still consists exactly **60 Parts** of WHT, **five to a Period**, as revealed by the 2Esdras scriptures in the entire Alphonso' 12th Phase Level.

This is all what I had derived from my understanding of the above Holy Scriptures and the several 'time constructions' that I had gone through over several months, before finally arriving at this one and accepting it as such. In other words, the reason for this acceptance was simply that it made complete sense to do so. This is because it would be proven eventually in this book for my coming to this acceptance, being strongly helped through the cosmic based construction process for the obtaining of the REVELATION beast' number which sum totals 666. The Chart A3 will make this somewhat clearer for your better understanding. The Appendix at the end of this book will provide you with the page reference for it.

Welcome back. OK you may have even more puzzling questions to ask me now. For example, you may want to know:

"How on Earth was I able to compute the very **age-sizes** with regards to the time taken for the expansion of the Universe through each of these Alphonso' 12 Phase Levels?"

Due to the obvious complexities within which this valid question is anticipated, it will be answered I hope, in due time and in due process within the context and limitation of this book and thereby of this author too.

So, for now, you just go on and accumulate this additional information as given to you in Chart A3 and Chart E.

We also need to understand very clearly from the very beginning, that when we are referring to the Ezra' **10 and a ½ Period**, as being referenced and described in these 2ESDRAS' Scriptures, these are actually WHT as derived from my understanding of it, as located in the Alphonso' 12th Phase Level **10 and a ½ Period**.

You will also discover as you study the Chart – A3, that each Phase Level is measured in **'Earth Time'** terms and representing in actual fact an ever increasing number of years in its expansion progress throughout the Phase Levels Universe expansion.

You will also learn how I had arrived at these **'increasing number of years'** in the very expansion of the Universe, as you continue your study through this Part Three of this book.

The scientific concept and proposition based on negative gravity that the Universe is indeed expanding at an alarming ever increasing rate, also provides me with the fundamental and important scientific support to my own similar concept as indicated on the previous pages, but having been totally derived from within the Holy Scriptures. This is also if I understand it correctly, is referred to as 'dark energy' (first proposed by Einstein), which led to the very thinking that the Universe is indeed **accelerating** in it' expansion, since the 'Big Bang' had occurred. Strangely, this is the case, though it should have been the opposite as scientist have informed us i.e. to be ever slowing down after the 'Big Bang' had first occurred so very long ago.

In fact it was Edwin Bubble's discovery in 1929 that the Universe is indeed expanding, and this had actually initiated the idea, that in the aeons ago, the universe must have been smaller. In fact Scientific Scholarship has informed us that it had begun from a highly compressed mass state until an explosion due to this compression must have had occurred within it as Dr Stephen Hawking had proposed, triggering this very expansion. It was this very idea that Fred Hoyle (a British cosmologist), though not agreeing to it, cynically called it the 'Big Bang'. I hope I am referencing all of this correctly.

> With all of the above in focus, you can seriously consider that **Science** is providing the necessary support or rather providing the understanding scaffolding for this 'Cosmic Based Universe Construction' of the 'number' of the second beast sum totalling 666.

> Also for me and the likeminded through this book, will discover this very cosmic construction has it' description or history firmly rooted in our **Biblical Scriptures** from the very first relevant referenced scripture as found in GEN 1:1.

This means for example in the Alphonso' First Phase Level, the Universe had expanded in the **allocated time sweep** from zero expansion to 0.9420336 years, as shown in Chart E. Similarly, in the Alphonso' Second Phase Level, it had expanded to 8.71381128 Years; which means covering a larger area/volume of Universe Space. Of course the rate of expansion or acceleration would be increasing gradually throughout the Phase Levels. I will however, only be taking into account this **overall change rate** i.e. it' final acceleration speed of expansion but not the gradual increase rate within the Periods/sub-periods of the various Phase Levels of Universe expansion. This means in essence that I will use the final rate of expansion possible in each Phase Level as the rate of expansion throughout that particular Phase Level.

Also take note, keeping this enlarging area/volume of Universe expansion into 'Universe Space', across all of the Alphonso' Phase Levels, through a similar amount of allocated 'time sweep'. You may be wondering, "What is this new concept, the 'allocated time sweep', being mentioned here?" Do not worry, keep plodding on, I will explain it to you very clearly soon.......I hope.

> This very model exposes the very **'acceleration'** in the Universe Expansion as time progresses forward from one Phase Level to the next Phase Level. This 'acceleration' was exactly what Einstein had proposed was indeed happening in the increasing rate in the expansion of the Universe through his 'dark energy' theory.

You need to also understand as a development of my 2ESDRAS' derived constructed model projecting the Universe expansion, that the Universe accelerates as a whole mass and thereby follows the same acceleration throughout every nook and corner in a particular time period.

So, as per my understanding, this means in reconfirming all of the above, although there were and still are definite changes in the rate of expansion within a Period or parts of a Period/sub-period, we are only taking into account the possible **total overall maximum change possible** from Phase Level to Phase Level as per this scriptural derived model.

My formula rate for the **expansion rate of the Universe** in these Alphonso' 12 Phase Levels, as having been supposedly triggered by the 'Big Bang', had been based on a specific time scale ratio, which I will introduce to you shortly. This will provide further answers to the questions that you may or would have with regards to the Chart A3.

Well anyway, let us not get bogged down with all of these technicalities and complexities that are certainly involved in the expansion of the Universe, and which is definitely way beyond my own understanding. This is because I am no Physicist, Mathematician, Astronomer or anyone that can be considered well learned; in fact I had voluntarily on my own accord dropped out of Engineering College, being primarily homesick and a bit disillusioned as influenced by my environment and circumstances at that time. Sorry to have disappointed you, if you may have thought, that I was learned at least to some degree to have taken such a task as this to be involved in.

It is not the scope of this book, neither it is of the **author' ability** to go any further on this. However, you can see that there is a definite increase in the **'age-size of the Universe expansion'** in the Second Phase, as compared to the First Phase Level. This is what I had wanted to express and achieve based on my understanding of the relevant scriptures.

It was not based on any particular science, although science does support this thinking on the matter too; of course without taking my scriptural derived proposed time scale ratio as being involved in their conclusion.

> You also need to take careful note, that I have kept the **allocated time sweep** the same in all of these Alphonso' 12 Phase Levels.

> So, in my **'Cosmic Construction Model'**, I have indeed followed the very expansion of the Universe, right from the very beginning of the 'Big Bang' in terms of it' increasing **age,** which directly relates to its increasing **size** too.

> In repetition: This model also takes into account the ever increasing acceleration or rather the increasing speed (though currently scientifically unknown rate i.e. referring to the speed of expansion) by applying my own scriptural derived or deduced **'time based scale ratio rate'** in its expansion too.

I know my stating this with such great 'simplicity' for such a huge and complex matter would certainly make me the laughing stock with many if not with all interested parties. Yet I have only this scriptural singular option to be presented here; so let it be.

However, even if you feel this way, please do continue to read it to the end if you can spare the time and have the patience to do so.

> It just might change your mind into at least understanding, how I did come to this very possibility, at the end of it all; well I hope so. Nothing to lose here, as I see it, but all to gain and for some perhaps a new Christian awakening and perhaps for others, possibly to being further strengthened, I sincerely hope in our Christian Biblical beliefs, just as I have too.

Scientists have devised several methods to estimate the age of the Universe. The most recent of which at the time of writing this book, which I have already mentioned earlier, is the NASA' Wilkinson Microwave Anisotropy Probe.

Another method amongst a few others as proposed by our scientists is the duration of light from distant sources such as stars, supernovas, etc., reaching the Earth. This study in particular would provide us with quite a good relative sense to the very age of the expanding Universe, but falling short in revealing to us, it' volume of expansion into the Universe Space. This is because our current science has yet to reveal to us or inform us of the speed and the acceleration for the expansion of the Universe.

However, there are two teams of scientists according to a recent article on Astronomy in our local national newspaper (NST dated 8 April 2001); who are now finding a way to measure the changes in the expansion rate of the Universe that has been going on over billions of years as per the current thinking. This they say is observable even now, so all the very best to them.

Anyway, coming back to some notes that I had written regarding Chart E:

This should be studied from the bottom upwards to understand it in it' proper perspective as it traces the development of the Alphonso' 12 Phase Levels in the expansion progress of the Universe. The values on the right hand side were obtained by multiplying the values on the left hand side by 60.

We multiply by 60, as the total number of Periods that we possibly may have in each of the 12 Phase Levels are 12 each and also each Period is possibly further subdivided into **5 equal PARTS**; just like that of Ezra' described model of WHT. I do not see any reason for not employing this here similarly and I indicated **equal parts** since I am overlooking the internal changing rates in the expansion but only considering the overall maximum expansion rate from Phase Level to Phase Level as already mentioned earlier. So the time that is being represented on the left is the time for a typical Part in that Phase Level. Thereby, distributing this overall expansion equally throughout the entire Period involving it' parts/sub-periods, etc., and in turn, throughout the entire expansion of the Universe, as that being possible through the Alphonso' 12 Phase Levels model. This you will come to understand better, later.

Therefore, having employed this in multiplicity, it would then give us a total of 60 equal segments of time separation for the Universe' expansion in each of the Alphonso' 12 Phase Levels.

> You must and should understand that the Universe expansion is actually a **continuous one**, although we are demarcating it by Periods or Phases of exponential growth as such in these Alphonso' 12 Phase Levels.

> In repetition once again: This means in the macro sense, we have only **one** continuous Alphonso' Phase Level which does indeed incorporates the entire Universe expansion (being still in progress) which had begun supposedly with the 'Big Bang' and also has these 12 Periods of Ezra' WHT-WFT towards the other end of it. However, behind the scenes i.e. through the 'hidden time structures' so to speak, are these Alphonso' 12 Phase Levels of Universe expansion for our easier understanding. Each of these Phase Levels have possibly 12 Periods that are each divided into 5 Equal Parts of AUET. This also keeps in line with Ezra' own 12 Periods of WHT structure, each having five equal parts each. This WHT as mentioned previously is in fact incorporated into the very last 12th AUET Phase Level.

This then seems to work into somewhat like the face of a time-keeping device. On the face, we only see the time results of the various cog wheel movements, which are operating inside and which are usually hidden from our view in most clock devices. These are so precisely made and precisely assembled to give us the accuracy in reading the time off its face with such ease. Based with this understanding, in our own AUET Clock System, each Alphonso' Phase Level could be understood as being time-phased through 12 Sectors of Universe Expansion, just as in our 12 Hour clocks. Therefore, one hour i.e. 60 minutes could be taken to represent 1 Sector of time, which can also be termed as being one Period of AUET. However, these 60 AUET minutes are **not the same time duration**, as our own Earth time minutes. It is far from it. You will understand this later better.

> However, you need to take careful note that when moving to the time registering of the next AUET Phase Level, the entire clock mechanism needs to be upgraded, so to speak, in order to accommodate a specific time scale ratio which will be introduced to you shortly. In fact this time scale ratio is exactly the same with the exponentially accelerating rate of Universe expansion into Universe Space as derived from within these 2ESDRAS' scriptures.

In other words, the **AUET MINUTE** in the first AUET Phase Level would have measured a time duration which would be relatively speaking **very much less** than what was the AUET MINUTE duration, as was represented in the second AUET Phase Level. This in turn is repeated similarly for the rest of the AUET Phase Levels. All of this up-scaling in the time measurement duration as just mentioned would be following a specific time duration scale/ratio which was specifically derived from within the Scriptures. You will find this remarkably amazing to say the least, when you do come across it and the manner that it was derived from the proper understanding of the referenced Scriptures.

> The upgrading as a suggestion if we are constructing such a device can be accomplished by changing all the cog wheels of the existing clock mechanism to be able to accommodate this time up-scaling duration from Phase Level to Phase Level. Another possible method would be to use a completely new clock each time with accommodating cog wheel mechanism to incorporate the next Phase Level AUET requirements. All of these new clocks, 12 in total, could then in turn be linked together into the overall AUET Clock System.

> I would personally prefer the second option as it would maintain the time records of the time that had expired of the immediate previous AUET Phase Level.

Of course we can only do this as a projected time model to incorporate what we think is happening in the expansion of the Universe as per our understanding of the relevant scriptures that have already been mentioned previously. Obviously, we cannot be recording it physically i.e. in real time terms due to our own very short life spans and our inability to maintain such a system over the duration. So we can only rely upon constructing such time models as in a lab setting unless someone finds a way to do it 'live' or in real time terms.

Every time the allocated time sweep for one part had been expired through one full revolution of the first cog wheel movement at the end of every **12 AUET MINUTES** of the particular AUET Phase Level, it would in turn drive another cog wheel, as in a normal clock movement mechanism. This divides each Phase Level Period-Sector into a further 5 Equal Parts of 12 AUET Minutes, each following that particular time scale of Universe Expansion rate that had been accorded to it.

So, by reading the second cog wheel movements off it' face, we can read at what stage is the particular AUET Phase Level was in at the time. Of course this is now redundant currently as all the 11 AUET Phase Levels have already been completed. However, I still need to continue describing this stage of the

AUET Clock System for you. This second cog wheel in turn would link onto another cog wheel (the third) to register every Period-Sector of the respective AUET. Once it had completed one full revolution or rotation, this third cog wheel would have registered in total, 12 Periods-Sectors of the particular AUET being time-phased at the time. This would then have indeed completed the registering of that particular AUET Phase Level.

From this stage, the third cog wheel of the first clock, as it completes one full rotation, then meshes into a fourth independent cog wheel which goes on to register the full AUET Phase Level that had been completed by the first clock. The fourth cog wheel can be considered to be connected to a clock face from which the universe expansion time phases can be read off one by one. Of course you would have to wait many, many million life times and more before you could see any movement. It was at this stage that the AUET Clock System would have linked into it' second clock and subsequently similarly into it' third, fourth and so on, until the final 12th such clock had expired reading all of the 2ESDRAS' WHT-WFT and what 'time' may be still left to fully complete or exhaust the 12 AUET Phase Levels.

We could name this fourth cog wheel as being the master cog wheel, for as each clock in the AUET Clock System becomes in turn redundant, it automatically disengages from the AUET Clock System after having it' entire time registered onto this master cog wheel as a corresponding AUET Phase Level. The master cog wheel then links up as already mentioned with the next clock' third cog wheel in the AUET Clock System to similarly register the next AUET Phase Level.

We must also take careful note that the master cog wheel is a special cog wheel with variable settings. This would then give the master cog wheel the ability to change it' dimensions and speed of rotation to accommodate all the intermediate up-scaling time durations of each of the 12 AUET clocks in the AUET Clock System accordingly.

If we so require, we can introduce as many hands to read off any amounts of smaller divisions of time even possibly to an Earth Day to Earth Day basis and even smaller than this too. We could also progress this clock design or rather the AUET Clock System to become a digital/computerised operating clock system.

> In conclusion to this clock design, at the micro level, each of the AUET Phase Level Clocks has also similarly **60 DIVISIONS** grouped into 5 equal Parts. This is why in Chart E we do multiply by 60 each Universe expansion, to get the total level of expansion for that Phase Level.

However, for the 12th AUET Phase Level, we also have another hidden time structure has already mentioned and that is each of it Ezra' WHT-WFT Period is further sub-divided into another 12 sub-periods each.

Also, when proceeding up the Chart E i.e. vertically, we multiply the previous Phase Level by the scriptural derived time scale factor or ratio, this being **9.25** times the time as projected at the end of the previous Phase Level. This is to get us to the next Level of Universe Expansion. In fact we get to the very end of this very next immediate Phase Level.

We can also obtain this final expansion per Phase Level by multiplying by 60 the time as projected on the left hand side of the Chart E for the respective Phase Level. This would obtain for us once again the **total level of age-size expansion** possible for the Phase Level.

> As mentioned above each AUET Phase Level progresses on in it' Universe expansion rate, exponentially being 9.25 times the AUET Phase Level' total expansion possible that was immediately preceding it.

> **9.25 times**

You will find out later in much more detail about this very important time scale factor or time ratio that has just been introduced here. Although, it may seem that I am proposing here a very orderly and very structured model of Universe expansion, however, I also do agree that this is not to be the case in reality. Despite this, I am assuming an overall view, which can be made to accommodate as far as this scriptural derived model is concerned, an orderly and structured Universe expansion, despite this definitely not being the case in actuality. Your study of Chart E, will also give you additional insight into Chart A3.

In reiteration: For your information, which has actually already been mentioned previously (forgive me for the several repetitions); we are intentionally ignoring the immediate rate of Universe expansion increase, within each of the Periods or Sub-Periods of the Alphonso' 12 Phase Levels. This does not at all interfere with this 'Cosmic Number Construction' of the second beast' number or for us to arrive at the desired results, which culminates with the Universe expanding into it' purportedly **GOD measured 39.96 billion year time frame**. This happens to be, the possible time projection for the ending of this present Alphonso' 12th Phase Level, based on my understanding of the relevant 2ESDRAS Scriptures, following this scriptural derived time scale ratio formula.

As mentioned earlier, unlike Fred Hoyle, who did not support or rather did not agree to the 'Big Bang' theory for the Universe Expansion cosmological model of their time, which as according to **Dr Stephen Hawking** (a brilliant, famous and currently living British cosmologist) began with the 'Big Bang'. I really do admire his tenacity to excel and to have inspired so many, even through his own personal health difficulties. He is indeed an impressive GIANT amongst us other mere mortals.

I have as mentioned several times previously, had calculated out, that the Universe expansion following the scriptural time ratio scale of **9.25** times will scripturally culminate at exactly **39.96 billion years** from the time the 'Big Bang' had occurred for this 2ESDRAS Cosmological derived model. This means taking the 'Big Bang' to be the starting point for the Universe expansion and thereby taking this as the referenced zero base point or starting base for the beginning of the Universe expansion and the ending to be the ending of the 12th AUET Phase Level. This would be also the end of the scriptural supported Ezra' WHT-WFT 12th Period.

Whether the Universe does keep on in it' expansionary journey after this time period if allowed to do so by the operating cosmic forces at the time is not within the scope of this book to offer any such suggestion. However, one thing is certain scripturally referring, and that is that it can only continue as long as it has not filled up all of the GOD measured 'Universe Space' that had been allocated to it from the very beginning of it' creation by our GOD ALMIGHTY – HEB 11:3 refers.

Somehow, although it is baffling to science as currently, that the Universe instead of slowing down is indeed increasing in it' speed of expanding away from the source base point of the Big Bang homogenously in all directions, I am of the notion that there must be some form of cosmic force that is actually drawing the Universe to expand increasingly in all directions as I had suggested previously and in a predetermined time frame too.

> Could this cosmic force be actually residing or existing in the very 'Universe Space-Time Frame' itself that was measured and constructed by GOD ALMIGHTY in 'OUTER SPACE' when GOD had allocated the measured 'Universe Space' into which **GOD** had put into it the Universe. This had allowed and still allows for the full expansion of the Universe to be limited within this 'Universe Space-Time Frame'. This is as I understand it from the Scriptures which refer – such as HEB 11:3 and others like it.

Well while those of you who may want to pursue this idea, it is also important for you to be clearly informed now that the very **beginning** of the 12th AUET Phase Level which has been progressively calculated from the very First AUET Phase Level using the scriptural time scale ratio of **9.25** exponentially, had begun precisely on the **4,320,000,000th year.** This was the year as calculated from the time that the 'Big Bang' as scientifically reported had occurred which had triggered this very expansion in the first place.

This Alphonso' 12th Universe Expansion Phase Level, as mentioning it again, is in progress at this very material time that we are currently living in.

> Strangely, you will see this period of time as calculated in this Scriptural based Universe Expansion Model i.e. the **4,320,000,000** years period, time and time again, in the ancient time systems.

This is as in the Indian/Hindu Cosmological Time Cycles where one Kalpa period equates to 4,320,000,000 years. Also, similarly found in the Babylonian Time System and perhaps even in other time systems too. It is also connected to our Sun, i.e. with regards to it' revolution around it' centre every 25 days as mentioned in the previous section. Also, this is almost the same period of time or rather the age that our scientist had estimated that the Earth is based on their science i.e. about 4.5 billion years old. Not being very far off from this time period cycle.

Also, if you had not taken notice of it as already previously mentioned, the beginning time period i.e. **4,320,000,000th** year describing the beginning of the 12th AUET Phase Level is actually synchronous with our very **heartbeats** too. Or rather, I should say, "It is the other way round, i.e. our very heartbeat is in fact synchronous with the very beginning age of this 12th AUET." For as already mentioned before, it beats every 100 hours at a rate of **432,000 heartbeats** or 4320 every hour. In fact if you do live for more than 115 years or so, which may be possible for some in this modern era but definitely not a problem for many in the Biblical Times of the OLD TESTAMENT as we have read in it; your heart would have beaten, yes, about **4.32 billion times**!!! It was as if it was destined to be so and it' implication is strongly emphasised in each of our very hearts and in a way fulfilling another cosmic mathematical pattern and affect.

Also, as mentioned previously, I am assuming for our ease of understanding and convenience for this **very complex** 'Cosmic Universe Accelerating Expansion', that the 'rate of expansion' is always consistently **increasing** from Phase to Phase. However, it may be also increasing and reducing at times from within each Period and part or sub-period, ever since the 'Big Bang' had occurred.

Dr Michael S Turner, an Astrophysicist at the University of Chicago, according to the same newspaper article being referenced, is one of those scientists who does support that there was a time in the Universe' Cosmic History, that the expansion of the Universe was indeed slowing down **due** to gravity, until negative gravity exceeded it and caused the Universe to **accelerate** in it' expansion instead

This scientific perspective to the Universe expansion, gets me thinking, whether this **slowing down and then acceleration** in the expansion of the Universe, is actually just one part of a phase, in the overall 'Universe History Cycle of Expansion'. Does this suggests, would it once again at some point have a situation where gravity begins to exceed negative gravity continuously again and increasingly at that, causing inevitably **slowing down** in the expansion or bringing to an halt the expansion or even perhaps reversing this at some point, to be contracting the Universe in this Cosmic Universe Space, instead.

This could eventually result in the **'Big Bang'** to re-occur again at the extreme end of the contracting phase. In fact this is not new in this thinking. Many have also recently suggested this possibility. This would then encompass the entire 'Universe Cycle' into an enlarged **'Universe Oscillating Cycle'**. This is somewhat like my own proposal with regards to the Planet Earth' 'Oscillating Cycle', as described in Book One. It is with regards to it' EAR oscillating speed from being first slow then increasing to a faster pace and then slowing down again, then repeating this cycle over and over again depending on the starting base point that you do choose.

Also, whether the Universe will once again go through this 'Big Bang' cycle or not is something which several scientists are currently exploring the very possibility. Perhaps it will oscillate within a definable 'safe period', without progressing or regressing into the extreme of another 'Big Bang' occurrence. Yet it should be well known that before the 'Big Bang' had occurred, GOD ALMIGHTY **had already created** the Universe from **ex-nihilo** (i.e. from nothingness it was). Now to further define this, "had already created the Universe", perhaps it may be better to call it the Pre-Universe state before the 'Big Bang' had actually occurred.

> Scientists would find it rather incomprehensible to accept or to fathom what does this really mean; from 'nothingness' into somethingness.

Well it is quite obvious that to many, generally speaking, the biblical creation concept, from 'nothingness' is an impossibility. However, for GOD 'nothingness' is no barrier or concern whatsoever. This in itself is just another demarcation to highlight why GOD is GOD and man is man. And it is quite obvious that the inspired Scripture writer of this particular Scripture in GEN 1:1, had not the slightest clue or inkling of it either (i.e. the manner in which the Universe had come into existence) but to express it as such, as was inspired by GOD i.e. to be from 'nothingness' or to be more exact to possibly imply as being as such.

> This once again exhibits an inspired Biblical writer having no prior knowledge of the subject, not even the slightest inkling, as in this case, about **'The Creation'**. It is quite obvious to all of us that the writer was not present at the time of 'The Creation'. Yet can be credited for that 'stupendous revelation', which the writer was inspired to write and which comes to us in it' briefest of forms in summary too, as evident in GENESIS 1:1 through just **ten scriptural words.** All of these in the very first opening verse of the Holy Bible and through others for the sequence of the creation events for the P & D (Preparation & Development) of the Planet Earth, as in the rest of the Genesis Chapters One and Two.

These stupendous revelations were so extremely brief in the description that it further cements my very proposition that the inspired writers had no prior knowledge of it but to have merely written it as it was divinely inspired of them to write as such. This is the underpinning meaning of being an inspired biblical writer.

> I do not think that there would be any dispute even from our scientific scholarship circles that for anyone to have been able to write **several thousands of years ago** about such a complicated and enormous event of the coming into existence of the very Universe and all that was and is in it, especially of the Earth, though in such brief summary and with such great amazing accuracy, was definitely indeed not of their own knowledge per se.

Their inspired revelations even about the sequence of the creation, first the matter and then the light, and the sequence of all that was brought into becoming alive on Planet Earth has indeed not been overturned as yet by all the present available ongoing scientific scholarship.

> This in itself from my perspective for what it is worth further testifies and makes these revelations just simply beyond us mere mortals at that time in our ancient science history and should provide some means for the totally scientific based mind and the atheist to crack a little and to hopefully come around to accepting that there is **GOD** after all which would further the possibility for **GOD** to reveal his majesty to them in an individual and personal way.

However, for us who do believe the fact of the matter is that it is the biblical version of 'The Creation', as described in the Biblical Book of Genesis and supported by other Biblical Books too in the library of books that make up the Holy Bible. It had all started with GOD ALMIGHTY. It was GOD' very own plan to have a Universe to exist and so it was brought into it' existence from 'nothingness' – REV 4:11 also refers.

All the 'matter' came into it' existence as GOD ALMIGHTY had willed it at the very beginning. What we have today is the awesome unending evidence all around us that cannot deny this biblical established truth that GOD Almighty had created the entire Universe and everything in it from 'nothingness'.

There are many learned, successful and famous scientists out there who have given their expert analysis and well supported theories and documentation of how all this matter that was generated by the 'Big Bang' theory and subsequently through the Inflation theory, had all come together to eventually form the Stars and the Planets and the Galaxies, etc. Yet they had never told us in the very first place **from**:

"WHERE DID ALL OF THIS MATTER COME FROM EVEN IN THE ATOMIC STATE OF IT' EXISTENCE, PRIOR TO THE BIG BANG ITSELF WHEN THE UNIVERSE WAS IN IT' PRE-STATE, LET ALONE, ALL THE 'LIFE' THAT ALSO EXISTS HERE ON PLANET EARTH".

> Okay, they had the theory of evolution for the many forms of life that had existed and for those that still do exist today, but what about 'matter' that had existed in the Pre-Universe before the 'Big Bang' as proposed by eminent Scientific Scholarship had even occurred?

This could be something for those who may become interested in this, to put some effort into, to explore and if possible to discover.

> To think of it, this had to be so, that what was created from **'nothingness'**, the very atom and all of it' structures and **energy** within itself, as a proposition, had also been divinely instructed or programmed into it by our **ALMIGHTY GOD,** a specific and unique **'behaviour'**

> This to my very understanding for my proposition here, was and is a type of 'desire', for lack of a better word to use here, to ensure the combining into the **required matter and the required molecules,** in the manner that the Universe could be brought into it' very existence element by element. This is from the very sub-atomic particles or nano structures generated from 'nothingness' to congregate into specific atoms and then these combining into elements, molecules and the matter that had eventually 'evolved' the Universe according to the **MASTER ARCHITECH'** plan i.e. GOD' PLAN.

> To me, being a total believer and ardent student of the written word of GOD ALMIGHTY and as such a total believer in CHRIST JESUS being GOD the SON; together with GOD the FATHER; and GOD the HOLY SPIRIT being the **THREE** in – The Holy Trinity; the existence of the Universe and/or the Pre-Universe was never left to chance. This is just as the 'life' that we have all around us was also not by chance association of some vital amino acids coming together at the appropriate time to be suddenly sparked into being from a **'dead'** chemical composition soup to becoming **ALIVE**. This was and is and will still be an awesome and spectacular transition; impossible by itself but because GOD had unanimously decided to be having us had taken place accordingly for GOD' greater glory. AMEN.

> This is the reason why exactly two parts of Hydrogen consistently combines with exactly one part Oxygen to form the molecule H_2O i.e. water; being paramount for the existence of 'life' that we have all around us.

This is the reason why the amazing and complex yet natural processes of photosynthesis which requires carbon dioxide, water and sunlight is possible.

In brief, regarding the process of photosynthesis, some organisms such as blue-green algae and especially all plants which uses the chlorophyll being mainly located in the chloroplasts of their leaves, to absorb **Solar Energy** from the Sunlight and together with the Carbon Dioxide and water is then used to convert these into sugar and other organic compounds such as lipids and proteins. These are then used by the plants to live and thereby to grow. This is essentially the process of photosynthesis.

Plants in turn become food for the wide diversity of animal life on land and in the sea and through the food chain, some plants and some animals on land and in the sea, eventually do become food for us Human Beings too.

> This is the reason why the '**GOD Created ECO-Balance**' also being applicable in the composition of the constituents in the atmosphere is as such that 'life' can continue to exist and thrive so well. Yet so unfortunately, is being destroyed on a daily basis, in a global way, due to our polluting of the atmosphere, which in turn destroys more and more of the Ozone Layer, which in turn threatens to unbalance this very GOD created eco-balance for 'life' to harmoniously and to progressively continue to co-exist.

This is the reason why the Sun is positioned exactly **93,000,000 miles away** from the Earth and is **'sized'** accordingly, so that it can generate the required amount of Solar Energy to ensure that 'life' and the ecology could exist without being annihilated if it was any closer or any further or any bigger in it' energy generation.

> Yet amazingly, all of this immense and unfathomable humongous structure of matter was and still is existing as fragile as probably egg shells, if I could use the metaphor, for it is being held together by **'Just SIX NUMBERS'!!!** The same that Sir Martin Rees was reiterating and informing us all about in his book of the same name.

So all of this could not possibly be existing exactly and precisely as it is currently due to 'Cause and Effect' principles which is indeed only earthly bound but that it does exists as such and operates as such due to our GOD ALMIGHTY being its Supreme and Divine ARCHITECH. AMEN

There is definitely indeed a mathematical pattern to all of this. Though it being very complex indeed for most of us to comprehend, yet from my understanding of the 'Biblical Creation', as revealed to us in the Holy Bible, this as a suggestion could have come about, due to this additional invisible dimension of the structured 'behaviour' having been inculcated by **GOD** directly into this very 'nothingness'. This was accomplished from the very beginning of it' 'conception' to the 'Big Bang', which had occurred at the GOD appointed time, which ultimately produced for us the Universe that we are having today.

> **This 'behaviour' as just mentioned, must have been 'genetically' ingrained into all of this created matter, even while it was in it' 'nothingness' state.**

In other words the 'nothingness generated matter' had to congregate into becoming the exact matter, which would eventually become the Pre-Universe and then after the 'Big Bang-Inflation', produce for us the Universe that we now have so evidently, as exhibited in the heavens all around us.

> This undeniably exhibits to me that the atoms or even before this, the very first energy structures, which would eventually come together to become the very atoms of the elements that we have now and then which progressed on to be joined together in varying and divers combinations to become the very first slivers of matter, were able to continue 'congregating' as such, solely because it was under the divine instructions ingrained into it' 'behaviour'.

These became eventually the various elements that were duly needed, so that this entire Universe could come into it' existence, structure by structure; atom by atom; element by element; matter by matter; and phase by phase the way it was and is and will be in the future with all the life in it too.

> It should be very clear to us by now that GOD did not create the Universe in a flash, but that it did take aeons and aeons to finally begin to materialise into the Universe that we do see now post 'Big Bang-Inflation' and even before time came into existence pre the 'Big Bang'.

Science had got it right, if I could dare say this from my point of view of being a Christian. It is this **'required time'** as scientifically established instead of the more popular Christian acceptable version of 'in a flash that the Universe was indeed created', that had actually prompted me or had driven me to understand the following. That the generated matter itself could not have become the Universe just by being left alone by itself to 'chance associate', but there must have been also this **divine 'instruction'** having been ingrained into it' 'behaviour', and in multiplicity or rather in it' combining 'desire', that had made all of this ever possible. Amen.

Therefore, through my viewpoint, it was definitely not by just 'chance association' or by any form of attraction, physical, chemical, nuclear or by any other means like gravity, electromagnetism, strong force, weak force, and etc., although all of these had helped too in the Universe creation process. However, I do propose that it was and is and will be, as according to my understanding of the Holy Scriptures, through this 'unseen' but GOD involvement in having programmed such 'instructions' into the 'behaviour' even at sub-sub-atomic levels and nano structures. These were then as per this proposal carried forward into the matter that eventually had brought the entire Universe from ex-nihilo into it' very pre-state existence and then gradually through the 'Big Bang' and the possible Inflation, the Universe that we have today.

If this was not the case then the destiny of the Universe itself would have been left entirely to chance and 'chance association', although, somewhat deliberate in coming about successfully, merely through the existing cosmic forces in operation, just as what our scientists have been saying about the beginnings of 'life' itself.

> Thereby, they and the likeminded, having accepted this, GOD had and has nothing to do with the Universe and so our belief of a GOD created Universe would become just a figment of our imaginations, inner yearnings and a way for us to explain away the 'mysteries' of the Universe existing and our own existence here on Planet Earth. This is what very much, is their stand on this matter. Whether it is shouted out aloud, or just quietly being implied that it is so.

Yet, there is an alternative and better solution to the one as offered partly by science and partly by our beliefs. That is, by combining both of these offerings into this 'solution'. That there is indeed a GOD-inbuilt ingrained 'DNA' or coded 'instruction programme' in the matter and in it' elements even drilling right down to it' atomic, sub-atomic particles, strings, structures, energy, etc., to bring the entire Universe step by step into it' very existence, as we have it in our midst. You could probably call this as being the 'evolving of the matter' from nothingness to eventually becoming the very stars, planets, galaxies etc., that it was intended to be by GOD ALMIGHTY to become, before we could even have the so called 'evolution of life' as we have it now.

A good example for this suggested inbuilt 'instructions' as programmed into the basic building blocks of all matter, which I am trying to offer explanation to you in order to help you to understand, "How it is possible for the 'matter' to behave as such as 'instructed' to, is akin to the particular **instincts** of multiplying and surviving as ingrained into all living things, plant and animals; birds; fish; reptiles, insects, MAN, etc., as I take the Monarch butterfly as a case in point." This example may be very fragile in it' appearance but nevertheless it would offer you a way to understand all that I am proposing to you as above; well I hope so anyway.

When the Monarch butterfly emerges from it' cocoon as reported scientifically somewhere in the south of Mexico and had matured into a graceful and beautiful butterfly; it **instinctively** begins it' own migration to the specific migratory destination from where it' parents (The Super Monarch strain) had come from **several thousands of kilometres** away in far off Canada!!!

Scientific scholarship informs us that the flight distance is about **3,000km one way.** However, this distance is not possible by the latest to emerge Monarch from the south of Mexico. These new butterflies would only be able to travel for about 3 weeks to the very first migratory stop. This period of travel time would enable the Monarch to cover the first **800km** distance from the time it left it' location in South Mexico. This in itself is a mighty feat to say the least. From here **another generation** of Monarchs will take up the challenge and continue for another greater distance to the final migratory 'rest-stop' where yet a **third generation** will then emerge to complete the journey somewhere into North Canada. It is here where for some reason we regularly have the **Super Monarch** strain to eventually emerge once again and does this unimaginable flight distance of **3000km** back to South Mexico. This would make it the **fourth** generation to finally complete this epic cycle journey, which if I am not mistaken, takes about five months to complete through the generations in a round trip as scientifically reported. You could probably check this out for yourselves in the INTERNET.

Just imagine that these delicate wings, which can so easily be crushed between just two fingers of a child, are yet able to accomplish such a gigantic feat physically and through it' mental capacity of such 'simplicity' relatively speaking to us humans, is just simply awe struck amazing.

Despite this enormous difficulty, which you can surely appreciate, the Super Monarch butterfly yet is able to for the very **first time**, navigate to the exact and precise location **3000km** away, is just simply awe struck amazing. We are even informed further by Scientific Scholarship, at times, to the very tree or plant that their great grandparents were even from about five months ago themselves!!!

No scientific study at the moment, if I stand correct, have been able to decipher exactly how this **instinct** or rather ingrained 'behaviour' to migrate back to where their great grandparents had first come from.

Take note that the young Super Strain Monarch butterfly emerging from North Canada had not the luxury of ever being led to South Mexico ever before. For this would be it' very first and sadly though it' only attempt. Adult Monarch guidance was absolutely not possible too, as all the adult female parent Monarchs had perished after laying their eggs and the male parent had finished it' life cycle some time before at the fertilization site. Mission accomplished. It was all now left to the next Super Strain Monarch generation to emerge and to take back their hopes and genes to the very distant destination from whence their great grandparents themselves had come from.

It also inevitably describes to us within this one fragile but incredible example of the 'Monarch Accomplishment' amongst the thousands and thousands of examples more out there, what an **AWESOME GOD** that we have been given such privilege to worship and to come know to some depth through THEIR WORD - the Holy Bible and THEIR creation. That is the Universe and all the life in it. Thank you, LORD GOD Almighty. Amen

This would be an excellent example to illustrate what I had meant when I had introduced the concept of having GOD inbuilt and ingrained into the atoms and subsequently into the matter it combines into and the specific quantity or size/volume that it would build itself to, that it would become someday the **grand Universe** that our LORD GOD ALIMGHTY had vision it to be as we have it now; all from nothingness.

This could not have taken place just because there was matter floating around everywhere in many spiralling gaseous clouds after the 'Big Bang-Inflation' had occurred despite the contributing effects of gravity and other cosmic forces. It had to be 'instructed' or designed to do so, to come together, as it had done even within it' atomic structure to become the Universe from first being in it' Pre-Universe state just as LORD GOD ALMIGHTY had planned it so to be.

If not two parts of Hydrogen would not have readily sought out to combine with just one part Oxygen and consistently at that in multiplicity to create the life sustaining **WATER** in the quantity and quality as 'The Creator' had required it so to be.

> When it was combining as such into the **WATER** molecule; the two parts of Hydrogen and the one part Oxygen had no idea of the future product that it' specific combining ratio as such, would be bringing about, and more so **why** it was doing so, now did it?

In other words, it could have just remained as such, i.e. as the elements - Hydrogen and Oxygen. I am not philosophising here or fantasising, but genuinely attempting to make an appropriate connection for this phenomenon to be taking place to our GOD ALMIGHTY being involved in it as the Supreme Master Chemist, Supreme Physicist; Supreme Biologist, etc., etc.

> Are you able to see the GOD connection in all of this through the **affinity** or the **'desire'** of the two different elements to be coming together as such as to address the specific **need** to combine as such in that specific ratio which would eventually become one of the pillar requirements to the sustaining of 'life' according to the MASTER SUPREME ARCHITECH; not everywhere but just on one single divinely selected and magnificently well prepared and developed 'Human Abode'; our PLANET EARTH.

> As such, in my understanding, all of this was indeed orchestrated by our God ALMIGHTY, which Science has been, still is and will continue doing somewhat paradoxically, in revealing to us these awesome GOD feats with such accuracy yet ashamedly without giving any due credit to the ALMIGHTY.

> **You could say that it is plagiarism of some sorts and nobody has yet been charged with the obvious crime!!!**

Of course in all of these very complex processes, the chemical, including that of photosynthesis; the nuclear; the physical;; the electromagnetism, the gravity (the strong force, the weak force); time itself and etc., all had also come together to enable this to become a huge success, as GOD had intended it to be. All of which was revealed to us through the most briefest of all summaries possible pertaining to an 'Universe size mindboggling GOD ALMIGHTY feat', which we get knowledge of it, as found in the Holy Scriptures and now through the Sciences.

Our eminent and learned Scientists, through their wonderful higher scholarship are discovering many aspects of how all of this had come about and their findings really amaze us too. However, I propose or if you do prefer of the opinion, that they will eventually come to an apex when and where they will not be able to probe any further and to discover any further, for that 'matter behaviour' and that 'GOD breathed life' being not physical in nature and thereby having not a process or processes to be deciphered and to be understood by any possible Science. For they must eventually conclude that it is of GOD, spiritual in nature as clearly expressed for **'life'** in GEN 2:7 and for the **'matter'** in GEN 1:1.

A simplistic and naive understanding you may think on my part and for those who may similarly share the same reasoning, but one which is very profound and deep if you would only give it a chance to....... breathe - Gen 2:7 and to desire – Gen 3:16b.

Nothing came into existence without the 'involvement' of the 'THREE PERSONS' in the Godhead being present for their momentous and gigantic event. We have John 1 – 10 reconfirming the Genesis accounts as were recorded in Genesis Chapters 1 and 2.

In most circumstances the scientific community has not fully addressed this 'Pre-Universe' or rather Pre-Big Bang state, but mostly having sidestepped it over the years as it is so scientifically glaringly evident. This they also do with the other creation miracle, i.e. our **'GOD breathed life',** which separates us from all of this type of 'dead' matter; for we are the **'living'** matter, although dust to dust we shall return without having any demarcation whatsoever with the other as far as the physical part of ourselves is concerned – GEN 3:19 confirms.

> Even this biblical revelation that our bodies would eventually return to dust is **SCIENTIFIC** in it' biblical presentation, long before any 'scientific mind' had understood it as such.

In the same light, an inexhaustible number of examples can be given to you to provide the facts, "Why GOD exists and thereby why we do too exist as such together with the rest of the Universe, yet if you still do not believe with that has already been provided you through all the available resources such as the Holy Bible Scriptures; through Christian writers; and Christian Evangelism, so help you GOD, we pray!!!

This continued unbelief as such could be taken to be similarly parallel to the biblical event as recorded in the Gospel of LUKE regarding the 'Rich Man and the Poor Man - beggar Lazarus'. Chapter 16: 19 – 31, refers. Our LORD and SAVIOUR JESUS CHRIST provided us with a parable rendered lesson in the Scriptures, that if we take quick heed of as we are still alive at this point in time, unlike the rich man who did not and found himself in torments in Hades – Luke 16:23 at the time of the parable lesson teaching, it would still not be too late for those who still do not believe. Please do come to your very senses and to become believers in the **GOD ALMIGHTY** who had created the very Universe and each of us including all the 'life' that was, is and will be in it. Do not be like the rich man whose name we do not even know!!!

Coming back to the task at hand: Take note that as the 12th Period in the Alphonso' 12th Phase Level comes to an end in the far distant future, it does not mean or even remotely suggest, that the expansion of the Universe would also come to an abrupt end. In fact through my very understanding of the relevant scriptures in 2ESDRAS and also in the Book of Revelation; it will continue as such. This is also stated at the very top of Chart–E, as the Revelation Scriptures substantiate it – Rev 21 & 22 refers and confirms.

Also, from the 2ESDRAS scriptures, we are informed or rather it can be deduced by employing my understanding, that a total of only **7 and a ½ parts** are finally left for the remaining future history of the World to be yet fulfilled. Dividing these 7.5 parts by 5 will produce for us the 1½ WHT-WFT Periods that are still remaining**.** These are the **1½ Periods** remaining of our Ezra' World History-Future Time. This can be derived only if you are able to understand and discern what the Holy Scriptures as in the 2ESDRAS 14:11-12 were actually depicting to us in a somewhat encrypted manner to resolve and to understand.

All of this then obtains for us our *Thirteenth Milestone* Achievement.

Progressive Expansion of the Universe According to the Alphonso' 12 Phase Levels and the Time Scale Ratio of 9.25 Times the Previous Phase Level, as Derived From the Understanding of the 2ESDRAS Scriptures - CHART A3

Pre-Universe in Pre-Expansion state
'Zero-Time/'Zero'-Size' (All the energy and all matter of the Universe already existing in here).

First Phase — First representation of the Universe after the 'Big Bang' and Inflation had occurred. Universe 'Age-Size' is now recorded as being 0.9420336 Years at the end of this Phase.

Second Phase — Universe continues to expand in 'Age-Size': 8.71381128 Years

Third Phase — Third Phase Age Size: 80.6027575458

Universe expansion is accelerating, despite some slowing down periods too.

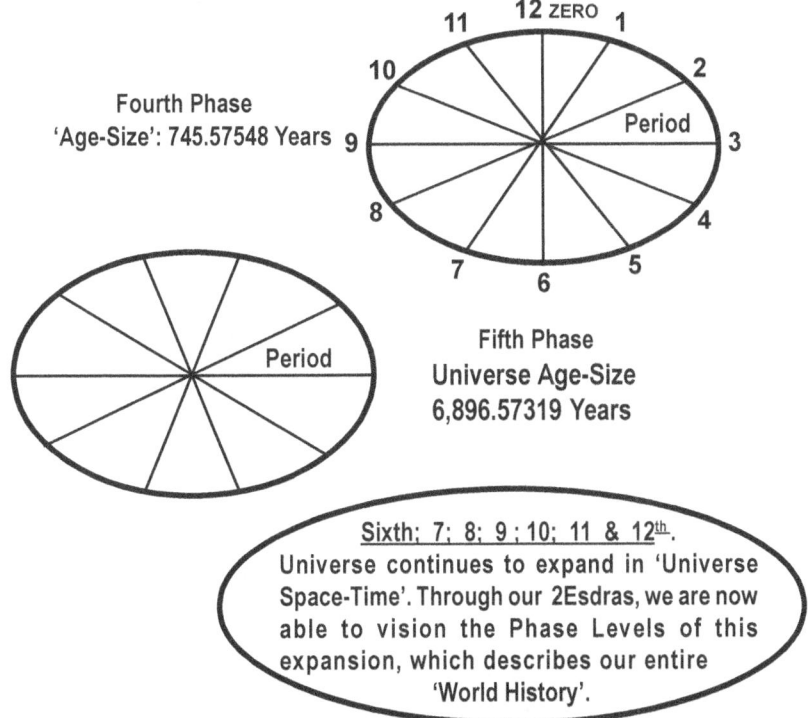

Fourth Phase 'Age-Size': 745.57548 Years

Fifth Phase Universe Age-Size 6,896.57319 Years

Sixth; 7; 8; 9; 10; 11 & 12th. Universe continues to expand in 'Universe Space-Time'. Through our 2Esdras, we are now able to vision the Phase Levels of this expansion, which describes our entire 'World History'.

Universe 'Age-Size' at the beginning of the 12th Phase Level was 4.32 Billion Years. At the end of the 12th AUET Phase Level, it will be 39.96 Billion Years

CHART- E Designed as per the 12 AUET PHASE LEVELS

However, the Universe Progresses On: 13th Level, 14th, 15th.....into Universe Space. This is supported by the 'New Heaven & New Earth Begins' - Rev 21 & 22 refers.

AGE - SIZE OF THE UNIVERSE

Elliptical Sweep in 12 AUET MINUTES Of Universe Space Expansion Time : 666,000,000 Years/6 Degrees,	End of 12th Phase Level: 39.96 Billion Years
72,000,000 Years/6 Degrees/12 AUET MINUTES	11th Level Ends: 4.32 Billion Years
7,783,783.783 Years/6 Degrees/12 AUET MINUTES	10th Level Ends: 467,027,026.98 Years
841,490.1387 Years/6 Degrees/12 AUET MINUTES	9th Level Ends: 50,489,408.322 Years
90,971.90688 Years/6 Degrees/12 AUET MINUTES	8th Level Ends: 5,458,314.4128 Years
9,834.800743 Years/6 Degrees/12 AUET MINUTES	7th Level Ends: 590,088.04458 Years
1,063.221701 Years/6 Degrees/12 AUET MINUTES	6th Level Ends: 63,793.30206 Years
114.9428865 Years/6 Degrees/12 AUET MINUTES	5th Level Ends: 6,896.57319 Years
12.426258 Years/6 Degrees/12 AUET MINUTES	4th Level Ends: 745.57548 Years
1.343379243 Years/6 Degrees/12 AUET MINUTES	3rd Level Ends: 80.60275458 Years
0.145230188 Years/6 Degrees/12 AUET MINUTES	2nd Level Ends: 8.71381128 Years
0.01570056 Years/6 Degrees/12 AUET MINUTES	1st Phase Level Ends: 0.9420336 Years

World History Time in progress, ever since the 'Big Bang-Inflation' had occurred.

9.25 TIMES SCALE RATIO EXPONENTIALLY APPLIED VERTICALLY TO BOTH SIDES WHEN MOVING UP TO THE NEXT LEVEL.

BEFORE TRIGGER (Big Bang-Inflation), ZERO UNIVERSE EXPANSION

Since the Big Bang was reportedly the possible trigger for our Universe Expansion, thereby, as it occurred the 'Pre- Universe Period' was immediately brought to a definite close.

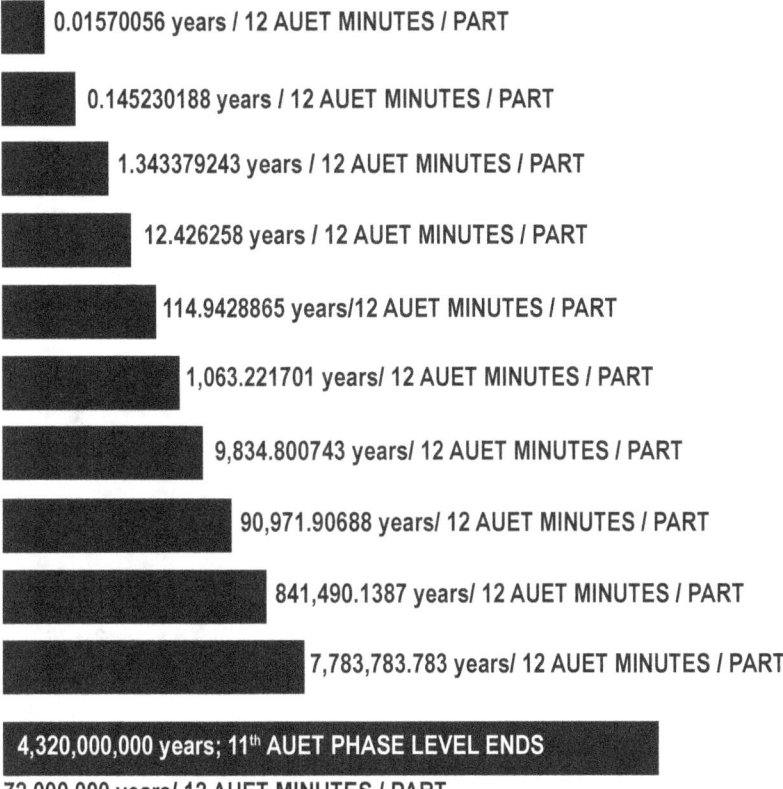

0.01570056 years / 12 AUET MINUTES / PART

0.145230188 years / 12 AUET MINUTES / PART

1.343379243 years / 12 AUET MINUTES / PART

12.426258 years / 12 AUET MINUTES / PART

114.9428865 years/12 AUET MINUTES / PART

1,063.221701 years/ 12 AUET MINUTES / PART

9,834.800743 years/ 12 AUET MINUTES / PART

90,971.90688 years/ 12 AUET MINUTES / PART

841,490.1387 years/ 12 AUET MINUTES / PART

7,783,783.783 years/ 12 AUET MINUTES / PART

4,320,000,000 years; 11th AUET PHASE LEVEL ENDS

72,000,000 years/ 12 AUET MINUTES / PART

12th Phase Level of Universe Expansion Progress Begins Now

666,000,000years/12 AUET MINUTES/PART

4,320,000,000 years begins the 12th AUET PHASE LEVEL

39.96 Billion Years Ends it

The coloured shaded boxes together with the Chart E, represents the Universe that is expanding in each of the Alphonso' 12 Phase Levels accordingly.

In the First Phase Level, the Universe Expanding Time (UET) of 12 AUET MINUTES/PART represents a time value of **0.01570056 years.** This is the 'Age-Size' of the Universe expansion ever since the 'Big Bang-Inflation' had occurred at the very beginning of this Phase Level, which began for us at the 'Zero Time Base Point'.

By the time it had completed in total the 60 Parts of Universe expansion in this First Phase Level, the Universe had expanded into an Age-Size of **0.9420336 years**.

'THE SCRIPTURAL COSMIC 666'
The Cosmic Based Construction, Leading to the 'Number' of 'The Beast'

BOOK TWO - PART THREE
Page 300

Now you can multiply this First Phase Level' complete Universe expansion being represented through it' age-size 0.9420336 years by the time scale factor or ratio, **9.25 times**, and you will get the next Phase Level' completed age-size Universe expansion. As in this case it will be the age-size, 8.71381128 years. This in fact can be repeated all the way up to the 12th Phase Level as similarly.

In the Second Phase Level, the UET of 12 AUET MINUTES takes **0.145230188 years** to expire.

By the time it had completed in total the 60 Parts of Universe expansion in this Phase Level, the Universe had expanded into an age-size of **8.71381128 years**.

In the Third Phase Level, the UET of 12 AUET MINUTES takes **1.343379243 years** to expire.

By the time it had completed in total the 60 Parts of Universe expansion in this Phase Level, the Universe had expanded into an age-size of **80.60275458 years**.

In the Fourth Phase Level, the UET of 12 AUET MINUTES takes **12.426258 years** to expire.

By the time it had completed in total the 60 Parts of Universe expansion in this Phase Level, the Universe had expanded into an age-size of **745.57548 years**.

In the Fifth Phase Level, the UET of 12 AUET MINUTES takes **114.9428865 years** to expire.

By the time it had completed in total the 60 Parts of Universe expansion in this Phase Level, the Universe had expanded into an age-size of **6,896.57319 years**.

In the Sixth Phase Level, the UET of 12 AUET MINUTES takes **1,063.221701 years** to expire.

By the time it had completed in total the 60 Parts of Universe expansion in this Phase Level, the Universe had expanded into an age-size of **63,793.30206 years**.

In the Seventh Phase Level, the UET of 12 AUET MINUTES takes **9,834.800743 years** to expire.

By the time it had completed in total the 60 Parts of Universe expansion in this Phase Level, the Universe had expanded into an age-size of **590,088.04458 years**.

In the Eight Phase Level, the UET of 12 AUET MINUTES takes **90,971.90688 years** to expire.

By the time it had completed in total the 60 Parts of Universe expansion in this Phase Level, the Universe had expanded into an age-size of **5,458,314.4128 years**.

In the Ninth Phase Level, the UET of 12 AUET MINUTES takes **841,490.1387 years** to expire.

By the time it had completed in total the 60 Parts of Universe expansion in this Phase Level, the Universe had expanded into an age-size of **50,489,408.322 years**.

In the Tenth Phase Level, the UET of 12 AUET MINUTES takes **7,783,783.783 years** to expire.

By the time it had completed in total the 60 Parts of Universe expansion in this Phase Level, the Universe had expanded into an age-size of **467,027,026.98** years.

In the Eleventh Phase Level, the UET of 12 AUET Minutes takes **72,000,000 years** to expire. By the time it had completed in total the 60 Parts of Universe expansion in this Phase Level, the Universe had expanded into an age-size of **4,320,000,000 years**.

In the Final Twelfth Phase Level, the UET of 12 AUET MINUTES takes **666,000,000 years** to expire. By the time the total 60 Parts of universe expansion in this current 12th Phase Level which had begun in the 4,320,000,000[th] year since the 'Big Bang-Inflation' had occurred to be finally fulfilled in it' entirety; the Universe would have had expanded into an age-size of **39,960,000,000 years**.

Now as already explained previously that the Universe in reality is actually expanding through one continuous Phase Level of expansion unlike what has been described to you as above; you now need to understand, if we are only taking into consideration just one continuous Phase Level of Universe expansion, then the Universe is expanding at a rate of **666,000,000** years every 12 AUET MINUTES ever since the 'Big Bang-Inflation' had occurred.

So, the Universe accelerating expansion into the GOD measured Universe Space-Time Frame, is indeed expanding at a rate of **666,000,000 years** every **12 AUET MINUTES**.

In other words, every 12 AUET Minutes segment of time would currently be taking **666,000,000 years** to expire or to be fulfilled with the 2ESDRAS WHT-WFT. And as one segment of 12 AUET Minutes is actually ONE PART out of a total of 60 PARTS in the Phase Level, then the total time that it would take to fulfil the entire Phase Level or to fulfil the entire 2ESDRAS WHT-WFT would be:

39,960,000,000 years

Therefore, we should be able now with the proper understanding of the above, collapse all the previous Alphonso' 11 Phase Levels of Universe expansion and time mesh it into the current 12th Phase Level to create just **ONE** continuous Phase Level of Universe expansion, ever since the 'Big Bang-Inflation' had occurred as illustrated below. This also means we would need to substitute the 12 Periods of Ezra' WHT-WFT with the same 12 Periods of this one continuous Universe expansion 12th Phase Level. The 11 Phase Levels then become the **'hidden time structures'** though still **existing as a time record** which I had derived and had developed from my very understanding of the relevant 2ESDRAS Scriptures. This had made it possible for me to discover this constructed Cosmic Time Model for the possible expansion of the Universe according to the relevant scriptures in 2ESDRAS.

Zero Time	
'Big Bang-Inflation'	**39.96 Billion Years**
4,320,000,000 years had expired	12th AUET Phase Level of Universe expansion begins in the 4.32 Billionth Year

11 AUET Collapsed Phases

All of the above time periods can now be substituted by the Scriptural Ezra' 12 PERIODS of WHT-WFT as follows:

EZRA' 12 PERIODS OF WHT-WFT BEING FULFILLED AT THE SAME RATE OF THE UNIVERSE EXPANSION of 666,000,000 years every 12 AUET MINUTES

1½ Periods remaining

1	2	3	4	5	6	7	8	9	10	11	12

4.32 billion years begins the First WHT-WFT PERIOD

Seven and a Half PARTS of Ezra' WHT-WFT remaining,

½	1	2	3	4	5	6	7

less the 500,000 years that has already expired within the ½ PART

Further to my understanding and interpretation of these relevant scriptures in 2ESDRAS, coupled together with what I had already discovered with regards to the 360 day Years; the remaining 7 and a ½ Part of WHT-WFT left remaining, as shown in the coloured shaded boxes above, had in fact already begun from the time of the Referenced Base Position (RBP), which I had named earlier as being an Earth Axis Rotation Speed Switch Over (**EARSS**) base i.e. **RBP18:24:12 (A)**. Also, in this particular case, this EARSS base was also indeed when this present EAR' **18th Oscillation Cycle** had also begun, as described in detail in 'The Addendum'. This also means that accordingly much of the remaining WHT is indeed 'World Future Time' (WFT) for us.

In repetition: This as you remember, happened at the 'Referenced Base Position 18:24:12 (A), which had a 24hrs 12mins EAR Period. This particular axial Earth Axis Rotation Speed Switchover (EARSS) base that we are concerned with here, took place in this '18th EAR Oscillation Cycle' from it being faster to becoming slower, following the science backed 'rate of EAR speed change' i.e. **1/1000th second every 100 years**.

You will understand this better, as you refer to the **Chart-B1,** a few pages down. You will also begin to realize, as you continue reading, the reasons for these 7 and a ½ Part of WHT-WFT that are remaining, being acknowledged as also beginning from this very important RBP18:24:12 (A).

> **This means, if we are now able to find out, "What does these 7 and a ½ PART of Ezra' WHT equal to in terms of Earth Time, then we will be able to establish the full extent of it spanning across the entire 12 PERIODS of Ezra' WHT-WFT being backed by the Alphonso' 12 Phase Levels.**

Although, I had already revealed the total WHT-WFT in terms of Earth Time, as being 39.96 Billion Years, you may have realized, I have not exactly calculated it out or rather offered any development proof for it as yet.

However, as just mentioned above, once we are able to establish what the 7½ Parts of Ezra' WHT-WFT equal in terms of ET, we would be then able to by simple progression establish the entire Earth Time for the 60 PARTS of Ezra' WHT.

Through the understanding of these Scriptures, we will be then able to establish the true **Biblical Age of the Universe.** Scientists have however been trying for centuries to determine by secular methods, even as presently, the current age of the Universe. It is not my personal intention to be in any conflict with Science, for I am only following the Biblical path (with my understanding) as expressed in this book to determine it. This is as a spin off from my present quests.

We need to recap here that the WHT Clock is structured per Period of WHT into 5 groups or rather 5 parts allocated with 12 AUET/WHT Minutes each per part. Therefore, 12 Periods have in total 60 AUET parts and each equating to 12 AUET/WHT Minutes. Whereas, our Earth Time Clocks are basically structured the other way round. That is they are grouped into 12 groups of 5 minutes Earth time each. However, both are reading the time similarly, although, a Minute in WHT is not a static period of 'time measure' for it is always increasing in time value according to the rate of expansion of the Universe as already shown a few pages ago. You also must realise that a Minute of WHT is indeed a very large amount of time spread across thousands if not millions of years at the more advanced end of our Universe expansion. Whilst a minute according to our Earth Time Clocks on Earth is exactly that, a minute of time only and has been as such ever since the Sun, Earth and Moon became operatives as a time keeping system for us.

However, despite these very large differences in time reading, we could still create a definite and direct relationship between both of these times. It then follows according to a proper time scale we can bridge these two time zones i.e. the ET and the AUET, so that we can convert our ET into AUET and vice-versa. The purposes for doing this are quite significant, as you will find out soon enough.

These **12 WHT AUET MINUTES**, which are equally equated to each and every Part of the 60 Parts of Ezra' WHT-WFT, which are driven by the Alphonso' 12th Phase Level of Universe expansion is the allocated time sweep, I was mentioning much earlier. Please take important note of this and more details of it will follow shortly.

We will continue after you have studied through the following Chart - B1.

THE EAR' 18th OSCILLATION CYCLE IN THE 12TH AUET PHASE LEVEL: CHART – B1

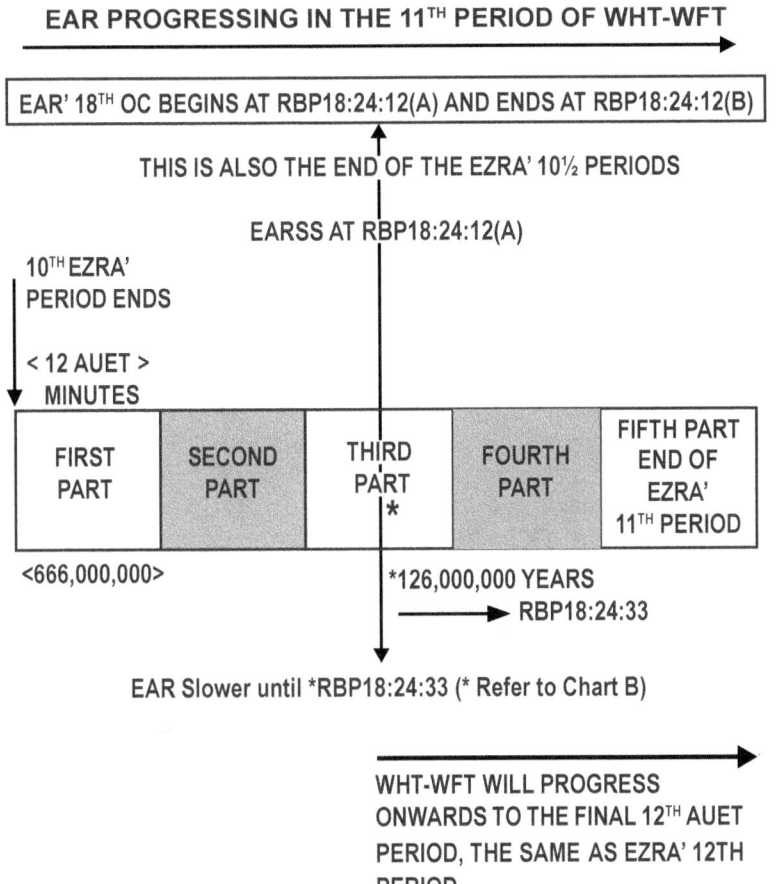

Some notes on the above Chart B1

Slower EAR from the RBP18:24:12(A), reducing at the rate of 1/1000th second every 100 years until reaching *RBP18:24:33 exactly *126,000,000 years later. This is the same time that it takes the EAR to reduce by 21 EAR minutes to reach *RBP18:24:33 which is the mid base of the 18th EAROC.

Faster EAR begins now once again from the *RBP18:24:33, increasing at the similar rate of 1/1000th second every 100 years as proposed by this OEARM until reaching the end of this 18th EAROC at RBP18:24:12(B), which takes another *126,000,000 years.

2½ Parts in this 11th Period + 5 more Parts left in the next and final 12th Ezra' Period i.e., 7½ Parts in total of WHT-WFT is still remaining, less about 500,000 years that have already expired since the 18th EAROC had begun at RBP18:24:12(A).

*RBP18:24:33 is the RBP when the Earth obtains the 24.55 Hours EAR PERIOD. As already mentioned, RBP18:24:12(A) is also the beginning of the EAR' 24.20 Hours EAR Period and the 18th EAROC. At *RBP18:24:33, we will have for the very first time in our Biblical Human History, the 360 Earth Days Orbital Years. It will happen as shown by the * which describes the 126,000,000th **year** from the beginning of the 18th EAROC. This is also the exact time period taken to add 21 EAR minutes to the EAR Period of 24.20 hours or rather 24 hours and 12 minutes to become 24 hours 33 minutes. From here the EAR speeds up again until reaching RBP18:24:12(B).

The 18th EAROC will finally end 252 million years later, at this RBP18:24:12(B). The 19th EAROC will then begin at this very same RBP but for it, this will become it' RBP19:24:12(A). It will then end 42 EAR minutes later likewise, just as all the other EAROCs before it and those that will come on-stream after it. This 19th EAROC will then end at RBP19:24:12(B), where once again the 20th EAROC will begin at RBP20:24:12(A).

I hope the above Chart-B1, makes it even more easier to visualize now, of what I have been trying to establish with regards to the further establishing of the 360 day years through the slowing down of the Earth' Axial Axis Rotation (EAR).

> **This is my 14th Milestone Achievement.**

To Recap:

The **7½ Parts remaining** equates to the remaining 1½ PERIODS in the Ezra' WHT-WFT in the Alphonso' 12th Phase Level. However, we need to less another 500,000 years from this remaining time which is left for us.

> So the time that we have left remaining, to my understanding and interpretation of the relevant Scriptures, would be also the **end of time for life on Earth** as we have it now.

However, I am not suggesting that I have just discovered when the 'End Times' would occur as prophesied in our Scriptures, but you will find out this 'time' that we have left remaining is directly connected to the 'time' left for our Sun to sustain life on Earth. So, if the 'End Times' had not come before this Sun ends it' life sustaining energy, then this would have to be it, for those who are possibly still 'living' somehow at that time.

I hope I have made this clear. In this respect, we are also very concerned with the ancient past, even that which was prior to our very existence, is also important to us, as it records the beginning of the creation of the Universe.

Also, GOD ALMIGHTY had designed 'Time' for us and by enabling us to read the signs and seasons, we have been able to record and track the passing of the days and the years gone by and those that are yet to come – Genesis 1:14 confirms.

Therefore, the remaining time in World History has to be pertaining to the remaining time left for the life supporting shining Sun. However, take note; this is **not the end** of the Universe.

Does this mean then, as a probable assumption, that we at some time in the future could move out or transfer human beings to another life sustaining Planet, if it at all exists, even outside our own Solar System??? Or perhaps even create our own means of survival on Earth without the need of the shining Sun. If we are able to do this someday, I still do not think based on Scripture and our belief in GOD ALMIGHTY and the Bible being the true Word of GOD, would make it possible for any to escape the **Judgment Day,** despite this human 'strategy' of survival being a probable possibility.

This Alphonso' 12th Phase Level of World (Universe) History-Future Time, can now be illustrated as such in consolidation on a typical 12 hour clock-face.

> **Therefore, following the time left for our World History-World Future Time; the clock hands must be set to read 10.30.**

However, we need to take note that in this case, the usual am and pm clock time references of the full day do not apply as it does not denote the time of a day but of the particular 'time' in our World History-World Future as to when these '7 and a 1/2 Parts' had begun.

Also, further to this fixing of the time as being 10.30, I have also equated it to the time when the Earth had an axis rotation period of **24.20 Hours** at the **RBP18:24:12(A),** which is the important RBP as it also, begins the **18th EAR Oscillation Cycle**. However, in repetition, we have in fact past this time a little bit in World History time terms already.

To be as accurate as I possibly could be in this circumstance; it should be about:

5.211936+ seconds

In normal Earth Time terms, these few WHT seconds (5.211936+) past the RBP18:24:12, which is similarly past the 10½ Periods in the Alphonso' 12th Phase Level, should be amounting to more than:

FIVE HUNDRED THOUSAND YEARS

On a more personal note: For each one of us, our own personal **'Judgment Day'** (i.e. our first death), could be very close at hand indeed. So it is important for us to be mindful of this always, so that we do not fall to temptation and sin, which leads us away from the presence of GOD, but to be always ready when our own time does come, whenever that may be.

Although, I have illustrated World History Time here somewhat similarly to our common clock, which is based on **Earth Time,** we must understand and take serious note, that the time scales are obviously very different. You will find out more about this in detail later, but to give you a brief hint right now, it is as follows:

> **One WHT MINUTE in the 2ESDRAS' World History Time Period is averaging towards the 55.5 million years span of time.**

During this Alphonso' 12th Phase Level, like all the other 11 Phase Levels before it, the Universe will continue expanding into a more larger area in the GOD allocated Universe Space-Time that is possible in this Period of time. The Universe in each Phase Level is recognised to be expanding according to the time scale factor or ratio of **9.25 times** in relation to the most immediate previous Phase Level. I will explain in greater detail, how I had obtained this specific time scale factor/ratio for our Universe Expansion constructed model, but again briefly for now, it is as follows:

> As shown on the previous page: 1 WHT MINUTE is currently equating to **55.5 million years** of Universe expansion.

Also, 1 EAR minute change in the axis rotational speed of the Earth will take **6 million years** to accomplish. This was indeed established based on the scientific provided speed change rate in the EAR for 1 second every 100,000 years. This then produces for us this important time scale ratio of **9.25 times** when comparing this time taken i.e. 6,000,000 ET years for 1 EAR ET minute speed change to the time of 1 WHT Minute which is currently equating to as being 55,000,000 ET years.

Then we can clearly see that:

The 6,000,000 EAR ET years x 9.25 times would equal to:

The 55,500,000 years that equates to 1 WHT Minute in the Universe expansion progress in the 12th AUET Phase Level.

9.25 EAR minutes speed change = **1 WHT AUET MINUTE in the 12th AUET Phase Level**

9.25 EAR minutes in ET terms = **1 AUET MINUTE in ET terms**
9.25 : 1

This time period comparison is in relation to our own Earth' Axis Rotational Oscillating Speed Changes as compared to the passing or fulfilling of Ezra' World History Time in the 12th Alphonso' Phase Level of Universe expansion.

Now here is something very important for you to understand so that we can have this time scale ratio to be established and understood better accordingly.

> This time scale ratio of 9.25 times, was as predetermined by GOD ALMIGHTY from the very beginning of the Universe Expansion Progress (UEP), even before the Solar System had come into it' existence as such. This is my very understanding and conclusion. And when it did come into existence and had become operative; it became synchronised into this time system in that particular ratio as it became an integral part of the Universe expansion accordingly.

> This is my *15th Milestone Achievement*, which was needed to be established to enable me to continue progressing in revealing the 'cosmic construction' of the **'number'** of the second beast to you.

Life as we know it now cannot continue on the Earth indefinitely as confirmed by scientific fact and Biblical Scripture as it is directly dictated by the life sustaining Solar System Sun. In this matter both Scripture and Science do equivocally concur. Then, if we do not have the Sun shining as we have it today, there will be little or probably even no life on Earth to possibly speak about in that future time. This is why I understood and proposed to you that the 7½ Parts remaining in our World History/World Future Time, in it' natural progression sense, cannot exceed the time left for our Sun to sustain human life on Earth. This then provides for the argument that as long as it is less this time left for the Sun, then it should satisfy the 7½ Parts remaining.

> However, on the other hand, taking all relevant issues into consideration such as the very **relevant Scriptures in 2ESDRAS** which equated the very 'end of time' with the 12th Period of Ezra' WHT-WFT that I had also similarly connected to my **Alphonso' 12th Period** in it' 12th Phase Level of Universe expansion, we can now come to only one basic and firm conclusion.

That is if you understand it correctly, then at best, these 7½ PARTS of World History time left, should be equated precisely to the remaining time left for our *Sun* and not to just any measure of time or to another event.

Also, you will learn as you progress through the remaining of this book, that the common time scale **9.25 times** also provides us with the additional support to the above reasoning.

> If you do recall from Book One, I did establish this time left for our Sun as being **4,995 million years**, as calculated from the RBP18:24:12(A), which is within the current scientific calculations for the time left for the Sun in it' life sustaining solar energy generation.

This was according to my previous **Eight Milestone Achievement,** which was achieved very much earlier. Please refer to the Appendix at the end of this book for the referenced page or you could go directly to page 124.

Then based with this understanding, we can now equate this **4,995 million years** to the **7½ Parts** remaining in world history/world future time as computed from the RBP18:24:12(A).

When this is further proven to you in the following pages, you will further understand the reasons why this has to be so and that there is no alternative route possible. Also, as mentioned, we need to commence this time period from the important RBP18:24:12(A). You will also understand this more clearly, as you study the equations below.

> **Therefore, 7½ PARTS of World History Time, is to be represented and equated precisely to 4,995 million years.**

With this having been established as such, then it has to follow that:

1 WHT-UET PART (equivalent to 12 AUET MINUTES progress) would equate to **666,000,000 years** in the Alphonso' 12th PHASE LEVEL expansion model of the Universe into the Universe Space-Time, as was measured by our **GOD ALMIGHTY**.

You will immediately see the infamous sum total of **666** in this time period of 666,000,000 years for the very first time in our context and interest, emerging now, if I had not mentioned it previously.

So, if we subdivide a Part of World History Time into a million equal subdivisions of time in years, you will be able to isolate for the very first time the mysterious sum total of the **'number'** of the beast, which is no other than the infamous **666** years.

> Remarkably, this sum total 666 has now become a basic unit of World History Time measurement. This is quite incredible, if you really think about it.

> On the clock-face, these 666 years, would be represented precisely by 0.00072 WHT-AUET SECONDS.

You can also further subdivide each unit or segment of 666 AUET years into further 666 sub-units; each representing just a year.

All of the above understanding has also made possible all of the following equations. This stage of the development in the **'cosmic construction'** of the **'number'** of the beast is very important and critical for our ongoing success towards revealing it.

The Equations are as follows:

1½ Periods of Ezra' WHT = 7.5 PARTS of WHT

7.5 PARTS of Ezra' WHT in the Alphonso' 12th PHASE LEVEL of Universe expansion would take 4,995 Million Years to be fulfilled.

> 4,995 million years is the time left for the Sun to keep on shining, as it is doing today. This has been calculated from the important RBP18:24:12(A).

Therefore, 1 PART OF A PERIOD in the Alphonso' 12th PHASE LEVEL, equates to 666,000,000 Years.

1 Division i.e. a millionth of a PART in the Alphonso' 12TH PHASE LEVEL = 666 years.

1 Division can be further segmented into 666 sub-divisions.

1 sub-division of a AUET Part = 1 Year

> We also should have already realized at this stage of this development, that we have indeed *two different 'Measurements of Time'* to contend with in this book.

Therefore, it needs very careful study to avoid grave mistakes, when referring one to the other.

> One 'Measurement of Time' which is the World History Time (WHT) is following the progressive expansion of the Universe into the GOD measured Universe Space-Time Frame or area which actually encapsulates the expanding Universe. So as to what was established previously; WHT is actually AUET in the 12th Phase Level of the Universe expansion.

Based on the previous Charts – A3 & E, you can see that each of the Alphonso' 12 Phase Levels was in fact unfolding like a spiral with 12 coils that were gradually enlarging with each Level upwards. This indicates that each coil of the spiral which was representing one Phase Level became bigger as the unfolding or uncoiling progressed, specifically to be indicating an expanding Universe. This uncoiling also increases in speed as we move up the conical expanding spiral. You can similarly establish as many cones that are required through all directions of the expanding Universe to be more specific. However, we must take note, that it is still just this UNIVERSE alone, which is expanding in all the various possible directions.

Based on this constructed expanding Universe model, the Alphonso' 12th Phase Level in its **ending** will complete the already pre-calculated **39.96 Billion Years of Universe expansion** from the time the scientifically reported 'Big Bang-Inflation' had occurred.

According to the Book of **Genesis**, Chapter 1:1 - In the beginning God created the heavens and the earth. This construction does not dispute this truth in anyway whatsoever, and therefore, is in total support of it. The author also personally believes 100% in this 'Word of GOD'. However, we must take careful note **not to be literally confused** by the time allocated for all of the Creation Accounts. This I have already changed for some of them to be understood as actually having been the **'Preparation & Development'** Accounts (P & D) of the Earth alone, ever since Gen 1:2 continued with the Creation Accounts. Most of the Creation Accounts since that 2nd verse were solely pertaining from my study of it, to the very explicit description for the transformation of the Earth to make it totally and ideally habitable for us from all aspects that were necessary to sustain our life here.

This understanding then also underpins that these P & D accounts were definitely not just six days long. To most of us, 'the Biblical Six Days', just means that; six Earth Days.

I am in full agreement with anyone who does believe that with GOD nothing is impossible. However, the scientific truth of the matter is that our **LORD GOD ALMIGHTY** did not do this in six days. In other words that was not GOD' intention in the very place to have done so, even though we have been eager or overzealous to express it as such!!! We must not always place our Christian values and understanding to be emotionally at tenterhooks with science at all times, but should consider all the provable evidences and should agree when these overwhelming scientific evidences are able to stand up to the critical analysis and the test of time, sometimes over hundreds of years. This does not mean that our Christianity will crumble but rather that Science is revealing more of the wonderful Creation of our LORD GOD ALMIGHTY for our better understanding and sheer amazement to it all.

Sure they also do make mistakes in their own zealousness to find the answers to all the 'mysteries' out there, but this is not intentionally. There are also times when they were absolutely right. A case in point is my referring to their correcting of the long time held notion that we were the very centre of the Universe, or at least the centre of the Solar System with the Sun and all the other Planets going around us. This wrong concept was also taken as being the scientific model of the day at that time just as similarly was the Church' stand on it, as it also had fitted well into the religious based understanding of it too.

This we now know is not the case, for the Sun is actually at the centre of our Solar System, which scientific scholarship itself had corrected. The Church however took a very long time to concur and to think of it with some good reasoning to do so too; slowly.

Due to our own understandable Christian motivation to uphold that with 'GOD all things are possible', have many a time in the past and even as presently, resulted in unfortunately having our Holy Bible to be label by many as a mere fantasy, fabrication and a work of fiction. Some of our critics have given us the concession that at best it is just a 'History Book of Sorts', and worse still by some others, as a corrupted text of the original authentic version, which as they say, "Had been lost to mankind a long time ago."

Anyway, many of us when it comes to regarding the time duration of an 'Earth Day' as compared with that of a 'Creation Day'; we do consider it to be similar for obvious reasons, including the fact, that in the first place we see no difference at all between these two.

> Our Earth Day, in my humble opinion and study of relevant scriptures as indicated below, is obviously a very much infinitesimally smaller amount of time, in comparison to a single Day of GOD' creation activity. These 'Creation Days' in my humble opinion once again, could have also varied in its time duration from one Creation Day to another and quite significantly at that too.

If you are able to keep an open mind, you may be able to see this specific difference, as you study these two portions of Scripture carefully: Gen 1:3-5 and Gen 1:14-18 refers.

The 'Light' which GOD had seen and which was described in the Holy Bible as singular in nature, (which GOD first saw) is not the same 'lights' that we are presently able to see as provided by our Sun and Stars and the Moonlight being the reflection of our own Sunlight. Who could say if this **first light** was indeed the background radiation that GOD could see being the possible radiation produced by the Big Bang or by some other cosmic occurrence and/or cosmic development?

For all of these 'secondary lights' which I would like to refer to these as such, became operative only in the 4th Day of Creation. This was long time after GOD had seen the first light.

These secondary lights are the stars in principle, and for us the Sun is our most important of them all. Together with the relevant planetary motions of the Earth, including that of it orbiting the Sun and the daily rotation on its own inclined axial axis, does provide us with our sense of 'daily and yearly time'. These motions and specific axial axis inclination amongst other factors also do in turn provide us with our various climate conditions and the seasons, being as important and necessary for all life too.

> These two sections of Scripture seem to me to be highlighting this very possible difference in these two types of 'lights'.

Also, our Lord' Day is very much different in the aspect of the 'time' and probably even the 'light' that it equates to from the 'time' and the 'light' that equates to our day.

This above could be somewhat the basis for the proper understanding of this scripture, in 2Peter 3:8, which is as follows:

> **But, beloved, do not forget this one thing, that with the Lord one day is as a thousand years, and a thousand years as one day.**

This seems to me to be a GOD expressed divine 'time ratio', as being expressed here.

No matter what you may think or conclude in the end with regard to all of these scriptures and my proposition as above, in order not to be dragged further into this very difficult and somewhat controversial discussion at this point in time, for this book is not the place or forum for this discussion; I will just proceed on with the task at hand which beckons me to continue.

Therefore, coming back:

This universe expanding constructed model which follows a specific expanding time scale ratio of **9.25 times**, expresses the possible overall creation progress and that also, only in the terms of it' **age**. And based on this from another perspective, it' possible '**size**' in the expansion of the Universe. This I have accomplished by using a combination of basic scientific data and through the employing of my very own scriptural based understanding with regards to this matter.

Therefore, the scriptural words 'In the beginning' as indicated in Genesis 1:1, had indeed taken place sometime long before the 'First Level of Universe Expansion' even had ever begun. This needs to be understood as such, because the Universe was already created by then. This directly means that the Universe was already in existence. This as I had stated previously was in the 'Pre-Universe' state, before the Big Bang had actually occurred. In other words, in a *'Pre-Big Bang'* state.

However, based on the above understanding, you can clearly see that I am actually equating **size** in direct relative terms to the **increasing age** of the Universe. Also, taking into account it' expansion too, as was described to you in Chart E and the subsequent supporting explanations given to you on the Chart itself.

In reiteration:

All of the above indicates that there was a **'Time'** which the Genesis Scripture 1:1 simply stated as being, **'In the beginning'**. This was the time when GOD had first created the Universe and therefore it had existed, or rather had to obviously exist even before the 'Trigger' that had initialized the very cosmic expansion of the Universe had even occurred. Somehow, this valuable point of understanding had been simply ignored that it had to exist before the 'Big Bang-Inflation' had occurred, which in turn unmistakably to me, actually points to a 'GOD created Universe' as the scriptures reveals accordingly.

> In repetition, God created the Universe, *ex-nihilo*. This Latin word means: from 'nothing' God created the Universe. This is Scriptural – Genesis 1:1 refers and is further confirmed by Hebrews 11:3.

The Chart–E, illustrates the 'Expanding Universe' into the **'GOD ALMIGHTYY MEASURED UNIVERSE SPACE-TIME FRAME'**, following the available or allocated **'Time Sweep'**, as accorded or deduced from my understanding of the 'WORLD HISTORY TIME' model. This was developed through the appropriate understanding and the application of the very important and extremely relevant Biblical Book, 2Esdras. I used the time scaling factor of **9.25 times**, to give us the possible expanded Universe' 2ESDRAS' scriptural model. This was depicted in this Chart-E according to **time** and not **distance**, which would have provided us, if we knew the speed of expansion, with an area/volume size of our Universe.

> Outside this '**GOD MEASURED Universe Space-TIME FRAME'**, there is still more **Space available**, mind you; but it does not belong to our expanding Universe. This understanding is also based on Scripture, since the Universe was measured and then put into it – Hebrews 11:3 refers and others like it too.

You will also notice that as the Alphonso' 11th Phase Level of Universe Expansion came to a close; the time period that had expired from the time of the 'Big Bang' was indeed only **4,320,000,000 years.** Quite a short time indeed when you compare it to the time spanned by the next single Alphonso' 12th Phase Level, i.e. 35.64 billion years, which is indeed the same 12 Periods of Ezras' WHT. This very important understanding was developed as you already know in repetition; solely through the Holy Scriptures, as based on the Biblical Apocryphal Book, 2ESDRAS.

> This exact time period of **4,320,000,000 years** is remarkably, if you do recall from the 'Bridging Section' of this book, being the similar period of time that **One Kalpa Period** as formulated through their astronomy in their 'Indian/Hindu Cosmological Time Cycles do represent or equates to.

In fact, these 4.32 billion years at the end of the 11th Phase Level or from another perspective, it was the beginning of the Alphonso' 12th Phase Level and therefore, was naturally the very first one (i.e. Kalpa Cycle), that our Universe had gone through quite obviously, since the 'Big Bang-Inflation' had occurred. There will be in total **9.25 Kalpa** time periods or similar cycles to the end of the Ezra' 12th Period of WHT-WFT.

Further to this, we also had come to know that another time period of a similar **4,320,000,000 years** does become the exact **'First Mean Motion'** of the Sun in a time period that is accorded to 12 Million Divine years, as propagated by the Indian/Hindu Cosmological Time Cycles.

This comes about when you convert these 12 million Divine years into becoming ordinary Earth years by multiplying these by a factor of 360. This naturally means as you have already been informed previously that One Divine Year equates to 360 ordinary Earth Years as per this Indian/Hindu Cosmological Time Cycles model.

Not only that, but you may also have noticed that the basic time unit (12 AUET Minutes) of this 11th Phase Level of Universe expansion, as shown in Chart-E i.e. **72,000,000 years** is indeed remarkably the equivalent or rather being exactly similar to the **'Second Mean Motion'** of the Sun, for that same converted divine time period. This is shown in my modified 'Sexagesimal Demonstration Chart'. Check the Appendix for the exact page to refer to it. This is again according to their Indian/Hindu 12,000,000 Divine Years, which was responsible for the clocking of these two time periods in the First & Second Mean Motions of the Sun accordingly. The First Mean Motion being the 4,320,000,000 years and the Second Mean Motion being the 72,000,000 years.

> In fact, the first mean motion is exactly 60 times the second mean motion just as we had used regularly 60 Parts to the next Phase Level of Universe expansion. You can refer to this First & Second Mean Motion of the Sun in the previous 'Bridging Section'.

These amazing and astounding similarities on many counts, cannot be just simply ignored as being just mere coincidental, now could it??? In other words there must be some basis, scientific and/or cosmic, being clearly supported by the proper understanding of the relevant scriptures, to be able to derive somewhat similarly these universal periods of time in the same cosmic events in these both time systems.

It seems to me that it may have been quite likely that the ancient Indian/Hindu astronomer/mathematician/scientist/sage, must have had somewhat similar knowledge of the Cosmos and this was their only way to describing it to the common man, and more importantly to their royalty without probably being killed for their **strange revelations** to the very 'superstition based society' of India at that ancient time. Anyway, most societies around the world were probably as superstitious too in those ancient times of human development and thinking.

So in my personal opinion to a point, I think that they came up with many fabricated stories of the divine and created their gods (such as Lord Brahma) and other deities accordingly around their astronomy.

Thereby, they were able to somewhat actually camouflage their astronomical discoveries, which some of these have come to us through their Indian/Hindu Cosmological Cycles.

Even the Christians had branded those who came up with ideas that were not supported by the Church of the day as being heretics and some considered even as witches and were subsequently burned at the stake for these specific reasons. We know too well what happened to Galileo Galilei, in relatively recent times, when he stated that it was the Earth that goes around the Sun together with the other planets and not that the Sun as held by the Church that goes around the Earth. For this they imprisoned him and kept him in isolation until he had died. They only spared his life due to his already advanced age at the time when he had published his findings.

I am using the CHARTS – A3 & E to simply illustrate the important **'TIME RELATIONSHIP'** between the time of the Earth' development towards it' 360 day years, to the continuing expanding Universe. This is with particular focus in the Alphonso' 12th Phase Level of Universe expansion, which I have now, substituted with the scriptural Ezra' 12 Periods of WHT-WFT. This then also incorporates our entire Solar System.

If and when these operatives of the triune system do change their 'fixed' relationship with one another; only then will the 'Earth Time' change accordingly.

The Book of Genesis in the Bible, Chapter 1:14-18 refers specifically to this 'fixed' relationship.

Since GOD purposefully designed this, it is quite unlikely this 'fixed' relationship would change until the 'End Times' or until when GOD decides to change it. This Earth Time as previously mentioned is also the time with which we are currently using for all time and speed/distance measurements, etc.

The remaining 7½ Parts of World History or rather to be more precise less the 500,000+ years, which as estimated has already been used up, is the remaining time left for our future.

Also, that it does establish the relationships as previously indicated is not by mere coincidences. This could then in turn provide in many ways the necessary support to my 'scriptural based cosmic' theories as described earlier.

Also, as previously mentioned, if we know the speed and acceleration with which the Universe is actually expanding, we (not I obviously but those who are able to) then would be able to calculate the present size of the Universe in this current Period; but unfortunately we yet do not.

However, as I have already established during the 14th Milestone achievement, that 12 WHT (AUET) Minutes allocated time sweep is to be equated to each Part of a Period of AUET; therefore these have to follow:

12 AUET MINUTES = 666,000,000 Years = 1 PART of an AUET PERIOD in the 12 Ezra Periods of WHT-WFT
6 AUET MINUTES = 333,000,000 years
1 AUET MINUTE = 55,500,000 years

'THE SCRIPTURAL COSMIC 666' BOOK TWO - PART THREE
The Cosmic Based Construction, Leading to the 'Number' of 'The Beast'

> **1 AUET SECOND represents 925,000 years of WHT**

> 1 Year of AUET/WHT which is a Sub-Division of the above AUET time period is represented by **0.000001081 seconds** on our timepiece.

If someone does decide to make a clock to read this Universe Expanding Time (UET), I envision it to be a really very gigantic clock. This is because in order for us to be able to read any time movement smaller than the 925,000 years; for it would take 925,000 years before we are able to register even one second movement, this will be way past our 'bedtime' and thousands more of our descendant generations (permanently).

Also, 1 Period of WHT-WFT accommodates 3,330,000,000 years of Universe expansion i.e. 3.33 Billion Years of AUET. Therefore, the Ezra' 12 Periods of AUET/WHT-WFT will be accommodating 39,960,000,000 years in total. That is 39.96 Billion Years being the final age of the expanded Universe at the end of the 2ESDRAS' WHT-WFT, which still has allocated time remaining to be fulfilled in our future.

> Our scientists currently provide for the present age of the Planet EARTH to being about 4.5 billion years. This too is acceptable for my scripture derived constructed Universe expanding time model.

To be a little more specific and in line with this Universe expanding constructed time model, the Solar System became operative only in the 29.97 Billionth Year, when the Sun began to shine 'life-supporting sunshine' upon the Earth for the very first time.

This value was obtained by simply taking away 9.99 billion Years. This was calculated as being the full life of our Sun based on this scriptural derived model and the science which also supports this. So, 39.96 billion years minus 9.99 billion years, will provide us with the **29.97th Billion Year as being the Solar System' operative date** as per this cosmological hypothetical model.

> This also means that the Solar System first beginning with the **Sun** itself had come on-stream within the first part of the **10th Period** of Ezra' WHT-WFT. Reading it in AUET clock time terms it would be within the 9.20 i.e. probably within the first 12 AUET minutes in the Ezra' GOD determined 10th Period.

> Although, my time construction also agrees with the scientific estimate for the age of the Planet Earth to be around 4.5 billion years, i.e. being a little younger than the Sun itself (about ½ a billion years younger), it could have in fact come into operative existence, more precisely to be habitable since around 4,329,000,000 years ago.

This would then without being over speculative in this, provide the Earth with about 171,000,000 years for it' P & D to have become a habitable Planet and not just one of the other lifeless Solar Planets as still evident today. This would also be keeping in line with the Genesis Creation Accounts as already described to you previously.

> If this could be acceptable, then the difference between the ages of the Sun according to this model being 4.995 billion years old and that of the habitable Planet Earth as being proposed here i.e. 4,329,000,000 years, would be actually exactly 666,000,000 years. This once again providing us with another complementing mathematical pattern towards the cosmic construction of the number of the second beast that sum totals 666, if this was indeed the case at that time.

At the very beginning of this effort, I had not the slightest clue whatsoever that it would materialise as such, as indicated in these two books. This is especially with regards to our Alphonso' 12 Phase Levels of Universe Expansion Progress, as already been made known to you, was developed based on the understanding of the relevant scriptures in 2ESDRAS. This records the expansion of the Universe in the allocated WHT sweep of 12 WHT minutes i.e. **666,000,000 years** per part.

This per Part Time Period, now being possibly the same amount of time that separates our Earth and it' only source of 'life sustaining energy' i.e. our Sun in age, is indeed quite interesting with regards to my intents and purposes for this book.

> I repeat that I did not make this linkage until just a few minutes ago. In order to give this discovery a date; today is actually the **8th of September, 2010** (around 11.00pm).

This further exhibits a Universe coming into existence not merely through a 'chaotic creation', but a Universe despite this chaos, emerging through a very specific and precise **mathematical pattern** operating behind the scenes, so to speak, though very complex in length, breadth and height, is understandably mindboggling to many of us.

However, it certainly exhibits a 'mathematical pattern of creation' having been designed into it; which clearly in my human mind once again reaffirms and points to our **LORD GOD Almighty**, being the Creator, as it was revealed to us in Genesis and other supporting Biblical Books in the Holy Bible.

> This is my **16th Milestone Achievement** which is absolutely necessary for us to continue this progress onwards.

This total time period of **39.96 Billion Years,** culminating at the very end of the Ezra' 12th WHT-WFT Period, would be the age of the entire Universe in just another 4,995 million years (less the 500,000 years or so which has also already been expanded), as was calculated from the RBP18:24:12(A).

Now as previously having explained, this obviously does not agree with the most current scientific (NASA') precise Universe age pegging discovery, as being 13.7 Billion Years old. However, you must take note this **39.96 Billion Years** would be the age of the Universe that I had arrived at through the 'Scriptural Based Process' as derived and adopted in this Book. Based on this, it also includes it' **future age** as per this Scriptural based model and so I am going to stick with it for our specific purposes.

Now prior to this scientific (NASA') Universe age pegging, the scientific community had estimated a very broad range of 10 to 17 Billion Years, for the current age of the Universe. Now who knows, that sometime later they may come up with some other theory or findings to even reduce this by more billions of years or perhaps even to add several more to their current claim. An **increase** would be definitely good for my scriptural based findings though.

Unlike their situation to be able to change either way according to the progress of their calculations and new findings based on new data and new technologies developed; I have to follow a singular path as dictated by the understanding as personally derived through these relevant Scriptures. However, the one similarity to a certain extent seems to be with the age of the Earth in both cases. It is good at least to have this consensus in this important matter.

Now through two charts, let me recap some of the above 16 Milestones achieved so far.

TYPICAL EARTH AXIS ROTATIONAL SPEED CHANGES IN EARTH TIME - CHART B

PROGRESSING CURRENTLY IN THE EZRA' 11TH PERIOD OF WHT-WFT

THE 18TH EAROC BEGINS AT RBP18:24:12 (A), ENDS AT RBP18:24:12 (B)

EARSS TO SLOWER BEGINS AGAIN HERE AT 24.20 HOURS EAR PERIOD

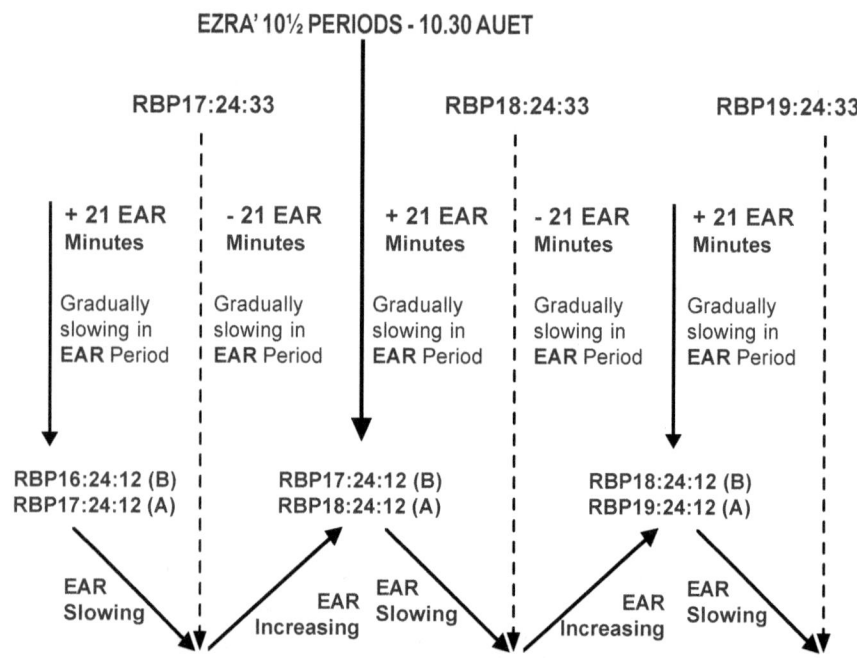

EARSS OCCURS EVERY 21 EAR MINUTES PERIOD TIME CHANGE AND EACH TAKES EXACTLY 126,000,000 YEARS TO COMPLETE

THE 17TH EAROC BEGINS AT RBP17:24:12(A), ENDS AT RBP17:24:12 (B)

17TH EAROC MID-BASE WAS REACHED AT RBP17:24:33 AND THE 360 DAY YEARS BEGINS ONCE AGAIN FROM HERE

18TH OSCILLATION CYCLE MID-BASE WILL BE REACHED AT RBP18:24:33 WITH A 24.55 HOURS EAR PERIOD. THIS WILL PROVIDE US WITH OUR VERY FISRT 360 DAY YEARS IN OUR ENTIRE BIBLICAL HUMAN HISTORY/FUTURE

EVERY 12 EAR MINUTES TAKES EXACTLY 72,000,000 YEARS TO COMPLETE

SOME IMPORTANT NOTES REGARDING CHART B

> Each 12 Minutes of EAR Period change which takes 72,000,000 ET Years can be divided into 500 equal divisions of time.

Thereby, each division of time = 144,000 years

> The Earth Time needed for our Planet Earth' EAR Period to acquire an additional 21 EAR Minutes, as an example, would be the same time that the Earth would need to move in any EAROC from the RBP X:24:12 (A) to the RBP X:24:33. This being 126,000,000 ET years distance away precisely.

> The X indicates any EAROC in at the time. Any less or any more years in distance travel between RBPs will defeat this whole OEARM and subsequently this entire effort would turn out to be erroneous.

Also, to have a reduction in the EAR Period, if that was the case according to this OEARM, then the opposite needs to occur precisely too.

As an example:

The Planet Earth would then need to move in any EAROC from the RBP X:24:33 to the RBP X:24:12 (B). This also being 126,000,000 ET years distance away precisely.

The first Earth Axis Rotation Speed Switchover (EARSS), for this present '18th EAR Oscillation Cycle' is also at the Referenced Base Position 17:24:12(B) but which is now referred to for this 18th EAROC to being RBP18:24:12(A). The second EARSS for this 18th EAROC will be located '21 EAR Minutes' away from here at RBP18:24:33.

This will be in fact the mid-base for this present 18th EAROC, which would come to an end at RBP18:24:12(B). The 19th EAROC also begins from this same RBP18:24:12(B) but for it, this will be called as RBP19:24:12(A).

We must also remember that increment (faster) in the Earth's Axis Rotation Period produces an increasing number of Earth Days in an Earth' Orbit around the Sun. Similarly, reduction (slower) in the axis rotation period produces a reducing number of Earth Days in a Year. The rate at which this changes whether in increase (as per my suggestion, if it does increase) or in reduction, which is scientifically indicated as being currently, depends on the scientific established change rate of 1/1000th second every 100 years in the EAR Period.

Also accordingly, this would then increase or reduce as the case may be, the length and number of the Solar Days in a year accordingly. The * as indicated in Chart B above, indicates the Earth beginning it' mean Solar Day of the current 24.20144776 hours (i.e. 24hrs 12min 5.211936sec). This provides us with a 365.242199 Days Solar Year as being currently observed according to our annual calendar.

The following Chart–C, would illustrate to you, the expanding Universe as it progressively expands in the 11th Period of Ezra' WHT-WFT. I sincerely hope that it is adequately designed for your better understanding.

THE EXPANDING UNIVERSE IN THE 12th AUET PHASE LEVEL ACCORDING TO EZRA' WORLD HISTORY TIME IN THE 11TH PERIOD - **CHART C**

PROGRESSING IN THE EZRA' 11TH PERIOD, WHICH BEGAN IMMEDIATELY ON THE **33.30 BILLIONTH YEAR** IN THE AGE OF THE EXPANDING UNIVERSE

→

RBP18:24:12(A) HAS ALREADY BEEN REACHED AND IS AN EARSS BASE

EZRA' WHT OF 10½ 'PERIODS' ALSO ENDS HERE AT RBP18:24:12(A)

THE EARTH IS NOW ABOUT 4.5 BILLION YEARS OLD AND HAS BEEN HABITABLE

THROUGH THIS PROJECTION (OEARM) SINCE ABOUT 4.329 BILLION YEARS

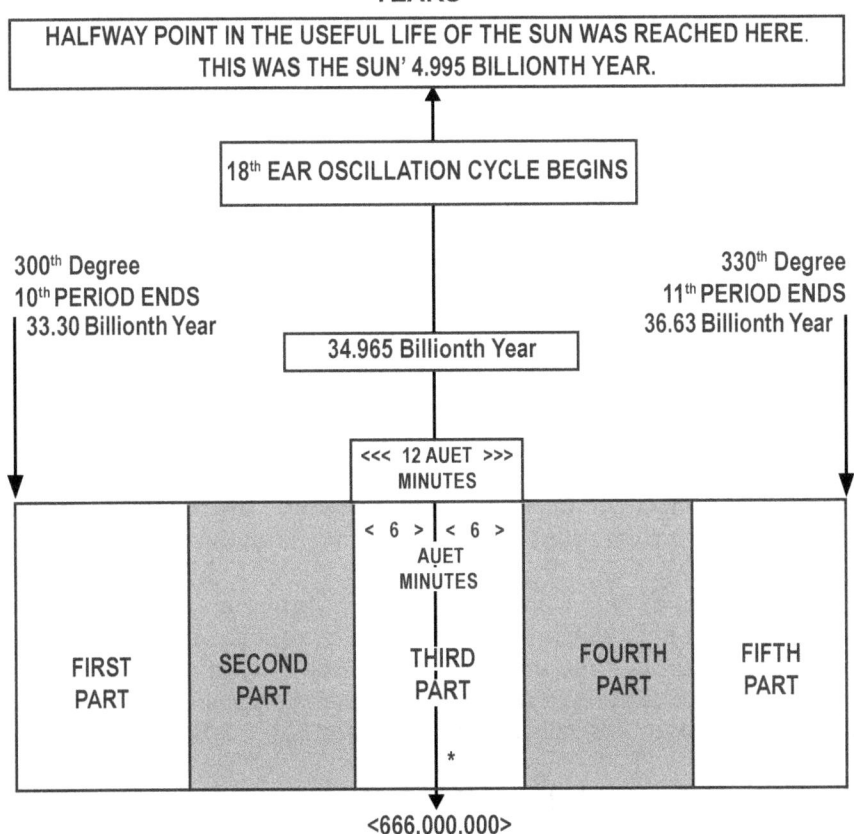

Notes on Chart C:

2.5 PARTS, less the 500,000 years that have already expired, + 5 more PARTS in the Ezra' last 12th Period of WHT is only that TIME which is still remaining for us and the Earth.

Each PART of the AUET as shown above takes up 666,000,000 WHT/ AUET YEARS. These can be divided into **4,625 equal time Divisions such as follows:**

Each Division of Time = 144,000 years

The Universe expansion continues progressing towards the EZRA' 12th and final Period of WHT-WFT, according to my understanding of the relevant referenced Scriptures. This also progresses towards the scriptural derived pre-determined 39.96 billionth year, which will be reached at the end of it. This would also be the end of the useful life of the Sun and probably could be equated to the Scriptural references, such as *Isaiah 13:10; Joel 3:15; Mark 3:24-25*. This however, as I understand it, specifically refers to Earth Time and also to it' 'End Times' only. For this is not from my understanding the end of the Universe though.

This * as indicated above represents the previously calculated 126,000,000th ET Year, as located in the EZRA' 11th Period of Universe Expansion. This is the specific time period as calculated from the RBP18:24:12(A) to RBP18:24:33. This is specifically pertaining to the EAR and the movement of the Planet Earth, as per it' 18th Oscillation Cycle within the overall context of the Universe' expansion and it' direct relationship with the Solar System and in turn with the Milky Way Galaxy.

The Earth at this very RBP18:24:33 will then begin having from here onwards until such time in the pre-determined specific time of the EAROC is reached, **360 Days Orbital Years. This Planetary Earth cosmic event will be indeed for the very first time in our Biblical Human History.**

Since the rate of reduction in the Earth' rotation on it' axis is only **1/1000th of a second every 100 years according to scientific scholarship,** we will have these 360 Days Years for quite some time. As you have already been informed, for the day to be reduced by even a single second of time in its EAR period, it will take a minimum of **100,000 years!!!**

Additional Notes on Chart – B and Chart – C:

Since One Second reduction and/or the assumed possible increase as per this OEARM in the Earth' Axial Axis Rotation Period would take 100,000

years, then it follows that: -
* 1 minute increase/reduction would take 6,000,000 years to fulfil.
* 12 minutes reduction/increase in the Earth' Axis Rotational Speed would therefore take exactly 72,000,000 years.
* Accordingly, 21 EAR minutes reduction in the speed of the Earth' rotation on it' axial axis, as already explained previously, will take exactly 126,000,000 years to accomplish.
* On this Chart-B, since 12 EAR minutes speed change takes 72,000,000 years to fulfil constantly, this time period then can be subdivided into 500 equal divisions of time measurement, with each division allocated a time period of 144,000 years. This number as you may know already is also found written in the Holy Scriptures – the Book of Revelation 14:1 refers.
* Each PART of a PERIOD, for all the 12 PERIODS of WHT, has also been equated to 12 WHT/AUET MINUTES.
* The time as in Chart C, can now be divided as in the previous Earth Time Chart–B, but not into 500 equal time measuring divisions, but into 4,625 equal Divisions of time measurement. In being able to be doing so, each equal Division of TIME also measures **144,000 years.** The same as shown in the Chart–B, a few pages previously.

Take note that so far in our progress, the continued accuracy and the reliability in the 'Cosmic construction of the second beast' number, has not been compromised in anyway whatsoever. This has been based through this perspective and understanding of the relevant referenced Scriptures, which had clearly helped me to develop this as such.

> The RBP18:24:12(A) was the position in WHT, about 500,000 years ago, when the Universe was 34.965 billion years old as derived through the relevant referenced scriptures of 2ESDRAS. This is also the Ezra' 10 and a ½ Period mark in the GOD revealed WHT-WFT, through this same biblical book. These are the same scriptures through which I had actually developed, as I had understood it, through my reading of the same, the very age of the Universe and the consequent 'End of Days' of the Earth.

Also, as previously explained, there are two rates of 'TIME' for us to contend with. This is not only being recognised as such in order to establish the 'number' of the second beast, but also because this must be the very case in the Universe, as I had discovered and derived it from within the relevant referenced Scriptures.

> This is indeed from this effort, as I had continued progressing through the development of this book, and thereby, of the opinion that it is indeed possibly a new discovery of one amongst the various other complex mechanisms of 'TIME', which are yet to be explored and understood accordingly.

With regards to the two possible measurements of 'Time' that I just pointed out above; one is the increasing or we could call it the 'Dynamic Time'. This came about directly due to the expanding Universe through each 'Level of Expansion' i.e. AUET which as you already know quite well by now was developed based on the relevant Scriptures as found in the biblical book, 2ESDRAS. The other is what I would refer to as simply being the 'Static Time'.

This 'Static Time' comes through our very own Solar System and is only possible due to the interacting but fixed triune cosmic time generating relationship between our Sun, Earth and Moon.

This important cosmic interaction of a Star, a Solar Planet (it' offshoot), and one single cosmic Earth satellite i.e. the Moon is singly relevant to us human beings only. This was ever since our GOD ALMIGHTY had set these into co-ordinated fixed motion, in specific relationship to one another for this exact purpose.

In other words, the Universe does exist because of us and not the other way round. An understanding as derived from my reading of the Holy Bible. This was the whole purpose for GOD having to create the Universe. This was so, that the Planet Earth could come about together with the rest of the unique Solar System in the Milky Way Galaxy and the Planet to be prepared as it had been, to be able to accommodate human life accordingly.

> As described in Chart–B, all of this is based on the cosmic design of our LORD GOD ALMIGHTY and as discovered; each segment of 12 EAR minutes (each representing 500 equal divisions of time) for the EAR speed change takes an unchanging 72,000,000 ET years to be realized.

Whilst the 12 AUET Minutes which accommodates each Part of the Universe expansion per 2ESdras' 12 Periods; each representing **4,625 equal time divisions** as described in Chart–C, takes **666,000,000 years**.

> Each equal time Division in both Charts B & C represents the same value in years i.e. 144,000 years in both Time Systems, despite following different change rates. Yet due to this common value per division in both systems, it can be used to establish a specific 'time linkage', interlocking these two cosmic based natural time measuring systems. This is to understand better their synchronous workings together as a whole, though operating independently of each other but through GOD' overall creation plan being completely in-synch with each other.

Now this specific 'time linkage relationship' that obviously exists between our Earth Time and the overall AUET will be described in greater detail in PART FOUR of this Book Two.

Now, as I was browsing through our local bookstore, I came upon a book which was authored if I do recollect correctly, by **John Leslie,** concerning our **Universe** to be having several natural occurring ratios and so I began to read it with some interest. How I stumbled upon it is also by sheer coincidence, but unfortunately, I do not recall the exact title of the book, but it could just be, 'A Universe Of Ratios' or something close to this. Anyway, I came to realise as I stood there in the bookstore scanning through the pages of this book, that he had actually listed several examples in the Universe, where specific natural occurring ratios which had already been discovered much earlier and were evidently documented as such in his book. While he did give several examples of these ratios and their relationships to the Universe, he did not list down the time scale factor or ratio that I am specifically using in my book. This is due to the simple reason; it had not been discovered by anyone until now and therefore this is the first time that my discovery is being documented as such in here.

> If there is anything that may possibly in the end hopefully, find you fascinated with my book, something that you may find after all to be of some significance or of some importance, this time scale factor or ratio could just be it; if unfortunately nothing else does.

This ratio that I had obviously been so very fortunate to actually have singularly discovered, is described in detail together with it' relationships in the Universe. Besides, it also regards to the 'Time' (UET), and also the recording of the time in UET units in the expansion of the Universe, which is still currently in progress. This time recording which is actually clearly evident in the 2ESDRAS' WHT-WFT relevant scriptures, was indeed provided to us through the revelation of it as specifically given by GOD ALMIGHTY through Ezra. He was also referred to as being Shealtiel in the opening scriptural verse of Chapter 3 in the Biblical Book, 2ESDRAS. In this Apocryphal Biblical Book, 2ESDRAS, we come to know of the 'Seven Visions' which was revealed and also interpreted to Shealtiel or rather to Ezra by the Angel Uriel. I am particularly focussed in this book which I am currently writing for you, with his receiving of the 'Seventh Vision'. Prophet Ezra is well known also in our Biblical History in the OLD TESTAMENT (OT). In fact the Bible has an OT Biblical Book, EZRA, which has been scholastically attributed to him as being the inspired author of it together with the other Biblical Books, Chronicles 1 & 2 and also some possibility for certain sections of Nehemiah. So Ezra is attributed with some very impressive and scripturally reliable credentials. He is a heavyweight with regards to the inspired writers and the biblical Prophets.

Furthermore, this ratio was also employed by me in such a way, making it possible for me to generate the unique cosmic construction of the 'number' of the second beast. So, there are numerous examples in this book of mine, where you will be able to easily discover the application of this time scale factor or ratio.

You will also discover for yourself as you proceed on, and if I may humbly add here, with some sheer fascination that had caught me too, of this very important time scale factor or ratio, 9.25 times.

> This had been originally developed as a time scale ratio between the EAR speed changes which are spread over great lengths of time and having directly compared it to the time as being progressed by the expanding Universe in even much larger periods of time, ever since the 'Big Bang-Inflation' had occurred aeons ago. Yet more remarkable than all of this, is that it was also discovered by me, to be embedded somewhat cryptically in the very Scriptures of the Biblical Book, Revelation!!!

> **This is indeed really amazing.** I just cannot express my joy enough in discovering this; for it further provides **important and exceptional evidential proof** that I am certainly on the right path in both the establishing of our future '360 Day Years' and my further discovering of the cosmic constructed 'number' of the second beast. You will find it very difficult to deny the Scriptural merits this fact alone offers to both of my quests.

The additional notes as already provided to you on Chart B & C, should make most, if not all of these complex matters easier for you to understand. I sincerely hope so, anyway. So, from all of these equations and specific divisions of time measurement, we were remarkably able to obtain the biblically important number of **144,000**.

The 500 Divisions of Chart B and the 4625 Divisions of Chart C can be quite obviously and clearly shown to also have a **9.25:1** time scale ratio in relation to each other and that each of these Divisions on both sides of this ratio measures the similar number of years. This of course, as you already know by now, is exactly the **144,000** years.

> This number, 144,000, as previously mentioned and of biblical common knowledge too, is found written in the Biblical Book of Revelation - Rev 7:4 and subsequently again in Rev 14:1 refers.

Now having said all of the above, what is to follow will surely blow your mind away. So, please be extra attentive to what develops next as below.

> Now, whilst I was studying and reading through the Book of Revelation, accidentally at first I thought, stumbled upon the decimal number **0.004625**.

Now you may become somewhat quite perplexed at this and rightly so, because research as much as you are able to and you will not be able to find this out yourself unless I do assist in revealing it to you. Yes, I am fully agreeable to be doing so, right now, without any undue delay and you on your own can decide whether it is an awesome discovery or not.

To me it is definitely in the same league as when the Physicist Leon M. Lederman together with his team of other Physicists, had discovered the sub-atomic particle, the bottom quark, which they named as 'Upsilon', making him to be the first amongst the six or seven so billion people that are possibly currently living in this world, to have been able to do so. This is simply awesome and please do forgive me if you think this linking with Physicist Leon' discovery, is indeed pushing it a way bit too much.

However, unlike these scientists, I had a lot of help from the Holy Spirit without which this would not be possible as such. Yet the elation for discovering this unique time scale factor or ratio is definitely of the same degree with that of Leon and his colleagues who had participated in the Experiment 288 in the Fermi lab.

This had been reported having taken place when in the summer of 1977 they had discovered the bottom quark sub-atomic particle.

If you are a football player (soccer), like I used to be in my younger days, it does not matter whether you are playing in the neighbourhood uneven hole-riddled grass-sand-mud patch field or whether you are playing for the Manchester United Football Club, in the UK. This is because for when you shoot a goal, it is the same elation and happiness that you and your team mates share with the multimillion dollar players of MUFC, when one of them shoots a goal too. It is just the same, no difference at all. Victory is certainly very sweet indeed and you will only know of this if you had the wonderful opportunity to have tasted it sometime yourself.

> I had surprisingly and I say this cautiously, obtained this very unique six place decimal, being the very significant quotient, as derived from my exciting discovery of the most significant Math Division at least in my life at the time, that being of the biblical **666** by the other biblical number **144,000**.

$$666/144{,}000 = 0.004625$$

> For some very compelling reasons, though not clear to me at the time of discovering this amazing possibility, but now I do personally know through the strong conviction in my heart, this was indeed the work of the **Holy Spirit**. Through GOD' grace this math division had been put into my mind. That is to specifically divide this particular Scriptural given number **666**, which as you already know now is the sum total of the number in question of the second beast with that of the other very significant Scriptural number; **144,000**.

Before I miss the opportunity, let me state this, that the Holy Spirit is the final THIRD GOD PERSON in the Holy Trinity, WHO we have come to know more intimately ever since the Gen 1:2 event. This is the very first mention of the Holy Spirit, where we had come to learn that the Holy Spirit was indeed hovering over the face of the waters (i.e. with regards to the Planet Earth when it was about to undergo the facelift, the renovation, according to the P & D accounts).

This 144,000 as you may know, is on the **opposing side** of the second beast. For it clearly represents the number of those who will be **sealed** i.e. with HIS (referring to Jesus) Father' Name (who is GOD the FATHER), written on their forehead. These will be as chosen from amongst the living **12 Tribes of Israel**, 12,000 from each, at that future time in our Human History - Rev 7:4-8 refers and Rev Chapter 14:1 also confirms.

This very significant divinely placed **'NAME SEAL'** on these very individuals found to be worthy of such a phenomenon, would protect these entire 144,000 special GOD selected Israelites. This is as per the actual biblical scriptural fact from which we can draw conclusion that they will be amongst the first to be redeemed from the Earth during the awful, horrible, devastating, dark days of Revelation to come in the future.

Now having done the math division and having obtained this six place decimal quotient of **0.004625**, I immediately realised that it was to be associated with the number of divisions per Period in WHT/AUET i.e. the **4625 Divisions** as described in Chart C. Of course, it is of different values, but bridgeable as you will see.

Despite discovering the above connection, I still decided to set it aside for the time being, thinking of it as just a strange coincidence that it was so and went on with my other routine business. Nevertheless, this six place decimal resultant quotient, **0.004625**, got indeed registered into my very own subconscious memory. Probably, just like any other thing that we think, see or experience in our daily living.

Some weeks later, after the above encounter with the decimal quotient **0.004625**, while driving one morning, 3rd **May 2001** to be exact; once again with the same Holy Spirit compulsion that I had experienced earlier, I began this time round to tinker with the calculated time-ratio scale, which I had developed originally i.e. **9.25:1**.

While still driving, in my mind I began to first reduce by half the value of this time-ratio scale. The answer that I had obtained was **4.625:0.5**.

Then still strongly compelled to continue with this process, I proceeded on to further reduce the value of this particular time-ratio scale representation by dividing it with 1,000. This entire quite basic arithmetic process came to my mind from out of the blue, so to speak. Yet it came with such purpose and authority as I recall; further suggested and convinced me, this was indeed the continuing revelation being received and as such guided by the Holy Spirit, to eventually reach some specific end result here.

What immediately then registered in my mind in particular was that the first part of this time-ratio scale, after going through this division of a thousand, resulted in the number, **0.004625**. This precise quotient number **0.004625** was indeed obtained a few pages earlier, by dividing the Scriptural given number **666,** by the other Scriptural given number being the **144,000**!!!

$$666/144000 = 0.004625$$

I began to initially realize and as it slowly sank in, "Have I made that tremendous connection of my original time-scale ratio of **9.25:1** (which was initially developed mainly with the Biblical help of the relevant chapters in 2ESDRAS **(an Apocryphal Biblical Book of the Second Canon)** and now directly with these two very significant Scriptural numbers as found written in the last arranged Biblical Book **(according to the First Canon)** in the Holy Bible." This being of course the Biblical Book:

'The Revelation of Jesus Christ'

This tremendous and amazing breakthrough which from the very beginning was orchestrated, as I do firmly believe by the Holy Spirit, if I may add even at this significant stage, for the successful continuation of this book that I am currently writing. In fact this entire book is way beyond my league, my human abilities; dear friends. So I want to reaffirm to you, this has to be the purposeful work of the Holy Spirit indeed, our Divine Helper, GOD THE HOLY SPIRIT - The **THIRD GOD Person.**

I rushed home to double check all of this. Also, to see whether I could really develop this already discovered ratio of mine, being the **9.25:1**, directly through the Revelation scriptures. This is to be obtained by using this very same scriptural derived six place decimal number quotient of 0.004625, which was first obtained when I had divided the two biblical numbers; **666** by **144,000**.

So, I worked backwards of course, by first multiplying 0.004625 by 1000, which obtained for me the number **4.625**. Then by just **doubling** it, I naturally obtained the number **9.25**, which as you know now, is the first part of my important developed 2ESDRAS scriptural derived time-ratio scale; **9.25:1**.

Then using this same arithmetic process also for the second side of the time-ratio scale **9.25:1**, I obtained the 4 place decimal number, **0.0005**. For as you know, that you do not change the intrinsic value or relationship that any ratio represents, if you do exactly with one side just as with the other. We then can put these first results together as follows:

9.25:1 is the same ratio as 4.625:0.5

Just as

0.004625:0.0005

is the same ratio with

9.25:1

This is truly amazing and I must personally take time here to prayerfully thank the Holy Spirit, for the most gracious divine help, in helping me in more ways than I could ever imagine, especially to also linking these Scriptural numbers of **666** and **144,000** in this profound and very significant manner. To have established this unique time-scale ratio once again, but this time round through the relevant Revelation scriptures is simply amazing.

This **9.25:1** time ratio scaling factor, if you do recollect, was originally applied as shown in the previous Chart E, describing the progressively expanding Universe throughout the AUET Phase Levels or rather throughout the 2ESDRAS' 12 Periods of WHT-WFT.

> If I had discovered this through Revelation instead then, at the very beginning of commencing this book, I would not have had the foggiest idea of what it had meant or how it was to be used. This timely discovery now has indeed cemented all the past effort and the numerous times I had indeed applied it.

I will now further show you, how this special scriptural derived resultant quotient **0.004625**, relates to Earth Time and WHT (AUET) and subsequently to the similar ratio relationship that so significantly exists unknowingly to any of us until just now, between the significant Scriptural numbers, **666 & 144,000**.

These relationships can be shown clearly to you, as follows:

Sub-divide each Division of a Period being represented respectively in both Charts B & C into 144,000 equal sub-divisions of time; each would be then representing 1 year.

It is also to be carefully noted, that the grouping of **666 years** being obviously represented by **666** sub-divisions of a Division similarly in both Chart - B and Chart – C, equals to **0.004625 of a Division** in both cases.

This obviously means, if you were to multiply the value of a Division on either side of the Chart ratio by THE RESULTANT QUOTIENT of 666/144,000 I.E. 0.004625; it will equate to **666** years. This is because a Division on either side of the ratio represents a similar time value of exactly **144,000** years, as previously established.

Similarly, we can divide the 'static' Earth Time of 500 Divisions per Period which amounts to 72,000,000 ET years as indicated in Chart B into 1,000,000 subdivisions, whereby, each will have a time value of **72 ET years** exactly. So, accordingly each of these subdivisions will then be 0.0005 of a Division in time value.

Therefore, **666/144,000** will produce for us the resultant quotient **0.004625** and similarly, **72/144000** will produce for us the resultant quotient **0.0005**.

> The **666** being amazingly a unit of time recording the expanding Universe into the divinely measured Universe Space-Time and the **72** being a unit of time in the Solar System regulated EAR speed changes of our Planet Earth.

Therefore, we now can put all of this together in yet another new version of the same time scale ratio **9.25:1**, by directly incorporating these two very significant Scriptural given numbers of **666** and **144,000** from within the Biblical Book, REVELATION, together with the **72** as just shown above, as follows:

> **Earth Time** relating to the EAR speed changes per every 12 EAR minutes as compared to the **Earth Time** relating to the Universe Expansion Time progress. That is UET per every 12 AUET/EZRA' WHT-WFT Minutes. Therefore, these will be in the time scale ratio of **9.25:1**.

In other words:

72,000,000 EAR years X 9.25 : 666,000,000 WHT-WFT X 1

This directly means, that for **every 1 AUET/WHT-WFT year** progress in the expansion of the Universe, it would be exactly equivalent to the **time progression of the EAR every 9.25 years.**

9.25 ET years = 1 AUET/WHT-WFT year
9.25:1

> This unique time relationship between the expanding Universe progress and the Solar Planet Earth had even existed **before** the Earth or the Solar System or even the Milky Way Galaxy had come into it' very own existence in this Universe. This I know is because GOD' workmanship and design is clearly evident in all of this.

> This unique situation then describes or underpins a **GOD ALMIGHTY** designed predetermined destiny for the Solar System together with the Earth and it' Milky Way Galaxy. This is obvious at least from this view point, as it finally came into it' very own existence having been predesigned and predestined by our GOD ALMIGHY. This then became synchronised as such, in that time scale ratio of time progression, which seems to dictate everything else with the continuing Universe Expansion accordingly.

There is in this structure, as you can clearly see, an overall time pattern which has divinely been inculcated into it, a mathematical influence according to GOD' very own 'MASTER ARCHITECH PLAN'.

As we continue establishing these time relationships here, it would become even increasingly clearer to you.

Therefore, as directly derived & developed from Chart B & Chart C; we have:

500 Div of EAR Time Period X 9.25 : 4625 Div of UET X 1

500 X 9.25 : 4625 X 1

Similarly:

0.0005 x 9.25 : 0.004625 x 1

These relationships above firstly describes that for every Division of UET through every 12 AUET/EZRA WHT-WFT being 144,000 ET years, is exactly equivalent to every Division of time being also 144,000 ET years, as per the EAR speed change every 12 EAR Minutes.

Secondly, as shown below, it describes that for every **72 ET years** progress in the EAR speed change per every 0.0005 of it' EAR Division; the Universe would have expanded as per 0.004625 of it' UET Division, which amounts to **666 ET years**.

This then relates to:

72 X 9.25 : 666 X 1

9.25:1

> In other words, for **every 1 AUET/WHT-WFT year** progress in the expansion of the Universe, it would be exactly equivalent to the **time progression of the EAR speed change every 9.25 ET years.**

Then finally Chart B & Chart C in direct combination with the relevant scriptural numbers as follows would also be found to be in the ratio of 9.25 times the former.

72/144000 as compared to 666/144000
0.0005 as compared to 0.004625

72:666

The latter is **9.25** times the former and thereby, they relate to each other in the ratio:

9.25:1

All of the above are in fact still directly relating to each other in that same ratio scale of **9.25:1** ratio. This is the very same original time-scale ratio relationship that I had first developed at the very beginning as was described and employed in CHART E; Chart A2 and Chart A3. This is which exists between the EAR speed changes and the EZRA' WHT-WFT progress of the Universe expanding into the GOD measured Universe Space.

> This as mentioned previously was originally obtained or achieved without having the faintest clue or inkling of this very possibility being repeated once again by remarkably engaging and employing the relevant Holy Scriptures as found described in the Biblical Book of **REVELATION**.

We can also introduce right here, our former establishing of this similar ratio by putting **One Kalpa Period**, which was developed by the ancient Indian/Hindu astronomers through their very own developed 'Indian/Hindu Cosmological Time Cycles'; against the predetermined **Age of the Universe** as at the end of the 2ESDRAS' 12th Period which I had calculated out as already proven to you.

4,320,000,000 x 9.25 : 39,960,000,000 X 1

This means that there are 9.25 Kalpa Cycles in one complete age of the Universe. Is this not simply awesome?

Besides all of the above, if you do still remember, according to the 'Indian/Hindu Cosmological Time Cycles':

One complete orbit of our Solar System around the Star Alcyone in the Pleiades galactic star cluster of nine white blue stars in the Taurus Constellation, will take 24,000 divine years. Therefore, in Earth Time Years, this equates to 8,640,000 Years (24,000 X 360).

So, in other words this period in Earth Year terms, can be taken to constitute One Solar System Orbit around Alcyone. This is the brightest star in this Pleiades cluster, being 10 times the mass of our own Sun and having an absolute luminosity of around 1000 times of our own Sun!!! It is approximately 380 light years away.

Therefore, One Kalpa period which equates to 4,320,000,000 Earth Years, constitutes **500 Orbits** around Alcyone. Also, as we too can equate the Age of the Universe as at the end of the 12th Period of Ezra' WHT to being 9.25 Kalpas; then through simple arithmetic, we will find this constitutes **4625 Orbits!!!**

Can you once again amazingly see the ratio **9.25:1** being also similarly developed through these very means, by converting the full age of the Universe at the end of the 12 Ezra' Periods of WHT-WFT into orbits around Alcyone and also converting similarly One Kalpa Period into orbits around Alcyone.

One Kalpa Period X 9.25 : One Age of the Universe

4,320,000,000 Years x 9.25 : 39,960,000,000 Years

In other words, what we can deduce and further understand from the last few 'representations' as above, is that through this very same 'Indian/Hindu Cosmological Time Cycles', by using it as a third source of verification and authentication, we can further substantiate that our overall understanding of the Scriptural Ezra' WHT-WFT Periods, could be well placed; meaning accurate.

This also in turn once again re-establishes and reconfirms the accuracy of our original conceptual use of this remarkable ratio of:

9.25:1

This not only has it' firm and first roots in the second Book of Esdras, but also just as firmly embedded in the **Book of Revelation** and also amazingly can be developed from another foreign non-biblical time system. This is indeed very encouraging and also very intriguing, to say the least.

There is something extremely important and exciting to take note here and that is from within a translation of the Holy Bible (i.e. which does not carry the Deuterocanonical Books/Apocrypha Books which includes the 2Esdras) i.e. such as in the AKJ and the NKJV; I have been able to develop, as you can study from all of the above; my original conceptual time-ratio scale of:-

9.25:1

So in conclusion, it was not that farfetched after all, when I first introduced this time-scale ratio to you and used it to develop a specific cosmic Universe expansion model as per the Alphonso' 12 Phase Levels of Universe expansion. This was to illustrate to you, in the first place, our overall increasingly accelerating expanding Universe, as described for you in Charts A3, E & A2 by using the Apocryphal Book, 2ESDRAS. Of course, as mentioned already, I did not know at the time, that I would be making all of the other connections too.

> Also, this is the actual time scale ratio that we had initially obtained, when we compared Earth Axis Rotation speed changes time to World History Time, as confirmed previously.

So, by Cosmic design i.e. by the 'Hand of GOD', you will also see in a larger time perspective i.e. 1 PERIOD in the Alphonso'12th Phase Level of WHT equates to 3.33 Billion Years **exactly**.

Without taking into consideration the great differences in the 'size of time', the number **3.33** is identical **i.e. to 3.33 seconds,** which is equivalent to one division of Babylonian Hour (3,600 seconds) of time which is also similar to our time reckoning per hour too.

1/1080 X 3600 seconds = 3.33 seconds

What was their need for such precise accuracy??? Perhaps some of you may be able to figure this out and when you do, please let me know without undue delay.

Also, although not wanting to be overly speculative here; Jesus Christ to my understanding was crucified when HE was probably around 33 and a third year of age (33S!). There could be some possible cosmic connection here too that could be identified and further explored, if you are interested in this.

Well at least now, we do not need to question them, why not 60 or 30 or ten as for their using of such a large number that they had selected i.e. **1080.** For it is quite obvious that it has been dictated quite definitely by cosmic design and not by sheer fancy.

I also want to draw your attention once again to some facts that I had written on the very first page when I started writing this PART THREE for you. Please refer to it now if you can.

For your further information, I had previously pointed out to you this particular number, through my **'360 Equation Series',** as in: **360 x 3 = 1080.**

'THE SCRIPTURAL COSMIC 666'
The Cosmic Based Construction, Leading to the 'Number' of 'The Beast'

These cannot be just mere coincidences in my opinion and study. This is why, I propose there are some definite relationships in these time scales with our historical past and the understanding of time usage by the ancient peoples, which is still valid, as the similar time-keeping controls have also continued into our present and will continue as such even into our future. For it is dictated by the same triune relationship of the Sun, Earth and Moon. This further establishes for me and hopefully you too, the Scriptural truth in the **Deuterocanonical/Apocrypha Book, 2Esdras.** More of these relationships are also discussed on the first pages of Part Four.

> I have also in the last previous few pages, further established the direct relationship of the sum total of the **'number'** of the second beast, which is indeed **666**, with the other Scriptural number of **144,000**.

Also, there is a further relationship of the scriptural number 1260 (REV 12:6 refers) and the scriptural time measurement of a time and times and ½ a time (Dan 7:25 refers), which when multiplied together, as already shown previously, generates the important cosmic time number, i.e. **126,000,000**.

> Also, 1260 days directly equates to the **42 months;** a time frame, which is also mentioned in Scripture. Through this 'cosmic construction', we will also discover this becoming a definite certainty in Earth Time terms in the future. This is when **each month** will take exactly **30 days** to complete, which in turn provides us with the 360 day years accordingly. Referenced Scripture - Rev 11:2-3.

> Besides this the number 42 is also again found reflected in the full length of an 'EAR Oscillation Cycle', which indeed takes 42 EAR Minutes in total to complete. This in terms of years is exactly 252,000,000 years. Remarkably, the above 126,000,000 years as previously calculated, is indeed exactly half an EAR Oscillation Cycle.

This was to further show you that it is unmistakable that there are specific relationships between all of these respective REVELATION Scriptural Numbers in some way or another, being connected with the overall 'construction' of the Cosmos, which further exposes to us glimpses of the **'MIND of GOD'** here and there.

We are in fact humanly gifted to have the opportunity to discover and to observe these very divine workings into the cosmos at large and in particular within our own backyard, our Solar System, although it is only just a glimpse, but an important one nevertheless in my humble opinion.

Also, as already shown to you, we have an **explosion** of time relationships, which are in the **9.25:1** unique time scale ratio, which makes it not just as a single coincident occurrence, but exposes that there is definitely a **GOD ALMIGHTY** designed purpose for it to be as numerous as it is, having been fortunately discovered and revealed to you as in this very book.

All of this as you will find out also, positively contributes to the construction of the **'number'** of the second beast. This also demonstrates that we are still indeed on the right track this far. I must say, just even to arrive at this stage, has been really mind boggling and indeed mentally exhausting for me. Therefore, do not hold it against me, if I state that I would not have been able to go through this, without the very necessary contributing help from the Holy Spirit. This is my belief.

Now, in further support to our understanding of all the above and to make it even clearer to you that the Universe is still currently expanding into it' measured area/volume (measured by GOD ALMIGHTY) in Space over time; we have another way of presenting this expansion, which would also fulfil the World History Time of 2Esdras.

Therefore, let us imagine a collapsible type **Elliptical Cone,** which is progressively expanding upwards or one that we can pull out at a certain changing pace and which is also obviously expanding breadth ways or rather sideways, in tandem with the similarly expanding Universe in all directions possible due to the 'Big Bang-Inflation'.

Let us also imagine, it' imaginary cone shaped wall, form the outer limits of the Universe Space and thereby limits the expansion of the Universe, in every direction that it is possibly expanding at every stage or Phase Level of Expansion. However, all of these will be operating or expanding within the SPACE-TIME as measured and allocated to the Universe by GOD AMLMIGHTY. In other words, not to exceed the area measured for it by **GOD ALMIGHTY** in Space and in the Space-Time dimension.

Looking from the open-ended cone downwards, as in a Plan View, and slicing it horizontally will produce **Ellipses** of reducing areas at every Phase Level, until we reach the bottom of the Cone, which ends practically into a base cone point.

This point is then taken to be the starting reference base of the expanding Universe in Space over Time in this imaginary constructed cone model.

> This means, at this most bottom point, 'Time' is actually reading Zero in relation to our Pre-Universe, Pre-Big Bang, which is also taken to be Zero in age/size at this base and 'Time' in Space.

This does not mean in anyway, that it does not exist, but rather that because of the heavy dense concentration of matter into a very, very small compact area; I have taken it to reference, **Zero.**

Furthermore, it is referenced as being Zero, for we need to recognise the expansion of the Universe at that point in time, had not been triggered as yet.

Now, instead of arbitrarily slicing the Elliptical Cone into ellipses at random, we will follow our specific time ratio scale of **9.25:1** once again, to establish these very ellipses at the various 12 scaled-levels of the Cone. This would describe the expanding Universe, according to the Alphonso' 12 Phase Levels, which in turn was derived through the relevant scriptures, as found written in the Biblical Book, 2Esdras.

The ending of the Alphonso' 12th Phase Level of Universe Expansion, is as far as our Biblical 'World History-World Future' takes us in the allocated 'SPACE-Time', as derived according to the understanding of these Scriptures in 2ESDRAS.

As I had indicated to you as previously, this is however, not to be taken as being the very end of the Universe. It could possibly be the end of our Solar System, particularly with regards to the three operatives that we are concerned with, i.e. the Sun, the Earth and the Moon in it' jointly sustaining of life on Earth.

One thing is for certain and that is, we will surely have a new heaven and a new earth. In other words our very own **'New World'**, as prophesied in Isaiah 66:22-24 and in Revelation – Chapters 21 & 22 (as found in the Holy Bible).

I know this must have been a tough section to go through without any serious hiccups in mind and in thought. Therefore, as a suggestion, probably another reading would be in order, so that you would be in a better position, to fully understand and appreciate the following final PART FOUR which holds even more intriguing new discoveries that would simply blow you away.

PRAISE BE TO GOD

END OF PART THREE

E: gcf@globalchristianfamily.com

PART FOUR

THE UNVEILING OF THE 'NUMBER' OF THE (SECOND) BEAST

We now come to the final and most critical part of this entire book. I must certainly congratulate you and thank you for having stayed with me through BOOK ONE and PART THREE of BOOK TWO. I must thank you for still staying on course with me, despite the many original mind-boggling concepts that have been established here and which may to many be completely too much to accept for various reasons. I however do accept this as being an inevitable outcome to some extent and therefore being part and parcel to my difficult but biblically necessary endervour to fulfil or if you wish to attempt in fulfilling our GOD ALMIGHTY established commission as specifically given to us in Rev 13:18. Thanks and Amen.

This is when we need to reconcile the two distinct and different time zones as described in Charts B & C, in such a way, that it remarkably provides us with the unique and **singular set of 'numbers',** which sum totals **666.**

> This phenomenon combined with the perturbation possibility to the Earth' orbit, gives it the required scriptural accuracy dictated by the relevant scriptures in Revelation and 2Esdras. Though being somewhat divinely encrypted as written, the unravelling of these has indeed become the utmost challenge for me in my life or for that matter even for any other human effort component brave enough to take it on.

How did I stumble upon this very thinking and realisation you may ask???

The only answer that I can still give you is that, it had to be the work of the Holy Spirit. If I have stated this in gross error, please do forgive me for this presumption. However, having given my sincerest apologies in advance, it could be the very case, this work does in the end identify who the second beast would really be or help to lead others through their own efforts to his identification at some point in time in the near or distant future. This book could awaken many I hope to take up the baton to continue seeking this conclusion for the benefit of all mankind if I have failed in doing so.

> **Even if this does turn out not to be the very case, my effort alone would still provide us with the understanding that we will at that precise period in time have the Biblical 360 Day Years which is also the 360 Solar Days too, and the real possibility to derive a series of cosmic related time values, that can be used to generate precisely the unique number that would sum total 666.**

From my personal perspective, this journey through these two combined books have given us additional information about ourselves; our very existence perhaps; and some possible data regarding our Solar Planetary System through the newly acquired interpretation of the relevant referenced Holy Scriptures. Also of the Universe at large, with regards to it' accelerating expansion as time progresses on, ever since the 'Big Bang-Inflation' had occurred.

These discoveries were of course realised not because I have some scientific evidence and scientific knowledge to all of these, but as mentioned that it were mostly based on the Holy Scriptures almost entirely, with a little help from the existing but quite basic scientific yet relevant information.

All of this now being timely revealed, as constructed through this very unique 'Cosmic Approach' in this book. Also, through this unique process of establishing the **'number'** of the second beast, I had realised the most significant spin off from this process including a few others too.

This is the specific time linkage of static Earth Time (I had previously explained, why I had termed it as being static) to the dynamic Alphonso Universe Expanding Time (AUET), which I had developed through 2Esdras' description of 'World History Time' (WHT-WFT). All of this has already been previously explained to you in very great detail.

In fact, you can say that the referenced Scriptures in 2Esdras (the last two verses of Chapter 13:57-58 and Chapter 14:1-13), is an extension or if you rather prefer, providing us with more 'Scriptural Information' to the history of the heavens and of the Earth, which **Genesis 2:4** was actually bringing to a conclusion in its narration. Please do read the Genesis Scriptures too. This revelation alone in my humblest opinion would hopefully contribute in enhancing its (2ESDRAS) authenticity and relevance, having been appointed by the 'Second Canon', and thereby being undeniably an integral part and parcel of the Deuterocanonical/Apocrypha Biblical Books.

> **The referenced Scriptures in 2ESDRAS were in a way dating the 'Creation Accounts' and the Universe' future to a more specific EZRA' WHT-WFT Period.**

As previously mentioned several times before and which is by now already obvious to you; this discovery, the **'number'** of the second beast, was based primarily on Scripture and some very basic astronomical facts as given to us. These were coupled together with some other new Earth-Sun-Moon relationship possibilities that I had offered in this book and with a fresh understanding of some of those Solar Planetary relationships that were previously established by Scientific Scholarship.

Let us once again examine the time-scales of Chart-B and Chart-C, though somewhat differently from the previous, as follows:

According to Chart-B:

> 1 EAR second change represents or takes 100,000 years to be accomplished. This is the time that it would take for a reduction or an increase of 1 second in the Earth' axis rotation period, whichever the case maybe at the time.

According to Chart-C:

> 1 WHT (AUET) second actually represents a time period of 925,000 years of World History-World Future time. Therefore, 1 Year according to WHT can be represented by 0.000001081 of a WHT second.

This follows that **1 Billion Years** of WHT, could similarly be represented by **1081 WHT (AUET) seconds**. I indicated this time equation for a particular reason, as this number **1081,** is so uncannily close to the number of divisions that the Babylonians divided their hour into i.e., into **1080** divisions per hour resolution.

The only explanation for this difference of one division that I can offer at this time is that as per my current proposition; it has something to do with the counting methodology of the divisions.

Probably, it is our counting of the value of the very first division in the hour being 0.000000000 - 0.000000001, as being significant which causes this difference of one. While in the other probable case i.e. the Babylonian', this initial division may have been ignored for their lack of understanding of the value for zero, when they divided their hour into 1080 divisions. This means perhaps the Babylonian had begun counting their divisions from 0.000000001 - 0.000000002 as being their very first division.

In fact besides offering the above explanation, I seriously do not know why we have this difference after all. For the actual matter could be that the Babylonian was right in their own way based on their cosmology and maybe I am also right in suggesting the above counting methodology, which may be the cause for this difference.

Now having said all of this, I accidentally discovered another possibility of how these 1080 divisions could have been developed by the Babylonian. However, I will describe this to you at the appropriate time, later, actually towards the very end of this Part Four.

If you do remember in Part Three of this Book, I made reference to these almost similar numbers, when I had indicated that the time scale 9.25:1 and it' other representations such as:-

72/144000	:	666/144000
500	:	4625
0.0005	:	0.004625

When divided one by the other for example:–
0.0005/0.004625 produces remarkably, **0.1081**.

This prompted me as you may recollect in making some important and probable linkages to the Babylonian System of calculating and keeping time. Also, both of these numbers, 1081 and 1080 represents time in seconds.

However, please take note, since the Babylonians divided the hour into 1080 divisions and we know that an hour equates to 3,600 seconds; this means 1080 divisions by right should also be equal to 3,600 seconds.

I also had read that the Babylonians had further sub-divided each of the 1080 divisions of an hour of time into 76 smaller sub-divisions of time measurement. I must confess that it really blows my mind just to think, "Why did the Babylonians need such infinitesimally small measurements of time in that day and age and how did they actually measure it"??? It is simply amazing. This also in turn provides us with the basis of understanding that they knew quite a lot about measuring time and due to their specific needs to do so with such accuracy.

The above smaller time sub-divisions also means that the Babylonians divided **an hour** into **82,080** equal **units** of time; each reading in parts of a second!!! This is truly amazing.

What was this accuracy for and in such ancient times? As a thought, it could be due to their astronomy. Even if we represent our **whole** day in units of seconds, it will amount to only 86,400 units of time. Whilst, they had in an averaged day of 24 hours - 1,969,920 units of time to contend with everyday!!! This is simply mind-boggling.

In fact amazingly and strikingly, we can also see this number of **1,969,920** similarly being reflected in the ancient 'Indian/Hindu Cosmological Time Cycles'. This is obtainable, when you multiply 5,472 Hindu divine years by 360; in order to convert these divine years into our Earth Years. This relationship is somewhat similar to when my extended 'Maya Long Count Calendar', had in common with the same 'Indian/Hindu Cosmological Time Cycles'.

Also, in continuing some more relationships with the 'Indian/Hindu Cosmological Time Cycles', in the same light, I had personally discovered, just before the conversion of Earth Time to the Alphonso Universe Expanding Time, we can easily see, each Yugapada being systematically reduced by 1,200 Divine Years. That is 4,800 Divine Years down to **3,600** Divine Years; then down to 2,400 and finally to 1,200 Divine Years. In fact the last pre-conversion Yugapada Period (Kaliyuga Period) does equate to 1,200 Divine Years. Amazingly, I personally discovered that If you were to divide 1,200; 2,400; 3,600 and 4,800 by our running in sequential order '360 Equation Series' totals or results, which means: 1,200 by 360 (360 X **1**); 2,400 by 720 (360 X **2**); 3,600 by 1080 (360 X **3**); 4,800 by 1440 (360 X **4**), you will indeed get **the value** 3.33 **Divine Years** for each of these simple arithmetic divisions!!!

This is truly amazing, for as you have just found out also, that the 3.33 is indeed also the value in *seconds* of One Division in an hour of Babylonian Time!!! It actually once again underscores that there is indeed some fundamental basic linkages with all of these ancient time keeping systems.

Besides the above Babylonian connection, you may have noticed from above, the ratio of 4, 3, 2, 1 being somewhat obtained, when I had **divided** each of the Yugapadas, which were systematically being reduced in the 'Indian/Hindu Cosmological Time Cycles' from 4,800 divine years to 3,600 then to 2,400 and finally 1,200 by my running in sequential order '360 Equation Series' totals.

This ratio of **4, 3, 2, 1** is also spoken about or mentioned in the English translation of the Sanskrit work, 'Aryabhatiya of Aryabhata', page 12 by Harvard Professor Walter Eugene Clark (1930). This translation work was published through, 'The University of Chicago Press', Chicago, Illinois. It also points out this 'ratio', to another work called the Suryasiddhanta, which may be worth exploring. This is shown in the extract taken of it as shown on the following page:

12 ĀRYABHAṬĪYA

3. There are 14 Manus in a day of Brahman [a *kalpa*], and 72 *yugas* constitute the period of a Manu. Since the beginning of this *kalpa* up to the Thursday of the Bhārata battle 6 Manus, 27 *yugas*, and 3 *yugapādas* have elapsed.

The word *yugapāda* seems to indicate that Āryabhaṭa divided the *yuga* into four equal quarters. There is no direct statement to this effect, but also there is no reference to the traditional method of dividing the *yuga* into four parts in the proportion of 4, 3, 2, and 1. Brahmagupta and later tradition ascribes to Āryabhaṭa the division of the *yuga* into four equal parts. For the traditional division see *Sūryasiddhānta* (I, 18–20, 22–23) and Brahmagupta (I, 7–8). For discussion of this and the supposed divisions of Āryabhaṭa see Fleet.[1] Compare III, 10, which gives data for the calculation of the date of the composition of Āryabhaṭa's treatise. It is clear that the fixed point was the beginning of Āryabhaṭa's fourth *yugapāda* (the later Kaliyuga) at the time of the great Bhārata battle in 3102 B.C.

Compare Brahmagupta (I, 9)

yugapādān āryabhaṭaś catvāri samāni kṛtayugādīni |
yad abhihitavān na teṣāṁ smṛtyuktasamānam ekam api ||

and XI, 4

āryabhaṭo yugapādāṁs trīn yātān āha kaliyugādau yat |
tasya kṛtāntar yasmāt svayugādyantau na tat tasmāt ||

(*op. cit.*, XVII [1926], 60–74). The *Pañcasiddhāntikā* also (XV, 20), "Āryabhaṭa maintains that the beginning of the day is to be reckoned from midnight at Laṅkā; and the same teacher again says that the day begins from sunrise at Laṅkā," ascribes the two theories to one Āryabhaṭa.

[1] *Op. cit.*, 1911, pp. 111, 486.

Since there were some 'Time Relationships' that I had also been able to establish with the **Maya**, as previously shown, I thought could there also be some more further relationship again through the relevant Holy Scriptures with how the Babylonians had marked their time. Some of these Babylonian 'Time Facts' were referenced from the Encyclopaedia Britannica, under the heading of the **Jewish Calendar** and also some others which were developed in the process of writing this book, which you may have come across and noticed earlier.

It is quite obvious, the Babylonians and/or the peoples from whom they had inherited their 'Time System', if that were indeed the case was also derived from the Cosmos. This is indeed the common source for all of our 'Time Systems', with the exception of the 'atomic second', which is actually independent of the cosmic motions of the 'time operatives' i.e. the Sun, the Earth and the Moon.

> You will also come to realize just as I had discovered that the **AUET Second** being on a very much larger time scale than the atomic time-keeping-second, is indeed the ultimate 'Cosmic Example' of time progression, being also **completely independent** of our triune time controlling operatives. Yet despite this, at the same time, can be timed according to a specific time ratio scale, which I have already had developed and should be well known to you by now, is for your convenience once again shown as below. This is actually built upon the time kept by our own three local time controlling operatives i.e., the Sun, the Earth and the Moon.

As a matter of record:

Chart-B : Chart-C

1 second speed change in the EAR Period is related to 1 second of Universe expansion in the Alphonso' 12th Phase Level of Universe expansion through the time scale ratio i.e. being 9.25 times the latter as shown below.

This is:
100,000 Years X 9.25 = 925,000 Years

Or our familiar
9.25 : 1

Again we see the same ratio of 9.25:1, but using **years** as the referenced value this time round being established here. In the previous ratio scale of 9.25:1, it was representing the both same Charts with regards to the equating of their respective **'Number of Divisions'**.

That is:

$$500 \times 9.25 : 4625 \times 1$$

The other common factor binding the two time zones would then be for each 'Part of a Period' of time in both Charts to being represented by a third party representation. In this case, it would be to being timed by our time clocks. This obviously then becomes the default common time system for these two time zones. As an example, our time clock measures each 'Part of a WHT Period', precisely to **12 WHT Minutes or 12 AUET MINUTES.**

Based with this knowledge, we can now convert or link the Earth Time and the consistent progress of the Earth' development towards it' '360 Day Years', as shown by Chart-B into WHT (AUET) terms as shown on Chart-C. This of course can only be accomplished with the proper understanding of the expanding and accelerating Universe, through the 'World History Time' of 2Esdras and it' relationship to Earth Time. All of this in fact had already been established in great detail, as previously, in this book.

With this understanding, we now can also finally proceed with the construction of the **'number'** of the second beast as follows:

Let us begin with our previously calculated **126,000,000 ET years.** This is the precise period of time that I had calculated, based on the scientific given data of 1/1000 second every 100 years EAR speed change rate that would take the Earth to have it' axial axis rotational speed to be progressively reduced by an additional 21 EAR Minutes. This was computed as previously from the **RBP18:24:12(A)**, which would give us our first 360 Earth Days Orbital Years at **RBP18:24:33**.

This would obviously be closely and quite immediately be also associated with our '360 Solar Day Years'. This we have already established in Book One and can be reviewed on Chart-B.

Now, we also know that on Chart-C:

> 1 WHT Year is represented by 0.000001081 WHT second. This 1 WHT Year would be the same amount of time that our Earth Year also represents in Earth Time terms.

> **With the above understanding, this '0.000001081' is then indeed the conversion factor that we need to use when converting Earth Time into WHT (AUET).**

We can convert this specific Earth Time period of 126,000,000 ET years as shown on Chart B, which was obtained through the previous calculations, onto this Chart-C. This specifically plots out the World History Time (AUET), by using the above conversion factor. We can directly convert this Earth Time Period of 126,000,000 ET years or for that matter any other Earth Time period into WHT (AUET), without losing it' original Earth Time value.

> This is possible because there is no change in the value of time in itself. In other words, the 126,000,000 ET years is still 126,000,000 ET years although converted onto the scale of the AUET.

> Also remember, that 'Earth Time' in terms of a year, is only concerned with the number of Earth Axis Rotations that the Earth actually takes to complete an orbit around the Sun, at any particular period in it' history

We can now proceed to convert this Earth Time period (ET) into WHT (AUET) Seconds as follows:

126,000,000 ET years X 0.000001081 = 136.206 WHT SECONDS

> This is indeed our **17th Milestone Achievement, which** is absolutely necessary for our continued and successful progress in this cosmic construction and the subsequent unveiling of the **'number'** of the second beast.

It is important for you to understand that in other words, the 21 EAR minutes of time reduction in the Earth' rotation as per it' axial axis, as calculated from the RBP18:24:12(A) (when the EAR was 24.20 hours/day); progressively reduces the number of Earth Axis Rotations per orbit, till we do obtain the 360 number of Earth Axis Rotations that is possible in this 126,000,000 years time period. This period ends at the RBP18:24:33, when the EAR would be 24.55 hours/day.

> In fact, it will be the very first time that it would occur in our Biblical Human History-Future.

This 'Cosmic Process' indeed lengthens the day even more then what it was at RBP18:24:12(A). This has already been previously explained to you in much greater detail. Therefore, we are able for these 'Earth Axis Rotational Speed Changes', to use this above newly established conversion factor, to represent it in World History Time terms.

> You must however, take very careful note of the actual time period or value that each WHT/AUET second represents, which is of course being 925,000 ET years.

In the above particular 'Earth Axis Rotational Speed Change', i.e. 126,000,000 ET years, this conversion can be read out on our time clocks, to be taking:

136.206 AUET SECONDS in the Alphonso' 12th PHASE LEVEL of Universe expansion.

> This 12th Phase Level as you already know, had it' 11 previous Phase Levels of Universe expansion consolidated/collapsed prior to the beginning of this 12th AUET Phase Level, which in it' turn has also become the AUET PHASE LEVEL which is the exact same time period as described by the 12 Periods of Ezra. In other words it is one and the same.

> Thereby, this entire time period consolidation, as now having been registered in UET and recorded as such, then it' First Period becomes the very First Ezra' Period of WHT-WFT. This indeed had begun in the 4,320,000,000th year. Similarly, all the 10 and ½ Ezra' Periods that have already been expired become the 10 and a half AUET Periods. Finally, the remaining Ezra' 1 and a ½ Period will become the remaining periods in the 12th AUET Phase Level. They are not running in parallel, but it is one and the same.

This is the reason why, I am able to use our own Earth Time Clocks, as the third party time-keeping device, to register this converted Earth Time into WHT by employing this very important and cosmically significant time ratio scale of 9.25:1.

We now need to place this very same **136.206 WHT SECONDS** into it' appropriate Minutes and Seconds time placing. This is done not just so that we can have it easily read in the normal time measurement reading format, but that it has indeed a very definite and defining reason for me having to do so. Therefore, this reads as follows:

2 MINUTES 16.206 WHT SECONDS

I found out in the process of writing this book that it is acutely critical that we get the WHT equivalent of 126,000,000 ET years, expressed as 2 Minutes 16.206 WHT Seconds, precisely. Even the most minute infinitesimal variation to this precise cosmically derived duration, would end in utter failure, without us ever achieving our ultimate objective of securing the number or rather to be more specific the proposed **'birthday date number identity'** of the second beast, which is described in it' biblical sum total form of **666**.

Yes, the number that will sum to **666** and which is constructed through this remarkable cosmic approach could indeed be the very birth date involving date/month/year, and etc., for this second beast being described in the Biblical Book of Revelation, Chapter 13.

This entire journey through these two books, which I have packaged as one for your very convenience, was to arrive at this very important stage. This is indeed to get this time conversion absolutely and precisely correct; converting from our own 'Local Earth Time Zone' to the overall controlling 'Master Universe Time Cosmic Clock', of the expanding Universe. This is so, that we would ultimately obtain for ourselves the greatly complex assumed 'birthday date of the second beast'. Hopefully, this would be the case, so that we could or rather those who would be living at that future time, possibly be able to ascertain, who the second beast would really be. Subsequently, exposing him to the world at large and as importantly, being timely at that too.

> This is greatly and very significantly important, so that, before all is lost at that future time, which in an accumulating evil process, had begun from Day One. This being that very day, when Adam and Eve were so easily and blindly duped, into such unthinkable acts of disobedience AGAINST GOD. This disobedience directly coerced by Satan was committed when they took off the fruit of the tree of knowledge of good and evil. This fruit was one of the two that GOD had instructed them i.e., they were forbidden to eat. This disobedience as mentioned inevitably was indeed directly against our LORD GOD Almighty. However, as the scriptures reveal in the New Testament, their future generations, would be given GODLY and timely provision of grace. This would be to GODLY being able to take the necessary rallying action worldwide, to be engaged against this last concerted stand of evil at that future time, being possibly our Biblical Armageddon.

> For your information, if you do not already know, this second beast being under the full control of Satan is in fact a man!!!

> This cosmic constructed sum total number, which was quite clinically designed as we progressively find out, though with such great complexity in-built into it by our CREATOR GOD HIMSELF, but yet, is set within the grasp of our **human understanding,** as is foretold in REV 13:18.

This human understanding element needed in resolving and to obtaining in this case the cosmic constructed number becoming possible or evident, was indeed only through the constant promptings and the spiritual guidance of the Holy Spirit (our GOD HELPER). GOD wanting to ultimately salvage the obedient remnants of mankind from the very last stronghold clutches of the evil one and his numerous willing cohorts.

Well anyway, this specific Earth Axis Rotation speed change time period of 126,000,000 years, in converting to the AUET being exactly

136.206 AUET SECONDS,

by engaging the appropriate conversion factor being **0.000001081**, is just one of it' many applications. Another important application would be in relation to travel and weather forecasting, and in fact there are several other applications too.

You also may already know that there are many other applications and purposes, similarly, which have made it absolutely necessary, to have agreed upon an 'International or World Time'.

In somewhat the same light, this means the master control time or master control clock, **for all that is in the Universe** is indeed the Universe itself. This may be quite ambitious to think of it as such, but at the moment there is probably no other in the offering. I have called this time keeping phenomenon, simply as the Alphonso' Universe Expanding Time or AUET for short. Or if you prefer the name by which our Scriptures in 2Esdras called it, then it would be, World History Time. I personally prefer using AUET, since for most of us, the word 'World' today refers to only our Planet Earth and the word 'Universe' in our language mind bank, incorporates the overall everything in our Universe Space.

So, if we the 'Human Race' were in fact first located or some of us are relocated to say, Planet Mars; then the local time on Planet Mars will have to be calculated based on it' relationship to our Sun. This will therefore be 'Martian Time' for those who are residing there. However, the 'Master Control Common Time' will still be according to **the AUET**, even for the **'Earthling Martians'**. This is somewhat comparable in a way to converting our own local time to 'International time'. This was done generally for the purpose of knowing, what is the time as presently or even later or even was in the past, as the case maybe, over at another location on Earth.

However, you must take note that we need to recalculate the relationship of Martian Time to **the AUET.** This means we need to calculate out the appropriate and correct **conversion factor,** to calculate out the correct AUET Martian Time before hand, in order to take the second step that would be to relate it to our Earth time accordingly.

We have to make reference to the **AUET,** so that, we on Earth and those on Mars can have our both times synchronized to a common time reference. This would enable us to do many things accurately between our two planetary communities. This is besides being able to tell what is the time immediately on any location on Mars, in regards to our own local Earth Time or as the case maybe, vice versa.

We would be able to do this also, for any other location, in our Solar Planetary System. Of course you can appreciate that it will really get very technical and very complicated, as we go further and further out into different universe time zones.

These common time based references to the **AUET** would in my humble opinion, come surely as a necessity and in greater use one day in our distant future. This would be when Space exploration and Space travel become a definite reality between human communities here on Earth and human based colonies located in other places in the great vastness of the Universe Space or at least within our very own galaxy or at the very least in the beginning, within our very own Solar Planetary System. This would essentially be a step by step, process by process human endeavour.

I believe that as Man through his technology, advanced innovation, creative intelligence and above all for the future survival of the human race (long before the post Sun era); will modify and engineer other planetary environments to become 'human friendly' if not even here on Planet Earth. Even fortifying and strengthening the entire human anatomy from every conceivable aspect of it, which would be extremely necessary for us to withstand and to stay alive successfully in other harsher planetary environments.

This would be certainly achievable, as I presently observe it, through the tremendous advancements seen even as currently, especially in the medical sciences. This being actually coupled together with the very fast pace biological-electro-mechanical-digital engineered body part enhancements and also the inventing of very highly specialised medical applicable materials, which together, would one day be used in replacing or assisting our internal organs, blood vessels, even to modify and to create super oxygenated enhanced artificial blood itself.

Not limiting to this only, but to also enhancing sight and hearing and the fitting of our limbs with highly specialised attachments and etc.

All of which would be to make us able to manage well in these harsher environments besides the ability to walk & run faster, jump higher and to go even much further in distances, beating all world records as currently being held by just only a few well trained and talented people. This would be at that time achievable even here on Earth by any 'specially assisted' human being and this common enhanced human ability too, would be also equally important at some future time in our own environment here on Earth.

All of these advancements would enhance the human race in several aspects; making us more resilient, much stronger, even disease free possibly, and perhaps the ability to regenerate damaged parts; making those future generations to live longer than we currently do. Perhaps even able to have really much longer lives, which would be probably very essential, when travelling into outer space, from one distant human colony to another, or even for more longer extended Space exploration missions. They probably could live much longer lives with all of these advanced medical improvements and bio-tech enhancements, just as those early progenitors and early peoples of the ancient Old Testament days, were so blessed to live for hundreds of years. The longest living progenitor, Patriarch Methuselah, biblically recorded as being **969 years old** at the time when he had died!!! – Genesis 5:27 confirms.

These people in the future will need to rely on **AUET** clocks or even any other time system clocks that may be developed for many related and useful purposes. It certainly would become a sheer necessity to do so.

Please do not think that my propositions above are or were influenced by that once globally popular TV show – Startrek (which has made yet another comeback) and it' famous Starship, The Enterprise, or even those previous popular space cartoons. For I am of the expressed opinion, colonising other possible 'sites' other than this First Human Base Planet Earth which had commenced it all with GOD creating Adam and then Eve would happen in the natural course of Mankind' future progress. Our very future survival could depend on it.

Coming back to our focus:

For our LORD God Almighty to have even warned us of this major impending attack on Mankind, by Satan, invoking this evil strategy (as the Book of Revelation reveals so clearly to us); this should be more than enough to alert us to the very seriousness of this most destructive and final assault that will be aggressively waged by Satan on all Mankind. Probably, this could be Satan' 'mother of all battles and wars', as directed indirectly against our LORD God ALMIGHTY through all mankind.

Please pay very careful attention now, for these are truly very important moments. For now comes the time to unveil to you and my fellow man, the actual **'number'** of the second beast that sum totals **666** through this very unique cosmic approach for the very first time ever.

This has always been an important **'Open Divine Commission'** to **any** who may have acquired the understanding (i.e. the knowledge & the wisdom), to be able to take up this awesome and divinely prepared challenge, as written and revealed in the Biblical Scriptures – REV 13:18 confirms. For GOD ALMIGHTY had provided it as a '**Universal Warning**' for all time (past, present and the future to come), of the impending dangers to our very precious salvation, which would ultimately ensure our safe and guaranteed entry into the Kingdom of Heaven to enjoy our eternal life together with the rest of the heavenlies.

This discovery, I sincerely and prayerfully hope, would bring a fresh awareness to us all, that Satan is not a figment of the imagination in biblical proportions, but indeed real and dangerous to our individual eternal future; yours and mine too.

Through the relevant Scriptures, I had discovered as already mentioned that the construction of the **'number'** is based on the Cosmos and therefore on it' cosmology. This is in furtherance with a direct relationship, relating to our Solar System. More directly relating to the triune solar party being the Sun, the Earth and of course it' sole satellite, the Moon. This is in the overall context of the Universe' expansion, which itself is progressing in 'Real Time' terms, as currently.

This particular AUET Period of **136.206 AUET SECONDS** is the AUET, as converted from the corresponding Earth Time of 126,000,000 years. It also occurs in this particular and probably the most important 'EAR Oscillation Cycle' to date, being the:

18th EAR Oscillation Cycle

It can be similarly equated to a specific cosmic solar event. In this case, it is the

'birth of the 360 Day Years',

in this biblical human history-future period. In other words, this would be the very first time ever that it would take place in our Human Biblical era. This is of paramount importance for your correct understanding in the process of establishing and constructing the **'number'** of the second beast.

For some compelling reasons, I began to construct 'time measurement headings' that you will read as below, in the graduated time measurement manner, as described herein.

MINUTES   SECONDS   TENTHS   HUNDREDTHS   THOUSANDTHS

I placed this specific AUET measurement of 136.206 AUET SECONDS, which I had earlier converted back into easy clock time reading; as being **2 Minutes 16.206 AUET SECONDS** as follows:

MINUTES	SECONDS	TENTHS	HUNDREDTHS	THOUSANDTHS
2	16	2	0	6

Following this time classification breakdown, I then advanced or rather re-tracked this time breakdown further backward into the AUET. Once again guided by the **HOLY SPIRIT,** to put in the next important time measurement period into this cosmic construction.

This was the time measurement period that we had much earlier referenced and had obtained according to the 2Esdras 14:9-11 Scriptures, which is the 10th Period of WHT, which had already arrived.

WHT PERIOD	MINUTES	SECONDS	TENTHS	HUNDREDTHS	THOUSANDTHS
10th	2	16	2	0	6

With this now as presented above, I just went on as per Rev 13:18 had required and added all of these numbers together as follows:

WHT PERIOD	MINUTES	SECONDS	TENTHS	HUNDREDTHS	THOUSANDTHS		
10th	2	16	2	0	6	=	36

After thinking of how should I progress or regress this further to achieve what we had set out to accomplish, I realised that if this is emerging into a specific time sequence measurement reading, then I must include the current 18th Earth Axis Rotation Oscillation Cycle into it now as follows:

Current EAR Oscillation Cycle	:	18th
WHT-PERIOD	:	10th
AUET MINUTES	:	2
AUET SECONDS	:	16
AUET TENTHS	:	2
AUET HUNDREDTHS	:	0
AUET THOUSANDTHS	:	6
		54

The next time sequence measurement reading to be slotted in came quite easily to me. This I quickly realised obviously needed to be included, though being of the 'hidden time structures'. These are the consolidated/time meshed 11 AUET Phase Levels + 1. The + 1, being the very last Alphonso' 12th PHASE LEVEL, which is now currently in progress. So, the expanding time sequence measurement reading does appropriately continue as follows:

Current Alphonso' Phase Level of Universe Expansion	: 12th
Current EAR Oscillation Cycle	: 18th
WHT-PERIOD	: 10th
AUET MINUTES	: 2
AUET SECONDS	: 16
AUET TENTHS	: 2
AUET HUNDREDTHS	: 0
AUET THOUSANDTHS	: 6
	66

You can most definitely and obviously take notice that the basic cosmic generated sum total number of **66** has now finally emerged. This looks very encouraging, as you already know, that the biblical sum total of the second beast' number is indeed **666**.

We now obviously need to resolve the further needed 600. All we need to do now is to find out all the appropriate time measurement slots to be added to the above expanding time sequence. Although, this seems to be looking relatively easy now, however, you need to take careful note that all of these 'new additions' should be part and parcel of this unique **'cosmic time sequence approach'**.

Something very interesting and which is also very relevant that I would like to share with you at this timely juncture, is that the Holy Bible without the Deuterocanonical/Apocrypha Biblical Books being included in the mainstream of the Holy Bible; that means to be considering only the First Canon Biblical Books, then it would contain exactly **66 Biblical Books.** This of course is already common knowledge but nevertheless wanted to share this with you just the same.

> **Furthermore, the Book of Revelation is indeed remarkably the 66th book in this biblical arrangement.**

Isn't this something to wonder about this strange or rather remarkable coincidence, if you prefer. As you already know, this is the same Biblical Book which contains the infamous sum total number **666** being indeed the **'sum total number'** of the second beast, who is a man – REV 13: 18 confirms.

> However, one thing is absolutely certain in my mind, i.e. without the Deuterocanonical/Apocrypha Biblical Books, and for our intents and purposes, specifically the 2ESDRAS Biblical Book; this entire work by no means would have been possible at all.

This underpins that without the 2ESDRAS Apocryphal Biblical Book, I would not have been able to reveal the entire workings nor the processes for the cosmic construction of the required **'number'** of the second beast. Neither the earlier effort of my establishing the actual commencement for the Biblical 360 Earth Day Years/**360 Solar Day Years** for the first time ever in our Human Biblical History-Future. I just cannot stress this enough to you.

Therefore, coming back to the removal of the Apocryphal books from most of the available Holy Bible translations as we have presently, in my personal opinion, was another way for Satan to cut up GOD' Word, so that his **'number'** (i.e. of the second beast) that would ultimately identify him to the world, would not be revealed but concealed until it is too late for us to take any measure of retaliation; whether it is secular in nature or through spiritual means or a good combination of both.

This, Satan has indeed already accomplished quite successfully to some damaging extent, by creating doubts on the canonizing of the Biblical Deuterocanonical/Apocrypha Books. This eventually had resulted for these Biblical Books to have been set aside from certain Bible translations, but not from the Roman Catholic translations – i.e. the Vulgate, the Jerusalem Bible and which is also maintained as such in more modern Catholic Bibles too. Thank God, they still do maintain these intact even as currently.

> Sadly and unfortunately though, even baffling indeed, how was it possible for the Protestant, being the other members of the body of Jesus Christ, whom have identified themselves more so with the Holy Bible than generally the Roman Catholic has, well at least in the past, and yet have indeed allowed this very thing to happen to the expressed and divinely inspired written word of GOD.

Satan, as we have biblically come to know of him, had twisted the very truth of GOD' **spoken Words** to Adam and Eve – Gen 2 & 3 confirm. Through this cunning ploy, both Adam & Eve were simply duped hook, line and sinker, into believing Satan' own evil laced twisted version of GOD' spoken word.

Through this very strategy, Satan had easily executed the immediate i.e. pertaining to Adam & Eve' destruction to a point and subsequently the **consequent downfall of all Mankind to come**, due to this single disobedience with this one well planned and timely attack!!!

If anything could be said in the defence of Adam & Eve, then it would be obviously their being unobtrusively naive to this devastatingly evil satanic ploy, as they were living in just pure innocence of anything evil and of evil doings. For as you may very well know, they both had lacked in this very knowledge of good and evil doing from the very beginning of their creation. For that matter having any awareness of these, to desire these in any measure at all, unlike the ex-angels who were in Lucifer's cohort; who had acted upon their own desires with their ring leader Lucifer himself, which had ultimately triggered their eventual fall from grace.

Both Adam and Eve, having no purpose for it whatsoever, which was probably GOD' plan for all of us too after the debacle in the heavens; until Satan (Lucifer) came onto the Earth scene at the very beginning, into their very midst, and destroyed all of this GODLY peace that the Eden garden tranquillity had to offer them; as they both succumbed to his satanic ploy quite uneventfully.

As it is biblically well known, Eve first then through Eve, Adam, were foolishly **duped** into being **disobedient** to GOD' specific **'forbidding'** command. In the same light, we can see this similar disobedience but not through ignorance but willfully being acted upon, being strikingly so common amongst us, even as of now, as we live from day to day, committing one sin to another and continuing unashamedly at that.

Once this was accomplished by Satan, the forces of good and evil, as a chain of events, were literally released to take hold over the 'minds and hearts of men', even our very souls. Simultaneously, this had caused the sad closing of the 'Gates of Heaven' to all of us, beginning with the very FIRST BIBLICAL HUMAN GENERATION - Adam and Eve themselves. It also had left us all with a resident sin (commonly referred to by the Roman Catholic teaching as the 'Original Sin') that was inherited from their disobedience - ROM 5:12; 19 confirms.

> This was in my most humble opinion, indeed the saddest day ever that we can possibly record in the history of Mankind and the World; the day Satan was successful in bringing the complete downfall of Mankind with just one stroke of such evil satanic genius.

Humanity was changed forever, to say the least since then, for Satan had hijacked GOD' very own 'PERSONAL PLAN' for all Mankind and had literally destroyed it or rather had been successful in derailing it for a duration.

GOD eventually through HIS mercy, grace and love for us all then renewed, reinstated, and got our special relationship well back onto the tracks with HIM and the Heavens. This renewed 'relationship', had also brought with it all the 'Perks of Salvation', as were made possible through our LORD and Saviour Jesus Christ, the Messiah, being 'GOD the SON', at the very CROSS through HIS subsequent resurrection on the third day of HIS crucifixion.

We have been well informed of these GODLY glimpses of **Jesus Christ being man and yet being GOD also,** several times throughout the Old Testament prophesies, also through the Gospels of the New Testament, and specifically through the Biblical Book of ACTS.

This is what sets **HIM** so uniquely apart from us all. Taking into consideration also, of **HIS most miraculous birth** that does inevitably sets the very beginning to this human demarcation difference between **HIM** and any of us.

Sadly though, this greatest and most unique of 'human' birth event, being probably never to be ever repeated again, had been quite oblivious to almost all but just a handful selected few. It would have been just so awesome to be most privileged to have lived knowingly of HIM during **HIS** short time here on Earth. This in fact was scripturally evident in the case of Simeon – Luke 2:25-35 confirms, and Anna, a prophetess (84 years old at the time when Jesus Christ was born) both of whom had lived to see and acknowledge HIM – read Luke 2:36-38.

In other words, we must realise there was a great difference between **JESUS CHRIST being human** and us, for whilst **JESUS** was in this human form, JESUS was always divine in **HIS** dual nature. Less we so easily forget, HE **is** GOD; **was** and **will continue** to be so even when JESUS had put on this human form for a GOD purpose. Yet only on occasion whilst in this human form did GOD invoke HIS divine nature for our specific purposes. These were revealed several times throughout the New Testament. Some of these though not limiting was that Jesus Christ had changed water into the highest quality wine possible ever for all time and in an instant too, during the 'Wedding at Cana'.

HE had calmed the frightening and overwhelming storm, whilst they (HE being amongst **seasoned fishermen** at the time) were out at sea.

HE walked on water, actually the Sea of Galilee, when it was most tempestuous at that material time.

HE had made the many that were lame from birth to walk **immediately**, as HE willed it, for the very first time in their lives.

HE cured many of the lepers in that region, completely.

HE made the blind from birth to see for the very first time ever in their lives.

HE had set demon possessed individuals free of them once and for all, so that, they could resume their very lives in blissful peace.

HE cured the sick and the dying.

HE commanded Dead Man (Lazarus) to rise up and ordered him to come out from his tomb, though dead and bound in burial grave clothes, to live again after four days of death!!!

HE forgave with such grace, mercy and GODLY love, at times even when not having been asked to do so. Well able to do this because............**HE is GOD.**

Also, with an overflowing abundance, rewarded those who were so very faithfully generous, even to have given all that they had at that material time; without even ever holding back anything for their own survival as they were willing to share in the same fate that was awaiting their needy recipient/s. This they did as we learn from the Scriptures, not by any form of coercion, or any psychological manipulation, tactic or fear having been instilled, but through their very own sense of giving, goodness and love.

Not limiting to all of the above, we also do see these GOD glimpses through so many other scriptural events and even more stranger biblical circumstances, despite of serious misgivings and misunderstanding of who HE really is, was, and shall be forever and ever.

For nowadays, it seems quite in common place for people from many walks of life, even from 'Men of GOD' to just any of us ordinary folks, to associate Jesus Christ as being no different from us, in the aspect or perspective of HIS 'humanness'.

Although, it is obviously an attempt, to bring GOD Jesus Christ as close as our human intellect permits to being one of us exactly in the humanness aspect; never should we just simply confuse ourselves that we human beings are of any equality to HIM at any level and under any circumstance whilst HE was in this earthly body.

> *IMMANUEL - JESUS CHRIST, our LORD and SAVIOUR, GOD THE SON was quite definitely not living here amongst us for the mere 'Human Experience'. He was tasked with an higher responsibility. AMEN*

Coming back into focus:

The Book of Revelation provides for all mankind, a divinely designed **red alert** warning. Just like we do similarly come to know, as in the first few Chapters of Genesis - when Adam & Eve were commanded by our LORD GOD ALMIGHTY not only about not eating of it, but also of **not even touching** the fruit of the tree being the tree of knowledge of good and evil – GEN 3:1-5 refers. We are now, through this Book of Revelation, somewhat being similarly warned by GOD ALMIGHTY to take care that Satan will be and is indeed making another stronger and better strategized attempt at destroying Mankind once and for all.

Satan is preparing to rob us of our very **Salvation,** being the key with which we have been given the very opportunity to have entry access when we individually qualify to enter the very Kingdom of Heaven. This as you may already know was made possible through the ultimate and the highest price of redemption ever possible for all time, having been paid for us all, through Jesus Christ on the Cross, being our Lord and Saviour. HE being GOD HIMSELF had set us free from the very wages of sin.

This only **'GOD who became Man'** - Jesus Christ, could possibly do as the situation had required; which is another insurmountable feat that sets apart **'HIS Humanness'** from all of us others.

In this impending Apocalypse to come, GOD is giving us some help in identifying for us the manner in which Satan will be coming to do this, very thing – REV 13 refers.

> I am also convinced, the fact that Satan exists as such although being at one time an highly anointed angel of importance in the Heavenly realm before his fall together with his agreeing cohort, confirms my personal belief that even when we earthly die, we will still possibly continue having our individual freewill for all eternity. As an assumption and weighed opinion; our GOD ALMIGHTY would not have it any other way.

This thinking is also inevitably based on the possible reason, of why and how, Lucifer (Satan) and the other fallen angels could do what they did to cause their eventual casting out from the very Kingdom of GOD itself. Then later out of possible rage and frustration for this sending out, through their continuing evilness began engaging in relentless efforts to destroying us, being successful at first with Adam and Eve which has to be their evil way of indirectly getting at GOD.

This is not the very first time that GOD had been doing this very thing i.e. giving help through divine intervention, for we can read from the very Scriptures of the Old Testament; where GOD ALMIGHTY had divinely intervened several times to level the field against the enemies of the Israelites as a people group, and even on an individual basis too as evident in both the linked Testaments

LORD GOD ALMIGHTY, please forgive me and always help me, I pray, to stay completely focused on YOU and on what the Cross through YOU had accomplished for me personally. For YOU, amongst all the other things that YOU have done so graciously for us; first loved us and died for us whilst we were yet still sinners. I pray that I will not stray from YOU ever, ever again. Holy Spirit, please be always my guide, my protector and my deliverer through my every weakness and every temptation that does come my way. Thank YOU GOD THE FATHER, GOD THE SON and GOD THE HOLY SPIRIT. Amen.

Coming back to our cosmic construction of the 'number' of the second beast:

The next step came almost naturally and all at one go. As you already would know, that the particular WHT period which was converted earlier, is indeed when the Earth for the very first time would actually have 360 Earth Days-Orbital Years and also quite obviously the 360 Solar Day Years too.

It is as if to strongly suggest that the second beast (the man) would be born on this very day in the future when the Earth experiences for the very first time in our **Biblical Human History**, a 360 Days Year. This could indeed be **his birthday** and if you do recollect, I stated earlier in Part One of Book One; that your birth date, also would become your natural 'number', identifying you from the rest, besides the name that was given to you.

> Therefore, this specific date possibly becomes the second beast' birth date and naturally also his 'number'.

However, another way to be looking at it from a completely different perspective, despite my consistent emphasising of the above concept, understanding and proposition; would be that the number which is being 'cosmic constructed' here, could be the very number that would identify the second beast at any time conveniently possible to him. This meaning that the second beast could actually exist at any time before this next 360 Day Years time period could ever be realized. This is by simply assuming this number to be his very own, at any time convenient to him.

Well, this is what I thought could be the case, but please do read on and you will find out something very interesting just as I had as I progressed on with this specific idea on the following page with regards to the scriptural fact as revealed in REV 13:18.

Meanwhile, in this possibly new scenario offering, the to be completed constructed cosmic related number in this PART FOUR, is quite definitely not related to my previous proposed possibility of it being referring to a birth date of an individual, but a unique number nevertheless. For it reveals to us amongst a few other cosmic events, when our Planet Earth for the very first time in our human biblical history and future, would be having the 360 Day Years period again. Subsequently, I would also be using it directly in the construction of this number that would sum total the biblical 666. In this very sense, it could also be referring to a birth date not of an individual though, but of the cyclic recurring 360 Day Years period, to be specific, every 252 million years. The very next 360 Day Years Period is commonly referred to by us Christians as being the 'Prophetic Years'.

At this stage of this cosmic construction number development, I must emphasise, that I now do agree to abandon this idea of linking Satan to become operative through the second beast at that specific future time only instead of it now being at anytime, as just suggested above.

> So in this new scenario offering, the second beast, would be using this cosmic constructed number that uniquely and biblically sum totals to 666, and thereby, inevitably identifying himself with it, just as REV 13:18 had revealed in it' prophecy.

Now be ready for the very interesting scriptural fact that I had missed when applying the REV 13:18 Holy Scripture.

This as being suggested here, Satan could do at anytime, but within obvious time limits, which being only known as such by GOD ALMIGHTY.

However, (now here it is) not being able to choose any other number but the number as such that was assigned to him (i.e. for the second beast), it becoming his number for this very purpose, as divinely appointed by GOD ALMIGHTY.

So, in this divine way, GOD ALMIGHTY is yet once again levelling the field for us and this time round it is against Satan himself.

> One thing is for certain, in conclusion being that, the second beast would be scripturally identified by a **divinely assigned number**, which uniquely sum totals to 666. Whether it would be this very 'cosmic constructed' number that I am attempting to put together in this book, which for me is quite definitely fixed by GODLY design into the cosmos and thereby sets it uniquely apart from any other is left to be seen.

> However, could I be wrong in this cosmic number construction? Certainly I could be, but for it to be proven either way, we need to wait and see the final outcome. Well at least for those of us who would be living in the time period when Satan does decide to act, will know for a fact. Until then, I can only propose that the cosmic constructed number as being the **divinely assigned number** which Satan has to use in the identifying of his second beast for the whole world to be made aware of; the same that whoever eventually follows them will have to be marked with as such.

All of this has been foretold in this Revelation 13:18 prophecy.

Hallelujah, Praise be to GOD

Please do study the REV 13:18 Holy Scripture and discover for yourself, whether my understanding of this scriptural revelation as above, is indeed correct or otherwise.

Satan nor any individual for that matter cannot get away from GOD' own 'Prophetic Announcements', as quite evident through that which had been foretold and have come to pass throughout the entire Holy Scriptures. This is the very testimony of it coming to pass. Satan may try to twist it and mask it for his own evil purposes but this time he would not be able to evade this prophecy which leads to his final destiny.

We must surely acknowledge that all the Biblical Scriptures in the Holy Bible do belong to GOD ALMIGHTY, being it' author and finisher. Thereby, the Biblical Scripture, which has foretold the fate of Satan and his cohorts, would be prophetically carried out to the letter when the time comes. This is exactly what is meant of the term 'Prophecy', which is indeed a foretelling of what is going to happen and will happen accordingly and in this particular case despite of any measures that Satan or any individual may employ or engage cannot change it' divinely time appointed destiny. This is unlike what 'fortune telling' is for those who are familiar with this practice. Only GOD ALMIGHTY HIMSELF can change it for HIS own GOD reason.

As far as I know it, this occurred only once or twice in the Holy Bible when GOD extended the life of king Hezekiah for a further fifteen years – 2Kings Chapter 20 refers, despite being prophesied to by Prophet Isaiah that he was going to die quite soon and that he should get his house well in order.

Just taking a few moments here to make a point:

Now, I would like to make one thing clear, that is, I definitely do not have all the answers but only attempting to with this regards through these two books of mine to offer the very possibility for obtaining this cosmic constructed number that sum totals 666. Only time and circumstance could tell if this is indeed the number of the second beast or perhaps would motivate someone else to take up this similar commission to offer another possibility or possibilities. Yet again, time and circumstance could only tell us, whether this other is indeed the correct number after all.

So, coming back into focus, to continue revealing the number:

Thinking about it over and over again, it suddenly dawned on me, that the headings of the graduated time sequence as being gradually obtained and quite obviously, which were being parts of a particular time measure, could be further enlarged to incorporate more time slots related to the cosmos.

I also knew, that it would be pointless to progress the time measure headings into smaller units of time measure, since the available time period was already fixed by all the previous calculations, which had culminated precisely at:

2 MINUTES AND 16.206 AUET SECONDS

So, this would make it rather impossible to move any further into that direction. Similarly, we cannot progress into larger periods of time than the Alphonso' 12th Phase Level of Universe expansion, as it is the largest parcel of time currently known to us biblically. So the only option was to move into intermediate time measurement periods; such as days, months and years. This you will see more clearly, as described below.

I also decided at this point that the months should be represented by the **12 Lunar months,** as I had already proposed that the Moon at that appropriate time in the future would be taking **30 days** to complete it' orbit around the Earth each time. This making it into an excellent LuniSolar Calendar system without having to reconcile any differences between it and the annual orbit of the Earth around the Sun, which would also be completed in exactly 360 days. Once this was settled, all that I needed to do now was to place the appropriate numbers **360 and 12**, in it' proper intermediate time measurement places, as follows:

Alphonso' PHASE LEVEL of Universe expansion	: 12th
Current EAR Oscillation Cycle	: 18th
WHT-Period	: 10th
(The Converted 126,000,000 years AUET Time Period)	
AUET MINUTES	: 2
AUET SECONDS	: 16
AUET TENTHS	: 2
AUET HUNDREDTHS	: 0
AUET THOUSANDTHS	: 6
Earth Lunar Months	: 12
Earth Axis Rotations	: 360
	438

At this stage of the development in the continuous time sequence, we are still 228 shy of the sum total 666. Still a long way off, though. After some very serious contemplation on this quite a big shortfall, I then soon after, quickly realised that I needed to accommodate the actual additional time of **½ a WHT Period**. This too had also become our 'history in time', as per 2ESDRAS, Chapter 14 verse 12 readily confirms.

However, it is to be correctly represented in this expanding and continuous time measurement sequence reading. In this very case, we then need to find out the actual number of **'sub-periods'** which makes up the Alphonso' 12th Phase Level of Universe expansion. These were indeed the time drivers behind these scriptural 2ESDSRAS' **10 and a ½ Period of WHT** and those that were to follow too.

This actually amounts to **126 sub-periods** out of a possible total of **144**. This 144 is another biblical used number as expressed in its totality as being the 144,000 from the 12 Tribes of Israel. That is from each Tribe will be elected 12,000 who first must qualify as per the requirements set out in the relevant Book of Revelation Scriptures and then consequently be graciously rewarded by being sealed with God the Father' name. This GOD seal will therefore be a sign to Satan and his cohorts that these 144,000 are being GOD protected from the attack of the second beast and the dragon behind it (Satan himself). This is clearly confirmed as in REV Chapter 7, 13 and 14.

Alphonso' Phase Level of Universe expansion	: 12th
Current Earth' Oscillation Cycle	: 18th
WHT-Periods that have expired	: 10
Sub-Periods that have already expired since the very beginning of the 1st Period of Ezra' WHT	:126

(The Converted 126,000,000 years AUET Time Period)

AUET MINUTES	:	2
AUET SECONDS	:	16
AUET TENTHS	:	2
AUET HUNDREDTHS	:	0
AUET THOUSANDTHS	:	6
Earth Lunar Months	:	12
Earth Axis Rotations	:	360
		564

This still leaves us short by a whopping 102 that still needs to be added to the above continuous time measurement sequence reading. I just could not close the gap for the life of me any further and thought for awhile that all must be truly lost, sadly, at this advanced stage of this time sequence development.

Several months had passed before I had finally realised a glimmer of hope as provided by our GOD HELPER - the Holy Spirit; that's what I propose anyway. I finally had realized that I could possibly advance this time measurement sequence reading above even further. This could actually be achieved by including the relevant RBPs, i.e. the Referenced Base Positions, which also had played a major and vital role in getting us started in the first place with this time sequence. In fact, I have a notion, that if you are interested, you could probably track the orbit of the Earth with the Sun through it' journey of the Milky Way Galaxy by plotting out these RBPs accordingly onto a Universe map.

If you do recall, our entire 126,000,000 Earth Years, were indeed calculated through the RBPs of 18:24:12(A) to 18:24:33. This covering a total of 21 EARs Minutes from the former RBP18:24:12(A) to the latter RBP18:24:33, which is yet to be reached. I do think that all of these time measurement sequence reading breakdown need to be also included too in this expanding time sequence, which is gradually moving towards the sum total 666. As these are also important relevant time posts in this cosmic number construction. These too are all an integral part of it.

I now need to be very careful in how I handle these cosmic time numbers and the values that they stand for, as I place them appropriately in their rightful places as follows:

Alphonso' Phase Level of Universe expansion : **12**th

Current Earth's Oscillation Cycle : **18**th

WHT Period that had essentially been over or had already ended, as was scripturally revealed and had been expressed as such in this Apocryphal Biblical Book - 2ESDRAS.

:**10**th **Period**

Similarly as above, the number of Sub-Periods which had also come to an end since the very beginning of the 1st Ezra' Period of WHT-WFT.

: **126**th

The Converted 126,000,000 years into AUET Period, essentially obtains for us in the future, our first ever 360 Day Years in our Human Biblical History of our Planet Earth. Also, taking into account the relevant Reference Base Positions (RPBs) that need to be clocked in from RBP18:24:12(A) i.e. (18 + 12) to RBP18:24:33 i.e. (18 + 33). The EAR period of 24 hours is not to be taken into account, as it is common all throughout and never changing in it' EAR period value. In other words, it can be taken to be silent and does not need to play any active part in this as it is assumed as such.

Start RBP	: 18 + 12
AUET MINUTES	: 2
AUET SECONDS	: 16
AUET TENTHS	: 2
AUET HUNDREDTHS	: 0
AUET THOUSANDTHS	: 6
End RBP	: 18 + 33

As you can see directly from above, that we need to get to the half-way time position of the 18th Oscillation Cycle to achieve the above which had taken a reduction in the EAR period to fulfil this being

Minutes away from RBP18:12	: 21 EAR Minutes
Earth Lunar Months, 30 days each	: 12
T/F Earth Axis Rotations/orbit	: 360 (Days)

666
=========

All of the above time progression will achieve for us for the very first time in our biblical human history-future the Rev 13:18 sum total 666.

This entire continuous time measurement sequence reading of the AUET progression through the Universe expansion since the Big Bang-Inflation had occurred and combining it also to the tracking of the specific 21 EAR Minutes in the current 18th Earth Axis Rotation Cycle (which describes for us the obtaining of the 360 day Years in our Human Biblical History) has culminated for me in the obtaining of that elusive and mysterious number set.

This does indeed sum total to the Biblical sum **666** of REV 13:18. This is just simply amazing. Please do take some time to re-study the above carefully.

Well having accomplished what I had embarked on beginning with the 360 day years, which then subsequently linked me with this other more important quest, to calculate out this unique set of cosmic constructed numbers, which sum total 666, I could actually end this book right here and now and leave it to your criticism, constructive or otherwise. However, I do need to continue on for a bit.

I would like to draw your particular attention to how the Babylonians may have possibly obtained the sum total number **666**. Yes, they did indeed. For it was associated to their pagan ways of worshipping the Sun. One important point to note here is that although most of us Christians and even others, who have read the Book of Revelation, would have come face to face with this sum total 666; this sum total number though unique in itself, was also used by the Babylonians!!! This was thousands of years before GOD THE SON had come to redeem and save us from the eternal death and thereby eternal condemnation. They had used it in their pagan worship.

As far as we are concern though, pagan worship has nothing to do with the things of GOD ALMIGHTY and the Kingdom of Heaven, but everything to do with the occults; superstition; witchcraft; sorcery; magic; worshipping of idols; worshipping of animals and objects and of course which includes the Sun, and etc., in it' various and diversified forms. Even to the extent of having direct dealings with mediums, demonic beings and demonic spirits too.

Just as I had found out that the sum total 'number' of the second beast, is to be obtained solely through the cosmos, as a cosmic time derived system based on the relevant scriptures referenced; we learn that the Babylonians in their own way, also had derived the sum total 666, through their own devising. Somehow, they connected it to their own conceptual perceptions of the Cosmos too.

We are informed that the Babylonians had divided the starry night into **36** constellations. Different talisman or amulets represented these and they contained all the numbers from 1 to 36.

According to a report, which I had extracted through the Internet, it seems there are drawings from photographs taken in 1910, which show actual amulets, which were in the Berlin Museum that showed the veneration that the ancient Babylonians had for their sun god.

According to this report, on the front side of the number 1, we have the 'god of the sun' standing on the lion. This according to the report indicated the sun' position in the constellation of Leo during August. On the back is inscribed "Nachyel," meaning 'intelligence of the sun,' and in 36 squares are arranged the numerals 1 to 36. This is done in such a way that adding the numbers of any column either horizontally or vertically and also the two diagonals crossing the square, the total is always the same; **111**.

The total sum of either the six columns or the six rows, i.e. six horizontals or six verticals (6 x 111), would total indeed to **666**!!! You could also get the sum total of **666** by adding the two outside columns with the two outside rows, together with the two diagonals!!!

Strangely, if you refer to the Sexagesimal Chart in the Ancient Civilizations Time Keeping Section in this book after the Addendum, which I had modified appropriately for our intents and purposes; you will find under **Year 111**, that the 'Second Mean Motion' of the Sun does indeed describe **666** Mean Motions.

Meanwhile, the 'First Mean Motion' of the Sun actually describes 39,960 Mean Motions.

> This is indeed a unique situation as you may recall that these 39,960 mean motions or rather 39,960 years does indeed describe a **'one millionth part'** of the future age of the expanding Universe. This Universe future age to be was discovered or derived based on the 2ESDRAS scriptures. This Age of the Universe at the end of the 12th AUET or rather at the end of the Ezra' 12th Period in it' full extension would be 39.960 billion years.

> This is simply amazing to say the least, as it also is directly responsible for delivering or driving the Second Mean Motion of the Sun through 666 cycles. Both numbers 39,960 and 666 being obviously so very relevant and important in this book, that it is simply amazing to discover this very connection that the Sun plays in all of this scriptural mystery, yet through another ancient source – The Indian/Hindu Cosmological Time Cycles.

These 39,960 'First mean Motions' of the Sun can be rewritten too, as being **60 cycles of 666 years**.

> This in multiplicity reveals that there are also **60 million 666 year cycles** of time measurement in our biblically derived age of the Universe (i.e. 39.960 billion years), as it ends the Alphonso' 12th Phase Level of Universe expansion. This is indeed very interesting too, as it can very easily represent or be consolidated into a very real cosmic time keeping system.

In both cases as you can plainly see, i.e. the 'Babylonian 36 Squares' and my Sexagesimal modified Chart of the 'Indian/Hindu Cosmological Time Cycles' does involve the Sun and the Cosmos. Well anyway, for your convenience, I have provided this 'Babylonian 36 Square' arrangement for you as follows:

6	32	3	34	35	1
7	11	27	28	8	30
19	14	16	15	23	24
18	20	22	21	17	13
25	29	10	9	26	12
36	5	33	4	2	31

It is also common knowledge now, that if you add all the numbers from 1 to 36, i.e. 1+2+3+4............+36, you will indeed again get the sum total, **666**!!!

The report goes on to say, that the second illustration is also a **Solar Seal**, but it honours the star Basilisco, which was the diminutive form of the Greek basileus (king), thus meaning the same as the Latin Regulus. Now, Regulus is the only first-magnitude star in the constellation of Leo. The sun and the moon are again clearly seen on this amulet, and on the reverse side is the same arrangement of numerals with the actual figure given of the total **666**!!!

This above second illustration of the 'square' carrying the numbers 1 – 36, is not of the Babylonian era quite obviously, since it has Greek and Roman influences. However, it is obvious the concept and design of this 'Square of Numbers', in the second illustration was indeed copied from the Babylonian. It is interesting to note that on this particular 'Square', according to the report, the actual number of the sum total **666** is given. Also, it is good to note that the New Testament manuscripts were available at the time, both in Greek and Latin. Latin as we know was the primary language of the Romans and parts of the region which was colonized by them at that time. This time, also obviously includes the Book of Revelation, which also holds the sum total of the **'number'** of the beast, **666**.

The Internet Report which was referenced provides this reference sources:

Unfolding the Revelation (Revised) by Roy Allan Anderson, pages 125-127, Published and copyrighted 1953, 1961, 1974 by Pacific Press Publishing Association, Boise Idaho, Oshawa Ontario, Canada. Library of Congress Catalogue Card No. 61-10884.

With regards to all of this Babylonian information, the more interesting question that comes up in my mind is that, "Why did the Babylonians concentrate on the production of such a mathematical pattern, which indeed did result in the sum total of **666** or rather sets of numbers that could be added together to sum total **666?**"

"How was their thinking channel into producing this very mathematical pattern through which they had clearly and amazingly achieved this particular sum total of **666?**" Even though we do know that it was based on their very understanding of the 36 Constellation divisions of their starry night sky; this is still amazing to say the least.

Oblivious to them, this would eventually become a center of greater focus and of greater importance, that GOD ALMIGHTY enables anyone of us, who has the necessary wisdom and understanding, to calculate out the **'number'** of the beast that sum totals to **666**. This was openly commissioned to us by GOD ALMIGHTY, as evidently expressed in the Book of Revelation – REV 13:18.

While you are pondering on this, the Internet report goes on to say that the entire square pattern, which carries these numbers 1 - 36, is also referred to in numerology as the Magic Square of the Sun. We are informed that there are similar Magic Squares for Saturn, Jupiter, Mars, Venus, Mercury and the Moon; all of which have been known for centuries.

So, **666** according to this Internet report, makes us to realize or deduce from it, that it is a number also associated with the pagan **Sun** worship. This worship had originated in the mysteries of ancient pagan Babylon.

Besides the Babylonian connection, it is also interesting to know that in the pursuit to find out this **'number'** of the second beast; had also led me to find out the time left for the Sun to continue shining based on my understanding of the relevant referenced scriptures. This is also similarly with the Universe' biblically derived future age as at the end of the 12 AUET expansion Phase Levels or rather at the end of the 12th being the final Ezra Period. Here again, the Sun would be involved, and it is also connected to the Biblical 'End Times'.

I have calculated the possible future age of the Universe being 39.96 billion years at the time when the Sun will also not have it' life sustaining shining power as it has today. In other words our Solar Sun would have been shut down by then, i.e. it' power operation, so to speak, that is relevant to our Earth sustaining life. Despite it' great difference to what NASA Scientist have most recently estimated it to be, i.e. at 13.7 billion years (**past age** or the current age of the Universe) with a 1% margin of error; I have no choice but to still uphold my biblically derived **projected** future age of the Universe as being the 39.96 billion years. This was derived according to the 'Scriptural WHT-WFT Model', which I had personally developed through the Holy Bible' relevant Scriptures.

This would be as the Universe completes it' expansion according to Ezra' 12th Period WHT-WFT, as developed through the understanding of 2ESDRAS' Chapters 13:57-58 and 14:1-13.

I also want to draw your particular attention to our previous '360 Equation Series' if you do remember, it is towards the very end of Part Two in Book One. We are able to generate this actual Universe age total, surprisingly, through this simple '360 Equation Series'.

The particular 360 Equation Series, **1110th,** in it' sixth and final progression ending unfolds as follows:

$$360 \times 111{,}000{,}000 = 39{,}960{,}000{,}000$$

39.96 Billion years

Here, you also see the highlighted digits of **111**, which once again connects us to the Babylonian Astrology Square; the Indian/Hindu Cosmological Time Cycles and to the sum total of the **'number'** of the second beast, **666**.

Also, as previously mentioned from the total age of the Universe, as at the end of the World History Time; we can remarkably and directly derive the sum total 'number' of the second beast, 666 as follows:

If we divide 39,960,000,000 years directly by 60,000,000; we will get the sum total 'number' of the second beast, 666. This could be interpreted as being exactly 60,000,000 time cycles of 666 years each from the time of the 'Big Bang-Inflation' to the end of 2Esdras' WHT-WFT.

It exhibits a precise cyclic mathematical time in-built cosmic design all through the expansion of the Universe, despite its very chaotic ongoing development, right from the very beginning. However, it does not suggest that the Universe would stop in it' expansion at the end of this time period as indicated above, but based on this scriptural model, it seems to be the end of the WHT-WFT as described in the relevant 2ESDRAS scriptures for the Solar System. This once again in my opinion reveals the 'Hand of God' divinely designing into all of this; this exact preciseness.

This also encompasses the end of the 'sunshine power' of the Sun, as we know of it as today.

Again in repetition, take note, this is indeed not the end of the Universe, just possibly, the very end of our Solar System operating as currently. Although, the above was achieved purely through very simple arithmetic and very simple analysis, it was derived through the Scriptures. It was purely developed through relevant biblical scriptures which are in support of this suggestion in the very first place if you understand it as I have done.

Now, although the Babylonian was indeed the very first people to contend with this sum total **666**, it had also surpassed their very history and existence. For with the above understanding in place, **666** had always been, the sum total of the beast' **'number'**. It was designed into the Cosmos from the very beginning and it was also coupled together right from the very existence of the Solar System in continuity of this GOD' cosmic design and architecture or rather cosmictecture.

This is very important for you to take note of here. This is so, that we become clear, although the 'Apocalypse Future' of Mankind and of the Sun and of the Earth, as described in the Biblical Book of Revelation, which was only revealed in writing sometime in AD 70 – AD 95; the **'number'** of the second beast sum totalling **666**, was already fixed by GOD ALMIGHTY and had been already instituted in this cosmictecture, when the very Universe itself was being designed by GOD ALMIGHTY.

The Universe' existence or cosmic structure and cosmictecture as it is appearing now, was not just by mere chance association over the aeons that it became what it did become eventually as we see it presently. As this in-built unique cosmic constructed number, which does sum total uniquely to being 666, is indeed promising to be a GOD instituted testimony and a GOD instituted check and balance to negate this very popular scientific thinking of it being just by mere chance association of surplus sub-atomic particles that had somehow survived the annihilation when particles first collided with each other; eventually becoming the atoms and matter progressively.

> In other words, through this cosmic constructed number mechanism, we can actually use it to disprove that the Universe was indeed not by mere chance association of particles coming together and building itself into the Universe that we have today.

> As a typical example in support of the above: Why did two parts Hydrogen had needed to seek out to combine specifically in the natural with one part Oxygen??? This is besides the very Chemistry that we had learnt in school.

Whilst you are contemplating your plausible answer to this poser, we already know for quite a while that this specific combination makes one molecule of water and to have repeated this process in the natural for trillions upon trillions number of times and more, and to have done it consistently in the natural to produce all the water that we currently have with us had not taken place just by mere chance association over and over and over again, but by the will of GOD ALMIGHTY.

I do not know whether the same process is still going on in the natural or it had reached it' equilibrium some time ago and therefore the process had indeed stopped according to GOD' plans. Anyway, I leave this to our scientific community to explore and to inform us accordingly.

To make another point, the way I see it, the Babylonian were indeed the very first people to have the foreknowledge or rather being the very first to contend with a specific series of numbers that when combined together properly would sum total **666.** This being possibly, before any other people group on Earth had come to know of it. Their foreknowledge and contention with these series of numbers could be taken to be somewhat like a precursor to this biblical sum total **666**, the same that would be eventually revealed by our LORD GOD ALMIGHTY through the Apostle John in the Biblical Book of Revelation – REV 13:18 refers.

Less we choose to ignore or rather forget or perhaps, many still may not know, that the Babylonians were indeed quite involved in many of the important Scriptural Old Testament events that were connected directly or indirectly to the People of Israel, i.e. the 'People of Promise'. All of this is quite clearly evident to those of us who have read through the Holy Bible. Even their (Babylonian) legends such as the 'Gilgamesh Epic', which is already well known amongst Biblical Scholars, Biblical teachers, those interested in Bible History and others too; this Epic should be also somewhat recognisable as having another classic parallel to the authentic and original description as written in the Holy Scriptures regarding the Biblical Noah' Flood.

This close but yet still distant similarity from my study of it with regards to the Gilgamesh Epic and the Noah' Flood (you can check about this, you know where) is mentioned here, with reference to the sum total number **666** being the sum total of a specific **'series of numbers'** as exhibited by the Babylonian Astrology Square of the Sun. This Epic was referred to, just so that I could make some Babylonian connection to this Biblical event. And there are more to come.

Therefore, once again, the reasons I had stated that the Babylonian' foreknowledge of the sum total **666** was indeed a precursor is firstly based on the fact that the Cosmos and the Solar System had already existed a long time, even before the Babylonian or any human had come into being, let alone when they had established their 'Square of the Sun'.

Secondly, in hindsight, the world must give due credit to the Babylonian for having discovered some of the 'cosmic secrets' that GOD had recorded for us in the Bible, although, they had primarily used their discoveries for their own occult and pagan practices. The credit is due for the mere fact that they were able to study the heavens in those very ancient days, which GOD had created. They had come to understand and appreciate this probably in the greatest of awe and sheer human wonderment that something bigger than themselves, more powerful than they, were operating all of this in the very heavens and of human life too.

Unfortunately for them, they only had access to the pagan road, whilst we have been given the awesome privilege to come to know to a certain extant our LORD GOD ALMIGHTY through HIS Holy Scriptures. How are they going to be judged on the 'Last Day'? God only knows the outcome.

This credit is also appropriately due just the same to all those scientists in any field including those who had discovered so many other 'cosmic secrets' along the way and are still at it today through new generations. These even being more successful than the past efforts combined. They are indeed revealing to us some really amazing stuff about the cosmos (the heavens).

Yet not only because of the Bible that we do believe GOD is the CREATOR of the Universe and everything in it, but because of how it exists and was put together, besides the very testimony of our very own marvellous existence with all the other life forms around us here on Earth.

Many of these 'secrets' were revealed through GOD' Word, which were first spoken and then handed down through descendant generations through oral tradition (as for the Old Testament), long before it was available in the written form.

Most of the events in the New Testament have already come to pass before having been recorded as such in written form by the very witnesses to the biblical events and other events were written through divine inspiration and through some spectacular spiritual experiencing episodes by them. This includes that of Prophet Ezra. All of these events were scripturally documented for you and me, not just to let us know of the event proper but to also encourage and fortify our Faith in the knowledge that our LORD GOD ALMIGHTY really exists. Fortunately, it also includes that there is **'ETERNAL LIFE after DEATH'**, through the very 'SALVATION' that was made possible through our LORD and SAVIOUR, JESUS CHRIST. This is the fundamental key which bridges us human beings with our amazing potential and future reality of becoming also spiritualised beings and thereby we would go on living for eternity without ever ending.

Most of these documented scriptural events have already been accomplished or fulfilled and thereby have indeed become our scriptural history, with the exception those pertaining to the Apocalypse, Armageddon and the JUDGMENT DAY events. These are pertaining to the 'End Times' and also some other prophesies which have yet to happen, but have already been foretold in written form too. This is indeed very interesting.

As already mentioned many major biblical events and biblical personalities as described in the Old Testament, also did involve the ancient Babylonians. Even the infamous Tower of Babel was probably located, as we are informed in Babylonia. This is according to Biblical Scholarship and Genesis 11:1-9, refers.

Also, less we forget, Abram later to be directly name changed by GOD to become Abraham, the most acclaimed Patriarch and biblical mentioned progenitor became the father of the Promised Land (Canaan) where the 'People of Promise' were to live and to claim it as their very own. These people were his direct and his other indirect descendants. He himself was from **Ur** - a Babylonian city.

Genesis 11:27-32 and Genesis Chapters 12, 13, 14, 15, 16, 17, 18, 19, 20, 21, 22, 23, 24, 25:1:11; refers to the life and times of Patriarch Abraham.

From this very extensive coverage of Abraham' life in the Holy Scriptures, spanning about 15 Chapters, almost as long as the Gospel of Mark in terms of Chapters and about 60% according to the number of content pages this Gospel has, biblically announces to us besides other scriptural factors, the tremendous, extensive importance, the Babylonian Abraham had been in the 'OT' times. This importance has indeed cascaded down even as presently into our own Christian History and the History of the Israelites; which continues even as of today.

It is also to be noted that Sarai who was Abraham' wife, whom God also had later renamed to become Sarah was also from **Ur**. This is besides the biblical fact that she was indeed his half sister – Gen 20:12 confirms, making her also to be a true Babylonian.

So it is quite obvious that the very **'First Parents'** of the future Israelites, had in fact Babylonian roots firmly embedded into their very culture and human make up. In other words they were indeed Babylonian and just like all Babylonians at that time, Abram himself included, together with his father Terah were indeed pagan worshippers. Of course this was before GOD had called Abram out of Ur to go to the Promised Land. It would be difficult for me and you to deny that Abram was not doing the same worship like his father Terah was doing at that time; before the call. I believe this to be exactly so, mainly because of his family' cultural and pagan background and their obvious influence over him on this matter.

Abraham in this sense was very fortunate and extremely gifted to be divinely selected from amongst the possible thousands and even millions living at the time by our LORD GOD ALMIGTY, to begin in a way a 'new generation' of People; the Israelites. This awesome accolade and divine appointed purpose was also somewhat shared with his Babylonian wife, Sarah.

If you care to read **Joshua Chapter 24** carefully, it would confirm somewhat the above thinking. For you will come to know that the chosen people of God (who were indeed the very descendants of Abraham either directly i.e. through his sons and their sons or indirectly through his daughters and their children) themselves had to make an important decision during Joshua' time, several centuries away later from Abraham and Sarah. It was whether to worship our GOD ALMIGHTY or the foreign gods (idolatry; paganism and etc.) of their fathers and even those that had influenced them and had been acquired during their long captivity in Egypt!

> This Chapter is also particularly very important, for it also re-emphasises the deeply entrenched 'Babylonian Connection' in the Israelites origin. So based on this, we can probably conclude that the Israelites evolved out of 'Babylonian Stock'.

Correct me if I am wrong with regards to this matter. This is just a matter of my biblical derived conclusion and in fact is quite well known in biblical scholarship circles too. In fact Abraham had appointed his own servant for the task of finding or locating a wife as preordained by GOD for his only son (recognised heir) Isaac, who had turned out to be Rebekah from his own country, which was situated in Babylonia. Even Isaac' second son (in fact a twin with Esau) and the eventual heir to succeed him, i.e. Jacob, got married to two sisters (both daughters of his mother' own brother, Laban - Genesis 29 refers), whilst he was in **Haran** (located in Syria), another city in ancient Babylonia. This indeed constitutes two successive Babylonian-Abraham direct descendant generations, whom together will eventually and further establish the 'Chosen People of God', as originally promised to Abraham by GOD.

The third and successive Babylonian-Abraham direct descendant generation was indeed Jacob' children i.e. his 12 sons (through whom the 12 Tribes of Israel would later be established) and his only daughter, Dinah. It is from these 12 Tribes that 12,000 Israelites from each would be fortunate enough to be selected worthy of receiving GOD' Name SEAL to protect them and set them apart during the second beast' time of rampage and destruction as foretold in the Book of Revelation.

So in total four generations, including the generation of Abraham and Sarah themselves; the bloodline was indeed pure Babylonian; both father and mother' side. I started counting the generations from Abraham only and not including his own father Terah, because GOD' Covenant was made with Abraham, which did not include his father - Genesis Chapter 15 refers.

Judah (one of Jacob' sons) finally inherits the birthright and leads the 'descendant generations' i.e. Abraham' Generations onwards; but he marries a Canaanite woman, which finally seems to have broken the pure Babylonian Bloodline, as shown in the genealogy that leads to David and beyond. However, stranger things had happened as you will shortly read below. So obviously, the descendants from here onwards are of mixed lineage, and yet they were named in the Biblical 'Genealogical Listing'.

In fact with Judah, this mixing of lineage becomes somewhat complicated, when Judah goes unknowingly into Tamar, his own daughter-in-law, of his former two dead sons; the second of which was given to her by their traditional/ Biblical 'Levirate Marriage' - Genesis Chapter 38 explains and refers. This one time relationship with Tamar, in fact produced twins; Perez and Zerah. Perez then is listed as having continued Abraham' descendant generations, onwards - Matt 1:3 confirms.

Several decades of descendant generations later, Joseph had a unique 'Son', Jesus Christ, without him ever 'touching' his betrothed Blessed Virgin Mary. This was naturally a gigantic miracle being the miraculous birth of our LORD and Saviour, Jesus Christ (The Second Person in the GODHEAD of the Holy Trinity that we have come to know through HIS WORD) into this physical world of ours. **However, what people generally do not know is that even Blessed Virgin Mary did not have any biological connection with JESUS CHRIST.** This is the further and deeper DIMENSION revelation to the mystery of this awesome miracle that has been played down very much by our distracters in the birth of our LORD and SAVIOUR JESUS CHRIST. You need to read more of this in my next book, if it does go to print.

The point that I am trying to make here is that Blessed Virgin Mary gives esteemed recognition to Patriarch Abraham, when she links him up to her lineage ancestry - Luke 1:55 confirms. This is quite amazing because even

Mary, through this scripture verse, informs us of her **Babylonian roots**, which she leapfrogs right through her genealogy to link right back to Abraham. This is of some particular importance to take note of here, as I want to establish the relevance of making the 'Babylonian Connection' in my own progress to discover the number of the beast.

So the 'Babylonian Connection' in Biblical Judaism and Christian History, is also indeed much more then what really meets the eye!!! These were the very reasons that I went briefly into the very subject of Abraham, the Israelites and Blessed Virgin Mary.

The Babylonians astounding understanding of what they understood about the heavens, in such ancient times is simply stupendous. Just like we are still unravelling the complex reasons, "Not why the Egyptians built the Pyramids, but how were those Great Pyramids at Giza built; three of the most prominent being positioned and aligned to the Orion Belt of Stars and so precisely at that too besides all the other construction feats that they had to accomplish with such amazing skills without the use of modern machinery, cranes, and etc???" This is just one of the many mysteries of the Pyramids that still need unravelling or perhaps it has already been discovered how it was actually done. Yet there are still many other unanswered questions and mysteries to be unearthed.

So, the Biblical **'number'** sum totalling **666** has a far more reaching and in-depth connection to the Cosmos, to the Solar Planets, especially the Sun and the Earth with it' Moon and also to the eventual revealing of whom the second beast really would be in the end.

> Every number as placed and positioned in the total cosmic construction of the **'number'** of the beast in this model has an impact or 'value' directly derived from the cosmos.

> This includes of course to our Solar System and as shown, it is specifically with regards to 'Time'. The 'number' is directly related to the AUET and the EAR speed changes of our Planet Earth. These are actually associated to it' reducing/increasing speeds during every EAR Oscillation Cycle, which we are currently in the 18th. So in the end, it was indeed appropriate, I think, to name this book:

'THE BIBLICAL 360 DAY YEARS
&
THE SCRIPTURAL COSMIC 666'

'THE SCRIPTURAL COSMIC 666'
THE UNVEILING OF THE 'NUMBER' OF THE (SECOND) BEAST

The cosmic number time sequence measurement reading, which sum totals **666** is as follows:

121810126181221620618332112360

Another time arrangement to represent the same above could be as follows:

121810126
18122162061833
21
12360

The first row constitutes the actual AUET time frame that has passed us by, according to the Apocryphal Biblical Book - 2ESDRAS. Yet we are all currently in the same 18th Oscillation Cycle (OC); the same that Adam & Eve were in with regards to the overall expansion of the Universe.

The second row bring us into the more specific time focus range to when we would be exactly, in the terms of the Earth, experiencing for the very first time in it' Human biblical history, the 360 Day Years. This eventual time period range culminating sometime in our distant future, being 126,000,000 years as calculated from the very beginning of the 18th OC i.e. from RBP 18:12 and ranging through to the midway of the 18th OC at RBP 18:33. This time range has been converted to AUET keeping, in order that it could be shown to be in synchronous with it, as depicted in this row.

The third row is recording the time progression being the 21 EAR minutes change in the Earth' axial axis rotation period as it orbits the Sun to accomplish for us the expected result as expressed in the final fourth row.

The fourth row is the expected outcome of the first, second and third row, all being in-sync time progression to finally obtain this outcome for us.

This is a 30 digit number, when read as above, in it' entirety, is actually describing the unique time sequence of the birth of the 360 day years for the very first time in our Human Biblical History-Future both in the AUET Zone level and also in the Earth Time Zone level.

When these two Time Zones are combined as such, it remarkably produces for us the unique cosmic derived number that sum totals 666. This actually fulfils the Open and Divine Commission of our LORD GOD ALMIGHTY, as was presented in Rev 13:18. In it we also do find the expressed revelation that we will indeed be able to unravel this mystery. It is within our human capacity to do so.

The above time format could be sized quite easily to fit any size of forehead or right hand, these locations as expressed per the scriptures in REV 13:16. An example is as shown below.

```
    121810126
18122162061833
        21
      12360
```

It is quite obvious that if required it is possible to size it even much smaller as the case may warrant.

> **This is my final 'Milestone Achievement' bringing the total to exactly 18.**

> This number 18 is indeed a significant number in itself in this cosmic based 'Revelation' mystery.

Before I finally bring to a close these Books, there is also some important information, which I would like to share with you at this final stage.

> Although, at first, I did not realise the very significance of the **number 18** in itself, which also happens to be the number of the Earth' Oscillation Cycle that we are currently in, and to a lesser degree also the number of the 'Milestones Achieved' to get us here; until I came across the several instances in the Scriptures, some of which were highlighted by others, in the relevance of this **number 18**.

I never knew this until arriving almost towards the very end of my quests. Strangely though or should I say rather by Divine design, the only one verse in which **666** appears in the entire Book of Revelation, is also the **18th verse** in that **Chapter 13**. Also, **6+6+6** equals to 18.

It is in this particular and specifically current 18th EAR Oscillation Cycle, in which future time, the 360 Day Years would begin for the very first time in our Biblical Human History. This singly makes it uniquely relevant to us from all of the other EAR Oscillation Cycles since past. As it is also in this 18th OC in which the 'number' sum totalling 666 as divinely assigned to the second beast is fundamentally derived in. Yes, here too it is the 18$^{th.}$.

It is also already well known that the word **beast appears 37** times in the entire Book of Revelation.

> I also had the wonderful opportunity to personally discover as described below; adding to all the others before me:

> That if you divide the biblical sum total of the second beast' number, i.e. 666 by the number of times the word beast had been used in the Book of Revelation i.e. 37 times; you will indeed get, surprisingly, yes again, the result 18.

Now somehow through further prompting of the Holy Spirit, **(that's my belief),** it was revealed to me that we can use this piece of information, which I had just recently discovered and to apply it remarkably as follows:

You have already been informed that the increasing size of the Universe, to expand fully into what it would be at the end of the Alphonso' 12th Phase Level/Ezra' 12th Period in Universe Space; would actually take **39,960,000,000 years.**

Also take note that the beginning of the Alphonso' 12th Phase Level of Universe expansion had begun precisely on the **4,320,000,000th year** or rather 4.32 billionth year into the overall expansion of the Universe which also became the beginning for the First Ezra' Period of WHT.

> Now, if we divide this expanded age of the Universe as at the end of it' Alphonso' 12th Phase Level, by the number of times the word **beast** had been used in the Book of Revelation, i.e. exactly by 37; we will remarkably get the result, 1,080,000,000.

Now I may be repeating myself but you can immediately see the familiar first level hour resolution of the Babylonian Time System, i.e. 1080 Divisions/ Hour in the above quotient. It is as if that the 37 number of times this word **beast** had actually been used in the Revelation Scriptures was orchestrated there for this exact purpose to reveal to us this connection of Earth Time zone to the AUET Zone, which I suspect had also been exposed by the Babylonian' use of the similar 1,080 divisions of time in an hour.

> So, from the above division of 37, we then have an AUET time-keeping system generated, whereby, we have **37 major segments** of AUET time; each equating to a whooping **1,080,000,000** years.

Now if we divide this amount of time into **1080 AUET Divisions**, just as the Babylonian had done with an hour of time; we will then have one AUET division equating to just **1,000,000 years**.

This then can simply be further sub-divided into a time resolution of 1,000,000 sub-divisions; then each unit of these AUET sub-divisions would be reading off just **one year**. From here we can further drill down to link this AUET system to our own Earth Time clock system of reading time on a daily basis.

This would also in turn generate an **ET Annual Calendar System** which would interlock with the other larger AUET System, which also begins reading off sub-sub-divisions of AUET, first in years and then sub-divisions of 1,000,000 years and then finally in Divisions of 1,080,000,000 year segments, which culminates this entire Universe cycle of reading the AUET. This is of course after completing a total of **37 AUET Segments,** which finally reads one **39,960,000,000 years** AUET cycle.

> Could this be the very reasons for the Babylonian to have such a time keeping system in the first place? Have I somehow stumbled upon the very reasoning for them in doing this type of time keeping construction? As such does this reveal that they possibly knew about this very **AUET?** Just like I do understand that the Indian Hindu Cosmological Time Cycles seem to indicate and perhaps to some extent even also similarly with the Maya's time keeping system too.

The Maya civilization seems to me, that they too also had this knowledge, whether knowingly or unknowingly. Their time-keeping system is also in my opinion, somewhat **independent** from the very static time-keeping of the triune time controlling system of the Sun, Earth and Moon and seems more inclined to the AUET time frame. This is amazing indeed if this is eventually proven to be correct, as it seems from their time keeping that they and others did not have to use the static time-keeping system of the Sun, Earth and Moon, but instead, possibly an abstract form of time keeping through the AUET. It may be still worthwhile to initiate a further study, if I could make this very suggestion.

> Well anyway, it also further tightens and confirms the unique connection between our AUET, with the relevant verses as used in the second canonized stream of Biblical Books, as in the 2Esdras (with which I was in the very first place able to establish this very AUET), together with the relevant verses as used in the mainstream (First Canon) Biblical Book of 'The Revelation of Jesus Christ'.

Also, as we are informed that the Babylonian and the Indian/Hindu Time Systems followed a base number of 60, we too can represent our AUET following this base number, just as well. For the number **39,960,000,000** can be divided by 60 and we can keep on dividing it by 60, to a very fine division time resolution is in fact reached.

In fact, 39,960,000,000 years divided by 60 is:

666,000,000

As indicated just above, each equates exactly to **666**,000,000 Years and you can immediately see the scriptural sum total, **666 – REV 13:18 refers.**

> By dividing each of these 60 Divisions into a million equal parts, we can read AUET in sub-divisions of **666** years!!!

Here, you can immediately see the second beast' number, in it' sum total form of **666** being isolated and established as a single unit of **time measurement** or time division.

Everything seems to be fitting in quite nicely now, mathematically and scripturally. This exhibits a 'purposefully designed Universe', obviously highly complex but overall in a harmonious balance with itself as seen or as discovered with regards to 'Time' being it' very dimension.

This demonstrates a huge massively **'GOD Controlled Creation'** of mind-boggling size but yet framed in a GOD measured Universe Space. It is definitely not **a 'Chaotic Creation',** which is a creation by association i.e., just through mere chance to evolve into, without GOD being at all involved in it into any size that it could eventually become.

Although, this to my understanding was indeed a very finely tuned 'GOD Controlled Creation'; it still allows the various 'components' of the Universe to migrate somewhat 'freely' within the GOD established confines and controls. That is with regards to Space & Time Laws of the 'Universe Space' and within it' accompanying 'Universe Time' restraints or constraints (i.e. AUET).

So, definitely not just a spontaneous one; as can be seen from every aspect of GOD' HAND and MIND in the creation of the Universe and everything in it. This includes even to the very early time of the trigger (Big Bang-Inflation), which had been 'Divinely Timed' to occur precisely at His appointed time to initialise the universe expansion; if it had occurred just as cosmologist Stephen Hawking explains it to us. This cannot deny our LORD GOD ALMIGHTY being brought into the **'Scientific Creation Equation'** and the reasons why the Universe and everything in it exists as it is in the broader sense. Furthermore, this lends some very necessary Scriptural support to the scientific community that the Universe had indeed a **beginning**. This very **beginning**, was in fact revealed to us through the Book of Genesis in the Holy Bible which is the very first Biblical Book in it' arrangement.

Now I want to just recap some information that I had already established as previously.

> One Earth Orbit currently takes 8,839.39 hours with a current speed of **66,000 miles per hour** or rather 105,600 km per hour typically. Here once again we can clearly see some influence of the Earth' speed of orbit to the generation of the unique biblical sum total number of the second beast; being 666.

Also, the Earth spins at around **11,000 miles per hour** at the equator, which provides another contributing linkage.

> The EAR speed switchover from faster to slower occurs regularly at the beginning of every EAR Oscillation Cycle. In this particular case the 18th Oscillation. It has already occurred at RBP18:24:12(A).

The EAR speed slowing down or increasing up as the case maybe at the time, would be at a consistent rate either way of 1/1000 second per every 100 years.

With the EAR Speed Switchover occurring at the RBP18:24:12(A) at the very beginning of this 18th EAR OC; the EAR begins actually slowing down in this phase until reaching the mid-base of the OC at RBP18:24:33. From here, it will speed up again until the very end of the OC to repeat it all over again as long as it is permitted to do so by the relevant cosmic and solar forces.

EARTH' 18th Oscillation Cycle began at RBP18:24:12(A)

EAR Period 24.20 (RBP18:12A)
24hrs 12mins : 365.264049586 Earth Days/Orbit

24.20144776 mean Solar day duration i.e. 24hrs 12mins 5.211936sec, establishes the current **365.242199047 Solar Days/Orbit**

EAR Period 24.21666666
24hrs 13mins : 365.012663455 Earth Days/Orbit

EAR Period 24.23333333
24hrs 14mins : 364.761623109 Earth Days/Orbit

EAR Period 24.25 (RBP 18:15)
24hrs 15mins : 364.510927835 Earth Days/Orbit

EAR Period 24.26666666
24hrs 16 mins   :   364.260576924 Earth Days/Orbit

EAR Period 24.28333333
24hrs 17mins   :   364.010569664 Earth Days/Orbit

EAR Period 24.30   (RBP 18:18)
24hrs 18mins   :   363.760905349 Earth Days/Orbit

EAR Period 24.31666666
24hrs 19mins   :   363.511583277 Earth Days/Orbit

EAR Period 24.33333333
24hrs 20mins   :   363.26260274 Earth Days/Orbit

EAR Period 24.35   (RBP 18:21)
24hrs 21mins   :   363.013963039 Earth Days/Orbit

EAR Period 24.36666666
24hrs 22mins   :   362.765663475 Earth Days/Orbit

EAR Period 24.38333333
24hrs 23mins   :   362.517703349 Earth Days/Orbit

EAR Period 24.40 (RBP 18:24)
24hrs 24mins   :   362.270081967 Earth Days/Orbit

EAR Period 24.41666666
24hrs 25mins   :   362.022798635 Earth Days/Orbit

EAR Period 24.43333333
24hrs 26mins   :   361.77585266 Earth Days/Orbit

EAR Period 24.45   (RBP 18:27)
24hrs 27mins   :   361.529243353 Earth Days/Orbit

EAR Period 24.46666666
24hrs 28mins   :   361.282970028 Earth Days/Orbit

EAR Period 24.48333333
24hrs 29mins   :   361.037031995 Earth days/orbit

EAR Period 24.50   (RBP 18:30)
24hrs 30mins   :   360.791428571 Earth Days/Orbit

EAR Period 24.51666666
24hrs 31mins : 360.546159076 Earth Days/Orbit

EAR Period 24.53333333
24hrs 32mins : 360.301222826 Earth days/orbit

EAR Period 24.55 (RBP 18:33)
24hrs 33mins : **360.056619144 Earth Days/Orbit**

> The EARTH would have now reached the important mid-base point of it' 18th Earth Axis Rotation Oscillation Cycle at **RBP18:33** with an EAR period of 24.55 (i.e. 24 hours 33 minutes).

It is also quite clearly evident from the above that we did not achieve the desired result of obtaining exactly 360 Earth Days/Orbit at the precisely appointed time of 126,000,000 years as calculated from the RBP18:12(A) culminating at RBP18:33. However, you would realise that we did achieve **360.056619144 EARs at RBP18:33**, which is quite close to our objective. The reason why we did not achieve the ideally required result of **360 Earth Days/Orbit** precisely is because we did not take into consideration or rather compensate for the affects of the possible occurring **perturbation** of the EARTH as yet.

Through this assumption if this does indeed occur then the perturbation should be effective enough to alter the orbit to a time period of **8,838 hours**, as required for our intents and purposes. This is instead of the currently followed non-perturbation 8839.39 hours orbit.

With Perturbation:

> **360 EARs X 24.55 Hours (EAR Period) = 8,838 Hours**

Without perturbation:

> **365.242199 Solar Days X 24.20144776 Hours = 8,839.39 Hours**

That is a total difference of only 1.39 hours or 1 hour 23 minutes 24 seconds in the time taken to complete the annual orbit at that future distant time almost 126,000,000 years away. Some possible study of this probable phenomenon being the perturbation of the Earth should also be carried out, as a suggestion.

However, the fact of the matter is that I am still able to establish that our Earth would surely experience the 360 day orbit **(i.e. 360.056619144)** even without the phenomenon of perturbation being ever involved.

Let us however, leave this to the 'BIG BOYS' to resolve this out for us. In the meantime, my obtaining of the unique scriptural based cosmic derived 'number' which indeed sum totals 666, still remains intact.

Also, just for your added convenience, I would like to index the 'Milestone Achievements' and the Charts used here, in the Appendices on the following pages.

So finally in sincere humbleness, I do believe the HOLY SPIRIT has finished with me in these revelations. So, I can conclude this work with the scriptural confidence that I have indeed possibly discovered the 'number' of the second beast, through a cosmic construction approach, but yet based on scripture, which remarkably sum totals to the **REV 13:18 - 666**.

PLEASE DO KEEP IN TOUCH

gcf@globalchristianfamily.com

Goodbye and God Bless You, Always.

charles alphonso
IN HIS MAJESTY'S SERVICE
ACCORDING TO HIS GOOD PLEASURE

Date and Time of Birth: 31 August 1952, 10.15 pm

TIME STAMPED BY THE SOLAR STAR

PRAISE BE TO GOD ALMIGHTY

AMEN

APPENDIX – '18 MILESTONE ACHIEVEMENTS'

TIME IS DYING - Pg 84 - 88

BOOK ONE - PART TWO

First Milestone Achievement - Pg 92

Second Milestone Achievement - Pg 97

Third Milestone Achievement - Pg 99

Fourth Milestone Achievement - Pg 104

Fifth Milestone Achievement - Pg 116

Sixth Milestone Achievement - Pg 118

Seventh Milestone Achievement - Pg 122

Eight Milestone Achievement - Pg 124

Ninth Milestone Achievement - Pg 128

Tenth Milestone Achievement - Pg 145

ADDENDUM

Eleventh Milestone Achievement - Pg 205

Twelfth Milestone Achievement - Pg 209

BOOK TWO – PART 3

Thirteenth Milestone Achievement - Pg 296

Fourteenth Milestone Achievement - Pg 306

Fifteenth Milestone Achievement - Pg 309

Sixteenth Milestone Achievement - Pg 321

BOOK TWO, PART FOUR

Seventeenth Milestone Achievement　　　-　　Pg 353

Eighteenth Milestone Achievement　　　-　　Pg 387

APPENDIX – CHARTS

THE EQUINOXES/SOLSTICE DIAGRAM　　-　　**Pg 114**

SEXAGESIMAL MODIFIED CHART　　-　　**Pg 256 - 258**

CHART A3　　-　　**Pg 297**

CHART E　　-　　**Pg 298 - 299**

CHART B1　　-　　**Pg 305**

CHART B　　-　　**Pg 322**

CHART C　　-　　**Pg 325**

THE BABYLONIAN 36 SQUARES　　-　　**Pg 376**

www.ingramcontent.com/pod-product-compliance
Lightning Source LLC
Chambersburg PA
CBHW051624230426
43669CB00013B/2179